Undergraduate Topics in Computer Science

Undergraduate Topics in Computer Science (UTiCS) delivers high-quality instructional content for undergraduates studying in all areas of computing and information science. From core foundational and theoretical material to final-year topics and applications, UTiCS books take a fresh, concise, and modern approach and are ideal for self-study or for a one- or two-semester course. The texts are all authored by established experts in their fields, reviewed by an international advisory board, and contain numerous examples and problems. Many include fully worked solutions.

For further volumes:
http://www.springer.com/series/7592

Philippe Lalanda • Julie A. McCann
Ada Diaconescu

Autonomic Computing

Principles, Design and Implementation

 Springer

Philippe Lalanda
Laboratoire Informatique de Grenoble
Université Joseph Fourier
Grenoble, France

Julie A. McCann
Department of Computing
Imperial College London
London, UK

Ada Diaconescu
Department of Computing and Networking
Télécom ParisTech
Paris, France

ISSN 1863-7310
ISBN 978-1-4471-5006-0   ISBN 978-1-4471-5007-7 (eBook)
DOI 10.1007/978-1-4471-5007-7
Springer London Heidelberg New York Dordrecht

Library of Congress Control Number: 2013936543

Printed on acid-free paper

Springer is part of Springer Science+Business Media (www.springer.com)

Foreword

The autonomic computing initiative—the creation of self-managing systems—was a call to arms from IBM (Paul Horn, 2001) to the industry and academic computing communities and signified the mainstream adoption of such research fields as intelligent fault management.

Although IBM set it in the context of coping with the ever-increasing 'systems of systems' complexity and dealing with the total cost of ownership (TCO), researchers expanded this to next generation of computing and communications, for instance, pervasive computing, ubiquitous computing, swarm-based computing, agent-based computing, smart grid, on-demand computing, next-generation Internet, adaptive communications and the latest trends, green and cloud computing. These streams of research have found focus through such research conferences as ICAC, EASe, SEAMS, MUCS and SASO (International Conference on Autonomic Computing, Engineering of Autonomic and Autonomous Systems, Software Engineering for Adaptive and Self-Managing Systems, Managing Ubiquitous Communication and Services and Self-Adaptive and Self-Organizing Systems, respectively). The decade of research also saw the creation of related initiatives such as Autonomic Communications and Organic Computing, as well as communities, such as the IEEE Technical Committee on Autonomous and Autonomic Systems (TCAAS) and the Autonomic Communications Forum (ACF).

Due to the complexity of the challenges that this subject brings to the fore, the Autonomic Computing has to rely on expertise from many fields—software engineering, systems engineering, control theory and AI (artificial intelligence), among others. As such it is hard to 'nail' down the field which is possibly the reason there hasn't emerged a good tutorial text—till now. As with many 'hot' research initiatives, the spotlight (and often the funding) moves on, yet the original long-term 2020–2030 needs have not. If anything, they have become more critical. The Software Crisis 2.0 (Fitzgerald 2012) highlighted more than ever the need to have our software self-managing, due to the demand for data from digital natives, coupled with the huge volume of data now generated through ubiquitous mobile devices, sensors and applications.

The success of the initiative has already been indicated by the notable move of 'autonomicity' from the previously mentioned conferences and communities to a standard topic in almost all computer- and communications-based conferences and communities. Ironically, the final success of the initiative may be marked as it no longer exists separately as a specialised field but as a standard, invisible and integrated part of our systems and software engineering.

For the autonomic systems research and development to make further leaps and bounds and move convincingly into the next decade to meet the Software Crisis 2.0 and its other longer term goals requires that it move beyond the research labs and PhD programmes to our graduate, undergraduate and CPPD (continuous professional and personal development) courses.

This book marks the enabler for that next stage.

University of Ulster, Northern Ireland   Roy Sterritt
12 December 2012

References

Fitzgerald, B.: Software crisis 2.0. IEEE Comput. **45**(4) (2012)
Horn, P.: Autonomic computing: IBM's perspective on the state of information technology. IBM T.J. Watson Labs, New York (2001)

Preface

Autonomic computing seeks to render computing systems as self-managed. In other words, its objective is to enable computer systems to manage themselves so as to minimise the need for human input. Autonomic computing as an approach is guaranteed to change the way software systems are developed. Indeed, this new field is addressing some of the issues resulting from the ever-increasing complexity of software administration and the growing difficulty encountered by software administrators in performing their job effectively.

This book provides a practical perspective on autonomic computing. Implementing self-managed systems remains a true challenge today. Thus, beyond giving necessary explanations about the objectives and interests of autonomic computing, this book goes through the different software engineering techniques that are currently available for organising and developing self-managed software systems. In summary, this book uniquely:

- Provides a structured and comprehensive introduction to autonomic computing with a software engineering perspective, as far as we are aware this is the first book to do so
- Presents highly up-to-date information on techniques implementing self-monitoring, self-knowledge, decision-making and self-adaptation
- Provides a downloadable learning environment and source code that allows students to develop, execute and test autonomic applications at an associated website

Authors have created the aforementioned learning environment and placed it on a web page that will be regularly updated. The environment represents an autonomic pervasive computing application that simulates a *digital home*. A dedicated development environment has been designed around this; it allows the student to execute autonomic code in a runtime simulation that provides concrete, visual feedback of the behaviours illustrating what the student has programmed.

This book is aimed at students and practitioners working on software projects where system self-management would redress maintenance complexity and cost issues. Several aspects of this book have been tested in a classroom, which makes this book ideal for a 10-week lecture programme.

Content Level: master student/professional

Keywords: Autonomic computing, Software engineering, Software architectures, Software monitoring, Software adaptation, Knowledge and reasoning

Related Subjects: Software engineering

Authors: Authors are practitioners and recognised researchers in the field. They have published more than 200 publications in international conferences and journals.

Grenoble, France   Philippe Lalanda
London, UK   Julie A. McCann
Paris, France   Ada Diaconescu

Acknowledgments

Many useful discussions with colleagues and students helped in the preparation of this book. The authors would like to thank the following people who, without reward, reviewed and critiqued the text; their comments and suggestions have been invaluable in ensuring the quality of this book:

Luciano Baresi, Charles Consel, Clément Escoffier, Catherine Hamon, Roman Kolcun, Pedro Martins, Iulian Neamtiu, Simon O'Keefe, Alessandra Russo, Poonam Yadav and Shusen Yang.

We are also grateful to Simon Rees of Springer who encouraged us to write the book and provided invaluable assistance in the production of the final copy.

We would also like to thank our colleagues, friends and family for their constant support, encouragement and patience. Ada thanks Mr. Smith for regularly changing the subject. Julie thanks husband Grant and son Carter—you can now use my laptop to watch 1950s cartoons. Philippe thanks his wife, now an expert in autonomic computing, and his two sons, Grégoire and Arthur—experts to come!

Contents

Software Engineering to Autonomic Computing

1

Software, as an artefact, has been tremendously successful. It has pervaded every aspect of our professional and social life, due mainly to the outstanding advances in hardware, but also to undeniable progress in software engineering practices that allow the timely production of high-quality computing products.

Software is however a victim of its own success. The software systems of today have to constantly face new and demanding requirements in terms of their availability, robustness, dynamism and pervasiveness. This is challenging, the way software systems are produced and managed. In particular, great pressure is put on the maintenance of software and systems; maintenance tasks are becoming increasingly difficult and correspondingly more time-consuming to carry out. Today, many believe that we have reached a barrier in terms of complexity and that innovative practices are needed to ensure the continuous delivery of software-based services.

In this introductory chapter, we present how software systems are currently being developed and managed. We show how the use of software has evolved and how this has impacted on the software development and maintenance processes. In particular, we show that much of the complexity involved with the software life cycle has moved from the development stage to the maintenance stage, which raises formidable challenges for practitioners.

Finally, we briefly introduce the field of autonomic computing, a relatively new spin on the ways we build and maintain software systems and whose purpose is to overcome some of these aforementioned problems we highlight. This chapter motivates the need for autonomic computing systems.

P. Lalanda et al., *Autonomic Computing: Principles, Design and Implementation*,
Undergraduate Topics in Computer Science, DOI 10.1007/978-1-4471-5007-7_1,
© Springer-Verlag London 2013

1.1   Software Complexity

Software systems can be amazingly complex. They can be difficult to conceive, to implement, to understand and to maintain. This raises significant challenges that gave birth to the *software engineering* approach to creating computing systems a few decades ago and has motivated the autonomic computing movement today. But what is a software system, and why is it so complex?

A software system is a collection of programmes and data deployed on one or several computers for execution. It is complex for a number of reasons. First, programmes are heterogeneous constructions. They can be made of a number of interacting computing entities, very diverse in the sense that they have their own structure, their own state at runtime and, sometimes, their own language. These computing entities are typically project specific. That is, they are created for the purpose of a single project, and this makes it difficult to reuse the experience obtained from one project to another, in terms of the development and maintenance of these entities across projects.

As observed by Frederic Brooks in his famous essay about software issues [1], as the size of systems increases, the type and number of entities to be assembled increase exponentially, meaning structural complexity can be amplified.

Brooks also pointed out that software is intangible. Accurately representing the computing entities that compose a system and their behaviour is a non-trivial task. It requires defining a number of views at different levels of abstraction and many relationships between these different views. This separates the software building process from other more traditional engineering disciplines, where entities are more concrete and can be represented and understood more easily.

A software project is not limited to programmes and data though. It also comes with various software artefacts built throughout the software development process, including requirements specifications, architecture diagrams, documents, code, test suites and configurations specifications. There are tight relationships between these artefacts that are hard to express and to maintain. Most of the time, they are not entirely completed to perfection and some artefacts can be lost over the course of a project (such as design rationales). For instance, it is not unheard of that a piece of code can no longer be directly related to the requirement that motivated it.

Software artefacts are many, and the sheer number of these artefacts (and their relationships) adds to the complexity associated with modern software systems.

Brooks also stated that an essential feature of software systems is their ability to change. The source of the pressure to change comes from the clients and users, a phenomenon not normally associated with objects that are traditionally manufactured. For those objects, evolutions are carefully planned and incorporated in subsequent releases. In contrast, most software systems have to be regularly updated to stay relevant. There are of course many good reasons for that: satisfied users want more functions, bugs need to be fixed, market conditions change, incoming load has increased, hardware or software resources have evolved, etc. But the bottom line is that most people do not understand enough about the software to comprehend the extent of the difficulty and risks involved with updating existing systems.

This pressure to regularly adapt software to varying conditions has deeply impacted software engineering in the past, and this remains true today. In recent years, for instance, software development practices have been made more agile. Indeed, in many cases, a development project has to be able to start even when some business and technical aspects have yet to be nailed down. Similarly, market pressures sometimes push companies to release 'unfinished' products, leaving bugs and missing functionalities for subsequent releases. There are of course advantages in releasing products early. An example of this is where a product is conceived for some purpose, but on release its usage changes and then its subsequent development follows that usage. *Flickr* is one such example, it was released as part of a multiplayer online game (from Ludicorp), but users availed of the photo storage capabilities and this popularity drove the focus to photo storage and exchange.[1]

The requirement for frequent changes continues when the system is deployed and in operation. Here again, evolutions are necessary to preserve system utility and relevance. Changing software while it is in use brings additional challenges. One such challenge could be where the developers, systems analysts and other staff associated with the creation of the software are now long gone. Another example is where systems have to be maintained with new resources, and sometimes this may be required to happen where documentation is poor or non-existent. Also, where the systems are in active use and cannot be stopped to carry out maintenance, the computational state, for example, the values of the parameters and the objects running, has to be preserved. As we will see later in this book, this brings about non-trivial problems.

In this context, time and complexity do not mix. As time passes and system evolutions accumulate, the complexity of a software system continues to grow. In fact, where evolutions have not been anticipated, their implementation can even alter the logical structure of the system. Invariably, the software system gets more and more complex: artefacts are more numerous, less coherent and more intricate. System evolution increases in difficulty, and each new evolution can make the situation worse! There may come a point in time where only a complete refactoring of the system can decrease its complexity. This task is however very costly and, generally, delayed as long as possible—often triggered when updates simply cannot be accommodated. This observation led to Lehman's law stipulating that when a programme is modified, its complexity will increase, provided that one does not actively work against this [2].

In spite of this considerable complexity, the software community has been tremendously successful. Software systems are everywhere: they have pervaded most aspects of our working and social life. In industrial societies, most people possess one or more computers that take different forms such as laptops, tablets and smart phones. Companies such as Google, Twitter or Facebook are known all over the planet, and their services are used by millions of people. They have created new ways to work, to learn and, above all, to communicate. Software systems are also

---

[1]http://www.ludicorp.com/about.php (2012).

becoming more distributed, and they are getting larger. Systems counting many millions of lines of code, and which are subjected to thousands of updates per year, are a frequent occurrence. They arguably constitute some of the most complex artefacts ever built by human beings. To give an order of magnitude, David A. Wheeler estimated that version 7.2 of the RedHat Linux operating system is worth 8,000 person years in terms of development time.[2] As a comparison, the construction the Empire State Building required only 3,500 person years!

It seems, however, that the situation is changing. New domains like Internet services, cloud or pervasive computing are emerging and placing new demands on software systems. Specifically, systems have to be even more distributed, more heterogeneous, more dynamic, developed more rapidly, etc. Many think we have reached a barrier in terms of being able to overcome such complexities. Software engineers are beginning to feel that they are unable to anticipate, design and maintain such systems using traditional approaches.

As a result, there has been a push towards more automated approaches to help develop and, above all, administrate and maintain software systems. IBM, in order to refer to this new set of practices, coined the term *autonomic computing*.

Autonomic computing is the main topic of this book. It can be viewed as one approach to the engineering of software systems and, as such, encompasses the broad scope of sub-disciplines in the computing field, encompassing requirements engineering, software architectures, design, development, testing, maintenance, configuration management and quality. For these reasons, we begin this book by providing a background introducing 'traditional' software engineering approaches. We believe it is of major importance to be familiar with such practices in order to understand why and how they have adapted to face new challenges. Inversely, it cannot be denied that most of these traditional techniques are still required in the implementation of future solutions. In this introduction, we focus on the notion of customisable software processes to guide the development and maintenance of software systems for it has had a deep and lasting impact on software practices. The software engineering processes acknowledge that the production of software systems can be managed and, in doing so, have encouraged the controlled production of reliable, high-quality, cost-effective, software systems.

Software processes describe the activities that are to be performed to enable software system production. There have been a number of models that describe the individual activities that occur during this process and how those activities interact, characterising the methodologies that define best practice. Activities are divided into development and administration cycles. Development activities deal substantially with the production of programmes meeting specified requirements. Administration activities are more concerned with system deployment and its day-to-day management and maintenance. Identifying the commonality of activities for a number of software development initiatives and then sharing the resulting knowledge, artefacts, etc. have had a great impact on software practices. That is, it has allowed the definition of the successful, repeatable techniques that are now taught in universities and widely used by practitioners.

---

[2] http://www.dwheeler.com/sloc/redhat71-v1/redhat71sloc.html.

1.2   The Software Life Cycle

1.2.1   Software Development

Software engineers identified the problem of complexity early in the history of computing. The famous so-called software crisis appeared in the late 1960s, when the term software engineering was coined. Put simply, software engineering focuses on how complex computing projects can be designed and then managed over the life cycle of a project.

Software engineering can be defined as a systematic discipline that aims to improve the specification, design, implementation and maintenance of software systems by increasing their quality and cost-effectiveness. Precise definitions of software engineering are not readily found; however, many books introduce the subject in detail [3, 4]. Nevertheless, its concepts are derived from the fields of mathematics, computer science and, of course, engineering practice.

Software engineering has developed successful techniques and processes to help build programmes and conduct projects. Many techniques rely on the principles of modularity and separation of concerns. Application of these principles to programming, for instance, has led to the definition of structured programming, object-oriented programming, software componentisation and so on. The implementation of these principles to better achieve software projects has resulted in the definition of development processes.

Development processes have been defined in order to decompose the production of software into a number of smaller and more controllable activities. Particularly, a software development process specifies and organises a set of interrelated activities that can be followed in order to properly deliver a quality software system. Because different software systems are required for each specific situation, processes are usually defined as models (i.e. defined in abstract terms) and then customised, case-by-case, to meet the specific needs of each particular software project.

Development activities include requirement management, design specification, implementation and the validation of software systems. A number of process models have been proposed to coordinate and implement these activities. The Waterfall model [5], for instance, relies on a sequential approach: requirements first, then design, coding and testing. However, this approach does not provide the opportunity to revise or review the work carried out in the initial stages of the life cycle when the project is in the development process (i.e. one cannot revisit the requirements and design stages when working in the development and testing phases).

Such sequential processes are less popular today because of their inability to deal with change. They are simply not suited to the way in which software is produced in the current fast-paced, dynamic business environments. Nowadays, the approach to the development process is incremental. As illustrated by Fig. 1.1, software systems are built through successive increments, where at each stage, requirements, design, coding and testing activities are carried out. This process is repeated until the software system is ready for delivery.

Each activity uses and produces software artefacts that are very diverse by nature. They can include textual documents, structured texts, graphical models, source files

Fig. 1.1 Software life cycle

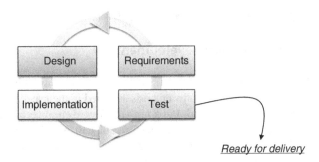

Ready for delivery

and binary files. These artefacts are complex because of their number and their volume. They can be made of many interacting elements and are consequently hard to integrate, administer and maintain. They are also characterised by a number of traceability links. For instance, systems architectural decisions are made to meet some requirements, so the pieces of code that was used to implement this should be able to be traced back to an architectural design and then to its requirements, etc.

These artefacts constitute the base elements of every software project and determine its success. They must be modular, with strong cohesion and weak coupling.[3] That is, where the cohesion of software artefacts is strong, its readability, maintainability and reuse are maximised. Likewise, minimising the coupling between artefacts is also good for readability, maintainability and reusability. These properties are then of utter importance when it comes to software evolution. Well-structured, coherent and decoupled artefacts favour evolution and limit the propagation of uncontrolled side effects. Maintaining relationships between artefacts is highly important. Not understanding the rationale behind an artefact's internal structure and its relationships makes it almost impossible to update a system without the risk of causing undesirable side effects.

A simple example could be where a component is used to determine the location of the user. This component is used to direct music to the nearest speaker to that user. The code that ships the music around the room uses a location component as a black box (i.e. the system is not interested in how it calculates location, just the integers that represent location co-ordinates resulting from executing the code in the component). This system has the advantage of having its functions and services represented as components, so it has the advantage of being decoupled and well structured. Therefore, when we find a better way to get the user's location, we can take out the old component and plug in the new. However, side effects can still happen. Perhaps the precision of the new location component is higher than the old one, so the numbers representing the co-ordinates adhere to a smaller location grid space. When added to our music system, this might have the side effect of not mapping to the locations of the speakers, and therefore, the system will direct music elsewhere.

---

[3]Cohesion is about the functional scope of an artefact (a component, a class, a design diagram, an analysis diagram, etc.). Coupling is about the number and nature of relationships between artefacts.

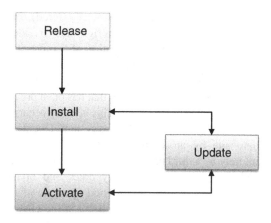

Fig. 1.2 Major deployment activities in the software life cycle

1.2.2   Software Deployment

Deployment starts when a software system has been duly approved for delivery. Its purpose is to produce a live software system to the user, and this may ensure that it is deployed and running on the client's site. It handles the transfer, installation, configuration and integration of concrete artefacts therein. It initiates the different executable components of the software system and deals with subsequent updates.

Deployment is normally carried out by authorised administrators. It is traditionally decomposed into the following (sub-) activities (Fig. 1.2): release, retire, install, uninstall, activate, deactivate, update and adapt [6].

Iterating through this list, the purpose of the *release* activity is to prepare the software so that it can be transferred to the client. Simply put, it consists of packaging the constituents of the software with the information required by the deployment processes that follow. *De-release*, or *retirement*, is the inverse activity of *release*. It is carried out when a software system is obsolete or is no longer needed.

The *installation* activity inserts the software in the target environment and configures it for execution. In the simplest cases, installation is about copying files to a target execution infrastructure. Most of the time, however, it requires a sequence of operations to be performed such as uncompressing files, selecting locations for installation, getting appropriate permissions, configuring some aspects of the software system and integrating the software system in the existing computing infrastructure.

The *activation* activity comes after the software system installation. Its purpose is to start the executable elements that have been previously installed. In the simplest cases, activation consists of calling a unique binary file (i.e. a programme) with the appropriate input parameters. In some situations, however, it requires several programmes to be initiated, and these may be installed on different machines.

Un-installation is the inverse activity of installation. It is carried out when the presence of the software system is no longer required. *Deactivation* is the opposite activity of activation. It is done when the execution of a software system is no longer required (or the service is no longer offered). *Deactivation* and *de-installation* are complex activities in their own right due to code dependencies. Their implementation may imply the reconfiguration of components that have a dependency relationship with the element that is being decommissioned.

The purpose of the *update* and the *adapt* activity is to change parts of the (or indeed the complete) software system that has been previously installed, which may or may not be activated at this point. This activity is carried out as many times as necessary during the lifetime of a software system. Updates are traditionally performed on the client site by an administrator. More regularly, however, updates are initiated remotely by a third party, for example, an operating system (OS) update from an OS vendor, who controls delivery dates and update frequencies. Periodic security updates to the software is a good example of this. Here, code that fixes security vulnerabilities is developed and put at the clients' disposal by software providers. A security patch can then be inserted by the client administrator or remotely pushed by the provider, with or without prior authorisation, depending on the vendor–user agreement.

Institutively, the *update* activity would appear to be a simpler task compared to installation and activation, but is it? Clearly, considerable configuration and integration activities have to be carried out during the early phases of the life cycle. However, a closer look reveals that the update activity is heavily constrained and often very complex. It has to respect the computing environment that uses or relies on the software component so as to not introduce new problems. Also, an update must preserve data, states, intermediary results, etc. Poorly designed updates can introduce new problems requiring the software to be regressed back to its previous state.

Deployment is a key software activity. It is technically very challenging in the sense that all sorts of operations are required: software artefacts have to be compressed, packaged, transferred, uncompressed, copied, configured, integrated, started, modified, etc. In addition, software systems can be required to stay in operation while further deployment activities are executed, which clearly increases the level of difficulty.

Deployment has long been underestimated and only now receives due attention. The recent availability of new tools, like the Chef configuration management tool,[4] for instance, facilitates the work of administrators, providing higher-level languages to automate complex infrastructures deployment. However, even with such new generation tools, the level of complexity remains high.

The complexity of the deployment activities is actually at the heart of the motivation for autonomic computing. Performing the various deployment tasks, in fact, is complex. For instance, the initial configuration stage can include hundreds of parameters to be set. Also, software systems may have to be integrated with heterogeneous systems, whose lifetimes can be dynamic and can be spread over local or wide-area networks. It is necessary, in this situation, to identify these systems and their configurations to correctly install and run the software. Over time, as software and its underlying execution platform change, some deployment activities,

---

[4]Chef—open-source, systems integration framework: http://www.opscode.com/chef.

including configuration, must be repeated (see next subsection). This activity comes at a great cost, the majority of which is not the computing infrastructure, but the time taken and salaries required for the staff (system administrators, etc.) that are involved with this process.

1.2.3   Software Maintenance

Maintenance starts after the software's initial installation. Its purpose is to modify the software being used in order to fix bugs, to improve quality of service or to address new conditions for execution. Maintenance comprises a number of activities, ranging from the 'simple' reconfiguration of certain parameters to more complex operations, like the development of new pieces of code or the migration to new running platforms.

It is important to understand that maintenance is not limited to minor changes in operational systems. Maintenance, in fact, has to deal with changing user requirements and operating environments (as explained in Sect. 1.1) and sometimes requires that major updates are carried out. In recognition of this, Lehman termed the maintenance function as evolutionary development [2].

Traditionally, maintenance activities are classified into four categories. *Corrective* maintenance takes care of faults and errors detected in delivered software. *Adaptive* maintenance is concerned with evolving the system to better match user and changes in the system's environment. *Perfective* maintenance deals with evolutions in the desired functions or related quality of service. Finally, *preventive* maintenance targets the detection and correction of latent faults in the delivered software. Contrary to common perception, correcting misbehaviours accounts for, on average, less than 20 % of the total maintenance effort [7]. That means that around 80 % of the maintenance effort is dedicated to software evolution (where adaptive maintenance accounts for 25 %, perfective maintenance for 50 % and preventive maintenance for only 5 %).

It is commonly accepted that maintenance is a complex, time-consuming activity that can take far more time than the initial development of the software. In fact, it is today acknowledged that between 50 and 80 % of effort spent on a computer system will happen after it has been delivered to the customer. As detailed in the previous sections, updating a software system is inherently complex. It can require changing unstructured or badly structured code, often in situations where documentation is lacking. As software ages, the software structure is likely to be altered by successive updates, and, as a consequence, changes become difficult and risky to perform (since side effects are more likely to occur).

Maintenance is carried out by one or several system administrators, often called the 'sysadmin'. The responsibilities of system administrators are many and vary according to organisations. In most cases, they require high technical skills in order to, for instance, configure databases, Web servers or networks, in accordance with what is expected of the system. They also need in-depth expertise to be able to solve problems affecting the behaviour of a software system: they need to understand

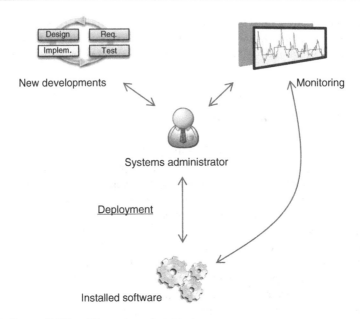

Fig. 1.3 Responsibilities of the system administrator

the purpose and nature of a software system in order to quickly determine what goes wrong and to fix it (or to report it to interested parties).

The administration job has often to be carried out under considerable stress. As we will see later in this and the next chapter, the complexity and stress faced by administrators can lead to bad decision-making with, sometimes, undesirable outcomes.

As illustrated by Fig. 1.3, we can distinguish two forms of administrative actions: the adaptation of software already installed and the integration of newly developed artefacts. New artefacts can correspond to expected updates or to specific answers to requests initiated by the administrator. In the latter case, the term 'software patch' is often used in maintenance terminology.

Let us develop these two categories of actions. In the first case, the purpose is essentially to monitor the software systems and to adapt the software artefacts that are already present. There are a number of ways in which this can be achieved. First, it can be executed through the appropriate tuning of configuration parameters, which can be tricky in some instances. Indeed, many systems are characterised by hundreds of parameters with tight interrelationships. Finding out the best values and the right balance between values requires advanced skills and expertise that are not easy to find. It may often require third party intervention of an expert or consultant. Complexity is so considerable that in many cases, most parameters remain unchanged, even at the cost of degraded performance. Adapting existing artefacts may take other forms. It may require that some programmes or data is moved to different computers or different middleware. That is, it can also involve the migration of some parts of the (or the complete) software to a new version of a supporting middleware. Such an achievement may be long and difficult and may demand code rewrites. In general, processes have been defined in order to guide such operations and minimise trouble.

In certain cases, reconfiguring existing artefacts is not enough to enable the system to adapt to new conditions. Here, deeper changes motivating system redevelopment are needed. Note, new developments generally use the same tools and processes as those used to develop the system initially (with the additional constraint that existing software has to be accounted for). Also, system administrators use the same deployment primitives in order to install, integrate and activate updates. In this regard, initial developments and subsequent maintenance-related developments are very similar. Their shared purpose is to produce code meeting current requirements and deploy it on the clients' site.

Relatively little effort has been dedicated to the deployment and maintenance activities (i.e. compared with the relative importance and cost of these phases). For a long time, the software engineering activity was focused on the development phase. This predominance is not anecdotal. This focus on the development aspects of software engineering is not surprising. Most research effort in the history of software engineering has sought to improve the way we produce software systems that meet the clients' expectations, minimising the chance of misbehaviour at runtime, etc. [8].

In this context, the software administrator has a difficult and sometimes unacknowledged task. Software administrators often have to carry out delicate and sometimes vital operations with poor tools that often are not well integrated or sufficiently abstract to aid the job. When a problem is detected, system administrators are often faced with a dilemma. Either they update the system, without all the necessary knowledge to be certain that they can avoid undesirable side effects, or they limit their actions and only report problems, waiting for problems to be fixed by developers (termed as new developments in Fig. 1.3). The latter may receive low prioritisation from project managers and from developers, and therefore, this task may take some time.

Many think that this situation has worsened in recent years. Indeed advances in hardware and networks, combined with ever growing demands for new features and the increased pressure on time-to-market, have deeply changed the software industry. Customers are longing for new software-based services, and companies are striving to supply these new services as fast as possible. This raises serious challenges since it means more complexity and more frequent updates, which in turn equates to more functionality and more code being required to be delivered in increasingly shrinking delivery times. Ensuring system correctness and dependability in these conditions becomes a real challenge.

1.3 Maintenance Challenges

Outstanding advances in hardware, communications and software engineering have contributed to place software at the heart of our society. This software 'invasion' is still going on, and nothing indicates that it will slow down soon. First, hardware performance is still increasing exponentially. Though, under reassessment due to the bounds of physics, Moore's law is still in evidence. That is, we can still observe that storage capacity and CPU speed will approximately double each 18 months. Also, all sorts of networks are spreading around us. They allow the connection of a myriad of equipment, some with a relatively small footprint, but powerful enough to host software-based functions. The pervasive and cloud computing paradigms, that either place computing into the fabric of the environment or alternatively move storage and heavy computing into the *cloud* (*a* virtual computer whose geographical location can be totally transparent to the user), merely reinforce this trend.

However, this constant evolution is not without serious problems. In fact, the way software systems are currently developed and maintained is called into question. In short, the development of software systems has to become faster and more agile, whereas maintenance has to be able to perform more functions more efficiently in order to remain in line with its environment.

To meet these demanding requirements, practitioners have adopted new development practices. First, the time when software was developed entirely for one project is over. Instead, due to reduced costs and production delays, software development is more like assembling external components—called COTS (components off the shelf)—which are often provided by third parties (such as corporations and open-source communities). COTS can generally be configured before being executed and administered during execution. But they are very heterogeneous. They frequently come with their own configuration methods, tools and vocabulary. Thus, parts of a single system can be configured via a specific XML-based language, for example, while others by a command line interpreter or via a Web interface. Moreover, COTS allow the configuration of many parameters, sometimes several hundreds, and this facilitates the system being tailored to user preferences as well as helping it fit with the current computing infrastructure that will be used to support it. Also, they have diverse goals and evolution cycles, so, the maintenance of COTS-based systems requires expertise in numerous technologies and tools. Moreover, it also requires being able to follow changes of components that are by de facto beyond the user's control.

Also, components that make up software applications are often distributed over networks of different kinds. So, more of the software maintenance activity includes the configuration and subsequent monitoring of a number of networks. Here again, networks are often not under the system administrator's sole control; they evolve according to their own strategies and schedules, not specifically following the exclusive needs of the software systems that use it. The proliferation of networks also brings the development of new software distribution methods.

With the arrival of cloud computing, many services are now remotely available, for instance, office automation suites such as Microsoft Office. These new applications constitute the main business of modern corporations like Google. However, the externalisation of services and data storage has led to stringent requirements regarding system availability and performance. Service consumers, especially corporations, may request availability rates of 99.999 %, in the knowledge that service interruptions imply heavy financial penalties and thus will be minimised. In 2008,

Fig. 1.4   Percentage of errors ordered by cause for three Websites in 2000 [10]

for instance, the cost of downtime for a corporation like Amazon came to tens of thousands dollars per minute.[5]

In order to reach such a quality, speaking in terms of performance and availability, maintenance operations have to be performed very quickly and reliably. However, currently, on large heterogeneous software, maintenance operations do not meet these requirements.

Thus, software applications have become heterogeneous, networked and vital for both the economy and the society overall. They are part of sophisticated *ecosystems* and evolve in unstable, even unpredictable, contexts. As explained earlier, a direct outcome is that maintenance has become increasingly complex and administrators have to face increasing pressure.

Of course, companies are aware of this issue and a number of counter measures have been taken. For instance, the heterogeneity and complexity of administration tools have required the specialisation of administrative staff and the setting up of specific training programmes. CISCO and Oracle, among others, provide qualification certificates to reward system administrators and show that they have successfully shown that they can control their specific system. Nevertheless, it is clear that software systems made of networked heterogeneous elements are still difficult to install, configure and maintain, not to mention, to optimise. Administrators, as skilled as they may be, are reaching the limit of human capability. Also, the cost of hiring experts is not affordable beyond a certain limit.

At the same time, the human resources needed for the deployment and maintenance of software has greatly increased over the last few years. Human beings are increasingly more involved in the day-to-day operations of software systems. However, until recently, human administration mistakes were not really taken into account. That is, the administrator was not considered as a potential source of errors during the deployment, updates and, more generally, maintenance and problem fixing stages of the software life cycle. This assumption is no longer reasonable. At the beginning of 2000, many surveys have published the causes of errors and repair costs in the information systems, for example, [9]. Figure 1.4 displays the result of a 6-month survey conducted in 2001 concerning three anonymous medium-sized

---

[5]http://news.cnet.com/8301-10784_3-9962010-7.html.

Websites. It shows very clearly that most of the errors were caused by the 'operations', that is, the system administrators. Today, it is estimated that the system administrators themselves cause approximately 40 % of errors resulting in breakdowns.

It is foreseen that this situation is going to get worse. In 1991, Mark Weiser has
described a world in which computers would be omnipresent and transparent to
users [11]. This vision has given birth to the pervasive computing field that is getting more concrete around us. Soon, non-expert users will have to carry out some
form of software installation, maintenance, etc. The technical skills of such users
may be relatively low, and even if it is reasonable to think that these skills will
increase with experience, it is not likely that it would reach a sufficient level for
facing the complexity of current and future computing systems. But, more than a
problem of skill sets, the users are not interested in being system administrators;
they simply want the smooth operation of the software.

On the other hand, the environment in which pervasive applications evolve is
highly fluctuating and depends, for instance, on the operation of the network infrastructure, energy availability and other conditions (sound level, temperature, etc.)
that occur at each instant. An extreme example of this dynamism lies at the cyber–
physical interface—the crossing point where the computer system and the environment meet. This issue pertains mostly to modern embedded computing systems
where the extreme dynamism and interdependency between the critical components
and the physical environment are as yet not well understood. Here, the gap between
software engineering and systems engineering needs to be bridged to allow systems
to adapt to change.

1.4   Autonomic Computing

As the development, maintenance and operation of computing systems became more
complex, communities began to emerge with a specific remit to examine ways to
overcome the problems mentioned in the previous sections. In particular, we have
witnessed in recent years the development of more automated deployment and maintenance strategies. Such approaches, based on dedicated tools, are aiming to automate
a number of administrative tasks such as installing packages and modules, defining
authorisations and updating configurations. Many approaches, however, are based on
low-level script-like specifications and still require strong technical system administration expertise in order to carry out specific operations. Also, these approaches only
address a few aspects of software administration. Essential maintenance tasks, like
architecture evolution, for instance, are still ignored or insufficiently supported.

One major initiative came from IBM, and this sparked off the use of the term
'autonomic computing' to characterise the notion of a computer system that is able
to adapt to internal and external changes with minimal intervention from the human.
Autonomic computing is the result of this trend of automating parts of the maintenance task.

Paul Horn—the research director of IBM—detailed this autonomic computing paradigm in a manifesto in October 2001 [12]. Here he identifies software complexity as being the major challenge for computer science for the beginning of the century. To paraphrase, he describes this complexity as a short-term obstacle to the evolution of services and software and, in the absence of any systemic change or paradigm shift, as a long-term threat where the complexity of software keeps increasing until human resources can no longer cope. In this view, system administrators will have to solve complicated problems, the causes of which will be difficult to comprehend. Consequently, the performance and reliability of such systems will be endangered, with, of course, knock on financial impacts.

With the drive for more profitability in corporations, it is unlikely that management committees will endorse colossal budgets to maintain systems. In addition, a further problem is that complexity also impacts on security: how can we guarantee the security of data, in such an open world, if we cannot make guarantees regarding the software that handles it? Similar statements can be made regarding systems availability or other non-functional software qualities.

IBM's premise is to enhance systems with self-management capabilities. Systems are thus able to evolve in an autonomous manner, fixing undesirable behaviours and adapting to their changing requirements and environment. This autonomy is introduced in order to soften the complexity of the administration task, and in doing so, the system administrators delegate a part of their workload to the system itself. That way, they can focus on the system's fundamentals and off-load more mundane tasks to the automatic administration software. Also, it is expected that administration tasks performed by the systems themselves can be of higher quality, decreasing the introduction of bugs during the maintenance phase.

The level of autonomy given to a system is a product of two aspects. They relate to the ability to map the administration function to a process executable by the machine and how easy it is to implant that function into the system. That is, some administration tasks are difficult to define so automating them is correspondingly difficult. Further, it may also be difficult to inject such automation code into some legacy systems where the source code is obscure or non-existent. As we will see later on, different levels of autonomy can thus be targeted.

The expected benefits of autonomic computing are numerous and obviously include the decrease of maintenance expenditure and risk. The goal is to obtain systems that are able to configure themselves automatically, and with a tendency towards zero configuration for the administrator, hence reducing costs. As a consequence, autonomic computing promises to allow a revaluation of the tasks allocated to the human system administrator, allowing them to focus on more strategic or poignant aspects of the system support function. Autonomic computing also has the potential to increase service availability. The anticipation of potential problems and the automatic system diagnosis can provide increased application dependability and many non-functional qualities. It can, for instance, increase security, so that the system can be better prepared to counter malicious acts.

Of course, these benefits are very appealing and have fostered lots of research work around the world. This endeavour has taught us one thing, however, that implementing autonomic solutions is also very challenging. That is, autonomic systems are more difficult to design, implement and validate than software systems without the ability to self-manage. This is quite understandable; complexity cannot just disappear. Like a computation law of thermodynamics, the complexity is simply moved from runtime to design time, as a countermeasure to the increasing complexity involved with runtime administration so that it can cope with dynamic, fluctuating environments. Therefore, in order to unburden system administrators and decrease ownership costs, autonomic software systems are certainly more difficult to conceive and implement.

In fact, implementing autonomic solutions has a profound influence on most of the software engineering activities previously presented in this chapter. Of course, these activities still have to be used to produce autonomic software systems, but they have to be refined to meet more ambitious goals. In particular, four major new requirements have to be considered so that a computer system can be administered with minimal human intervention:

– A computer system must be able to monitor itself at runtime in order to know its internal situation. It also has to monitor part of its execution environment in order to follow relevant evolutions.
– A computer system must be able to keep some knowledge about its goals, its past and the current situation. Then, it has to integrate some type of reasoning capabilities to decide on corrective actions whenever needed.
– A computer system must be able to adapt itself at runtime in order to implement the corrective administrative actions that are required. Such adaptations must not endanger or corrupt ongoing operations.
– A computer system should provide a high-level interface, allowing human administrators to specify or modify system goals, tune reasoning processes and observe the system ability to attain its objectives.

In order to achieve these demanding requirements, most software engineering activities must be revisited. The requirements phase, for instance, must decide on the (types of) adaptations and monitoring data that are desired so that the system can self-manage. Some high-level requirements—the administrative goals—must become explicit and formally defined so as to be interpretable and manoeuvrable by the software system, at runtime, since these drive the system's operation. That is, the self-managed, autonomic system adapts its behaviour to best maintain these sets of goals.

As a self-managed system must be aware of its own operation, the design phase must decide not only on the adaptation but also on the monitoring features that must be incorporated in the software system. This can be complex and tricky. Since monitoring can be extremely costly, only relevant information has to be collected. If possible, monitoring should also be configurable so as to be adapted to the current needs of the system that strives to meet its goals. In some situations, monitoring can even be disengaged for performance reasons. Anticipating and allowing runtime adaptation is also very challenging. It means building up appropriate architectural styles and design approaches to enhance flexibility and enable safe runtime change. It also calls for specific mechanisms preserving ongoing computations during code adaptation. Finally, some part of the implementation has to be self-described and possibly available online (e.g. from repositories) so as to enable its automatic instantiation (deployment) or replacement depending on the runtime needs.

To some extent, the software engineering phases are progressively pushed into the runtime. The ultimate goal is then to extend or evolve current software engineering practices so that they can be partially performed during runtime. That is, a software system should be able to interpret (or even create) formal requirements (goals) at runtime, to apply existing designs for adaptation, to create or change implementations, (re)deploy and (re-)instantiate them, etc.

Clearly, there is a strong relationship between autonomic computing and software engineering. Autonomic computing will force software engineering to come up with new techniques and new approaches to software development and maintenance. This is truly an exciting challenge but a really difficult one indeed. This observation is one of the early motivations of this book. Beyond necessary explanations about the objectives and interests of autonomic computing, it seems important to us to go through the different software engineering techniques that are currently available for organising and developing self-managed software systems.

However, a comprehensive study of all modern software engineering techniques is beyond the scope of this text. Instead, in introducing the field of autonomic computing, we discuss software engineering implicitly; we introduce the elements of software engineering that are either relevant to a particular capability necessary for making a system self-managing or that are impacted by the move towards autonomic computing systems. More precisely, we present the principles and methodologies applicable to building autonomic computing architectures (Chap. 4), enabling systems to self-monitor (Chap. 5) and self-adapt (Chap. 6) and then the methods that systems can use in order to make adaptation decisions (Chap. 7). Finally, we provide some pointers on how software engineering can intervene for developing evaluation solutions for self-managed systems (Chap. 8).

Unclear or immature software engineering techniques with respect to their applicability to autonomic computing are not addressed in this book. For instance, the problem of discovering and formally representing requirements related to autonomic needs is not covered here for much research is still required in this subject. However, the more futuristic aspects of this field will be touched upon in the conclusion and the last sections of Chap. 9.

1.5 Book Structure

The structure of this book reflects the observations made in the previous section. Specifically, this book is made of the following chapters:

- *Chapter 2: Autonomic Systems*
  The purpose of this chapter is to define the autonomic computing paradigm and to introduce the related terminology. It discusses the main notions that are

essential to any autonomic computing system, including the concepts of goal, context and *self-** capabilities. It also presents in more detail the initial motivations behind the autonomic computing initiative.

- *Chapter 3: Sources of Inspiration for Autonomic Computing*
  The purpose of this chapter is to provide a (certainly biased) overview of the most relevant sources of inspiration for autonomic computing and to offer pointers towards more extensive specialty literature. We pay particular attention to biology, control theory, artificial intelligence and complex systems.

- *Chapter 4: Autonomic Computing Architectures*
  The goal of this chapter is to introduce the main architectural elements of an autonomic system at a high level of abstraction. It shows how self-managed software systems can be developed based on control/feedback loop elements and how such control/feedback loops can be constructed and integrated with other feedback loops. To some extent, this chapter sets up the rest of this book in that the chapters that follow aim to provide answers, partial in some cases, to the issues raised by this architectural chapter.

- *Chapter 5: The Monitoring Function*
  This chapter focuses on the monitoring function, which is the systematic collection of relevant information with the purpose of understanding, evaluating and controlling the system. Precisely, we look at different ways to design and implement monitoring. We focus on the establishment of absolute measureable technical metrics that represent the performance or state of the system.

- *Chapter 6: The Adaptation Function*
  This chapter focuses on the adaptation function. It defines precisely what it means and what it takes to modify a software system in terms of structure and behaviour. It also discusses the related challenges and presents a set of techniques that can be used to implement adaptable software systems.

- *Chapter 7: The Decision Function*
  The purpose of this chapter is to provide a brief outline of the various techniques that can be used to represent knowledge in autonomic computing systems and to conduct reasoning. There is a large choice of approaches available to the autonomic system designer, and the choice will depend on how much resources are available to represent and process this knowledge. This chapter is not an exhaustive list of techniques; rather, it gives a flavour of the most popular approaches found in the literature as well as approaches used in the past by the authors and practitioners.

- *Chapter 8: Evaluation Issues*
  This chapter presents the challenges to evaluating an autonomic system, what to look out for and what others have attempted to do. It aims to enable the reader to be able to design tests and metrics that can be used to compare autonomic computing systems with a particular focus on the aspects that make an autonomic system different from those without self-management features.

- *Chapter 9: Autonomic Mediation in Cilia*
  The purpose of this chapter is to show how the Cilia mediation framework has been rendered autonomic, using many of the techniques presented in this book. The Cilia framework is essentially used in pervasive settings in order to integrate

different forms of data sources and destinations. This chapter also presents ongoing work offering further management capabilities and aiming to progress towards endowing the Cilia technology with fully autonomic life-cycle management capabilities.

- *Chapter 10: Future of Autonomic Computing and Conclusions*
  The purpose of this final chapter is to recap the key points tackled in this book and to introduce the reader to the open issues in autonomic computing. Precisely, this chapter aims to look ahead and foresee the future of autonomic computing.

The purpose of this book is hence to clarify the software engineering techniques used by autonomic computing. It is a practical guide to introduce the concepts of autonomic computing to advanced students, researchers and system managers alike. Through the combined use of examples and practical projects, the aim is to enable the reader to rapidly understand the theories, models, design principles and challenges of this subject while building upon their current knowledge, thus reinforcing the concepts of autonomic computing and self-management.

We hope that this book allows the advanced computing student and researcher to be able to consolidate their programming, artificial intelligence, systems architecture and software engineering courses to allow them to better architect robust yet flexible software systems capable of meeting the computing demands for today and in the future.

We also hope that this book can help those responsible for the development and maintenance of real world systems currently in operation to understand the benefits that the autonomic computing approach can bring. We hope that the concise nature of this book allows them to rapidly catch up with the work that has been carried out in this field as well as to get introduced to some fundamental aspects of self-management that are beyond the scope of traditional computing training (e.g. control theory). This should therefore provide a greater grounding in the subject, and when combined with the practical nature of the examples and projects, readers should be in a better position to design and engineer self-management features into current systems as well as developing strategies for the development of new systems.

1.6   Key Points

In this chapter, we have introduced the following important points:

- Software systems are very complex constructions. They are made of a number of heterogeneous artefacts interacting in complex ways. Furthermore, software systems are intangible constructions, which make them difficult to represent, manipulate and update.
- Software production is structured into software development, deployment and maintenance. The purpose of the development phase is to build the software artefacts making up a software system. The goal of the deployment phase is essentially to transfer, install, start and update software systems. Finally, the maintenance phase is concerned with the day-to-day administration of running systems and their update.

- Much of computing engineering research effort has been dedicated to the development phase of the software life cycle. Relatively little attention has been given so far to the maintenance phase. Simply put, system administrators observe the systems at runtime, change minor things when needed and, otherwise, send a request to developers if something serious happens. However, this is no longer a suitable approach when software gets complex and its environment ever changing.
- Despite its inherent complexity, software has pervaded our professional and social life and users want more functions today, accessible anywhere and anytime. These new demanding requirements change the way software systems are structured and managed.
- Great emphasis is now put on the runtime aspects of the software life cycle: software management gets more complex and ambitious. Engineers are beginning to feel that they are unable to maintain new systems using traditional approaches.
- Motivated by this problem, a major initiative came from IBM. This sparked off the use of the term 'autonomic computing' to characterise the notion of a computer system that is able to adapt to internal and external change with minimal conscious intervention from the human. In the autonomic computing vision, human administrators merely specify the computer system's high-level business goals or policies, and software takes on this task through self-management.
- Self-managed systems demand us to rethink most software engineering activities in order to push them into the runtime. This book is structured according to this statement. It seeks to provide software engineering ideas that are required to understand and build autonomic systems.

References

1. Brooks, F.: No silver bullet: Essence and accidents of software engineering. In: Kugler, H.J. (ed.) Information Processing 86, pp. 1069–1076. Elsevier, Amsterdam (1986). Reprinted in Computer, 20, 4 (April 1987), pp. 10–19
2. Lehman, M.M.: On understanding laws, evolution, and conservation in the large-program life cycle. J. Syst. Softw. 1, 213–221 (1980)
3. Sommerville, I.: Software Engineering, 9th edn. Addison Wesley, Boston (2010)
4. Ghezzi, C., Jazayeri, M., Mandrioli, D.: Fundamentals of Software Engineering. Prentice Hall, Englewood Cliffs (1991)
5. Benington, H.D.: Production of large computer programs. In: Proceedings of the 9th International Conference on Software Engineering (ICSE), Monterey, CA, USA, pp. 299–310. IEEE Computer Society Press, Los Alamitos (1987)
6. Carzaniga, A., Fuggetta, A., Hall, R.S., Van Der Hoek, A., Heimbigner, D., Wolf, A.L.: A Characterization Framework for Software Deployment Technologies, Technical Report CU-CS-857-98, Department of Computer Science, University of Colorado. http://serl.cs.colorado.edu/~carzanig/papers/CU-CS-857-98.pdf, April 1998
7. Lientz, B.P., Swanson, E.B.: Software Maintenance Management: A Study of the Maintenance of Computer Application Software in 487 Data Processing Organizations. Addison-Wesley, Reading (1980)
8. Baresi, L., Ghezzi, C.: The disappearing boundary between development-time and run-time, FSE-18, 7–11 Nov 2010, Santa Fe, New Mexico, USA (2010)
9. Patterson, D.A.: A simple way to estimate the cost of downtime. In: Proceedings of 16th Systems Administration Conference, LISA, pp. 185–188. http://roc.cs.berkeley.edu/papers/Cost_Downtime_LISA.pdf (2002)

10. Patterson, D.A.: Availability and maintainability performance: new focus for a new century. In: Key Note at Conference on File and Storage Technologies (FAST), vol. 2, Monterey, CA (2002)
11. Weiser, M.: The computer for the 21st century. Sci. Am. **265**(3), 66–75 (1991)
12. Horn, P.: Autonomic Computing: IBM's Perspective on the State of Information Technology, *IBM*. http://www.research.ibm.com/autonomic/manifesto/autonomic_computing.pdf (2001)
13. Boehm, B.: A view of 20th and 21st century software engineering. In: ICSE 2006: Proceedings of the 28th International Conference on Software Engineering, pp. 12–29. ACM, New York (2006)

Autonomic Systems

2

The purpose of this chapter is to define the notion of autonomic systems and to introduce related terminology. It discusses the main ideas that are essential to any autonomic computing system, including the concepts of 'goal', 'context' and 'self-*' capabilities.

The chapter also presents the initial motivations behind the autonomic computing initiative. It subsequently discusses the relevance of these motivations in light of both research and real-world implementations since this initiative was launched in the early days of the millennium.

We highlight the most important benefits that autonomic computing promises to bring to the IT domain as well as the equally important challenges that must be surpassed before computer systems can be endowed with autonomic management capabilities. An incremental approach to autonomic computing is presented in this context, proposing a five-step roadmap for progressively transforming current IT systems from their current (non-autonomic) status to full autonomic management support.

Finally, the chapter aims to position the relatively new autonomic computing initiative with respect to similar technological fields, supported by industry, governments or academia, as well as with respect to existing computing domains. Further relevant fields are discussed in the following chapter highlighting the inspiration that autonomic computing has and can draw from existing domains.

P. Lalanda et al., *Autonomic Computing: Principles, Design and Implementation*,
Undergraduate Topics in Computer Science, DOI 10.1007/978-1-4471-5007-7_2,
© Springer-Verlag London 2013

2.1   Autonomic Computing

2.1.1   Definitions

Autonomic computing (AC) seeks to render computing systems as self-managed. In other words, its objective is to enable computer systems to manage themselves so as to minimise the need for human intervention. In the autonomic computing vision, human administrators merely specify the computer system's high-level business goals. These goals subsequently serve as guidance to the underlying autonomic processes. In such settings, human administrators can more readily concentrate on defining high-level business objectives, or policies, and are freed from dealing with the lower-level technical details necessary to achieve such objectives, as these tasks are now performed by the autonomic system. Moreover, for specifying high-level systems goals, administrators may employ domain-specific concepts and languages, rather than having to permanently translate such concepts into low-level computer-specific terms (Fig. 2.1).

As explained in Chap. 1, autonomic computing is motivated by the increasing complexity inherent in today's software systems and the associated total owner-ship cost (TOC) of software systems. Software complexity mainly stems from the multitude of interrelated business requirements that systems must meet, from the significant number of interconnected software and hardware elements involved in system implementation and from the high distribution and heterogeneity of such elements. Some noteworthy examples of such complex software systems include enterprise applications, cloud platforms, grid applications, pervasive or ubiquitous software systems, management of massive data collections, communication and processing systems. While software complexity poses difficulties to system devel-opment, this complexity brings a further challenge during system execution, when the user experience and business revenues are at stake.

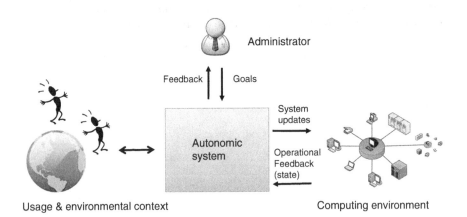

Fig. 2.1 Autonomic system

Complexity also comes from the frequent runtime changes that affect both business requirements and system implementation. Unpredictable change during system execution is practically guaranteed to occur over the entire lifetime of any complex system that interacts with our dynamic world. Change can be either intentional and carefully planned or unintentional (due, for instance, to external context modification or internal failure). Swift interventions are required to warrant correct, efficient and uninterrupted system execution. In the context of complex systems, ensuring such timely interventions raises massive administrative challenges, incurring significant costs and risks. In these circumstances, the prime goal of autonomic computing is to enable computing systems to autonomously deal with (unpredictable) change, so as to fulfil the objectives they were constructed for. Many administrative tasks are automated and carried out by autonomic processes rather than by manual intervention.

In general, the term *autonomic*[1] implies occurring involuntarily, unconsciously or automatically, or resulting spontaneously, from internal causes (e.g. autonomic reflexes). The term *autonomous*, originating from the Ancient Greek *autonomos* (from *auto*—'self' and *nomos*—'law'), signifies one's capability of *self-governance* or of defining one's own law, also implying self-containment and self-direction. In the context of biology, *autonomic* implies being a part of, related to, or controlled by the autonomic nervous system (ANS). Accordingly, *autonomicity* signifies the state of being autonomic. In the context of philosophy, finally, the terms *autonomy* [1][2] or *autonomous* have been used to signify one's ability to take one's own decisions, imposing one's free will and being independent of external control. In Kantian philosophy, autonomy is also considered in relation to *moral responsibility*.

Automating a system's management function implies adding further system complexity overall. Hence, paradoxically, dealing with existing system complexity compels us to exacerbate this complexity. To escape from this apparent paradox, it is important to note that the purpose of the autonomic computing paradigm is to decrease system complexity as perceived by *external* administrators at the cost of additional development being required to establish such a system. From this perspective, an autonomic computing system will absorb the complexity of commonly manual administrative tasks and leave simplified, intuitive and high-level interfaces usable by human system administrators. This approach will indeed increase internal system complexity overall, but will do so at the added advantage of minimising perceived system complexity for administrators and users.

---

[1]Definitions based on combined, adapted input from Merriam-Webster's online dictionary, 11th edition—http://www.merriam-webster.com, American Heritage Dictionary of the English Language and Oxford Dictionaries—http://oxforddictionaries.com

[2]While a discussion on such matters would be well outside the scope of the current publication, it could raise useful considerations regarding the purposes and limitations of the autonomous systems we are going to build.

Fig. 2.2 Onion diagram representing goal structures that influence autonomic management

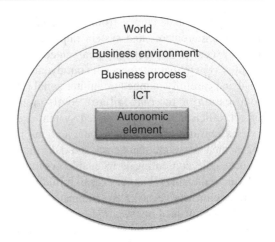

2.1.2 Goals

Autonomic computing relies on the notion of high-level business *goals* or policies specified by human administrators. Consequently, administrators' workloads and stress levels are being eased since they no longer have to deal with the lower-level technical details necessary to achieve such objectives.

Goals are the system objectives that must be achieved. Most of the time, they are expressed as criteria that characterise desirable system states, while the task of finding how those states are to be achieved is left to the autonomic system. For example, in the context of an enterprise application, a goal can specify that the response time of the Web server should be under 3 s, while that of the application server less than 1 s. In this example, goals are rather high-level directives so that they can be assigned by most administrators, even inexperienced ones. At the same time, more precise goals may also be specified, in order to allow skilled administrators to influence the detailed operation of the autonomic software. That is, the high-level goals are somehow mapped to low-level processes.

In this book, as illustrated in Fig. 2.2, we mean goals to be anything from business goals, such as 'to accrue a higher profit margin', to lower-level technical goals, such as 'to require that any Web transaction is satisfied within one second'. These then can map to lower-level policies and rules. For example, to ensure the latter goal is satisfied when client workload increases a rule mapping might indicate that a new computing server is added to the server pool to take on some of the load and speed up transactions accordingly.

Goals are at the centre of some interesting development approaches, such as the i* framework[3] or the Tropos project,[4] whose discussion nonetheless remains beyond the scope of this book.

---

[3]The i* agent- and goal-oriented modelling framework: http://www.cs.toronto.edu/km/istar
[4]The Tropos project: http://www.troposproject.org

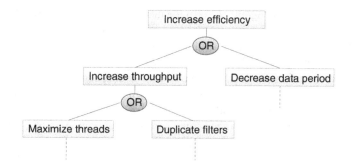

Fig. 2.3 Example of a goal hierarchy showing interrelationships

They may originate directly or indirectly from business process models that have obvious links to the business environment in terms of service expeditions and to the world at large. For example, where a Service-Level Agreement (SLA) exists between software providers and clients, it is usually refined into a set of Service-Level Objectives (SLO) that can be more easily measured and checked during runtime. Hence, there is a well-defined set of states that are required, a time period over which those states must hold, and clear metrics that are specified.

Goal-based expressions can be highly complicated. In fact, they express the administrators' business expertise at a high level of abstraction. This expertise guides administrators in their first steps when solving a problem. Figure 2.3 provides a partial example of such goal decomposition for a classic *pipe and filter* software system, where data are successively transformed by filters interconnected by pipes. We can see, for instance, that the goal 'Increase throughput' can be refined into either the subgoal 'Maximise threads' or 'Duplicate filters'. These represent the choices available that will affect throughput increases, by either increasing the number of threads dealing with incoming data in selected filters or by duplicating some selected filters and rearranging the data flows or by implementing both actions. In all cases, parallelism is utilised to improve the performance of the pipe and filter system. Otherwise, administrators have to decrease the data period, as indicated in the figure, in order to avoid unsafe and inefficient pipe overflows due to memory or buffer limitations for instance.

In simple autonomic systems, an administrator can globally specify abstract goals that can be at different depths in the goal decomposition hierarchy, as depicted in Fig. 2.3. However, the situation becomes significantly more complicated when dealing with autonomic systems comprised of several autonomic elements (this decomposition is discussed in more detail in Chap. 4). That is, the management responsibility and function is distributed. Generally, in such cases, goals have to be refined into different subgoals depending on the targeted autonomic elements. If we return to the *pipe and filter* example, we can imagine that each filter is an autonomic element. Then, each one may receive a different subgoal: one may have to create new threads and carry out related administration actions, while others may have to duplicate themselves and, again, perform the necessary adjustments that this action entails.

If sufficiently skilled, the administrator may decide on the subgoals for each autonomic element. Otherwise, it is up to the autonomic system itself to decide on the subgoal distribution starting from the overall goal specified. Several solutions may be envisaged. Centralised solutions come down to the creation of a super autonomic element that is able to decide on the goals of the other autonomic elements. More decentralised solutions demand some sort of collaboration among autonomic elements that consider themselves as peers. Centralisation, of course, is easier to implement and to control, but it does not scale. Decentralisation, on the other hand, scales up more easily but is difficult to design, follow and control, even in some of the simplest cases.

Finally, administrators can express further directives, including constraints and strategy specifications. Constraints are invariants and have to be maintained during all system evolutions. Strategies are specific directives set by the operator, often via a domain-specific language. They influence the way in which a goal has to be achieved by an autonomic element. More generally, administrators can even change the directives and knowledge employed by an autonomic element, as necessary over the system's lifetime.

2.1.3 Context

The notion of *context* has generated much debate, and there are still many schools of thought examining this notion and its relationship with computing. One school of thought approaches the subject with an open definition of context awareness— simply the understanding of what the current situation is. Other schools of thought believe that context should be more formally defined as the situation outside of an autonomic system's management function. Yet again, others think that the internal states of the autonomic system are also context.

In this book, we assume a notion of context that refers to anything that is relevant to an autonomic system while remaining external to its range of action. In other words, an autonomic system's context represents the part of its execution environment that is significant to its management process. When an autonomic system wishes to adapt so as to fulfil a goal, it will typically require an understanding of both the external world (the context) and its internal self (its state); see Fig. 2.1.

Context can be defined as any information that can be used to characterise the situation of an entity that is relevant to an autonomic system [2–4]. Hence, such entity can be a person, an object or a program. An autonomic system uses its understanding of an entity's state to make decisions and achieve its self-management goals. Obviously, the notion of context is very much application specific. Depending on the autonomic system at hand, different entities and different characterisations of these entities will be used. For example, an autonomic database management system will not necessarily use the same contextual information as an autonomic cellular phone.

Within the subject of context, we now make the distinction between *computing context* and *usage context*. The *computing context* contains the computing resources that an autonomic system may use to its advantage and those that in some way can impact the autonomic system's goal achievement. In the former case, the autonomic system can request execution of the resource (e.g. via service calls). Such context resources can include any computing entities that can be used to get information, perform calculations or contribute to the achievement of the autonomic system's goals. It can be, for example, a server, a sensor, an *app* store, a component repository, a network, a legacy application holding important business knowledge, a cloud infrastructure offering on-demand computing power and so on. In the latter case, the autonomic system may not have the ability to call the resource directly or to exercise any explicit influence over it (e.g. through negotiation). Nevertheless, the activity of an autonomic management process affects the administered system and this in turn can have an impact on other external systems without accessing them directly. In cases where an autonomic system consists of several autonomic elements, the state of a certain autonomic element can be considered as part of the internal state with respect to the global system and at the same time as part of the context with respect to another autonomic element in the same system.

The *usage context* refers to the *persons or external systems* that interact with the autonomic system in question and also to the *way* in which they interact with the system and to the *places* where the interactions take place. Human-related information is difficult to capture and to express. It is actually strongly dependent on the context sensors that measure the environment. Such measurements can be obtained via virtual sensing, derived from past usage of an artefact to illicit preferences, for example, or via actual sensing—using a device or service such as the user's current GPS location, for example. As such, contextual information can only be made available through the programming interfaces provided by these sensors. With the proliferation of smart devices, more and more context information sources become available. For instance, sensors can be embedded into physical spaces and provide information about a room's brightness, temperature and the movement of people therein.

Contexts can be characterised by a wide range of properties. Some contexts may be fully observable. This means that an autonomic system can require any piece of information at anytime. On the contrary, some contexts are only partially observable. This means that some information cannot be obtained or that it cannot be obtained on demand. For example, pervasive contexts are generally partially observable. This is due, in particular, to volatile components or nonresponsive devices that can be faulty or simply out of battery power. An autonomic system has to be aware of such situations and behave accordingly. For instance, an autonomic system may have to build and maintain a representation of the world in a best effort manner.

From a different classification perspective, a context can be deterministic or stochastic. This is especially interesting when the autonomic system attempts to influence its context, indirectly, as it has no direct control access to it. For example, in a smart home application, the autonomic system's objective may be to control the ambient temperature, even if it only has access to devices such as thermostats and windows. In a deterministic context, an autonomic system knows perfectly the effects of its actions given the context. The future state of the context is *determined* by its current state and by the actions performed upon it. In a stochastic environment, the future state depends, of course, on the actions performed on it but also on some unknown factors that cannot easily be predicted. Pervasive contexts can be seen as stochastic contexts, since their computing states change regularly due to unpredictable human-related actions, such as introducing a new smart phone into a room, or due to physical evolutions, such as sensor failure. However, even in what would be considered a more deterministic system, there may be less predictive elements; for example, an operating system has to cope with random key presses when the user types on the keyboard or when data arrives from the Internet.

Finally, a context is also characterised by its dynamicity. Namely, a context is said to be static when it does not change while the autonomic system is analysing the situation. Conversely, it is said to be dynamic if it can change during the autonomic system's reasoning (thinking) time. Pervasive contexts are, by their embedded nature, dynamic, and an autonomic system therein is governed by this dynamism.

The aforementioned context properties also hold for an autonomic system's internal state. Most of the time, an autonomic system has to perform in rather unstable conditions since its external context cannot be directly controlled and its internal structures and behaviours are also shifting.

2.2 The Origins and Motivations Behind Autonomic Computing

IBM launched the autonomic computing initiative in 2001. In a *call to action* manifesto, IBM's senior vice-president Paul Horn, supported by IBM scientists[5] and industry experts, identified complexity as a 'grand challenge' facing the IT industry and heralded self-managed systems as a means to overcome this challenge [5].

To emphasise the criticality of dealing with complexity in computing systems, the autonomic computing manifesto makes analogies with other domains that had already been confronted with complexity, namely, the telephony and agriculture industries, and described how automation revolutionised them.

Indeed, the rapid adoption of private phones in the 1920s was bringing about a fast expansion of the telephone network, raising worries for companies that had to administer them, for example, the American Telephone & Telegraph Company (AT&T). At that time, analysts predicted that if the pace of network growth was

---

[5]One could say that autonomic computing is a marriage of many subjects; therefore, it is no surprise that many of the early proponents of the field from IBM originated in physics (e.g. Paul Horn), computer systems (David Chess) and agent-based computing (Jeffrey Kephart).

sustained, by the 1980s, the demand for human switchboard operators would surpass the available supply [6]:

> Experts predicted that by 1980, every single woman in North America would have to work as a telephone operator if growth in telephone usage continued at the same rate. (At that time, all telephone operators were women).

AT&T/Bell Systems reacted to this situation by introducing automated switching protocols, which allowed them to avoid the predicted crisis.

A similar analogy was made in the autonomic computing manifesto with respect to the agriculture domain. According to the US Department of Agriculture (USDA) [7], in 1790, farmers in the USA represented 90 % of the total labour force of a population of almost 4 million. By the 1990s, this percentage dropped to 2.6 % from a population of more than 246 million. The report indicates that the dramatic improvement in the efficiency of food production was largely due to the technological innovation and automation of manual labour, compared with the preceding two centuries.[6]

These examples provide illustrations of the significant impact that task automation has on the advancement of any societal domain. Alfred North Whitehead's[7] insight into the progress of human society concisely highlights this aspect:

> Civilization advances by extending the number of important operations which we can perform without thinking about them.

In line with the general thinking of the time, IBM indicated that it was the IT domain's turn to consider the automation of its management processes, as a necessary step towards ensuring and sustaining its continuous, swift advancement. In 2001, IBM pointed out that the IT domain was being increasingly challenged by the complexity that ensued from its rapid and extensive development. As the advantages of computing systems rendered them increasingly popular, the rate of their development, integration and insertion into key societal domains consequently accelerated. At the same time, the management of such increasingly complex computing systems remained a largely manual endeavour, leading to a soaring demand for skilled and expensive system administrators. Consequently, in the initial manifesto [5], IBM indicated that '... the growing complexity of the IT infrastructure threatens to undermine the very benefits information technology aims to provide'.

---

[6]While decreasing numbers of farmers could also be caused by factors other than technology, such as massive food imports, the US Department of Agriculture (USDA) provides data indicating clear increases in farming productivity throughout the US history. For example, data available in this USDA article—National Institute of Food and Agriculture: http://www.csrees.usda.gov/qlinks/extension.html—points out that producing 100 bushels of corn necessitated around 14 labour hours and 2 acres of land in 1945, under 3 labour hours and little over 1 acre in 1987 and less than 1 acre of land in 2002. This and a discussion on bioengineered food are well beyond the scope of this book.

[7]Alfred North Whitehead (1861–1947)—English mathematician and philosopher.

In short, the IT domain was being prompted to face the complexity brought about by its own success! IBM's prediction in 2001 was that within the decade to follow, the IT domain's demand for workers would reach as high as 200 million, which is comparable to the entire labour force of the United States. At the time this prediction was made, hundreds of thousands of IT jobs in the United States remained unfulfilled. The trend at the time was indicating that the existing demand was to further increase by 100 % over the following years, raising significant concerns about the capability of a human task force to keep the society's computer systems running.

Certainly, one decade later, the situation seems less critical than IBM predicted in 2001 [8]. Various factors have contributed to this development, including the economic downturn of 2007–2009 [9], outsourcing and job delocalisation and reluctance of CEOs to increase enterprise spending by adopting new technology and hiring IT staff (e.g. [10]). In a possibly vicious circle, the high risks and total cost of ownership (TCO) associated with computing systems may discourage companies from renewing or extending their technological base. Limits on the numbers of available systems administration experts may already play a part in preventing the development of new, more ambitious IT applications. While a deep analysis of the exact causes behind IT development trends is outside the scope of this book, we discuss possible reasons in the following sections, drawing from official data on US employment statistics over the last decade.

While exact employment data in the particular domain of IT system administration is difficult to pinpoint, current statistics and predictions related to the IT domain in general do not seem to indicate an extraordinary growth in job openings in this sector. For example, according to the Bureau of Labour Statistics (US Department of Labour)[8] [11], the number of employees in 'computer occupations' taken together in 2006 reached around 3.1 million employees, then increased to around 3.4 million employees in 2010 (6.9 % growth). A further 22.1 % increase was estimated over the next decade, predicting to reach a total of about 4.2 million employees by 2020 [11]. This places the computer occupational group as the 6th fastest-growing occupational group (out of 22 groups[9]).

A further refinement of this data [12] highlights the progression of occupations, such as IT system administration. This refinement estimates that the number of employees in Database, Network and Computer System Administrator jobs was around 458,000 in 2010 and predicts an increase to 588,500 employees by 2020 (i.e. 28.5 % growth). Similarly, the number of *computer support specialists* is estimated at 607,100 in 2010 and predicted to reach 717,100 by 2020 (i.e. 18.1 % growth). While these numbers point out a need for a substantial system administration task force, they remain modest in comparison to the autonomic computing manifesto's initial prediction of 200 million required employees.

Based on this data, one may assume that the expansion of the IT domain may have already been limited by the lack of system administration support. Yet,

---

[8]Bureau of Labour Statistics—United States Department of Labour: http://www.bls.gov

[9]The fastest-growing groups being may be not surprisingly related to *healthcare.*

existing data and predictions from the US Bureau of Labour Statistics indicate quite the contrary. From the perspective of business growth and revenue output, the *information industrial sector* is predicted to be the fastest growing compared with other major sectors. At a 4.7 % per year growth in real output, the information sector is predicted to reach 1.9\$ trillion real output by 2020 [13]. This is higher than the sector's previous 2.3 % growth rate from 2000 to 2010 when real output rose from \$950.9 billion to nearly \$1.2 trillion. More refined data indicates that the expected growth in the information sector is to be mostly driven by *software publishers, data processing, hosting, related services* and *computer systems design and related services* industries.

Industrial growth correlated to employment statistics seem to indicate that even though the IT industry is experiencing considerable and increasing growth and development, employment in the area is to progress at a somewhat slower pace than initially thought. According to the report in [13], 'While real output in the information sector is growing faster than the overall economy, employment in the sector is growing more slowly than the overall economy'. This may be due to an increased productivity, which tends to accelerate output while slowing down employment.

Hence, with respect to system administration, it may be that increasingly automated management tools are already being introduced, subsequently limiting the demand for human employees to intervene. At the same time, the situation may also be due to IT outsourcing overseas and/or to increasing workloads on the existing task force [10].

Nonetheless, the increasing complexity of computing systems is starting to surpass the capacity of the human administrators to manage them. When introducing the autonomic computing vision, IBM was mainly concerned with enterprise systems. As the number of interconnected, heterogeneous components and layers involved in such systems increases, a point will be reached where human administrators will no longer be able to react rapidly enough to ensure continuous system availability, safety and security. At that point, or ideally before, automation should be introduced to help or replace such manual interventions.

As emphasised in the first chapter, computing system administration challenges are by no means confined to the enterprise domain. The recent proliferation of ever smaller and smarter electronic devices like smart phones, tablets, mini PCs and a variety of sensor and actuator devices, combined with the introduction of wireless communication and mobile software technologies, has brought about the construction of a large variety of pervasive and ubiquitous applications. These have targeted applications concerning smart buildings, home supervision and healthcare assistance, smart electrical grids or ad hoc social networks, to name but a few. These new domains introduce additional complexity factors, including low device resources; energy becoming an extra constraint to consider; significantly higher numbers of constituent hardware and software elements; increased dynamicity as mobile elements join, move about and leave the system; and so on.

Hence, the inherent complexity of such systems, combined with the lack of technical computing expertise of many of their users, reinforces the need for autonomic management solutions.

2.3   Self-* Properties and Expected Qualities

The characteristics of autonomic systems are typically described as some form of reflection of the self. In the context of this book, the self is typically the autonomic element. This section describes the different from of self-reflection.

2.3.1   Autonomic Key Features

In its autonomic computing manifesto [5], IBM identifies eight key characteristics to define an autonomic system:
1. To hold self-knowledge and consist of elements which possess system identity.
2. (Re-)configure in reaction to, potentially unpredictable, environmental changes.
3. Continuously strive to optimise functioning so as to reach predefined criteria.
4. Detect and recover from component failure so as to maintain global dependency.
5. Anticipate, detect and eschew various threats so as to maintain integrity and security.
6. Acquire knowledge of the environment and behave in a context-sensitive manner.
7. Implement open standards so as to be able to survive in a heterogeneous ecosystem.
8. Hide complexity by bridging the gap between business goals and underlying IT resources.

These general properties were subsequently summarised via four fundamental objectives or features (e.g. [5, 14–20] or [21]):
1. *Self-configuration*: the system sets and resets its internal parameters so as to conform to initial deployment conditions and to adapt to dynamic environmental changes, respectively.
2. *Self-healing*: the system detects, isolates and repairs failed components so as to maximise its availability.
3. *Self-optimisation*: the system proactively strives to optimise its operation so as to improve efficiency with respect to predefined goals.
4. *Self-protection*: the system anticipates, identifies and prevents various types of threats in order to preserve its integrity and security.

To achieve these objectives, a system must feature several essential attributes and capabilities. Hence, objectives can be described as the broad system requirements (*what* objectives to achieve), while attributes and capabilities as the key features for meeting those requirements (*how* to achieve the objectives). Since the autonomic computing initiative was initially launched, numerous such attributes and capabilities have been progressively identified by researchers in the area and categorised according to various criteria or domain-specific preoccupations. This extended list of self-managing (sometimes referred to as self-*) considerations forms an increasingly comprehensive set of crucial and, in some cases, redundant autonomic system properties.

The four fundamental features of autonomic systems are further discussed in Sect. 2.3.2, while the more extensive self-* capabilities list is presented in Sect. 2.3.3.

2.3.2 Fundamental Self-* Features

The four self-* features considered as fundamental for any autonomic system, and therefore most cited in the autonomic computing domain, are self-configuration, self-healing, self-optimisation and self-protection—also referred to in short as *self-chop*. This section discusses these four fundamental features.

Self-configuration: an autonomic system configures and reconfigures itself in order to adapt to various, possibly unpredictable conditions, so as to continuously meet a set of business objectives. This allows system administrators to merely specify high-level policies (*what is desired*) without having to worry about low-level technical details (*how to achieve it*). As a relevant example, an autonomic system would deploy and set itself up, based on predefined user objectives and current platform resources. At runtime, the system would support the dynamic addition/removal of servers to and from its infrastructure without requiring human intervention and without disrupting its service. Self-configuration must not be concerned with autonomic elements in isolation but the integrated system as a whole. Similarly to the way a new cell is integrated into a body, a new autonomic element must be able to integrate itself into a system's infrastructure, and the existing system must be able to adapt to the new element. From this perspective, self-configuration becomes an important enabler for the other self-* objectives, such as self-optimisation, self-healing and self-protection.

Self-healing: an autonomic system detects, diagnoses and recovers from routine or extraordinary problems while trying to minimise service disruption. Consequently, fault-tolerance is an important aspect of self-healing behaviour. Moreover, a system may predict potential problems and take pre-emptive action to prevent their occurrence. The purpose of self-healing is to attain overall system resiliency and robustness by being able to deal with the failure of any of the system's constituent parts. Self-healing implies that the system must first be able to detect symptoms pointing out an existing or potential future problem—for example, a bottleneck or an unresponsive system element. Second, it must be able determine a viable solution for avoiding or recovering from the problem. Discovering the root cause(s) behind detected or predicted problems (e.g. miss-configurations, bugs or failure in software or hardware elements) may help selecting an appropriate repair solution while involving more complicated analysis and planning procedures. Recovery methods may include finding alternative resource usage, downloading software updates, replacing failed hardware components, restarting failed elements or simply throwing an exception to notify a human administrator. Similarly to the way a damaged brain may use unharmed areas to re-implement lost functions, an autonomic computing system may dynamically integrate redundant or underutilised components to replace failed parts to maximise its availability. At the same time, it is important to ensure that the self-healing process does not inflict further system damage (e.g. by introducing new bugs).

Self-optimisation: rather than settling for the status quo, an autonomic system always seeks ways and seizes opportunities to improve its operation with respect to multiple, possibly conflicting, criteria (e.g. business objectives). Self-optimisation may be executed reactively or proactively, continuously aiming to improve system performance, cost or quality of service (QoS). For example, a system may continuously attempt to optimise its performance by adjusting current workloads to available resources or vice versa. Indeed, certain optimisation criteria may be conflicting—for example, performance versus security in an enterprise system or electricity consumption versus user comfort in a smart building. This requires autonomic systems to make various compromises when establishing optimal system configurations. High-level optimisation objectives may imply the simultaneous tuning of numerous interdependent parameters. Yet, optimisation of individual system elements does not guarantee system optimisation overall. Hence, self-optimisation must be approached from a holistic system perspective, with respect to both its multiple objectives and its numerous adjustable parameters. Just as an organism's muscles become more efficient with exercise, an autonomic system must be able to optimise itself over time, by learning and improving the various value combinations for its internal parameters.

Self-protection: an autonomic system anticipates, detects, identifies and protects itself from internal and external threats, in order to maintain its integrity and achieve security, privacy and data protection. Security represents one aspect of self-protecting behaviour, in both software and hardware (e.g. TCG[10]). Self-protection addresses various types of threats, including malicious attacks especially when exposed to insecure environments, accidental hits when being operated by insufficiently skilled or overly stressed users or cascading failures that persist despite repair attempts from self-healing mechanisms. In addition to reactive self-protection activities, an autonomic system may proactively anticipate security threats and take pre-emptive action to prevent their occurrence. Self-protection actions may include taking resources offline when detecting intrusions, increasing security checks when suspecting potential threats or generally alerting system administrators. Just as computer hacker attacks and virus infections are being increasingly automated for more dramatic impacts and faster spread across systems, defence procedures must be automated accordingly to enable suitable and timely responses to such incidents. Similar to a biological immune system, autonomic systems can make use of a 'digital immune system' to protect them while requiring minimum or zero user intervention or awareness.

These fundamental mechanisms are undoubtedly interdependent. For example, self-configuration represents a supporting feature of all the other self-* objectives. As another example, failure of a system's self-healing procedure may trigger the system's self-protection reaction in order to isolate and limit the impact of the affected

---

[10]TCG—the Trusted Computing Group™ (http://www.trustedcomputing.org)—a non-profit organisation formed to develop and promote open, vendor-neutral standards and frameworks for supporting trusted computing technology. The goal of trusted computing technology is to render computer systems safer and less prone to viruses, malware and unauthorised access.

system element. Conversely, a breach through the self-protection mechanism may affect various system parts, consequently triggering self-healing and self-optimisation attempts; learning and future avoidance of similar threats may also be achieved by the self-protection system.

2.3.3   Extended Self-* Capabilities

Since the launching of the autonomic computing initiative in 2001, the list of self-* properties for autonomic systems has been substantially extended. It now consists of a set of interrelated properties that a system should possess in order to achieve various degrees of autonomicity (Sect. 2.3.3). Most of the extended self-* properties are necessary for achieving the fundamental self-*chop* features (Sect. 2.2) and can therefore be subsumed into those four key objectives.

Some of the most important self-* properties identified so far are briefly highlighted as follows:

- *Self-**: a system's self-management properties in general.
- *Self-anticipating*: a system's ability to predict future events or requirements, whether with respect to the system's internal behaviour or to its external context. An anticipating system should be able to manage itself proactively.
- *Self-adapting*: a system's ability to modify itself (self-adjust) in reaction to *changes* in its execution context or external environment, in order to continue to meet its business objectives despite such changes.
- *Self-adjusting*: a system's ability to modify itself during runtime, including modifications to its internal structure, configuration or behaviour.
- *Self-aware*: a system's ability to 'know itself', to possess knowledge of its internal elements, their current status, history, capacity and connections to external elements or systems. A system may also possess knowledge of the possible actions it may perform (self-adjustment) and of their probable consequences (self-anticipating). Such knowledge is essential for achieving the self-chop objectives.
- *Self-chop*: the four fundamental self-* properties—self-configuration, self-healing, self-optimisation and self-protection.
- *Self-configuring*: a system's ability to (re-)configure itself—(re-)setting its internal parameter values, so as to achieve high-level policies or business goals.
- *Self-critical (self-evaluation)*: a system's ability to determine whether or not its high-level goals are being attained.
- *Self-defining (communication perspective)*: a system's ability to describe itself to other systems. A system's description should represent a subset of the system's self-knowledge, as relevant to targeted systems. A description should contain both data and metadata (data describing that data). Conversely, an autonomic system may need to understand and interpret other systems' descriptions.
- *Self-defining (high-level policies or goals perspective)*: a system's ability to determine and modify its own objectives.

- *Self-destructing (apoptosis)*: a system's embedded capability to destroy itself, either because it determines that it is no longer capable of reaching its goals (e.g. a corrupted system shuts itself down in order to prevent affecting user safety or infecting neighbouring systems) or because it has reached a predefined expiration date (e.g. autonomic military systems).
- *Self-diagnosis*: a system's ability to analyse itself in order to identify existing problems or to anticipate potential issues.
- *Self-governing (self-managing)*: a system's ability to administer itself in order to achieve high-level policies or business goals.
- *Self-healing (self-repair)*: a system's ability to recover from the failure of any of its constituent elements (reactive) or to predict and prevent the occurrence of such failures (proactive).
- *Self-installing*: a system's ability to deploy, configure and execute new constituent elements (e.g. patches or drivers) or to re-execute such operations for updating or repairing existing elements (e.g. fixing bugs or recovering after a crash).
- *Self-managing*: a system's quality of being autonomous.
- *Self-monitoring*: a system's ability to retrieve information on its internal state and behaviour, whether globally, or for any of its constituent elements. Self-monitoring is essential for attaining self-awareness and self-chop objectives.
- *Self-optimising*: a system's ability to improve its operation with respect to predefined goals (e.g. resource management for optimised system efficiency).
- *Self-organised (self-assembled)*: a system's property of being automatically formed via the decentralised assembly of multiple independent elements, which become the system's constituent elements.
- *Self-protecting*: a system's ability to protect itself from malicious or inadvertent attacks.
- *Self-recovery (self-healing)*: a system's ability to recover from partial or general failures.
- *Self-reflecting*: a system's ability to determine whether its self-* functionalities conform to expected operation. This may involve self-simulation operations. Within an autonomic system, self-reflection may be considered or implemented as a higher autonomic management layer (meta-management) that supervises and adapts the activities of the basic autonomic management layer, which supervises and adapts the managed system resources.
- *Self-simulation*: a system's ability to test and evaluate scenarios without affecting the executing system (e.g. it should not impact provided services). This allows replying to 'what would happen if' questions and hence facilitate the selection of self-adjusting actions when pursuing various self-* objectives.
- *Self-stabilising*: a system's ability to attain a stable, legitimate state, starting from an arbitrary state and after a finite number of execution steps. This property has been traditionally linked to fault-tolerance in distributed systems [22], but is receiving increasing attention from the self-management system community (e.g. ensuring that self-repair or self-optimisation operations converge towards a system state that complies with high-level policies).

Besides self-* properties, *context awareness* specifically represents an additional key capability of an autonomic system. Namely, an autonomic system must be able to detect and adapt to changes in its execution environment. This may include user behaviour, available resources or interactions with neighbouring systems. A context-sensitive system may improve its provided services based on knowledge about service contexts. For example, it can adapt responses to be returned to the user based on their perceived expertise or the resource capacity of client devices, ensure reliability under a wide range of predicted or unpredicted circumstances, discover 'relevant' elements in the environment and integrate them to perform self-repair or self-optimisation operations. Hence, context awareness becomes an essential system property for ensuring the aforementioned self-chop objectives.

Certainly, such self-* properties cannot be implemented in separation, or only for isolated system elements; rather, they must be considered *holistically*, from a global system perspective. Hence, a systemic approach is required for integrating and coordinating self-managed elements across entire computing systems. In addition to autonomic computing machines, self-management must equally be achieved at the level of inter-machine *communication*. Hence, autonomic communications [23, 24] should be an integral part of the general autonomic computing paradigm and of the engendered, *self-managed system* solutions [8] (further discussed in Chap. 10).

2.4   Benefits, Challenges and Degrees of Autonomy

2.4.1   Benefits of Autonomic Computing

As explained, the goal of autonomic computing is to address the escalating complexity of modern computing systems by automating system management and alleviating demand for skilled administrative interventions. In the short term, autonomic computing can benefit the IT domain by reducing both the dependence on human involvement and the system total cost of ownership (TCO). More specifically, near-term benefits of autonomic systems include (also introduced in Chap. 1):

- Improved user experience due to better system quality of service
- Facilitated user access to services due to more 'natural' human–machine interaction facilities
- Lower maintenance costs due to reduced requirements for human intervention
- Lower usage costs due to better resource management

In the longer term, achieving autonomicity at a systemic level can create a whole new range of opportunities for complex computing applications that would have otherwise been impossible to set in place, due to prohibitive costs or lack of available expertise. As autonomic capabilities are progressively embedded across multiple heterogeneous resources, they will cover entire systems or federations of systems. This would enable the extension of autonomic properties from the level of individual system resources to the global level of integrated or collaborating systems.

2.4.2   Challenges of Autonomic Computing

The importance of autonomic computing is matched by the significant difficulty involved in attaining autonomicity. This difficulty is rooted in the very objective that autonomic computing is aiming to attain, namely, managing *complex* computing systems. Automating the administration procedures of complex systems requires the development and maintenance of complex autonomic management logic. Indeed, setting in place autonomous solutions for administering large numbers of highly heterogeneous, distributed and dynamic system resources is no easy task. Also, taking into account multiple, possibly conflicting and evolving management goals exacerbates the situation.

In launching the autonomic computing manifesto, IBM recognised that the development of autonomic systems represents a 'grand challenge' for the entire IT domain. Addressing this challenge requires concerted efforts from numerous IT companies, businesses, institutions and academic organisations. Since the inception of the autonomic computing initiative, important progress has been made in the IT domain towards enhancing the automatic management support of computing systems. Yet, important progress and innovation remain to be achieved before autonomous computing systems can become the norm in the IT domain.

The autonomic computing grand challenge can be decomposed based on various criteria (yet, any attempt to fully categorise the work on this subject is bound to be imperfect). Major difficulties are raised by both scientific and technological challenges, requiring innovations and integration of advances from multiple areas, both within and beyond traditional computer science. This section provides a mere overview of the various challenge types involved.

First, at a conceptual level, the computing paradigm must change from one based on implemented functions and processing power to one based on data and high-level objectives. Recall that the purpose of autonomic computing is to enable administrators to abstract away from system implementation and configuration details and to focus instead on business objectives and adaptation policies. Consequently, the conceptual way of thinking about computer systems must evolve from one focused on technical aspects (*how* to implement and provide computing services) to one focused on provided business services and QoS properties (*what* services to provide and *what* policies to use for adapting them). In this context, for example, the focus of system performance should shift from resource capabilities and usage to perceived responsiveness and attained business objectives.

In order to follow this conceptual shift, the definition and design of computing systems must accordingly change. Autonomic system designers must be able to identify the necessary abstractions for understanding, specifying, controlling and implementing autonomic behaviours. Traditional computer science theories and techniques must be adapted to support dynamic and possibly unpredictable system change. From an architectural perspective, system designs have to adopt open standards and support the dynamic integration and collaboration of multiple heterogeneous elements. Global performance and dependability objectives have to be attained in the presence of continual changes in the system constituent parts and interconnections.

From an architectural perspective, the autonomic computing challenge can be split according to the targeted managed elements and their level of granularity [25]. Self-management challenges must be addressed at the level of both individual auto-nomic elements and of entire autonomic systems. At a fine granularity level, innova-tions are required for introducing autonomic management capabilities at the level of specific managed elements. At a higher granularity level, achieving autonomicity requires coordinated interaction among multiple autonomic elements.

Human–computer interaction (HCI) approaches must also evolve in response to the conceptual shift in the way in which administrators and users should interact with autonomic systems. Multiple, possibly conflicting business objectives and user actions, at both local and global levels, will have to be taken into consideration in tandem and translated into coherent technical parameters that can be managed via the self-* processes.

2.4.3 An Incremental Approach to Autonomic Computing

When introducing the autonomic computing paradigm, IBM promoted an *incre-mental approach* for making the transition between existing computing systems and future autonomic systems. Right from the start, IBM realised that it would be unre-alistic to attempt to revolutionise the IT domain by seeking to suddenly replace all existing systems with a new generation of autonomic systems. First, the IT com-munity is not yet fully *au fait* with the ideas of autonomicity. Secondly, customers that have invested significantly in existing IT environments would be reluctant to completely replace them overnight, especially in the absence of solid reassurances regarding the value of new self-management systems.

In contrast, an *evolutionary* approach addresses both challenges, as self-management can be progressively phased in and integrated bit by bit into the continuously evolv-ing IT system. In this context, IBM proposes an Autonomic Computing Adoption Model [15, 16, 19, 26] describing five incremental levels of system management (Fig. 2.4):

Level 1—Basic (Manual): Represents the starting point, where skilled administra-tors manually control each system computing element—setting it up, monitoring and potentially modifying or replacing it. This is the level that IBM considered IT systems to be at when launching the autonomic computing initiative initially. At this level, system management is completely non-autonomic or manual.

Level 2—Managed (Instrumented or Monitored): Employs monitoring technolo-gies to collect data from disparate managed resources and presents this intelli-gently for both offline and online system management. This approach improves productivity and reduces human administrator effort required to manually collect and synthesise data.

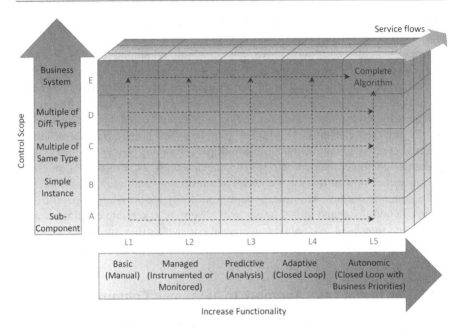

Fig. 2.4 (Reproduction of) IBM's Autonomic Computing Adoption Model *x*-axis: increasing autonomic functions; *y*-axis: increasing scopes over which the autonomic functions can be applied; and *z*-axis: service flows to which autonomic functions can be applied

Level 3—Predictive (Analysis): Employs analysis technologies that can correlate data from various managed resources, identify a range of patterns, predict optimal configurations and then advise human administrators on the corresponding actions to take. This reduces dependence on expert management skills, while rendering administrative decisions more efficient. As human administrators gain confidence, management can then progress to the next automation level if desired.

Level 4—Adaptive (Closed Loop): Enables the system to take automatic action and adapt the managed system from within itself; this is based on the monitoring information available and overall system knowledge. Service-Level Agreements (SLAs) may guide the automatic system management operation. Namely, an SLA can provide a formal, machine-readable specification of the high-level business objectives to be achieved and of the administration policies to be followed by the automated management processes. This autonomicity level improves system agility and resiliency while requiring minimum human intervention.

Level 5—Autonomic (Closed Loop with Business Priorities): Enables the system to self-govern by following high-level policies or business objectives defined by the teams of people responsible for the system reaching its objectives. This frees administrative staff from performing technical system management operations. Instead, users merely interact with the autonomic system for monitoring business processes and possibly for modifying the system objectives.

2.5   Similar Initiatives, Current Status and Relation to Software Engineering

2.5.1   Autonomicity in Existing Systems

It is important to note that, as in many areas, actions have preceded qualification. The intense necessity for autonomy is hardly new, and various systems have had autonomic-like properties well before IBM offered their approach. Some relevant examples include network algorithms employed for constructing and maintaining routing tables or protocols based on spanning trees. Many administrative tasks have also been automated. Among several utilities created for automatic update, we can cite the example of package managers in UNIX systems, which automatically resolve package dependencies. USB and network self-configuration (e.g. UPnP) are examples of autonomic features that have helped the general public to adopt computing at home.

More recently, an increasing number of platforms and applications have been progressively enriched with automatic management capabilities, including automatic application updates, device detection and driver downloads, self-sizing and self-healing computer clusters or context-sensitive identification procedures for accessing private accounts (such as email accounts). While the direct influence of the autonomic computing initiative on the development of such capabilities may prove difficult to establish, the important fact remains that automatic management is becoming an increasing concern for IT system providers. The exemplified administration solutions, while still relatively simple and focused on a single objective, should represent first steps towards more complicated autonomic facilities addressing broader and more heterogeneous administrative goals.

Some of the most significant application areas adopting and developing autonomic computing include: power management or 'smart grids'; industrial systems such as clusters, grids and data centres; pervasive and ubiquitous computing, such as smart buildings, medical assistance platforms and sensor networks; and completely unmanned systems including those necessary for military, space or rescue missions.

2.5.2   Top-Down Versus Bottom-Up Approaches

As autonomic computing was proposed, related fields with similar needs began emerging in parallel. Research initiatives aiming to render computing systems self-managed can be categorised with respect to two principal approaches.

First, top-down approaches aim to enhance the self-management capabilities of existing systems by essentially introducing various forms of control loops that can deal with targeted system resources. These approaches require administered systems to be based on technologies that support runtime monitoring and modification (Chaps. 5 and 6). These include, for example, technologies that employ dynamic component models. At the same time, beyond such technological requirements and their non-negligible impact on system design and implementation, top-down approaches impose no radical changes in the manner in which software systems have been traditionally architected and developed.

Conversely, a second family of initiatives address the system complexity problem from a quite different angle, arguing that self-management must become inherent via the very manner in which computing systems are being built. Such initiatives typically adopt a completely decentralised, bottom-up approach to designing and developing software systems. They essentially rely on self-organisation and/or emergence principles for obtaining desirable system structures and behaviours. The separation between offline development and runtime adaptation becomes blurred as the same core principles apply to ensure both initial system creation and subsequent self-* capabilities. Hence, self-management capabilities become inherent system properties rather than having to be explicitly coded for. Sometimes these systems can be called self-adaptive systems.

Regarding the positioning of autonomic computing, it is important to note that the main contribution of this initiative consists in introducing a new *paradigm* into the computer science domain—rendering computer systems *self-managed*—rather than in imposing a precise methodology, architecture or technology for implementing it. The generic architecture initially proposed by IBM (discussed in Chap. 4) does indeed seem to separate the autonomic management process from the resources it administers and also to implement this process via a single feedback loop. This logical architecture, if implemented as such, would correspond to a centralised, top-down approach, which was actually the case in many of the initial autonomic application developments. Nonetheless, the actual autonomic computing paradigm does not in any way constrain the development of self-managed systems to this approach, leaving open for exploration the entire solution spectrum between top-down and bottom-up approaches. This point is considered all along this book, as we will see, for example, in Chap. 4 when discussing autonomic system architectures.

2.5.3 Similar Initiatives

2.5.3.1 Industry

In parallel to IBM's autonomic computing initiative, several major industrial actors in the IT domain were promoting similar initiatives aimed at enhancing management support for complex computing systems [27]. The aim of these initiatives was to provide enhanced support for managing large-scale, dynamic, networked infrastructures, most notably including clouds, grids and enterprise systems. Virtualisation for data centres was a core principle driving most of these initiatives. Examples include Compaq's Adaptive Infrastructure[11] vision (2001) and HP's subsequent Utility Data Center (UDC) (2001–2004) and Converged Infrastructure[12] (2009) initiatives, Sun's N1 technology[13] (2002), Microsoft's Dynamic System

---

[11] 'Compaq Redefines IT Landscape with Adaptive Infrastructure', December 2001—http://www.hp.com/hpinfo/newsroom/press/2001pmc/pr2001120501.html

[12] HP Converged Infrastructure : http://www.hp.com/go/ci

[13] 'Sun Introduces N1 Architecture, Looks To Manage Networks As A Single System', by Joseph F. Kovar, CRN, September 2002 – http://www.crn.com/news/channel-programs/18821653/sun-introduces-n1-architecture-looks-to-manage-networks-as-a-single-system.htm

Initiative (DSI)[14] (2003), Cisco's Data Center 3.0 strategy[15] (2007) and VMware's Virtual Data Center Operating System (VDC-OS) paradigm (2008).

From a different domain perspective, in the ubiquitous system context, the European Commission Information Society Technologies Advisory Group (ISTAG) specified the ambient intelligence (AmI)[16] vision (1999), emphasising on more seamless, efficient and natural system support for human interaction. Finally, as a more generic, domain-agnostic vision, Intel's Proactive Computing [28] (2000) promoted the necessity for rendering computing systems more reactive, shifting the focus from traditional, human-*centred* computing to more autonomous, human-supervised computing.

2.5.3.2 Military

In addition to such industrial initiatives, several self-management research projects have been launched by DARPA[17] for military applications. A first set of DARPA projects was launched starting in the late 1990s enabling a new generation of self-forming, self-repairing, self-defending and heterogeneous networks[18] to provide critical advantages in unpredictable, unstable and dangerous environments. These included the Small Unit Operations—Situational Awareness System (SUO-SAS) program, Future Combat Systems Communications (FCS-C) program, the Optical RF Combined Link Experiment (ORCLE) program or the Wireless Networks after Next (WNaN) program.

A further series of DARPA programmes was subsequently launched for addressing additional autonomy issues in battery-powered wireless systems, such as unattended ground sensor (UGS) networks. These included the Connectionless Networks and the Wolfpack programs. The main goal of these programs was to develop techniques and technologies for enabling randomly deployed or mobile sensor devices to form highly efficient, low-power radio networks. Solutions involved support for forming ad hoc radio networks based on dynamically discovered neighbouring sensors, adapting sensor functioning modes to detected contexts so as to maximise battery lifetime, reconfiguring network communication in response to predicted transmission demands and collaborating within neighbouring sensor groups to equilibrate loads, implement coordinated strategies or track moving targets. Both initiatives involved individual sensor adaptations and collective collaborations, requiring adaptations at both processing and networking levels to provide fully autonomous sensor systems.

---

[14] 'Microsoft Announces Dynamic Systems Initiative', March 2003—http://www.microsoft.com/en-us/news/press/2003/mar03/03-18dynamicsystemspr.aspx

[15] http://www.networkworld.com/news/2007/072407-cisco-new-data-center.html

[16] Introduction to Ambient Intelligence from ERCIM News 2001: http://www.ercim.eu/publication/Ercim_News/enw47/intro.html

[17] DARPA: Defence Advanced Research Projects Agency—http://www.darpa.mil

[18] Henry S. Kenyon, 'Networks: Adapting to Uncertainty', DARPA, http://www.darpa.mil/WorkArea/DownloadAsset.aspx?id=2570

Another interesting research programme funded by DARPA was the Dynamic Assembly for System Adaptability, Dependability and Assurance (DASADA), started in 2000. DASADA was concerned with the development of technology for ensuring the dependability of mission-critical systems. Research carried out in this project has initiated architecture-driven solutions for self-managing large-scale distributed systems. Such solutions rely on extracting runtime software 'gauges' for monitoring system dependability properties (e.g. security, safety or architectural coherence), analysing collected information for detecting variance from predicted behaviour (e.g. runtime architecture diverging from prescribed template) and dynamically adapting the system so as to prevent violations of acceptable behaviour (e.g. self-repairing running system).

Still within the mission-critical systems domain, DARPA initiated the Self-Regenerative Systems (SRS) program in 2004. SRS aimed to develop technologies for ensuring the continuity of system-critical functionalities, in spite of damages caused by unintentional errors or sustained attacks. To achieve its goals, the program promoted biologically inspired diversity as a means of minimising damage inflicted by single attacks. This idea implied introducing multiple, functionally equivalent variants of system components, intended to limit the impact of any single attack to only a subset of the available variants. In addition, the program promoted cognitive immunity and regeneration techniques for detecting system parts damaged by successful attacks and implementing regenerative measures that ensured system recovery.

More recently, in 2012, DARPA launched the Assured Arctic Awareness (AAA)[19] program soliciting innovative technology for ensuring unmanned, remote, year-round surveillance of vastly isolated and environmentally extreme environments. Here, autonomous system operation becomes essential, involving support for unattended distributed sensing, long-range communication, mobility and energy management, persistence and survivability capabilities.

DARPA also planned to launch a Robotic Challenge[20] program (October 2012), aiming to bring progress to robotics technologies that can help in natural or man-made disasters. Particular attention is given to robots capable of autonomously driving trucks, walking through rubble or operating power tools to break walls and perform repairs. This challenge will capitalise on results obtained from DARPA's previous Urban Challenge[21] for autonomic vehicles (2007), which were required to drive in traffic and perform complicated operations including overtaking, negotiating intersections and parking.

---

[19] DARPA 's Assured Arctic Awareness (AAA) program: http://www.darpa.mil/NewsEvents/Releases/2012/03/16a.aspx

[20] DARPA's announcement (April 2012) of future Robotic Challenge program (to be launched in October 2012): http://www.darpa.mil/NewsEvents/Releases/2012/04/10.aspx

[21] DARPA's Urban Challenge, held in November 2007, at the former George Air Force Base in Victorville, California, USA—http://archive.darpa.mil/grandchallenge

2.5.3.3 Space Exploration

NASA[22] has also been showing interest in developing systems with autonomic capabilities, due to the nature and requirements of its unmanned space missions [29]. During such missions, communication between terrestrial control centres and spacecraft is frequently unavailable and continuously hindered by long round-trip delays. In such contexts, the success of expensive explorations becomes essentially dependent on the autonomous capabilities of spacecraft devices, enabling rapid control decisions to be taken to adapt to extraordinary situations. Self-reconfiguration and self-repair become equally critical capabilities in such missions, as direct intervention to replace faulty or damaged elements is utterly impossible. Hence, most such missions provide good examples of systems that must be autonomous, or self-governed, on the one hand, since vehicles are unmanned, and most often also autonomic, on the other hand, since unpredictable situations require vehicles to self-manage in order to adapt to changing contexts.

Traditional autonomous abilities in NASA space missions include star-tracking based self-navigation, self-directing antennas, automatic fault reactions and data storage and retransmission. For example, the AutoNav[23] autonomous navigation system [30] was employed on board the Deep Space 1 (DS1) (1999) and Deep Impact (2005) spacecrafts for enabling high-speed encounter missions to small bodies, such as comments and asteroids.

In contrast to space travel, which involves navigation through relatively simple and well-known environments, planet surface exploration requires autonomous rovers to find their way through challenging and unknown territories. In such contexts, autonomic rover software must analyse sensory information and take decisions for controlling the rover's driving actuators. The challenge increases as terrains may be sensed under widely different lighting conditions and sensor data may become faulty or incomplete. High radiation levels and widely varying temperatures raise further difficulties by limiting available computational resources.

The significance of autonomy for the success of this type of space missions was highlighted in one of NASA's 50th anniversary articles (2008) [31], in the context of Mars exploration programs:

> The vehicles used to explore the Martian surface require a high degree of autonomy to navigate challenging and unknown terrain (sic), investigate targets, and detect scientific events. Increased autonomy will be critical to the success of future missions.

The autonomic capabilities included in NASA missions have been significantly enriched over the years and consequently enabled the design of increasingly ambitious space endeavours.

---

[22] NASA: National Aeronautics and Space Administration—http://www.nasa.gov

[23] AutoNav: NASA's autonomous navigation system uses the relative positions of well-known bright asteroids with respect to a background star for positioning a spacecraft and guiding it to its destination. AutoNav has been successfully tested for guiding the Deep Space 1 spacecraft (1999) and Deep Impact (2005).

In 1997, NASA's Mars Pathfinder mission deployed *Sojourner*—the first space rover to autonomously drive on another planet. The vehicle was able to navigate on flat rocky Martian terrain in order to reach locations specified by Earth-based operators. The rover's autonomic functions were mainly reactive and did not build or employ a surface map. In 2004, the Mars Exploration Rovers mission deployed other two autonomous spacecraft—*Spirit* and *Opportunity*—for exploring the Martian surface for a projected 3-month period. Four years later, the two rovers had covered distances of over 4 and 7 miles, respectively, while well surpassing their initially predicted lifetime. The rovers possessed enhanced autonomous capabilities including 3D terrain mapping based on video cameras, selecting best paths to follow based on detected obstacles, estimating current rover position and orientation and finally approaching and studying designated targets.

More recently, in November 2011, NASA launched the Mars Science Laboratory (MSL)[24] mission for studying Martian surface and assessing the planet's 'habitability' (capacity to sustain life). The exploration rover—*Curiosity*—landed on Mars in August 2012 and started its autonomous surface exploration, as planned over the following two years. Curiosity was designed to autonomously detect and approach 'interesting' targets and autonomously collect and analyse corresponding samples for assessing Martian environment. In the near future (2020–2022), a joint mission between NASA and ESA[25]—Mars Sample Return mission[26]—aims to collect Mars samples and bring them back to Earth for further analysis. Considering the extended distance to cover and the limited survival time of the return vehicle on Martian surface, this mission will require an unprecedented level of autonomy from the exploration rover. Such autonomous abilities should allow selecting various navigation strategies based on rover models, terrain learning and prediction techniques; reusing learned knowledge to speed up navigation back to the ascent vehicle; learning normative measures and detecting off-nominal values indicating 'interesting' scientific events; and sensing and adjusting drilling positions in order to avoid damage to the coring tool.

As a future projection and an alternative approach to more 'traditional' missions, NASA launched the Autonomous Nano Technology Swarm (ANTS)[27] program (2000) [3]. ANTS proposes a generic architecture for human/robotic space missions based on an ant colony analogy, in order to ensure outstanding system survivability and goal achievement capabilities for deep-space unmanned missions. Drawing inspiration from social insect colonies, ANTS projects capitalise on self-specialisation and self-organisation principles for attaining massively resilient, adaptable and relatively cheap exploration systems. Generally, ANTS architecture involves numerous miniaturised, autonomous, self-similar, self-configurable and addressable elements,

---

[24] NASA's Mars Science Laboratory (MSL) mission: http://marsprogram.jpl.nasa.gov/msl

[25] ESA: European Space Agency—http://www.esa.int

[26] Mars Sample Return mission: http://www.esa.int/esaMI/Aurora/SEM1PM808BE_0.html

[27] NASA's Autonomous Nano Technology Swarm (ANTS) program—http://ants.gsfc.nasa.gov

with high social interaction capabilities that enable them to self-organise into various structures for achieving predefined goals.

As a concrete example of the ANTS application, Prospecting Asteroid Mission (PAM)[28] aims to analyse an asteroid belt in search for materials of astro-biological relevance. PAM plans to drive a carrier spaceship into deep space and have it self-assemble and launch 1,000 small exploration spacecraft ('picocraft') that are to travel through and analyse the asteroid belt. Spacecraft belongs to one of ten specialist classes, which include processing specialists (leaders), communication specialists (messengers) and several instrument specialists for diverse measurement types (workers). Once launched, spacecraft opportunistically self-organise into several sub-swarms, containing specialists from all classes, and simultaneously analyse different asteroids over the several years belt traversal. Each sub-swarm can repeatedly search for, detect and navigate towards 'interesting' asteroid targets; measure and create 3D models of analysed asteroids; and send adequate asteroid models to an Earth centre.

2.5.3.4 Academia

In addition to industrial, military and space exploration initiatives for developing self-managing computing systems, several similar initiatives have been launched from within the academic community.

These research initiatives aim to render computing systems capable of adapting to their dynamically changing environments, of self-configuring, self-healing, self-optimising, self-protecting and possibly self-developing via self-organisation and self-assembly processes, in order to reach predefined business objectives. While sharing a common goal, each initiative promotes a slightly different paradigm, focusing on different core principles, for addressing the system autonomicity challenge. Providing a comprehensive description of all the existing initiatives and their intricate interrelations could constitute the subject of an entirely different book. Here, we merely aim to exemplify some of the most relevant programmes, highlight their core principles and challenges and show how their advancement can contribute to progress in the autonomic computing domain.

Organic computing[29] (OC) is probably the most similar initiative to autonomic computing (AC). OC is based on a vision of future information-processing systems consisting of myriad autonomous devices, equipped with sensors and actuators, aware of their execution environments and organising themselves in order to provide various business services. In this context, the *controllability* of the emergent

---

[28]NASA's ANTS Prospecting Asteroid Mission (PAM), expected timeframe: 2020–2025, http://ants.gsfc.nasa.gov/pam.html

[29]Organic computing (OC) initiative: http://www.organic-computing.de. The OC initiative has been launched by a group of researchers from three German universities (Universität Hannover, Universität Karlsruhe and Universität Augsburg). In 2012 the initiative comprised more than 70 researchers from many institutions across Germany and other European and non-European countries. OC has been initially funded by the German Research Foundation (DFG) as part of the priority programme 1183 organic computing (2004–2011).

system behaviour becomes an important challenge. The OC community argues that self-organisation is becoming a fact (e.g. like the Internet) rather than a research hypothesis [32]:

> It is not the question whether self-organised and adaptive systems will arise but how they will be designed and controlled.

Therefore, OC aims to first understand the principles of self-organisation and emergence as present in many natural systems, in order to be able to develop theories and techniques that enable *controlled* self-organisation and emergence in computing systems. As its name indicates, OC draws inspiration from organic-inspired, biological systems, such as brains, swarms, social insect colonies or lifeless chemical compounds. It aims to apply the self-organisation and emergence mechanisms observed in such natural examples to artificial, technical systems.

The notions of system autonomy and control are central to both organic and autonomic computing. Autonomic computing concentrates on the feedback control loop as the main means of introducing system self-* capabilities. The manner in which multiple control loops can be integrated in order to ensure the coherence of a more global system is an important problem in autonomic computing (see Chap. 4). Yet, autonomic computing research has only recently began to focus on this significant challenge. Conversely, controlling the emergent structure and behaviour of self-organising autonomous systems has been the defining challenge of the organic computing (OC) initiative. The OC community also introduces feedback control loops, interconnecting the managed system with a system observer and controller. The purpose of the OC control loop is to influence the self-organising system elements in order to steer the emergent system state towards the targeted business or user objectives. Similarly to autonomic computing, the degree of autonomy of an OC system is defined by the level of automation in the system's control, ranging from completely manual (only human intervention) to fully autonomous (only automatic feedback control). In many research projects, the exact borders between autonomic and organic computing become hard to delineate.

Pushing self-organisation and emergence principles even farther, amorphous computing[30] aims to develop novel architectures, algorithms and technology for constructing and programming computational systems based on massively parallel and identical elements with reduced computational capabilities and limited local communication [33]. The purpose of amorphous computing is to capitalise on the availability of cheap information-processing devices while avoiding the need for extensive device reliability testing and expensive processes for exactly positioning and interconnecting parts into coherent systems. Hence, amorphous systems should be relatively cheap and fast to build while featuring important fault-tolerance properties with respect to individual malfunctioning devices or state perturbations.

Similarly to organic computing, self-organisation and emergent phenomena are at the core of the amorphous computing approach. Consequently, the chief

---

[30]Amorphous computing project, defined at MIT: http://groups.csail.mit.edu/mac/projects/amorphous

challenge remains the identification of organisational principles and programming methodologies for *controlling* amorphous systems. Addressing this challenge requires answering fundamental questions on the manner in which massive numbers of programmable, unreliable entities, interconnected in unpredictable ways, can be observed, directed and organised in order to obtain a coherent global behaviour that meets predefined goals.

Not surprisingly, amorphous computing draws inspiration from successful cooperation found in natural systems. Relevant examples include cells cooperating to form a multicellular organism, ants in a colony cooperating to build an anthill or humans in a society cooperating to develop a town or a city. As with organic computing, the common principles guiding such diverse natural systems should be understood and applied for designing novel technological systems.

Once achieved, the theoretical foundation of amorphous computing can be reused across a wide range of system applications, rendering the hardware substrate irrelevant, enabling materialisation via silicon chips as well as via living cells, as best suited for each application. For example, microelectronic mechanical components could be mixed with bulk materials such as paints, gels or concrete to obtain programmable materials. Resulting 'smart paint' could be smeared over a bridge structure for reporting on temperature, traffic conditions and structural integrity or to colour a building for detecting fires or intrusion threats. As a different example, digital circuits could be developed from biological cells and used as vehicles for drug delivery or for sensing threatening health conditions and deciding to inject an appropriate drug.

In addition to the aforementioned initiatives, multiple projects inspired by biology or by nature in general have been launched over the last decade, addressing either the issue of computing system complexity in general or more particular problems related to specific system domains or to precise challenge types. Of foremost importance are approaches providing solutions to the control challenge raised by self-organising or emergent systems. Several such solutions aim to find the right balance between flexibility and control, introducing various levels of compromise between exerting more control on self-organising and emerging systems and introducing adaptability into 'traditional', fully engineered systems. We can only enumerate a few of these initiatives here and show how they relate to previously discussed projects, principles and applications.

Multicellular Computing[31] indicates that the fundamental organisational principles of multicellular systems—including specialisation, messaging, stigmergy and apoptosis—can be reused for architecting computing systems, in order to surpass the spiralling control problem posed by their ever-increasing complexity. Morphogenetic engineering[32] [34] proposes to adopt principles from developmental biology—notably cellular differentiation and morphogenesis—in order to combine

---

[31] Multicellular Computing Website: http://www.evolutionofcomputing.org

[32] 'Morphogenetic engineering weds bio self-organisation to human-designed systems', R. Doursat, PerAda Magazine: Towards Pervasive Adaptation, 18 May 2011—http://www.perada-magazine. eu/view.php?article=003722-2011-05-18&category=Agents

the advantages of both purely self-organised systems and completely designed systems. In this approach, a designed *genotype*—specified as a set of rules, for example—dictates the self-organisation and self-differentiation procedures followed by system elements and guarantees the general structure, behaviour and/or properties of the emerging *phenotype*, the final executing system.

Within the broader organic computing initiative, Chemical Computing[33] promotes the chemical metaphor as a programming paradigm for enabling control in complex computing systems. Here, programming artificial chemical systems involves defining the interacting molecules, their reaction rules and the global topology and dynamics of their interaction space. The programmed molecular structures and reactions space set in place for each system element, at 'microscopic' level, lead to the emerging behaviour for the overall system, at 'macroscopic' level.

A significant challenge for any approach that relies on self-organisation and emergence consists in identifying the correct organisational rules, codes or processes that can give rise to the desired global states and behaviours. For example, it is tremendously difficult to identify a genome design that produces phenotypes with desired structural and functional properties. Unsurprisingly, nature provides a significant source of inspiration for addressing this intricate challenge, notably via the process of Darwinian *evolution*. This process relies on genome inheritance, mutation and natural selection to find solutions to the aforementioned problems—determining the micro rules (genotype) that will develop into macro systems (phenotypes) that are fit within a targeted environmental niche. Evolutionary computation has developed a wide range of algorithms and methodologies inspired by this process, including various genetic algorithms, evolutionary strategies, learning classifier systems, memetic algorithms, cooperative or competitive co-evolution techniques or combinations of evolutionary and developmental techniques (evo-devo).

The list of enumerated examples of programmes, projects and products similar or relevant to autonomic computing is by no means exhaustive. Our main purpose was to indicate that self-management is becoming a real concern in most IT system domains, with the exemplified self-management initiatives merely representing a significant reflection of this important fact. Further fields of interest are discussed in the following Chap. 3, which emphasises the influences that these areas have on the development of autonomic computing.

2.6 Key Points

This chapter has discussed the following important topics:
- Autonomic computing is a relatively new initiative that was launched in response to the increasing challenges raised by complex software systems. Autonomic computing aims to enable computing systems to manage themselves (self-management),

---

[33]The chemical metaphor as programming paradigm for organic computing: http://users.minet. uni-jena.de/csb/prj/organic

so as to minimise the need for human intervention, while rendering administrative interfaces more human friendly and less technology intensive.

- The autonomic computing initiative was launched by IBM in 2001. Similar initiatives have been launched in parallel by industry, academia and government organisations, with the purpose of attaining autonomicity in various types of complex computing systems. Most notably targeted systems include data centres, clusters and grid systems, ubiquitous and pervasive systems and unmanned robotic systems.

- The notions of 'goal' and 'context' are essential to any autonomic system. Goals represent the high-level business objectives or policies that human administrators specify and that the autonomic system must meet or follow, respectively. Context consists of all the significant facts about the state of entities that are relevant to an autonomic system but that are external to it and hence that the autonomic system cannot directly access and modify.

- In the autonomic computing context, system autonomicity is commonly resumed via four key properties—self-configuration, self-healing, self-optimisation and self-protection—sometimes also referred to as *self-chop*. Achieving such properties imposes several system capabilities, most notably including self-awareness, self-knowledge, context awareness, self-monitoring and self-adjustment. Since the domain's inception, the list of self-* features has been continuously extending, in order to explicitly highlight more precise or domain-specific capabilities. However, many of the latter features can be subsumed in the self-chop list.

- Autonomic computing promises many short-term and long-term advantages, including improved user experience, facilitated system management capabilities, reduced system ownership costs and new opportunities for computing system applications.

- The ambitious goals of autonomic computing raise important conceptual, theoretical and technological challenges, requiring the study and adoption of concepts from multiple scientific domains, the development of novel computer design paradigms, the introduction of supporting capabilities at various architectural levels and the integration of multiple autonomic elements into globally correct and coherent autonomous computing systems.

- The autonomic computing domain proposes a progressive path for introducing autonomic capabilities in computing systems. The Autonomic Computing Adoption Model was defined for this purpose, comprising five incremental levels of system management: basic (or manual), managed (or monitored), predictive (or analysed), adaptive (or closed loop) and autonomic (or closed loop with business priorities).

- Well before autonomic computing was defined as an individual IT domain, many computing systems were already featuring capabilities that were similar or identical to those involved in self-management. Examples include automatic configuration and optimisation algorithms, fault-tolerant applications and communication protocols, dependable, self-adaptive and reflective applications. While totally compatible with such existing features, autonomic computing proposes a new paradigm that explicitly targets autonomicity as an essential capability of complex computing systems.

- Autonomic computing should be best considered as a new *paradigm* in the computer science domain, promoting the idea of introducing self-management capabilities in computing systems rather than imposing a concrete methodology, architecture or technology for achieving system autonomicity.

References

1. Christman, J.: Autonomy in moral and political philosophy. In: Zalta, E.N. (ed.) The Stanford Encyclopedia of Philosophy (Spring 2011 Edition). http://plato.stanford.edu/archives/spr2011/entries/autonomy-moral
2. Dey, A.K., Abowd, G.D.: Towards a better understanding of context and context-awareness. In: CHI 2000 Workshop on the What, Who, Where, When, and How of Context-Awareness, The Hague (2000)
3. Truszkowski, W., et al.: Autonomous and autonomic systems: a paradigm for future space exploration missions. IEEE Trans. Syst. Man Cybern. Part C **36**(3), 279–291 (2006)
4. McCann, J.A., Huebscher, M., Hoskins, A.: Context as autonomic intelligence in a ubiquitous computing environment. Int. J. Internet Protoc. Technol. (IJIPT), special edition on Autonomic Computing, Inderscience (2006)
5. Horn, P.: Autonomic Computing: IBM's Perspective on the State of Information Technology. New York: IBM T.J. Watson Labs. http://www.research.ibm.com/autonomic/manifesto/autonomic_computing.pdf, October 2001
6. FitzGerald, J., Dennis, A.: Chapter 1: Introduction to data communications – "a brief history of communications in North America". In: Business Data Communications and Networking, 10th edn, pp. 5–7. Wiley (2009). ISBN 978-047005575-5
7. U.S. Dept. of Agriculture, Economic Research Service.: A History of American agriculture 1776–1990, Washington, DC, 1993. Summaries are also available online as teaching material, such as from the Library of Congress: http://www.loc.gov/teachers/classroommaterials/connections/hist-am-west/history.html
8. Dobson, S., Sterritt, R., Nixon, P., Hinchey, M.: Fulfilling the vision of autonomic computing. Cover feature. IEEE Comput. Soc. **43**(1), 35–41 (2010)
9. Sum, A., Khatiwada, I. The Nation's underemployed in the "Great Recession" of 2007–09. Monthly Labor Review, Nov 2010, http://www.bls.gov/opub/mlr/2010/11/art1full.pdf
10. Schwartz, E.: Bureau of Labor Statistics reports big drop in tech jobs – almost 50,000 IT positions lost in last 12 months. InfoWorld, 6 Aug 2008, http://www.infoworld.com/d/adventures-in-it/bureau-labor-statistics-reports-big-drop-in-tech-jobs-863
11. Lockard, C.B., Wolf, M.: Employment outlook: 2010–2020. Occupational employment projections to 2020. Bureau of Labor Statistics, Occupational Employment, Monthly Labor Review, Jan 2012, http://www.bls.gov/opub/mlr/2012/01/art5full.pdf
12. U.S. Bureau of Labour Statistics.: Employment by Occupation. Employment Projections, 1 Feb 2012, http://www.bls.gov/emp/ep_table_102.htm
13. Henderson, R.: Employment outlook: 2010–2020. Industry employment and output projections to 2020. Bureau of Labor Statistics, Monthly Labor Review, Industry Employment, Jan 2012, http://www.bls.gov/opub/mlr/2012/01/art4full.pdf
14. Kephart, J.O., Chess, D.M.: The vision of autonomic computing. IEEE Comput. **36**, 41–50 (2003)
15. Ganek, A.G., Corbi, T.A.: The dawning of the autonomic computing era. IBM Syst. J. **42**(1), 5–18 (2003)
16. IBM.: An Architectural Blueprint for Autonomic Computing, 3 edn. IBM Whitepaper, June 2005
17. Parashar, M., Hariri, S.: Autonomic computing: an overview. In: Proceedings of the 2004 International Conference on Unconventional Programming Paradigms, pp. 257–269. Springer, Berlin (2005)

18. White, S.R., Hanson, J.E., Whalley, I., Chess, D.M., Kephart, J.O.: An architectural approach to autonomic computing. In: Proceedings of the First International Conference on Autonomic Computing, 17–19 May 2004. IEEE Computer Society, New York (2004)
19. Huebscher, M.C., McCann, J.A.: A survey of autonomic computing—degrees, models, and applications. ACM Comput. Surveys. (CSUR) **40**(3) (2008). ISSN: 0360–0300
20. Wolf, T.D., Holovoet, T.: A taxonomy for self-properties in decentralised autonomic computing. In: Parashar, M., Hariri, S. (eds.) Autonomic Computing: Concepts, Infrastructure, and Applications, pp. 101–120. CRC Press/Taylor & Francis Group (2007)
21. Hinchey, M.G., Sterritt, R.: Self-managing software. Computer **39**(2), 107–109 (2006)
22. Dijkstra, E.W.: Self-stabilizing systems in spite of distributed control. Commun. ACM **17**(11), 643–644 (1974). doi:10.1145/361179.361202. http://doi.acm.org/10.1145/361179.361202
23. Smirnov, M.: Autonomic Communication: Research Agenda for a New Communications Paradigm. Technical report, Fraunhofer FOKUS (2004)
24. Dobson, S., et al.: A survey of autonomic communications. ACM Trans. Auton. Adapt. Syst. **1**(2), 223–259 (2006)
25. Kephart, J.O.: Research challenges of autonomic computing. In: ACM International Conference on Software Engineering (ICSE 2005), pp 15–21, St. Louis, MO, USA, May 2005
26. Miller, B.: The Autonomic Computing Edge: The Role of the Human in Autonomic Systems. IBM developerWorks, Nov 2005, http://www.ibm.com/developerworks/library/ac-edge7
27. Murch, R.: Autonomic Computing. IBM Press/Prentice Hall, Englewood Cliffs (2004) New Jersey (Chapter 14 – Other Vendors)
28. Tennenhouse, D.: Proactive computing. Commun. ACM **43**(5), 43–50 (2000). doi:10.1145/332833.332837. http://doi.acm.org/10.1145/332833.332837
29. Sterritt, R., Hinchey, M.: SPAACE IV: Self- properties for an autonomous & autonomic computing environment – Part IV A Newish Hope. In: 7th IEEE International Conference and Workshops on Engineering of Autonomic and Autonomous Systems (EASe 2010), 22–26 Mar 2010, University of Oxford, England
30. Riedel, J., Bhaskaran, S., Desai, S., Han, D., Kennedy, B., McElrath, T., Null, G., Ryne, M., Synnott, S., Wang, T., Werner, R.: Using autonomous navigation for interplanetary missions: the validation of Deep Space 1 AutoNav. In: International Conference on Low-Cost Planetary Missions, Laurel, MD, USA, May 2000, http://hdl.handle.net/2014/14133
31. Bajracharya, M., Maimone, M.W., Helmick, D.: Autonomy for mars rovers: past, present, and future. IEEE Comput. **41**(12), 44–50 (2008)
32. Schmeck, H., Müller-Schloer, C., Çakar, E., Mnif, M., Richter, U.: Adaptivity and self-organisation in organic computing systems. In: Müller-Schloer, C., Schmeck, H., Ungerer, T. (eds.) Organic Computing – A Paradigm Shift for Complex Systems, pp. 5–37. Springer, Basel (2011). e-ISBN 978-3-0348-0130-0. ISBN 978-3-0348-0129-4
33. Abelson, H., Allen, D., Coore, D., Hanson, C., Homsy, G., Knight Jr., T.F., Nagpal, R., Rauch, E., Sussman, G.J., Weiss, R.: Amorphous computing. Commun. ACM **43**(5), 74–82 (2000). doi:10.1145/332833.332842. http://doi.acm.org/10.1145/332833.332842
34. Doursat, R., Sayama, H., Michel, O.: Morphogenetic engineering. In: Toward Programmable Complex Systems Series: Understanding Complex Systems. Springer, Berlin/Heidelberg (2012). ISBN 1244 978-3-642-33901-1

Sources of Inspiration for Autonomic Computing

3

Autonomic computing can capitalise on advancements available from several scientific fields, both within and beyond the computer science domain. This chapter provides an overview of such fields and highlights their possible contributions to autonomic computing systems. The manner in which concepts, mechanisms and processes can be adopted and reused as software engineering approaches is highlighted across this chapter.

We discuss biology as the first source of inspiration for autonomic computing. While the bio-inspired *autonomicity* concept is highly relevant to autonomic computing, the potential of biology to inspire this field largely surpasses this metaphor. We therefore enlarge our discussion to biological systems in general, especially nervous systems, highlighting how their implementation in different species can inspire various solutions to autonomic computing systems.

We also show how autonomic computing shares many of its goals and necessary underlying constructions with some well-established engineering and computing fields such as automated control systems, robotics, artificial intelligence and multi-agent systems. The chapter summarises some of the most relevant concepts and approaches available from existing fields and indicates the manner in which they can be adopted to serve the autonomic computing initiative.

A number of interrelated theoretical fields provide a potentially significant link between natural and artificial autonomic systems. Areas such as complex systems theory, cybernetics, networked systems theory and artificial life have set out to decipher the inner workings of complex adaptive systems and ultimately to control or to build artificial ones. We briefly point out the relevance of such fields and the core concepts that seem most readily applicable to autonomic computing.

Certainly, the chapter cannot provide a comprehensive view of all areas relevant to autonomic computing. Rather, its purpose is to provide an (probably biased) overview of the most relevant sources of inspiration and to offer pointers towards more extensive specialty literature.

P. Lalanda et al., *Autonomic Computing: Principles, Design and Implementation*,
Undergraduate Topics in Computer Science, DOI 10.1007/978-1-4471-5007-7_3,
© Springer-Verlag London 2013

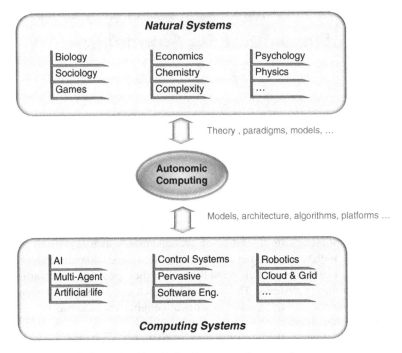

Fig. 3.1   Sources of influence and inspiration for autonomic computing

3.1   Overview of Influences

3.1.1   Introduction

In the first two chapters of this book, we saw that software complexity and its related costs are the main motivations behind autonomic computing. We also introduced the fact that many initiatives with similar goals preceded this initiative. Indeed, autonomic computing can be seen as an attempt at consolidating different domains [1] that have until now remained mostly isolated. In this chapter, we take a closer look at the influences that the autonomic computing initiative has had and investigate some of the existing domains that can support the development of autonomic computing systems.

As indicated in Fig. 3.1, we may distinguish two important realms of influence: the study of complex natural systems and the development of complex computing systems. Computing systems come from diverse software and hardware domains ranging from traditional automation systems to smart systems based on artificial intelligence techniques. They provide algorithms, architectures, models and techniques that can be directly reused in autonomic computing. In turn, natural systems are not software; their study can include domains as diverse as economics, biology, chemistry or physics, but they can also provide significant contributions to autonomic computing in terms of theories and models.

3.1.2 Natural Systems

In the beginning, autonomic computing was inspired by biology. In addition to the important paradigm of *autonomicity*, autonomic computing can draw significant inspiration from many principles and mechanisms driving biological systems. This is investigated in detail in Sect. 3.2 of this chapter.

Enlarging the system scope from a single autonomic application to several mutually influencing applications (or application components) brings about further significant challenges. These may in turn reveal additional research domains relevant to autonomic computing. In cases where autonomic components feature relatively basic behaviours and simple interactions, several disciplines such as physics and chemistry can provide reliable theories and models for describing the resulting behaviour and properties of an overall system encompassing such components. As indicated in Chap. 2 (Sect. 2.4.3), several computing science initiatives have already been defined relying on inspiration from such fields, including the amorphous and chemical computing initiatives.

Things can become more complicated when the autonomic components are data processing applications, capable of making independent decisions. Here, system designers must additionally consider the manner in which individually reasoning applications will impact the possible outcomes of the overall system considered. The disciplines concerned with societal, political, economic and psychological issues can offer useful inspiration, especially in regard to strategic decision-making and its consequences on the system behaviour and outcomes. These include mathematical models and interactive decision theories that have been developed and applied in the context of large-scale, dynamic, asynchronous and generally open systems.

In particular, interesting ideas and models for autonomic computing can, and have been, derived from the microeconomics domain. This branch of economics examines the way in which local, mutually influencing behaviours and decisions, channelled by high-level rules and regulations, give rise to different supply and demand patterns, product prices and production levels in individual markets. In this context, an interesting application of such models can be envisaged for addressing resource allocation problems. Indeed, several autonomic computing projects have introduced virtual currencies as a means of negotiation among computing processes competing for limited resources, such as processing cycles, storage space or communication bandwidth [2]. Autonomic agents have also been proposed for searching and comparing goods and services in the e-commerce market on behalf of consumers [3].

Game theory represents another important domain dealing with strategic planning concerns. Game theory can provide paradigms and mathematical models for decision-making schemes that can be usefully applied to 'multiplayer' autonomic systems. Namely, game theoretical principles can be employed for enabling multiple autonomic decision-makers to collaborate or to compete, in order to achieve common optimisations or overcome conflicting objectives, respectively. Based on such principles, system designers can determine the necessary rules to be set in place so as to ensure that the global system state will converge towards an equilibrium point that meets the system's business objectives. Examples of interesting game theoretical contributions include Nash equilibrium, Conjectural equilibrium, *Best Response* strategies or the *Stackelberg leadership model*, which we now briefly discuss.

The *Nash equilibrium*[1] is defined as a set of strategies, one for each decision-maker, where none of the participants can benefit from unilaterally changing their strategy. In other words, none of the players has an incentive to change its strategy provided that all other players maintain their strategies. This theory applies well to non-cooperative games, where each player attempts to maximise its benefit, possibly to the detriment of the group benefit. In the context of autonomic computing, Nash equilibrium would mean, for example, that each application takes the best decision it can while considering the decisions of all the other applications. However, as indicated above, it may happen that the established Nash equilibrium (or local optimum) is not a *Pareto optimal*[2] (or global optimum). Ensuring that a multiplayer system operates at the Pareto boundary generally requires some sort of *cooperation* among the players. Also, adopting a Nash equilibrium strategy requires that players are fully rational and hold perfect knowledge of each other's strategies. Alternative variants have been developed for situations where such requirements are impractical or impossible to attain. Notably, the *Stackelberg equilibrium strategy* can be applied when one particular player holds private knowledge of all its competitors and accordingly optimises its responses. Interestingly, this strategy has been shown to improve the performance of all participating players even if they continue to behave myopically. For cases where players cannot obtain perfect knowledge on each other's strategies, *Conjectural* equilibrium has been proposed to replace knowledge with *beliefs*, which can be obtained through repeated player interactions with their environments [4].

Considering the management of system complexity in general brings to the fore the necessity for understanding fundamental complexity and systemic principles. More precisely, to manage complexity one would need to first comprehend the key characteristics, inner workings and resulting behaviours of the targeted (complex) systems and to understand where the complexity comes from, how it manifests itself in the system and how it can be influenced or controlled. Hence, from a more theoretical perspective, autonomic computing may also benefit from the developments of general fields that have studied such issues, including systems theory, complex

---

[1]Nash equilibria: named after mathematician John Forbes Nash (1928) who invented the theory and received the Nobel Prize in Economic Sciences in 1994.

[2]Pareto optimality (or efficiency): named after economist Vilfredo Pareto (1848–1923), who employed the concept in the context of economic systems. In a Pareto efficient allocation, no individual can be made better off without rendering at least another individual worse off. In this state, no Pareto improvements can be made.

systems and the related subfield of complex adaptive systems (CAS) [5–7]. Notably, the many research areas related to the complex (adaptive) system domain can provide useful theories, models, algorithms and techniques for understanding and building complex autonomic computing systems. These comprise studies covering networked systems [8, 9], nonlinear dynamics and chaos theory [10], spontaneous synchronisation [11] and finally self-organisation, emergence, autopoiesis, adaptation and evolution [7, 12, 13]. Similarly, the field of cybernetics may provide insightful theories and studies for understanding complex, self-regulating systems [14–16]. Most existing theories in these domains have been based on, as well as applied to, scientific fields including biology, sociology, economy, physics, chemistry or engineering. Autonomic computing represents another challenging domain where such studies can find useful applications.

3.1.3   Adaptive Computing Systems

From an automatic control perspective, traditional automation systems have influenced autonomic computing right from its inception. Such domains include control theory and control engineering applications, which have long been studied and applied to mechanical, electrical, chemical or financial systems. Automatic control systems are discussed further in Sect. 3.3.

Within the system automation realm, robotics represents another important area from which autonomic computing can draw valuable inspiration. Indeed, robots must often operate in highly dynamic environments where adaptation abilities are essential and opportunities for human intervention are limited or undesirable. Considering the similar foundations and requirements of these two domains, it is hardly surprising that autonomic computing has borrowed multiple concepts, architectures and decision techniques from robotics. Most notably, these include modular and multilayered designs for complicated and dynamically adaptable reasoning and behaviour, as needed when operating in uncertain environments.

Additional sources of inspiration can be easily identified when focusing on a system's actual control strategies. When such strategies must dynamically adapt to internal and external changes, the decision logic may no longer be hardwired. On the contrary, it must be sufficiently generic and flexible to respond correctly to a wide range of unpredictable situations. This brings about the concept of automatic system 'reasoning', which must rely on an available body of knowledge. Consequently, autonomic systems start raising very similar issues that the artificial intelligence (AI) field has been trying to solve. Such issues include the provisioning of support for abstract representations, automatic decision-making, learning techniques and reasoning based on incomplete or uncertain information.

The field of multi-agent systems (MAS) has been developed to address many of the ideas and challenges raised by applications in artificial intelligence and other scientific fields. The key strength of these systems lies in their capacity to address complicated computing problems by dividing and distributing them among a set of specialised reasoning[3] agents. Carefully designed interactions among context-aware, adaptive and autonomous agents lead to the global behaviours that address the targeted problem. Hence, autonomic computing and multi-agent systems share a number of principles and objectives, including the use of autonomous, context-sensitive and adaptive entities. Indeed, MAS paradigms have been introduced from the earliest stages of autonomic computing architecture specifications (Chap. 4), showing that autonomic systems involving multiple interconnected feedback loops could be modelled and designed as a set of interacting agents. Section 3.4 provides a brief introduction to the AI domain and to the notion of rational agents.

Certainly, software engineering (SE) will provide an essential base for developing autonomic computing systems. From a design and implementation perspective, autonomic computing can adopt many of the existing paradigms and technologies that software engineering has introduced in the computing domain for ensuring application robustness and flexibility in execution contexts susceptible to frequent (dynamic) change. These include concepts and platforms provided by service-oriented computing, virtualisation technology, grid computing and the dynamic variants of aspect-oriented programming or component-oriented software. They also include reusable architectures, frameworks and design patterns that have been conceived considering extensibility, adaptability and evolvability as core requirements. The software engineering field and its contributions to autonomic computing are emphasised throughout the book and hence not further detailed in this chapter.

Finally, from a domain-specific perspective, several IT fields have been striving to address challenges that are similar or identical to those confronting autonomic systems. These include pervasive and ubiquitous systems, smart buildings and ambient intelligence, smart grids, self-adaptive and context-aware applications and middleware, dependable computing systems, reflective applications, mobile ad hoc networks and cluster infrastructures. Hence, autonomic system designers can adopt and reuse many of the research results that have been produced in these adjacent domains. At the same time, it is essential to stress that while information technology is inspired by, and welcomes approaches and techniques from other fields (including other IT fields), these constitute fields in their own right and as such possess their own 'difficult points'.

In the following sections we discuss some of the most important influences and sources of inspiration for autonomic computing—biology (Sect. 3.2), control theory (Sect. 3.3), artificial intelligence and multi-agent system approaches (Sect. 3.4) and finally complex systems (Sect. 3.5).

We focus on developing the biology angle on autonomic computing, since biology represents both the domain that provided the original idea behind the autonomic computing paradigm and the domain that is the least present in typical computer science curricula. A disambiguation of some essential principles in autonomous nervous systems may allow readers to better grasp the autonomic computing paradigm and to draw richer benefits from its relationship to biology.

---

[3] 'Reasoning' is quite loosely defined in the MAS context, as it can range from basic reactive behaviours to complicated and proactive learning, predicting and planning capacities.

3.2   Biology

3.2.1   Overview

The term autonomic refers to the autonomic nervous system (ANS), which is responsible for regulating vital functions. One might think that the complexity of the human body, given the variety of its parts, could make it impossible to coordinate all the necessary actions to keep the human system in a stable state, which is essential to its survival. However, in spite of this complexity, living organisms are prime examples of the power of adaptation to new environments that has yet to be equalled. These capabilities are possible thanks to internal coordination. It is not possible for a unique central organ to reign without sharing. Two distinct parts[4] must agree with each other in order to control the organism and ensure its survival: the brain orders the conscious, purposeful acts, while the autonomic nervous system (ANS) controls subconscious activities that are beyond wilful control. Both the brain and the ANS are part of the human nervous system (NS).

The ANS' main purpose is to ensure homeostasis—a system's ability to maintain internal equilibrium despite changes in its external environment and its internal state. The ANS[5] uses external and internal sensory information to regulate the activity of internal organs so as to maintain a set of vital parameters (body temperature, oxygen levels or glucose concentration) within a 'survivability' zone.

The ANS extends from the brain to the spinal cord via the brain stem and has branches to every gland and organ of the human body and is composed of several subsystems that interact to ensure the functioning of our bodies without our awareness. It is then possible to carry out intellectual activities without worrying about bodily functions. It is important to emphasise that these systems are interdependent and that the actions of one may affect the other. For example, the brain, and therefore conscious actions, can impact the ANS' unconscious behaviour. For instance, a scary thought, which causes stress, may lead to changes in heart rate and increased sweating to enable one to stay and fight or run away.

Within the biological realm, the ultimate goal of an organism's autonomic nervous system is to ensure the organism's survival. Similarly, in the IT domain, the goal of an autonomic computing system is to ensure the continual provisioning of the system's functional services and associated quality of service (QoS) properties in the presence of external and internal changes. In this scenario, the role of a human administrator seems to be equivalent to that of the conscious brain. That is, human administrators merely specify a computing system's high-level objectives and then only intervene in case of system failure or for changing system objectives and behaviour. To do this, system administrators are provided an overview and summary of the environment in order to make decisions, but a large part of the burden of administration is in turn managed by a variable amount of autonomous

---

[4]This of course represents a simplification of the human nervous system.
[5]Sometimes in conjunction with the endocrine system.

subordinates. They will have a very localised and detailed view of the situation of a resource or a particular resource pool. All in all, the sum of their actions defines the overall system behaviour.

3.2.2 Introduction to Biological Nervous Systems

A *nervous system* (NS) is an integrated biological system consisting of interconnected, specialised cells—nerve cells (called *neurons*) and non-neural support cells (called *glial* or *glue cells*). A nervous system has an essential role in controlling an organism's inner changes. Most importantly, the neurons of a nervous system are specialised in sending fast signals between different body parts, hence playing a key role in coordinating an organism's actions and reactions.

Nervous systems first appeared in the Cambrian period, around 542 million years ago. At that time, they represented a key enabler in the emergence of animals—multicellular, eukaryotic, *motile* organisms (i.e. capable of moving about in their environment). Static organisms, like plants or fungi, were rooted in their environments, hence presenting no stringent need for a nervous system. But *motility brings about change*. This represents both a great advantage and a great challenge for survival. Indeed, any organism enjoying movement can get away from predators and find more food but must immediately face the consequent disadvantages, namely, finding itself in ever-changing environments. Active motility implies perpetual changes in the animal's environment. In such conditions, the chances of survival of a motile organism will be greatly enhanced by its capacity to adapt to environmental changes, not to mention the capacity to avoid moving into fatal environments.

Hence, as a movement enabler, the nervous system can improve an animal's motion efficiency by coordinating the actions of its various body parts. Also, as a 'change manager', a nervous system helps an animal move in intelligent[6] ways—the more complicated the animal, the more intelligent the movement.

The key underlying functions of a nervous system rely on fast long-range communication and support for data processing. Such functions enable the formation of swift connections from sensors to actuators, passing through various control centres. They can also enable the conception of a more or less sophisticated representation of the external world, which is essential for predicting the consequences of actions. This type of *model-guided control loops* can bring about a wide choice of adaptations, ranging from simple reflex reactions to more complicated strategic action suites.

Interestingly, a similar developmental trend can be observed in computer systems. In this context, *programs* can be seen as means of controlling the behaviour of a computing system. Initially, programs were isolated entities, confined to static environments and performing well-defined calculations. They are now increasingly

---

[6]*Intelligent* is broadly used here to imply well-adapted behaviour for achieving a set of objectives—for example, the organism's survival and implied subgoals, like keeping warm, eating and avoiding being eaten.

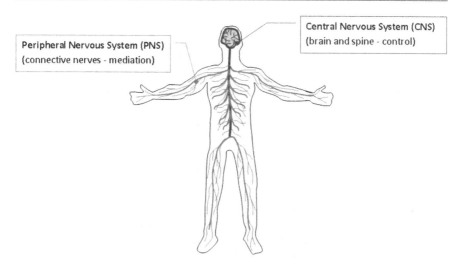

Fig. 3.2 Human nervous system

agile and mobile, operating in often unpredictable environments, possibly in collaboration with other computing systems. In this context, biological nervous systems can provide a great source of inspiration to software engineering. They show how the interconnection of basic system elements into rapid communication circuits can enable the efficient and coherent adaptation of complex systems. Furthermore, numerous examples show how diverse nervous system topologies, with various sizes and degrees of complexity, endow different species with various characteristics and capabilities.

3.2.3 Structure of the Human Nervous System

The human nervous system (HNS) is the most complex system making up the human body. As illustrated by Fig. 3.2, it consists of the central nervous system and the peripheral nervous system [17–19]. The central nervous system (CNS) is the largest part of the nervous system and principally consists of the brain and the spinal cord. It integrates information received from the different body parts and sends out signals (consciously or unconsciously) for controlling and coordinating the body's actions. The peripheral nervous system (PNS) connects the CNS to the different body tissues. It consists of cranial and spinal nerves and of different types of nerve clusters called ganglia. An intricate network of neural pathways interconnects the different nervous system parts.

From a theoretical system perspective, the CNS can be viewed as a data processing centre and the PNS as a data-mediation infrastructure for connecting the CNS to peripheral sensors and actuators. Data processing in the CNS is performed at various complexity levels from straightforward spinal connections between input

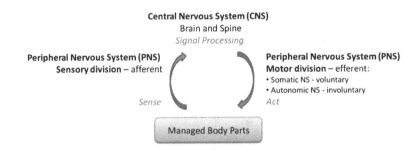

Fig. 3.3 Central, sensory and motor nervous system divisions

and output PNS paths (forming *reflex arcs*) to complex data-processing tasks in the brain (like pattern recognition, planning or learning). In addition to data communication, the PNS can also transform transmitted signals by amplifying their strengths or by filtering them out at various levels.

As illustrated in Fig. 3.3, the PNS can be further broken down into several subsystems,[7] in particular the *sensory* division and the *motor* division. The *sensory NS* conducts impulses from receptors to the CNS. It can be viewed as a monitoring infrastructure relaying sensory inputs towards data-processing centres in the CNS. Input data can originate from both external receptors like eyes, ears, nose or skin and from internal receptors like chemical concentrations, pressure or temperature sensors in blood, lymphatic circuits, glands and viscera.

Conversely, the *motor* division transmits signals from the CNS towards external and internal effectors. Two types of activator pathways can be distinguished: *somatic* and *autonomic*. The *somatic* division typically conducts impulses from the CNS to the skeletal muscles, hence playing an essential role in voluntary motor functions. Involuntary actions pass by the *autonomic* division to reach internal organs, including cardiac muscles in the heart, smooth muscles in the stomach or hair follicles in the skin. Hence, the *autonomic* division affects unconscious activities including heartbeats, widening and narrowing of blood vessels, breathing, digestion, metabolism and pupil dilation. The *autonomic NS (ANS)* provides a particularly enticing source of inspiration for the design of adaptive systems. This is due to its capability of using sensory information for regulating internal processes, while relying on a combination of relatively simple, unconscious and mostly hardwired circuits.

As illustrated in Fig. 3.4, the *ANS* is classically divided into two subsystems[8] consisting of circuits with opposing actions. On the one hand, the *sympathetic NS (SNS)* is concerned with adaptations that prepare the body for stressful or emergency situations—'fight or flight'. On the other hand, the *parasympathetic NS*

---

[7]Various neuroscience sources promote different PNS divisions (e.g. placing part of the sensory division within or outside the ANS), yet a discussion on this topic is well outside the scope of this publication.

[8]Various neuroscience sources also include the *Enteric* nervous subsystem as part of the ANS, yet for clarity reasons we avoid presenting this detail here.

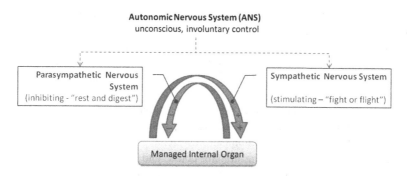

Fig. 3.4 Sympathetic and parasympathetic divisions of the autonomic nervous system

(*PSNS*) controls adaptations for ordinary situations—'rest and digest'. Based on these opposing circuits, the ANS can react to sensory information, from internal organs and the environment, by stimulating body processes via the SNS or inhibiting them via the PSNS.

The two autonomic subsystems (SNS and PSNS) typically work together to control the same organs. They constantly keep each other in check via stimulatory/inhibitory effects, which form various *negative feedback circuits*. From an engineering perspective, it is interesting to note how these two parallel circuits, sensing and acting upon the same managed elements, and implementing opposite reactions, can perform regulatory actions and maintain designated parameters within a targeted range.

A simple example is the use of these opposite circuits for autonomously maintaining blood glucose levels. In this case, the PSNS uses information on sugar concentration in the blood to detect high concentrations and stimulate the secretion of insulin hormones—this stimulates the extraction of glucose from the blood and its storage as glycogen in liver, muscle and fat tissues, hence decreasing glucose concentration. Conversely, the SNS uses the same information to detect low concentrations and secrete glucagon hormones—this stimulates the conversion of glycogen into glucose and its release into the bloodstream, hence increasing sugar concentration. Additional autonomic regulation examples show the same implicit coordination between the two opposite processes: the SNS increases blood pressure, heartbeat rate and breathing while the PSNS decreases them.

In order to enforce different actions on the same organs, the two ANS subsystems employ different types of chemical messengers (*neurotransmitters*)—in general, *norepinephrine* for stimulating effects (SNS) and *acetylcholine* for inhibitory effects (PSNS). Similarly, in a computing system, messages of different types can be employed to induce dissimilar behaviours in the same receiving components.

3.2.4 Function of the Human Nervous System

At the most basic level, the main function of the nervous system (NS) is *communication*—rapidly transmitting signals between different body parts (that are not necessarily adjacent). An alternative long-range communication mechanism is also available, relying on the release of hormones into the internal circulation. Nonetheless, signal transmission by means of hormone diffusion is slower and less accurate than NS-based transmission. Indeed, nerve circuits can more accurately connect specific target areas, with the fastest nerves transmitting signals at speeds exceeding 100 m/s.

From a computing perspective, diffusion resembles peer-to-peer broadcasting while nerve signalling resembles fast, precise, point-to-point communication. In biological systems, the two communication systems are used in parallel and sometimes combined. The engineering domain could, and already has to some extent, begin to study the advantages and disadvantages of such means of communication and the manner in which they could be combined.

At a higher abstraction level, the nervous system (NS) is responsible for controlling various body processes. This is achieved by extracting internal and external information via sensory receptors, processing the information so as to detect potential problems and to determine suitable responses and finally sending signals to the muscles or glands that can activate such responses. Not surprisingly, this process is highly similar to the one implemented by autonomic system control loops (as we will see in Chap. 4).

NS circuits offer important insights for software system engineering since they provide efficient means of achieving complex, adaptive control behaviours. At a basic level, such characteristics are based on several key constructions that enable neural circuits to simultaneously transmit and transform information (some details discussed below). From a higher, conceptual perspective, neural circuits can transmit signals of different types and strengths, amplify or decrease signal strength during transmission and achieve content-based routing based on signal types. On a neural circuit's effector end, similar constructions allow converting signal types and strengths for triggering diverse actions with different intensities. At a global system level, the integration of parallel circuits with mutually influencing effects leads to the emergence of complex, adaptive and convergent control behaviours. For example, the previous subsection showed how the parallel actions of sympathetic and parasympathetic circuits can form opposed feedback loops with highly efficient regulatory behaviours. Finally, in a biological nervous system, the occurrence of certain signals, whether punctual or repeated, can engender certain modifications in the functioning of a neural circuit—for example, different routing or increased signal amplification. This may in turn enable an NS to achieve adaptation and *learning*. Such capabilities based on repeated circuit usage and engendered results are also essential to autonomic systems, which can learn from their experience and adapt as best as possible to their environment.

Let us now provide a brief description of the main neural principles enabling biological nervous systems. Here, *communication* relies on the transmission of neural signals. Neural signals travel as *electrochemical waves* via neuron nerve fibres and pass from one cell to another via *synaptic connections*. Signal transmission across one neuron relies on the formation and propagation of an *action potential*[9] in response to some stimulation. Stimuli can be received concomitantly from different sources—sensors or other neurons. The sum of stimuli on a neuron must cross a critical *threshold* in order for the neuron to 'fire'. According to an 'all-or-nothing' principle, once a neuron's threshold is crossed, the signals transmitted are almost identical irrespectively of the intensity of the initial stimuli. Nonetheless, while signals at the neuron level are the same, significant differentiation can be achieved over neural circuits, by varying neuron interconnections, synapse types and signal synchronisation.

Most common and most diverse synapses are chemical. In a chemical synapse, the termination of a 'sending' neuron (activated by a signal) will release neurotransmitter chemicals into the space between the 'sending' neuron and the 'receiving' neuron. These chemicals bind to the receptors of the 'receiving' neuron. Here, different receptor types will have different effects: excitatory effects contribute to the neuron's activation and subsequent signal propagation; inhibitory effects do the opposite. Alternatively, electrical synapses can also transfer signals between neural cells, the main difference being the increased speed of signal transmission when compared to chemical synapses.

Similarly, communication between neurons and effector cell types (e.g. muscle cells) is also based on synaptic connections. As before, depending on the type of receptor in the receiving cell, the resulting effect can be excitatory, inhibitory or modulatory. For example, an excitatory effect on a muscle cell would manifest as rapid cell contractions. The NS uses over a 100 types of neurotransmitters,[10] with diverse effects on different kinds of receptors. Hence, a single sending neuron may have both excitatory and inhibitory effects when connected to different receiving cells with different receptor types.

While signal transmission between cells only lasts for a millisecond's fraction, longer-term effects may also occur in the synaptic connection. For example, the number of receptors in a receiving cell may be multiplied, subsequently increasing the sensitivity of the synaptic bound. Such changes may last for variable periods, such as days, weeks or longer. This type of mechanism provides an essential base for the formation of *memory traces* and *learning*. *Reward-based learning* may also occur based on the reinforcement of frequently activated neural connections and conditioned by an extra reward signal (that uses a dopamine neurotransmitter). These capabilities give the nervous system certain *plasticity*, enabling it to adapt to variations in its environment.

---

[9] Action potential (spike or impulse): the sequential polarisation and depolarisation of a neuron's membrane, caused by stimuli (in a neuron's dendrites or soma) and travelling through the neuron (soma and axon) towards its extremity (axon terminals). Importantly, only stimuli that cross a certain *threshold* cause the action potential to travel across the neuron, causing the neuron to 'fire'. Once triggered, all signals have the same action potential amplitude.

[10] The most common neurotransmitters include acetylcholine, dopamine, GABA, glutamate and serotonin.

3.2.5 Reflexes and Autonomic Control Loops

Autonomic computing can draw further inspiration from biological control systems by looking into the way they can integrate several reflex control circuits with more extensive control processes in order to achieve adaptive control behaviours, occurring at various time scales.

The simplest type of neural control loop (called a *reflex arc*) is involved in rapid, unconscious, *reflex* actions. It takes input from a sensory neuron, acts using a motor neuron and passes through a number of connection neurons. The circuits of such involuntary reflexes are hardwired during an individual's development. They may involve both skeletal muscle effectors and visceral effectors [18]. In addition, *conditional reflexes* may be *learned* during an individual's lifetime (e.g. how Pavlov's dogs adapt in the famous experiment).

Let us take an example that illustrates the functioning of a single reflex arc as well as the global behaviour resulting from the integration of several reflex circuits. We consider the case of a human foot stepping on a sharp object—as soon as this occurs, the foot lifts up promptly before the brain can consciously realise it [20]. This reflex process starts with a pain receptor sending a signal to a *sensory neuron*, which activates another neuron in the spinal cord. Within the spine, a connector neuron relays the signal to a *motor neuron*, which induces contractions in the leg muscle. This simple reflex arc only involves neurons in the peripheral system and spine, without involving the brain. Generally, the process is typically more complicated, involving the synchronous activation and implicit coordination of several other reflex circuits. Namely, signals in the spine must also be relayed to the other leg and torso muscles, balance the person, avoiding them tumbling over as the injured leg lifts. In addition, the same signal is also projected up the spine and through the brain stem to reach the sensory cortex. This subsequently excites the primary motor cortex, which contracts face muscles into contortions that help communicate the victim's distress to the external world.

This simple example shows how one alarm signal can be used to simultaneously activate several reflex circuits, tuned to act in tandem so as to quickly get an entire system out of danger.

Conversely, signals from multiple sensors can be aggregated in order to determine a single reflex's output or action. The example in [21] indicates how contextual information on a cockroach's current positioning can drastically influence its reaction when faced with a threat:

> Activity in dorsal giant interneurons of the cockroach initiates flight movements if leg contact with a substrate is prevented. The same interneurons initiate activity associated with running when leg contact is maintained. Thus, which one of two completely different behaviours the giant interneurons evoke depends on the presence or absence of leg contact.

In addition to such passive, stimulus–response reactions, the NS of several species is also capable of controlling the body via intrinsically generated activity patterns, which do not require external stimuli. From an engineering perspective, this is the equivalent of comparing *reactive* processes, such as methods triggered by external calls in object-oriented programs, to *proactive* processes, such as internal timers and goal-oriented planners in agent-based systems.

In humans, such proactive behaviour is achieved by means of internal activity cycles, based on neurons that can generate rhythmic sequence of action potentials, even in isolation. A good example of such activity is the *circadian cycle*—a sleep–awake pattern with about 24 h periods—inducing important behavioural fluctuations. While influenced by light, the circadian cycle continues to operate even when light intensity is maintained at constant levels (though some studies have shown that the cycle may get deranged over time in such cases).

Finally, let us have a look into the construction and functioning of control loops in the autonomic nervous system (ANS). Neurons belonging to the ANS form autonomic pathways that connect neurons located in the brain stem and spinal cord to effectors located in the internal organs.[11] Such autonomic pathways are activated by upstream signals from the Sensory NS or by motor signals from the CNS, consequently generating involuntary internal regulation. For example, signals indicating a high level of activity, such as running, will prompt the ANS to increase heartbeat and breathing rates and maybe to contract blood vessels for augmenting blood pressure. Since it is connected to centres in the CNS, the ANS may also be influenced by conscious processes and emotions. For example, a person's heartbeat and sweating may increase when they get angry and slow down as they adopt a more Zen attitude. Autonomic system designers can draw inspiration from the way in which autonomic pathways structured as relatively simple control loops can ensure prompt, unconscious regulatory functions for essential system parameters. Moreover, the connectivity and mutual influence between the ANS and higher brain functions in the CNS can provide valuable hints towards layered architectures for system designs.

3.2.6 Different Nervous System Architectures and Features

While most members of the animal kingdom, from jellyfish to humans, posses some type of nervous system (NS), the complexity of such nervous systems may tremendously vary [17].

Some of the most primitive animals do not possess nervous systems, but are still able to provoke coordinated movements of their entire bodies. For example, sponges can trigger whole-body contractions that expel water out of their hollow structures. This can be considered as a basic example of self-maintenance and context-aware self-protection.

Most of the more complicated animals possess various kinds of neural systems, featuring different types of architectures, or organisations. *Radiata* animals (radially symmetrical animals such as jellyfish or hydra) possess primitive nervous systems

---

[11]More precisely, the nervous projections of neurons situated in the spinal cord or brain stem connect to neurons located in the autonomic ganglia. To complete the circuit, the nervous fibres of neurons in the autonomic ganglia reach and connect to the internal organs.

consisting of a loose *nerve net*, with no central brain or spine. The interlaced nerve network of such animals allows them to react to sensory inputs such as light, touch, temperature or chemical concentrations. However, such uniform, unspecialised nets provide insufficient accuracy for locating the sources of sensory inputs, hence engendering identical reactions to inputs from different locations.

To improve coordination and movement accuracy, starfish feature a different organisation of their neural nets—several radial nerves extending through each arm and a radial nerve ring connecting them all in the middle. Starfish represent interesting examples of extensive self-repair capacities, being able to fully regenerate any of their arms. Even though such capacities are not directly enabled by the NS, they show how the particular NS topology renders it well-suited to extensive self-repair.

Most complex NS organisation can be found in Bilaterian animals, which represent most of the vertebrate and invertebrate animal species (including humans). All Bilaterian animals possess a central nervous system (CNS) comprising a brain, at least one central cord and numerous nerves. Certainly, the NS *size* will vary significantly across different Bilaterian species, from a few hundred highly specialised neurons and glial cells in simple worms to about a hundred billion adaptive neurons and glial cells in humans. As can be easily observed, the size and flexibility of an NS have a critical impact on the complexity and adaptability of its generated behaviour.

Within an NS, some neural circuits are genetically preprogrammed. These most notably include the neural circuits involved in basic survival mechanisms. At the same time, most NSs also feature various degrees of *plasticity* (or *neuroplasticity*), which enables them to undergo structural and/or functional changes based on input from the external environment. Changes may occur at reduced scales, like cellular changes and new synaptic connections involved in learning; or at larger scales, like extensive reorganisations of cortical mappings following brain injury.

3.2.7   Summary of Inspiration from Nervous Systems

Autonomic computing, as well as software engineering, can draw great inspiration from various aspects of biological nervous systems. Most notably, it is interesting to observe how behaviours that are complex and adaptive, yet coherent and reliable, can be obtained based on diverse decentralised networks of simple and similarly structured elements.

At a low, fine-grained level, engineers can look into the way in which relatively simple processes and constructions in neurons and synaptic connections allow for simultaneous, parallel and reconfigurable data transmission and transformation. At a slightly higher structural level, the simplicity and efficiency of autonomic and reflex control loops provide an immediate source of inspiration for the design of simple, single-goal, autonomic software. At a more global level, it is interesting to observe how adaptive behaviours can emerge from the coordinated integration of mutually influencing neural circuits. Observation at this level should aim to decipher the manner in which such emergent behaviours can be achieved via the careful interconnection and synchronisation of processes, as well as via higher-level structural organisation, specialisation and self-organisation capabilities, within a targeted environment.

From a networked system perspective, understanding NS topologies, at various scales, can provide a good base when designing control systems adapted to various contexts. Existing network topologies are worth exploring and range from the rather uniform, *random topology* of the jellyfish nerve net, through the more organised, *small-world topology* of the *C. elegans* worm [22] and to the combination of small-world and *scale-free organisation* of the complex dynamical system that makes the human brain [23].

At the periphery of any control system, the types, number and connectivity of sensors and actuators seem worth studying to pinpoint tradeoffs between the resources employed, engendered NS complexity and richness of supported input and output facilities enabling context-aware behaviour. To complement sensor-based reactive processes, inspiration can also be drawn from the use and implementation of proactive, self-triggering neural activities occurring in some biological species.

From an architectural perspective, it is interesting to note the structural separation of neural functions into several layers and components, as well as the coordination and cooperation among the different components and layers that ensure an efficient and coherent control behaviour overall. Most notably, in more complex neural systems, such architectures can be observed in the separation and interaction between higher-level neural functions and basic lower-level functions such as reflex arcs. This separation enables the isolation of different types of control concerns so as to prevent them from interfering with each other. As previously shown, reflex arcs and autonomic processes must provide fast, efficient and relatively simple functions. Conversely, high-level brain functions must engage in more complex data-processing functions, such as planning and learning, which may be performed over longer periods. Certainly, the two control types must cooperate so as to best ensure the organism's survival over the long term. Reusability of such separated concerns can be another incentive, as can be observed by studying the evolution of increasingly complicated biological species.

3.2.8 Bio-inspiration Beyond Nervous Systems

It is important to note that a biological system's autonomy does not solely rely entirely on the system's autonomic nervous system or on the nervous system in general. Additional, interrelated biological structures and processes can prove tremendously useful as sources of inspiration for engineering autonomic systems. These may include diffusion-based communication (based on the release of chemicals into the blood or lymph circuits) or context-sensitive processes taking place inside individual cells and propagating across groups of cells. A noteworthy process in this context is the *genotype–phenotype* transformation that enables the creation of a fully functional biological system, well-adapted to its environment, by the replicable and context-aware self-organisation of reusable resources collected from that environment[12] [24]. Such processes can also play a key role in system self-optimisation (the continuous renewal of constituent parts depending on resource availability and context), self-repair (by enabling the *regeneration* of system parts such as the arms of start fish or the tail of gecko lizards) and even self-protection (by detaching renewable body parts to avoid capture).

The mechanisms and processes behind species evolution provide great inspiration for engineering automatic solution-search algorithms and infrastructures, such as has already been shown via genetic algorithms. Such processes mainly capitalise on the capacity to represent an organism's blueprint in the form of an efficiently compressible information code, the possibility of mutating and mixing different blueprint variants and the capability of selecting the most suitable blueprints from the new resulting variants, based on the fitness evaluation of individuals.

Overall, the entire biological realm seems to open a wide range of opportunities for novel, alternative design solutions suitable for sustaining the production and maintenance of complex, adaptive IT systems. Certainly, caution must be taken when getting inspiration from the living systems domain. On the one hand, the underlying environmental restrictions and the targeted objectives can prove quite dissimilar for biological systems and engineered IT systems. Hence, engineers should search to merely extract inspiration from the biological realm rather than blindly attempting to copy its mechanisms without a thorough understanding of their primary constraints and motivations—for example, [25].

Finally, engineers should take considerable care when considering the long-term impact of the autonomic IT systems they develop and deploy into the real world. Indeed, the very advantages of an autonomous system could turn into notable disadvantages should an autonomous system no longer serve our purposes—that is, no need for human intervention. From this perspective, the context and lifespan of an autonomic system must be considered during its design and suitable solutions included into its very structure and function. Within this context, the Apoptotic Computing project has been defined with the goal of developing 'Programmed Death by Default for Computer-Based Systems' [26]. This project aims to introduce a *self-destruct* property into autonomic computing systems in order to help prevent catastrophic scenarios. This approach is inspired by the apoptosis mechanism in biological systems. Here, programmed cell death intervenes as part of immune responses in multicellular organisms, for eliminating damaged or diseased cells, in a controlled and non-toxic manner.

3.3 Control Systems

Automatic control systems have been around for some time to regulate industrial processes such as power stations and chemical plants. Like autonomic computing systems, the feedback loop is central to such systems. A control system consists of

---

[12]R. Doursat, 'Morphogenetic engineering weds bio self-organization to human-designed systems', *PerAdaMagazine*,May2011;http://www.perada-magazine.eu/view.php?source=003722-2011-05-18

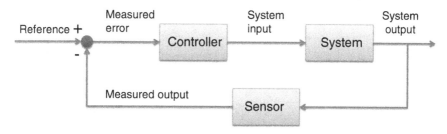

Fig. 3.5 Feedback loop

an interconnection of components specifically configured to achieve a desired purpose. Modern control engineering practice includes the use of control design strategies for improving manufacturing processes, the efficiency of energy use and advanced automobile control, among others. It is these processes (plant or components) that are under the management of the control system.

3.3.1 Introduction

The traditional goal of automatic control systems is to maintain parameters in a certain threshold without human intervention. These parameters are usually physical measurements or quantities such as speed and temperature. Control techniques have been developed to meet these needs [27], which include the use of feedback loops. As illustrated in Fig. 3.5, below, a feedback loop is composed of three elements: the system that one wishes to regulate, a set of sensors and a controller. From reference values set by the user, the controller's role is to observe the system through the sensors and make changes to ensure both system stability and compliance to the user's reference values. To achieve this, it is necessary to have an accurate representation of the system. That is why regulation techniques use mathematical models of the environment that define system state and the values of input and output that are possible. This concept of feedback loop has been present in autonomic computing from the beginning [28].

For completeness we describe a general process for designing a control system. This section provides a very simplistic and brief introduction to the subject, enough to understand some of the main concepts that tend to affect autonomic systems. To this end, much of the calculus has been removed; therefore, we direct the reader to the many introductions to control theory that exist for more full review.

Typically a representation of the control systems is modelled, and there is a gap between the complex physical system under investigation and the model used in the control system synthesis (see Chap. 7—Knowledge, for a more thorough discussion). Through the use of the feedback loop, the iterative nature of the control process allows us to effectively handle the design gap while trading-off complexity, performance and cost in order to meet the system's goals.

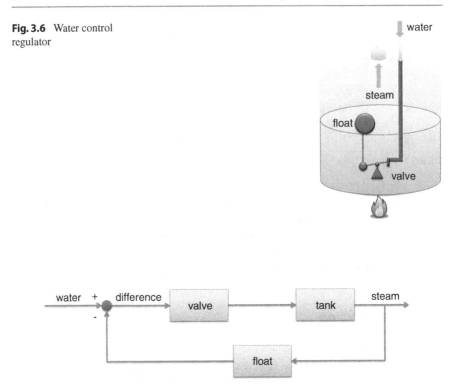

Fig. 3.6 Water control regulator

Fig. 3.7 Control model for water regulator

One of the earliest examples of a control system is a water control regulator (Fig. 3.6.) A float is used to measure the water level and ensure that the water tank does not run out of water to convert to steam. The water is released to the tank when the float decreases far enough to move the valve.

Figure 3.7 shows the control model for the water regulator depicted in Fig. 3.6. This can be described as an example of a closed-loop control system whereby the output (steam) directly affects the input (water) level as the steam 'consumes' the water moving the float.

Building a control system is not unlike building any adaptive or autonomic system. We need to establish what the goals of the system are (maintaining steam) and the corresponding variables to control (water level). From this the configuration of the system needs to be established which includes the sensor and associated actuator that will change the system to meet its goals. For our example the actuator is the valve and the float is the sensor. The controller is then specified and the key parameters to be adjusted (water level) detailed. Finally, the performance of the control system needs checking. Here it would be that the float is registering the decrease in water fast enough for the leaver to move the valve to let water flow: if this is too slow, which would cause the tank to boil dry, or too fast which would cause flooding. In this case then the controller needs adjusting.

As mentioned above, the type of controller in our example is that of a closed *feedback loop controller*. There are two alternative controllers, *feedforward* and *open-loop controller*. In feedforward control, disturbances (i.e. the aspects of the environment that cause the error) are detected and, before the resulting change is detected by the sensors, the actuator is triggered. An example of this is the heating system of your house that detects a window is open and puts the heater on before the thermostat detects a fall in temperature.

The open-loop controller calculates the appropriate inputs to feed to the control system in order to make it produce a desired output by using only the state of the system and a model of its behaviour. Thus, for this sort of controller to perform appropriately, it needs complete prior knowledge of the system. This is very difficult for systems in non-deterministic, dynamic environments. Therefore, instead of trying to understand the complex environment, the system uses feedback regarding how well it is matching its goals (or not) to steer its operation. A simple example of a closed-loop system is that of power-assisted steering in a car that uses sensors to monitor pressures on the turning components to increase power to help steer the car. Alternatively, a car without power-assisted steering is an open-loop system whereby the steering is controlled by the driver and the degree of turning is directly related to the amount of movement the driver forced on the steering wheel. One could argue that the driver uses human sensory feedback to compensate and adjust the steering wheel however.

We are more interested in feedback control, where the current output of the managed system compared to a reference value serves as an input to a controller that will calculate the appropriate input to send into the system to regulate it. These sorts of controllers do not require complete knowledge of the managed systems and so can perform well under dynamic environments or in the presence of unpredicted noise and disturbance. This is the sort of controller that would mirror the autonomic computing MAPE-K loop more closely (this is described in Chap. 4). In this case the system would be the managed system, the sensor would be the sensor touchpoint in the managed system and the controller would be the autonomic manager. The actuator touchpoint would be another component sitting between the controller and the system.

3.3.2 Feedback Control

Similar to our previous example, we now examine the general case where only one variable is being managed and another variable controls the managed system, s, such that the output is correlated to the input. The Input value often represents the value that is desired to be output. The aim of the feedback system to understand the difference between the input and output values, and this difference drives the control. Here when the output settles out to the required value, it is said to be in a steady state. We can model the system with the circuit in Fig. 3.8.

In order to analyse the feedback controller and how to make it efficient, a typical technique is to calculate the transfer function of the system. Here, we discuss this by means of the convention of using capital letters to represent the transformation of the signals and impulse responses.

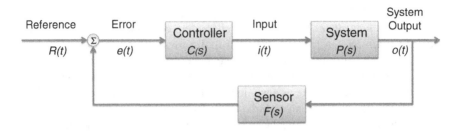

Fig. 3.8 General model of a single-input single-output feedback control system (SISO)

In this model of a control system, we have the system being controlled, a sensor that monitors the outputs from the system and a controller that regulates the system. Assuming the sensor in this system does not change the output value in any way, that is, $F(s)=1$, meaning it has no *gain*, which is typical of computer-controlled systems converting analogue signals to digital signals, for example.

The error at a given time, $e(t)$, is the value calculated as the difference between what was expected from the system (given the initial reference value $r(t)$) and what the sensor read as the actual value output. The error is a measure of how well the system is performing at any instant. If the error is large, this means the measured output is not matching the desired output. Here, the controller must adjust the input value to reduce this error and typically if the difference is large then the control action (also known as gain) is large.

$P(s)$ is the transfer function that goes from input $i(t)$ to output $o(t)$. The advantage of the feedback controller is that only simple knowledge about the managed component, or system, is required and not the environment. The controller's goal is to minimise the error. Because the system measures the effective error by subtracting the output to the reference, the system can directly react to previous system output.

3.3.3   The PID Controller

What we have described in the previous section is essentially a PID (proportional–integral–derivative) controller. It is one of the most widely used controllers and has been widely adopted for controlling a single variable in order to make it reach a desired set point. This controller is composed of a generic feedback loop, as depicted in Fig. 3.9.

After the error signal is calculated, the controller then applies three distinct operators to adjust this signal and each signal has a very specific role in the control loop:

- *Proportional* (*P*)—The proportional controller, as we have already discussed, simply applies a multiplicative constant to the error signal. Constant adjustment provides an input that aims to correct the current error signal. Here we see that K_p is the proportional gain, and $e(t)$ is the error signal, obtained by subtracting the reference signal (set point) and the present value $o(t)$. The proportional gain affects how

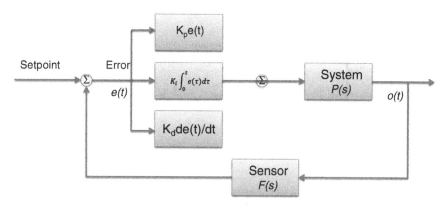

Fig. 3.9 Proportional–integral–derivative controller (PID controller)

much the system should be tweaked in order to respond to an input error, for example, like an amplifier. Higher gains will make the system adjust quicker. However, adjusting the proportional gain too high can cause the correction value to overshoot (Fig. 3.9) which in turn can produce large errors that need compensating for. Again if the gain is large it will overcompensate and essentially make the system oscillate more or even become unstable. Proportional control alone will usually not make the system arrive at its set-point value, but will only approximate it.

• *Integral (I)*—This controller integrates the error signal and so provides the response to the past behaviour of the system. It provides a control signal that attempts to correct the errors that should have been corrected previously, that is, it aims to eliminate bias. This accumulated error is then multiplied by an integral gain to weight the contribution of this component to the controller. Here, K_i is the integral gain. The integral term accelerates the system to the desired set point and, when used in conjunction with the proportional controller, eliminates the constant error. The gain needs to be carefully tweaked to avoid the system over-responding to the previous error and overshooting the desired value. Setting the integral gain higher will eliminate the error more quickly but with the risk of a larger overshoot, as every negative error integrated needs to be compensated for by positive error in order for the system to reach a steady state; see Fig. 3.10.

• *Derivative (D)*—The derivative component of the controller, as its name implies, compensates the derivative of the error over time. K_d is the derivative gain that will reduce the signal amplitude when overshooting and so can be very useful for decreasing the overshoot produced by the PI controller, while retaining the high speed of adjustment provided by it. However, setting the derivative gain too high can significantly slow the response.

The PID controller, having all of these components weighted, then produces the final control signal by adding all their contributions together:

$$P_{out} + I_{out} + D_{out} = K_p e(t) + K_i \int_0^t e(\tau)\,d\tau + K_d \frac{d}{dt} e(t)$$

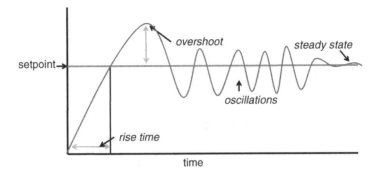

Fig. 3.10 Overshoot, oscillations and steady state of a system

There are many methods for tuning a PID controller in order to ensure that the system behaves optimally under the desired circumstances. Manual methods usually start by adjusting the proportional term until it starts to oscillate and then adjusting the integral and derivative terms to make sure the system adapts quickly and does not overshoot too much or become unstable. This controller is particularly useful in cases where there is very incomplete knowledge as to how the system will respond to the control signal. In cases where more complete knowledge of the system is available, the PID controller can be combined with feedforward mechanisms to provide a more suitable control.

3.3.4   Oscillations, Overshooting, Damping and Stability

A very important consideration with control systems is of course stability. In real-world applications, if the controller forces the system's output into approaching infinity, that is a serious issue that must be addressed. Thus, when using more complicated controllers, it becomes essential to use mathematical techniques to assess the stability of a system. Because this can be such a serious issue in engineering applications (where infinity in a system can mean physically dangerous situations), there has been significant research into this area. Firstly, we need to define what is meant by stability.

We have mentioned overshooting in the previous sections, depicted in Fig. 3.10. Overshoot, as the name suggests, is simply where the signal exceeds its steady-state value. Where the aim is to get the system to a steady state as soon as possible (i.e. reduce rise time; see Fig. 3.10), yet this causes conflict with the minimisation of overshoot. That is, typically where we have a steep line to attain steady state quickly the system will have a tendency to overshoot the set point. The magnitude of overshoot depends on time and the degree of damping.

Overshoot combined with a correction causing undershoot can in turn cause subsequent over and undershooting. This phenomenon is the system oscillating and is illustrated in Fig. 3.10. The net effect of this can cause the system to not converge

Fig. 3.11 Showing the effect of damping on overshoot

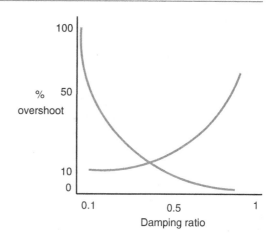

to a steady state, and in an autonomic context, this can be manifested, for example, as the system binding to different components and unbinding and rebinding again. This obviously causes problems with performance as the overheads to carry out the autonomic management are essentially dominating.

Damping is an effect that tends to reduce the amplitude of oscillations (e.g. friction can be described as a damping force). Figure 3.11 depicts the relationship between a damping ratio and the percentage overshoot. Obviously the more damping of a state change we provide, the less overshoot will occur. However, the more damping of error correction leads to a less responsive system and could increase the time taken for the system to reach stability.

The stability of a system relates to its response to inputs or disturbances. It can be described as a system which remains in a constant state unless affected by an external action and which returns to a constant state when that action is removed. Therefore, a system is stable if its error correction response approaches zero as time approaches infinity. Control theory is concerned not only with the stability of a system but also its degree of stability which can be described as marginal whereby the system is stable for a time and then when a disturbance is injected, the system becomes unstable for a time. The degree of stability, therefore, is an indicator of how close the system is to instability and how much disturbances will affect the system's ability to return to its expected output.

3.3.5 Control and Autonomic Computing

To simplify the engineering of managed systems, it is best to reduce the number of control loops in the system and keep them as independent as possible. The autonomic feedback loop concept helps this in that it focuses the abstraction to controlling each managed resource and hence one control loop per element. However, as will be seen in Chap. 4—Architecture, an autonomic system may comprise many managed elements (or resources) or a hierarchy of managed elements, and these may be controlled, tuned and managed very separately from each other. In this way, the ability to understand how the autonomic system is behaving becomes a more tractable process.

At the same time, the control processes of autonomic systems can become increasingly difficult to design, track and maintain as targeted systems, and their goals become increasingly complex, and as several managed systems may have to coexist in shared environments—such as is the case in smart grids or cloud systems. Here, the number, heterogeneity and interference among feedback loops can increase considerably as each managed resource in a large-scale dynamic system may simultaneously have to address multiple goals, while being constantly impacted by the activities of other managed resources, which may dynamically join or leave the overall system. Developments in modern control theory may become useful sources of inspiration for dealing with such situations in autonomic computing. Such developments most notably include nonlinear, adaptive, multivariable and robust control theories.

3.4   Artificial Intelligence

3.4.1   Introduction to Intelligence

John McCarthy[13] defines artificial intelligence (AI) as a 'science and engineering of making intelligent machines, especially intelligent computer programs' where 'intelligence is the computational part of the ability to achieve goals in the world'. AI is an important field that has generated a huge amount of work. Clearly, we do not attempt here to provide a detailed or comprehensive description of this field but simply seek to highlight the main aspects of AI that can affect autonomic systems. The interested reader is referred to the many books addressing this broad topic [29, 30].

The common purpose of all AI research is to construct computing machines that can solve problems. Autonomic computing can be included in this category if one considers that the particular problems to solve, as specified by human administrators, centre around the administration of software systems. Within this context, autonomic computing aspires to a considerably more modest objective than AI. The minimum level of intelligence required will depend on the complexity of the targeted computing system to administer and of its execution environment. This implies that rather than creating intelligence as a goal in itself, autonomic computing simply aims to endow computing systems with capabilities that render them more autonomous. Featuring such capabilities may or may not imply a certain level of artificial intelligence.

In the AI field, achieving intelligence means that artificial systems must be able to carry out *problem-solving* activities in order to *reach goals*. The more

---

[13]John McCarthy (1927–2011): computer scientist and cognitive scientist, considered to have coined the term 'artificial intelligence' (AI). John McCarthy has been a key figure in the development of the artificial intelligence field, for which he received a Turing award in 1971.

complicated and unpredictable the goals and the conditions in which they must be met, the more intelligence the system must possess. The actual manner in which problem-solving capabilities are designed and implemented in computing machines highly depends on the adopted view on the concept of *intelligence* (briefly discussed below). Irrespective of the adopted perspective, intelligence cannot develop or perform in complete isolation from the world in which it must operate. Hence, perception and action on the environment, communication and coordination with other intelligent systems become key capabilities. Such capabilities are also essential in autonomic computing.

As highlighted by Russel and Norvig [29], intelligence has been studied from several perspectives, and this has generated different lines of work. First, while some concentrate on the *thinking* processes that seem to enable intelligence, others focus on the observable *behaviour* that intelligence renders possible (or that generates the illusion of intelligence). Second, various schools differ on whether intelligence is strictly considered with respect to *human capabilities* or with respect to an *ideal form* (also referred to as *rationality*[14]).

Cognitive science views intelligence from the perspective of human-like thinking and consequently focuses on the study of the mind and its processes. This approach to AI is only relevant to autonomic computing in so far as insight into human cognition and its physiological support can be used to create knowledge representations, reasoning models or neural networks that can be implemented in a computing program to help render it autonomous.

The rational thinking approach to AI emphasises processes based on logic. Here, relevant facts and their interrelations are formally represented, and different types of reasoning are used for inferring new conclusions from existing facts. Based on this approach, a computer program should, in principle, be able to solve any solvable problem that is expressed in logical notation. However, serious limitations are encountered when attempting to develop programs that can solve real problems. These stem from the difficulty of formally representing knowledge about a complex and often uncertain environment and of actually executing logical inference within reasonable timeframes and with available resources. Within autonomic computing, logic-based approaches can be employed to solve clearly defined problems, such as straightforward analysis and planning (see Chap. 7).

Adopting a human behaviour perspective, identifying intelligence becomes a matter of comparing artificial system behaviours to human conducts. Based on this perspective, Alan Turing[15] proposed a test—known today as the Turing test—offering an operational definition for intelligence. In order for an entity to be considered

---

[14] 'A system is rational if it does the 'right thing', given what it knows' [29].

[15] Alan Turing: English mathematician, logician, cryptanalyst and computer scientist. He can be considered as one of the key predecessors of artificial intelligence (AI), as he defined a vision of AI in a 1950 article called 'Computing Machinery and Intelligence', where he has introduced the Turing test, genetic algorithms, machine learning and reinforcement learning. He has also introduced some fundamental AI concepts in a less-known article submitted in 1948 and entitled 'Intelligent Machinery', but which remained unpublished during Turing's lifetime.

'intelligent', it has to be able to reply to a human interrogator so as to make it impossible for him/her to determine whether the answers are coming from a human or a machine. From an autonomic computing perspective, the mechanisms and methods required for an entity to feature intelligent behaviour are certainly relevant. However, while an equivalent of the Turing test could be defined to evaluate system autonomicity, passing such test shouldn't be considered as a goal in itself. Just as the purpose of a plane is to actually fly rather than to fool other birds, the purpose of an autonomic system is to actually be autonomous rather than to trick other autonomic observers.[16]

Finally, intelligence can be viewed from the perspective of rational behaviour. Here, intelligence can represent whether an enabler or a reflection of rational action. Behaviourist approaches have mainly pursued the development of AI by employing the concept of rational *agent*.[17] A software agent fulfils the role of a virtual autonomous entity representing the interests of a human being. To pursue its goals, it must be able to perceive its environment, carry out autonomous control, adapt and survive in changing environments and possibly cooperate with other agents. Software agents seem the most suitable AI paradigm for achieving autonomic systems. We concentrate on introducing this concept and its possible applications within autonomic computing.

3.4.2 Introduction to Software Agents

An agent is an autonomous entity that perceives and acts in a given environment in order to achieve predefined goals [29]. An agent's internal control logic determines the agent's response to perceived stimuli or to other triggers, possibly considering internal states, histories of perceived events and so on. The agent's internal function is typically implemented via a computing program. There is a clear similarity between autonomic systems and software agents. Indeed, both types of computing systems:

- *Perceive Their External Environment.* They are context-aware in the sense that their behaviour can be affected by evolutions in the computing environment in its broadest sense. Also, environments can be categorised according to similar criteria. They can be fully or only partially observable, deterministic or stochastic, episodic or sequential, static or dynamic, discrete or continuous and comprising a single or multiple agents [20].
- *Pursue Their Own Goals with Minimal Intervention from Human Beings.* They may use different techniques and formalisms to achieve high-level goals,

---

[16]Analogy inspired by Russel and Norvig's discussion [29] on intelligent machines passing the Turing test.

[17]Agent : from the Latin *agens*—(noun) advocate or pleader; (adjective) efficient, effective or powerful; also from the Latin *agere*—(verb) to act, to urge or to conduct (Latin dictionary—http://www.latin-dictionary.net.)

predefined or specified by their creators. They utilise their inputs so as to establish an appropriate course of action that meets their initial requirements.

- *Act Upon Accessible Resources in the Pursuit of Their Goals.* While the targets of actions can be different—agents typically act upon their environments, while autonomic systems upon their internal resources—the actual action mechanisms are similar in the two system types.
- *Employ Progressively Sophisticated Control Logics for Achieving Increasingly Complicated Goals.* Hence, both agents and autonomic systems can either rely on simple reflex designs to promptly react to current situations or utilise more complicated data acquisition and processing techniques for also reasoning about the past and the future [31] (Chap. 7). For instance, such systems may build models of the real world and consider past events in order to make a decision. They may also be able to anticipate and foresee unsatisfactory situations.
- *Collaborate with Other Entities in Order to Achieve Their Goals and Carry-Out Concerted Actions.* Here, cooperation and competition algorithms developed in the multi-agent domain can prove highly relevant for integrating multiple autonomic elements or subsystems into coherent autonomic systems [32].
- *Are Organized in Complicated Architectures Based on Various Collaboration Patterns*, which can range from hierarchical organisations to fully decentralised structures (see Chap. 4).

Compared to software agents, the scope of an autonomic system is more limited. Autonomic systems are focused on programming structures and configurations and are interested in the management of artefacts. This is, of course, less ambitious than agents that could be usable in many domains. At the same time, self-management imposes some quite stringent specific requirements. In particular, an autonomic system has to be able to adapt its computing structure, which in turn demands advances in the supporting execution infrastructure. This aspect has not really been investigated by the agent field.

To achieve rational behaviour, agents can carry out logical inferences but must also exhibit some default or exploratory behaviour when uncertainty or limited computing resources prevent logical conclusions. In addition, in emergency situations, agents must act quickly and cannot spend precious time on lengthy deliberations. Hence, perfect rationality can become unfeasible in complicated environments. This point is important in the context of autonomic computing. In complex situations, even if autonomic management processes can outperform human administrators, they may, just as humans, take decisions that when analysed in retrospect prove to not have been the best possible. Technical and societal implications of such limitations must be carefully pondered when developing autonomic systems.

To evaluate an agent's success, agent designers typically introduce an objective performance measure. Rational agents always act so as to maximise their performance measure. Actions considered as rational depend on several factors, including the success criteria specified in the performance measure, knowledge of the environment, available actions and knowledge of their probable impact and history of perceived events and their impact on internal agent states. Such notions are highly relevant to autonomic systems, which must also be evaluated with respect to their ability to reach predefined goals.

While the concepts and paradigms related to intelligent agents directly apply to autonomic computing systems, the actual design and implementation of autonomic computing elements and systems proves just as difficult as the design and implementation of agents and multi-agent systems. Indeed, just as with complicated agent systems, the global architecture of large-scale, distributed, multi-objective, dynamic autonomic systems can quickly become fuzzy and hard to implement and maintain.

3.4.3 Building Artificial Intelligence

Several communities have progressively developed within the AI domain, since its beginnings in the late 1940s and early 1950s, mainly differing in their approaches to modelling and developing intelligence. In the following we briefly discuss the specificities of available approaches since we consider that similar choices will have to be made when developing different autonomic computing systems.

The traditional AI approach relies on the definition and manipulation of symbols from the problem domain. This *symbolic* approach follows a top-down strategy, trying to imagine, model and set in place the processes that can solve problems within a certain category. If problems are too complex to resolve in one step, a reductionist approach is adopted to progressively divide them into simpler parts for which solutions can be found. Partial solutions are then recomposed into a global solution for the entire problem. The symbolic approach has dominated most developments in the AI domain. Some notable application examples include expert systems, specific robotic applications, game playing like IBM's Deep Blue[18] program, language understanding and problem solving like IBM's 'Watson' Computing System.[19]

A second, bottom-up approach, referred to as the *connectionist* model, adopts an opposite strategy to building intelligence. It starts off with smaller simpler elements, such as those modelling the functions of brain cells (or neurons) and their interconnections, and attempts to progressively interconnect and combine such capabilities in order to obtain more complicated problem-solving functions. This approach more accurately models the actual structure and mechanisms that seem to underlie human intelligence –that is, brain structure and physiology. The connectionist approach has been proposed from the beginning of the AI domain, for instance, via Alan Turing's B-type neural networks, but has only recently gained popularity, mostly via neural network-based models. Some notable application examples include computer vision

---

[18] IBM's Deep Blue computer program managed to defeat the chess champion Garry Kasparov in May 1997 (http://www-03.ibm.com/ibm/history/ibm100/us/en/icons/deepblue).

[19] IBM's 'Watson' Computing System challenged and beaten Jeopardy Champions in February 2011 (IBM Jeopardy Challenge: http://techcrunch.com/tag/watson).

and image recognition, for example, identifying objects from video footage; heuristic classification and decision-making, for example, advising on whether to accept credit card purchases; or natural language skills, for example, predicting the past tense of English verbs.[20]

Symbolic and connectionist approaches feature specific advantages and limitations[21] [33]. Symbolic approaches facilitate rich expressiveness, explicit architecture and procedural versatility, which render them suitable for goal-based reasoning. They facilitate the conception of processes that use complex knowledge representations to perform systematic search explorations, parsing and recursive procedures. Explicit knowledge representation and architecture enable various parts to be reused, rearranged and modified independently. As a main limitation, symbolic approaches are highly sensitive to incomplete or incorrect data and perform rather poorly at 'common sense' reasoning tasks, where analogies and approximations are more suitable than precise formal procedures.

Conversely, connectionist approaches can inherently handle fuzziness and adapt knowledge fragments to specific contexts. They prove particularly well-suited at addressing ill-defined problems and weakly linked facts such as involved in pattern recognition, clustering, categorisation, optimisation and knowledge retrieval. Their main limitations are essentially due to the rigid, uniform and flat structure imposed by neural networks. Indeed, lack of larger-grain architecture makes it impossible to isolate a part of the network as a reusable piece of reasoning; to express, extract, share or reuse acquired knowledge; to address complicated situations by problem decomposition and integration of partial solutions; to learn to perform new tasks once trained; or to perform several tasks in parallel.

A radically different approach to building intelligence challenged existing AI communities by proposing an exclusively behavioural approach to robotic systems [34]. Namely, Rodney A. Brooks argued that intelligent behaviour can be achieved while exclusively relying on collections of simple, well-integrated reflexes. This approach eliminates intelligence as a necessary, explicit element that mediates between perception and action and rather defines it as a virtual concept induced in the mind of external observers. To help build complicated robotic systems based on this vision, Brooks proposes the *subsumption architecture*, which organises reactive reflexes into multiple, interdependent layers, representing different abstraction levels and goal complexities. This is not unlike some of the processes found in the natural ANS. However, in robotics, goals pursued by reactions in the highest layers, such as searching for food, must rely on and subsume reactions aiming to achieve simpler

---

[20] A well-known connectionist experiment conducted by David Rumelhart and James McClelland at the University of California at San Diego and published in 1986 consisted in training a network of 920 artificial neurons (organised in two layers of 460 neurons) to form the past tenses of English verbs.

[21] Cognitive sciences studying the human mind are similarly split into different communities. Cognitive psychology takes a top-down, knowledge-oriented approach, focusing on internal mental processes and states, including beliefs, desires, knowledge, ideas and motivations. Conversely, cognitive neuroscience takes a bottom-up approach by studying the biological substrates, or the brain's neural network, that underlie and enable cognition.

goals in the lower layers, like avoiding obstacles. Successful examples of this approach include the first autonomous spacecraft—Deep Space One—developed as part of NASA's Remote Agent program ([29], pp 27).

A more recent AI approach, called Evolutionary AI, uses bio-inspired evolutionary concepts to develop solutions that can solve predefined problems. An interesting application example consists in modelling the evolution or growth of a business within a simulated market place. Notably, Evolutionary AI has been used to model artificial life forms within the artificial life (A-Life) domain. Among other centres of interest, artificial life studies the self-organisation processes that lead to swarm intelligence, such as can be observed in the simple flocking patterns of birds, movement synchronisation of fish schools or more complex constructions of anthills, honey bee combs and human embryos.

While the debate on the merits of each of these approaches persists in the AI domain, some AI researchers propose hybrid solutions that can capitalise on the advantages of both these designs. Notably, Marvin Minsky argues that AI must employ and be able to integrate many, heterogeneous approaches, each one specialised in handling a different type of knowledge representation [33]. This view is further developed in Minsky's SOM theory[22] [35], where human intelligence is modelled as a collection of simple agents, each specialised in performing a specific type of task. The agent interactions lead to the formation of an agent society, or 'society of mind', capable of performing complex intellectual tasks.

Last, but not least, learning was proposed and developed by the AI community as a particularly potent element in creating and maintaining intelligence. Rather than having external programmers carefully design and implement intelligence all at once, learning enables intelligence to develop progressively and adaptively by automatically modifying a base of existing artefacts, in order to better achieve problem-solving capabilities within a current environment and with respect to present goals. Learning can apply to create, disable and tune reflexes in purely reactive entities, enrich and update knowledge in more sophisticated designs and finally identify suitable goals or even improve inherent learning methods.

In addition to initial development, learning constitutes a powerful and essential adaptation enabler. Most importantly, it allows the reuse of generic designs and implementations within a wide range of specific execution contexts and for attaining a large spectrum of goals. For example, an intelligent entity (or agent) can be designed so as to merely detain an initial reflex-based behaviour, enhanced with learning capabilities that progressively enable it to develop more sophisticated, knowledge-based behaviours. This renders a common design reusable for enabling any individual agent to develop, starting from a generic but basic set of capabilities that match all foreseeable environments to an efficient and sophisticated behaviour specialised for a certain environment.

---

[22]Society of mind (SOM): a conceptual theory about the workings of the mind and thinking, initiated by Marvin Minsky with Seymour Papert in the 1970s and later developed and published by Minsky in the 'Society of Mind' book, published in 1988.

3.4.4   Summary of AI Relevance for AC

Considering the aforementioned objectives and developments of artificial intelligence (AI), the field of autonomic computing seems strikingly similar. Initially, some critics have even accused IBM of having introduced a neologism to lull the reluctance of some companies to implement techniques inspired from artificial intelligence. This is a baseless accusation. In fact, artificial intelligence covers far broader areas of use and is much more ambitious than autonomic computing. First, the original purpose of artificial intelligence was/is to build machines able to compete intellectually with humans [29]. The goal of autonomic computing is much more modest since it is 'simply' to give autonomy to computer systems. This notion of autonomy is, in particular, much more important for autonomic systems than the relative 'intelligence' of the system itself. On the other hand, the level of 'intelligence' is difficult to quantify and highly dependent on the field. The concept of autonomy is much easier to evaluate. Intelligence is not the end, but a mean of giving autonomy to the system. Finally, an autonomic system is defined as a system that is subordinate to a human administrator with the precise goal of assisting with administrative tasks, while this is not necessarily the case for an intelligent system. However, the work developed in the field of artificial intelligence is clearly crucial to understanding and building autonomic systems. In addition to the generic, theoretical and developmental approaches promoted by various AI communities, more specific AI works are also relevant to autonomic computing, including studies on search algorithms, pattern detection and extrapolation, knowledge representation and inference, learning techniques, planning, epistemology, ontology and heuristics. Yet, autonomic computing remains a stand-alone discipline rather than an AI branch; the same way AI is a well-defined field rather than a branch of one of the many disciplines it relies on or gets inspiration from—mathematics, control theory, cybernetics, philosophy, psychology, neuroscience, economy, sociology and linguistics.

3.5   Complex Systems

Complex systems are systems that consist of numerous interconnected parts and that exhibit properties and behaviours that are not necessarily obvious from studying the properties and behaviours of the individual parts. The study of complex systems focuses on the way in which interactions among parts give rise to overall system behaviours and relations to the system environment. Complex system examples include social systems, involving interrelated humans; weather dynamics, led by differences in temperature and moisture densities; climate systems, based on long-term interactions among atmosphere, hydrosphere, cryosphere, land surface and biosphere; or chemical systems, where interactions among chemical elements can give rise to cyclical or oscillating reactions. Complexity Theory[23] focuses on the

---

[23] Here we refer to Complexity Theory as studied in relation to complex systems. This is not to be mistaken with the field of Computational Complexity Theory—a branch of the Theory of Computation (from theoretical computer science and mathematics) that aims to classify computational problems according to their difficulty and to relate identified classes of problems to each other.

study of interactions, iterations, emergence and pattern formation, all of which may prove relevant to advancements in autonomic computing.

Complex adaptive systems (CAS) represent a special category of complex systems, where in addition to being complex, systems are also adaptive, in the sense that they modify themselves in response to changes in their environments and potentially learn based on experience. CAS examples include ecosystems, social insects and ant colonies, brains and immune systems, cells and developing embryos, financial systems and stock markets and political and cultural communities.

It is important to note that the term 'complexity' is employed across different research communities in software engineering and computer science with quite diverse meanings. For example, 'complexity' may imply that a system is either extremely complicated, that the composition of its parts is nonlinear, or that the resulting overall behaviour is unpredictable. These differences aside, it remains clear that available CAS research can provide useful concepts and models for designing complex self-managing computer systems. Some of the most notable CAS concepts to be considered include *self-organisation* and *emergence*.

Moreover, several specific research fields that have emerged from the general CAS domain may prove particularly relevant with respect to autonomic computing systems. These include the study of networked systems (small-world and scale-free networks, dynamic and adaptive networks, graph theory, scalability and robustness properties), pattern formation (cellular automata, reaction–diffusion systems, self-replication and differentiation), nonlinear dynamics (attractors, chaos and stability analysis), evolution and adaptation (genetic algorithms, artificial life, evolutionary computing, artificial neural networks, machine learning, co-evolution, goal-oriented behaviour) or collective behaviour (ant colony optimisations, synchronisation, swarms or phase transitions).

Cybernetics (defined by Norbert Wiener[24] in [36], for instance) is another important interdisciplinary field specialised in the study of complex systems. Cybernetics focuses on the understanding and specification of the self-regulatory aspects of complex systems, where closed signal loops play an essential role. It is fundamentally concerned with principles such as coordination, communication, information, feedback, control and regulation, which can be employed to explain and predict possible system behaviours and functions. Such principles apply across a wide variety of complex self-regulatory systems, from IT to physical and social systems. They are definitely relevant to autonomic computing systems.

A noteworthy example of cybernetics' relevance to autonomic computing consists in W. Ross Ashby's[25] brain studies within this domain [15, 16]. Ashby regards the brain as a physiochemical system that reacts to its environment and learns from its experience to adapt its behaviour. The brain becomes a key adaptation enabler

---

[24]Norbert Wiener (1894–1964): American mathematician, considered as the main originator of cybernetics.
[25]W. Ross Ashby (1903–1972): English psychiatrist, carried-out pioneering work in the cybernetics domain.

and hence an essential contributor to an organism's survival. More precisely, adaptation is viewed as a means of keeping an organism in an equilibrium state within its environment. The organism remains *alive* for as long as the values of a set of *essential variables* are maintained within some 'physiological' limits or viability zone. Hence, change is only important in so far as it ensures the constancy of the essential variables. Beyond the adaptation mechanisms for achieving such ends, any goal-seeking intelligent behaviour is considered as merely in the eye of an external observer.

In this context, the brain's role is to control and adapt the organism's behaviour—the way it acts upon its environment—so as to maintain essential variables within limits. For this purpose, Ashby introduces a double-feedback control system design, which he refers to as *ultra-stable system*. A first, reactive feedback loop opposes external disturbances via a complicated sensor and actuator system. When the value of an essential variable is pushed towards its viability limit, a triggered reaction brings it back within the physiological zone. However, default reactions may fail to do this when more dramatic changes occur in the environment; essential variables may continue to diverge in this case. The second feedback loop, intervening over a larger time scale, is introduced to address this issue. It senses when the value of an essential variable becomes critical (reaches the viability limit) and triggers an adaptation in the default reaction behaviour (the initial feedback loop). Hence, an ultra-stable system reacts to small environmental disturbances on the short term and adapts its reactive behaviour in response to more significant changes over the longer term.

This approach appears directly applicable to autonomic systems, if administrative goals can be mapped to value ranges for well-defined variables. In this case, the double-feedback solution can correspond to a multilayer design for autonomic management processes, where a meta-management layer adapts the behaviour of a basic management layer, which in turn administers the managed resources. Several such architectures have already been proposed within the autonomic computing domain.

3.6   Key Points

In this chapter, we have discussed the following important points:
- Since its inception, autonomic computing has been drawing inspiration from several scientific domains, which share their concern for the study of the inner workings and control of systems, natural or artificial. Some of these scientific domains include biology, physics, chemistry, sociology, ecology, economy and psychology and from the computing science domain: artificial intelligence, multi-agent systems, robotics, self-adaptive computing systems and artificial life.
- At its core, autonomic computing relies on the concept of autonomicity, which it has borrowed from biology, or, more precisely, from the human autonomous nervous system (ANS), which regulates vital internal functions so as to ensure homeostasis. Additionally, autonomic computing may draw broader inspiration from the biological realm by analysing the underlying support for diverse control and regulation capabilities in different species.

- Autonomic computing's goal of regulating parameter values while minimising human intervention brings it close to the automated and control systems domain. Namely, control theory provides extensive studies on the design of regulating feedback loops, which can be readily adopted when engineering feedback-based autonomic computing systems.
- Autonomic computing's need for a decision process that links sensory inputs to actuating outputs brings it close to artificial intelligence (AI). Various AI communities have advanced on complementary approaches for solving complicated problems in complex environments, which is precisely the task of autonomic systems. The wide range of available AI learning techniques provides relevant means for knowledge accumulation and adaptation in autonomic computing.
- Multi-agent systems, initially developed as a subdiscipline of AI, have been adopted and applied across many disciplines for modelling and implementing complex systems of various types. Autonomic computing makes no exception, meaning that agent-based techniques and platforms represent a promising means for developing and maintaining autonomic software applications.
- Autonomic computing's goal of rendering machines autonomous brings it close to the preoccupations of the robotics domain. This is especially the case when autonomic systems must interact via sensors and actuators with the real environment and become progressively more mobile and capable to adapt to changing execution conditions.
- The related research fields of cybernetics, networked systems, complex systems and artificial life aim to provide a link between the natural and artificial realms: they use computational resources to simulate and understand natural complex systems, and they use the obtained knowledge to create and control complex artificial systems. Such studies can prove highly valuable to autonomic computing, which aims to develop similar artificial systems.
- Despite its strong similarities and rich inspiration from the aforementioned research fields, autonomic computing remains a stand-alone discipline rather than a branch of an existing domain, such as artificial intelligence, multi-agent systems or automated control systems.

References

1. Kephart, J.O.: Research challenges of autonomic computing. In: ACM International Conference on Software Engineering (ICSE 2005), pp 15–21, St. Louis, MO, USA, May 2005
2. Hansen, J.G., Christiansen, E., Jul, E.: The Laundromat Model for autonomic cluster computing. In: IEEE International Conference on Autonomic Computing (ICAC '06), pp. 114–123, Dublin, 13–16 June 2006. doi: 10.1109/ICAC.2006.1662389. http://ieeexplore.ieee.org/stamp/stamp.jsp?tp=&arnumber=1662389&isnumber=34794
3. Kephart, J.O., Greenwald, A.R.: Shopbot economics. Autonom. Agent Multi-Agent Syst. 5(3), 255–287 (2002). doi:10.1023/A:1015552306471. http://dx.doi.org/10.1023/A:1015552306471
4. Su, Y., van der Schaar, M.: Conjectural equilibrium in water-filling games. In: IEEE Global Telecommunications Conference (GLOBECOM 2009), pp. 1–7, 30 Nov 2009–4 Dec 2009, doi: 10.1109/GLOCOM.2009.5425333. http://ieeexplore.ieee.org/stamp/stamp.jsp?tp=&arnumber=5425333&isnumber=5425208

5. Waldrop, M.M.: Complexity: The Emerging Science at the Edge of Order and Chaos. Simon & Schuster, New York (1992). ISBN 13: 978–0671767891

6. Holland, J.: Hidden Order: How Adaptation Builds Complexity, 1st edn. Basic Books, New York (1996). ISBN 13: 978–0201442304

7. Kauffman, S.: At Home in the Universe: The Search for the Laws of Self-Organization and Complexity. Oxford University Press, Oxford (1996). ISBN 13: 978–0195111309

8. Watts, D.: Six Degrees: The Science of a Connected Age. W. W. Norton & Company, New York (2004). ISBN 13: 978–0393325423

9. Barabasi, A.-L.: Linked: How Everything Is Connected to Everything Else and What It Means. Plume, New York (2003). ISBN 13: 978–0452284395

10. Strogatz, S.H.: Nonlinear Dynamics and Chaos: With Applications to Physics, Biology, Chemistry, and Engineering. Studies in Nonlinearity, 1st edn. Westview Press, Cambridge (2001). ISBN 13: 978–0738204536

11. Strogatz, S.H.: Sync: The Emerging Science of Spontaneous Order, 1st edn. Hyperion Book, New York (2003). ISBN 13: 978–0786868445

12. Holland, J.: Emergence: From Chaos to Order. Oxford University Press (Sd), Oxford, UK (2000). ISBN 13: 978–0192862112

13. Maturana, H.R., Varela, F.J.: Autopoiesis and Cognition: The Realization of the Living. Boston Studies in the Philosophy of Science, vol. 42, 1st edn. D. Reidel Publishing Company, Dordrecht (1980). ISBN 13: 978–9027710161

14. Wiener, N.: Cybernetics, or the Control and Communication in the Animal and the Machine, 2nd edn. MIT Press, Cambridge (1965) (1st edn published by The Technology Press/Wiley, New York, 1948). ISBN 13: 978–0262730099

15. Ashby, W.R.: Introduction to Cybernetics. Chapman and Hall Ltd., London (1956)

16. Ashby, W.R.: Design for a Brain: The Origin of Adaptive Behaviour, 2nd edn. Chapman and Hall Ltd., London (1960) (1st edition published in 1952). ISBN 13: 978–0412200908

17. Nervous System. The Columbia Encyclopaedia. Columbia: Columbia University Press. 6th edn. (2004) (entry available from Questia online encyclopaedia: http://www.questia.com/library/encyclopedia/nervous_system.jsp)

18. Leong, S.K.: An Introduction to the Human Nervous System. Singapore University Press, Kent Ridge (1986) (Reflexes, pp. 155–161; The autonomous nervous system and visceral afferents, pp. 500–543). ISBN 9971-69-107-8

19. Gray, H.: Chapter IX: Neurology. In: Anatomy of the Human Body (Gray's Anatomy). Lea and Febiger, Philadelphia (1918). ASIN: B000TW11G6. Available online from Bartleby.com: http://www.bartleby.com/107

20. Macaulay, D.: The Way We Work: Getting to Know the Amazing Human Body. Houghton Mifflin/Walter Lorraine Books, Boston (2008). ASIN: B004TE780I. ISBN 10: 0618233784

21. Ritzmann, R.E., Tobias, M.L., Fourtner, C.R.: Flight activity initiated via giant interneurons of the cockroach: evidence for bifunctional trigger interneurons. Science 210(4468), 443–445 (1980). doi:10.1126/science.210.4468.443. http://www.sciencemag.org/content/210/4468/443

22. Watts, D.J., Strogatz, S.H.: Collective dynamics of 'small-world' networks. Lett. Nat. (Nature) 393, 440–442 (1998). doi:10.1038/30918

23. van den Heuvel, M.P., Stam, C.J., Boersma, M., Hulshoff Pol, H.E.: Small-world and scale-free organization of voxel-based resting-state functional connectivity in the human brain. NeuroImage 43(3), 528–539 (2008)

24. Doursat, R., Sayama, H., Michel, O.: Morphogenetic engineering. In: Toward Programmable Complex Systems Series: Understanding Complex Systems. Springer, Berlin/Heidelberg (2012). ISBN 1244 978-3-642-33901-1

25. Hinchey, M.G., Sterritt, R.: 99% (Biological) inspiration.... In: Proceedings of the Fourth IEEE International Workshop on Engineering of Autonomic and Autonomous Systems (EASE '07), 26–29 March 2007. IEEE Computer Society, Tucson

26. Sterritt, R.: Apoptotic computing: programmed death by default for computer-based systems. IEEE Comput. 44(1), 59–65 (2011). doi:10.1109/MC.2011.5. http://ieeexplore.ieee.org/stamp/stamp.jsp?tp=&arnumber=5688151&isnumber=5688134

27. Golnaraghi, F., Kuo, B.C.: Automatic Control Systems. Wiley, New York (2008). ISBN 13: 9780470048962
28. Kephart, J.O., Chess, D.M.: The vision of autonomic computing. IEEE Comput. Soc. 36, 41–50 (2003)
29. Russell, S., Norvig, P.: Artificial Intelligence: A Modern Approach, 3rd edn. Prentice Hall, Englewood Cliffs (2009). ISBN 10: 0136042597, 13: 978–0136042594
30. Nilsson, N.J.: Artificial Intelligence: A New Synthesis. The Morgan Kaufmann Series in Artificial Intelligence. Morgan Kaufmann Publishers, San Francisco (1998). ISBN 13: 978–1558604674
31. Kephart, J.O., Walsh, W.E.: An artificial intelligence perspective on autonomic computing policies. In: Proceedings of the 5th IEEE International Workshop on Policies for Distributed Systems and Networks (POLICY) 2004, 7–9 June 2004, pp. 3–12. IBM Thomas J Watson Research Center, Yorktown Heights, New York (2004). doi: 10.1109/POLICY.2004.1309145. http://ieeexplore.ieee.org/stamp/stamp.jsp?tp=&arnumber=1309145&isnumber=29053
32. Horling, B., Lesser, V.: A survey of multi-agent organizational paradigms. Knowl. Eng. Rev. 19(4), 281–316 (2004)
33. Minsky, M.: Logical vs. analogical, or symbolic vs. connectionist, or neat vs. scruffy. In: Winston, P.H. (ed.) Artificial Intelligence at MIT, Expanding Frontiers, vol. 1. MIT Press, Cambridge (1990) (Reprinted in AI Magazine, 1991, http://web.media.mit.edu/~minsky/papers/SymbolicVs.Connectionist.html)
34. Brooks, R.A.: Cambrian Intelligence: The Early History of the New AI, 1st edn. A Bradford Book, Cambridge (1999). ISBN 13: 978–0262522632
35. Minsky, M.: The society of mind. Pages Bent edition. Simon & Schuster, New York (1988). ISBN 13: 978-0671657130
36. Wiener, N.: Cybernetics: Or Control and Communication in the Animal and the Machine, 1st edn. The Technology Press/Wiley, Cambridge/New York (1948). ASIN: B000RJDZXI

Autonomic Computing Architectures

4

Software architecture specifies the structure of the components of a system, their interrelationships, principles and the guidlines governing their design and evolution over time [1]. This is the very purpose of this chapter: defining the main constituents of an autonomic system and understanding their structural and temporal relations.

Such exploration of the internal structure of autonomic systems will allow us to better understand the challenges in building autonomic systems. It will permit us to identify the major design and implementation barriers and their needs in terms of techniques, technologies, formalisms and methods.

This chapter highlights that there are not common agreements as to what an autonomic system is and what its constituent parts are, yet alone what those parts actually do. In some way, this chapter sets up the rest of the book in that the chapters that follow aim to provide answers, partial in some cases where research is still required, to the issues raised by this architectural chapter.

P. Lalanda et al., *Autonomic Computing: Principles, Design and Implementation*,
Undergraduate Topics in Computer Science, DOI 10.1007/978-1-4471-5007-7_4,
© Springer-Verlag London 2013

4.1   Autonomic Elements

Autonomic systems rely on the notion of an autonomic element. An autonomic element is an executable software unit that exhibits autonomic properties, that is, the self-* properties previously introduced in Chap. 2. To do so, it implements a control loop in order to constantly meet high-level goals set by authorised entities.

Specifically, an autonomic element regularly senses the possible sources of change through sensors, reasons about the current situation and arranges adaptations through actuators when and where it is necessary. An autonomic element is smart in the sense that it can make its own decisions and is able to modify its internal structures and behaviours as a response to external or internal events. It is rational in the sense that any management action it decides to perform is done in order to better satisfy its base requirements given the available knowledge. Its behaviour at any point in time can depend on what it perceives, on what it has perceived or on what it has *not* perceived.

As illustrated by Fig. 4.1, an autonomic element can be seen as a smart software island that can take care of itself, pursuing its own personal goals.[1] However, it is not a completely independent island. First, an autonomic element is driven by information provided by administrators, human or not, including goals to be pursued, policies and strategies to be employed and even knowledge to be used. Also, if an autonomic element has the autonomy to control itself, it still has to report to administrators. It has to provide them with understandable feedback so that they can be aware of its internal situation at anytime. Administrators can thus adjust goals or revise strategies where they deem it appropriate.

Then, an autonomic element is executed in a context. As explained in Chap. 2, this notion of context has generated much debate in the computing community [2]. In this book we assume the broad notion of context including the computing

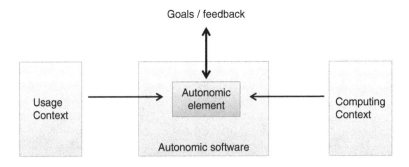

Fig. 4.1 Autonomic element

[1]A Trojan horse program can also be seen as an autonomic element, but this is not in the spirit of autonomic computing!

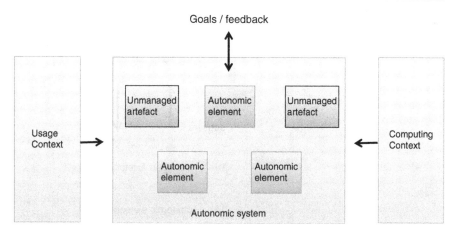

Fig. 4.2   Multiple autonomic elements

context, internal and external, and the usage context. Let us remind that the computing context contains the computing resources that the autonomic element can use and those that influence its actions. The usage context refers to the persons or systems interacting with the autonomic software. The behaviour at any point in time of an autonomic element can depend on these two forms of context.

An autonomic element can form a complete software system. In this case, an autonomic system and autonomic element are the very same, single software entity. In most cases, however, an autonomic element is simply a part of the whole autonomic system. Here, the autonomic element is really some sort of smart island taking its own decision in conformance with high-level directions. Outside of the island, administrators regain control of software artefact management in the traditional way, not simply via high-level directives. Unmanaged parts of a system represent any software or hardware resource that cannot be self-administrated. The reason for this may be that they are sufficiently stable regarding the system administration goals and so do not require runtime management intervention. Another reason may be that data and/or the means to self-administer these elements are simply lacking. Unmanaged elements can however provide valuable information to an autonomic element and clearly belong to the computing context.

Most of the time, though, the situation is much more complex (see Fig. 4.2). For scaling and scoping purposes, autonomic systems include a number of autonomic elements managing well-defined software regions or providing well-delimited functions. These autonomic elements may cooperate as they would do with any other software artefacts, being within or beyond the autonomic system they belong to.

Building an autonomic system comes down to specifying the features that have to be self-managed and to defining autonomic elements, usually an iterative process. Depending on their goals and constraints, for example, the time available to react or the number of events to consider, autonomic elements build upon different techniques and formalisms. Similarly, many interaction patterns can be employed to

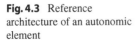
Fig. 4.3 Reference
architecture of an autonomic
element

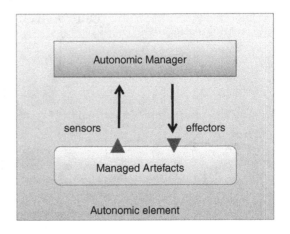

ensure cooperation among autonomic elements. Some systems, for instance, implement hierarchical organisations among the autonomic elements, while others are based on peer-to-peer interactions. Another challenge, of course, is to give a simplified vision of these different elements, autonomic or not, to the administrators. In particular, administrators should be able to define and redefine goals without intimate knowledge of the internal structure of the autonomic system.

4.2 Architecture of Autonomic Elements

4.2.1 IBM Reference Architecture

Autonomic elements are structured according to a simple, widely accepted, architectural model introduced by IBM [3]. This architecture, depicted in Fig. 4.3, is considered by many as the reference architecture. It clearly defines two distinct types of modules: managed resources and autonomic manager. Managed resources (or managed artefacts) are the software or hardware entities that are automatically administered in an autonomic element. The autonomic manager is the entity in charge of the runtime administration of the managed resources. IBM's reference architecture should be seen more like a *logical architecture*, identifying the main types of entities involved, defined via their roles, functions and interactions. For example, in certain cases, the autonomic manager and the managed resources may be more intertwined and less clearly separated than shown in this conceptual reference architecture.

A managed resource represents any software or hardware resource that is endowed with autonomic behaviour by coupling it with the autonomic manager. A managed resource can be a Web or database server, a specific software component, the operating system or a component therein, a cluster of machines in a grid environment, a rack of hard drives, a network, a CPU, a printer, etc. However, all managed resources share a common feature: they need to be adapted at runtime as a function of internal or external change where that change impacts on their goals. Adaptations are needed in order to provide a better quality of service, to take into account a new element in the context, to better satisfy user expectations, etc. They can be triggered by anything from someone with a mobile device has moved to a new room, a device's availability has changed, the component is not performing as expected or the size of the environmental data to be processed has changed.

Managed resources provide specific interfaces, called control points or *touch points*, for monitoring and adaptation. Two types of control points have to be differentiated: *sensors* and *effectors*. Sensors, often called probes or gauges, provide information about the managed resources. This could be some information regarding the elements' state or some idea of their current performance. For a Web server, for example, that could include the response time to client requests, network and disk usage figures or CPU and memory utilisation. Effectors provide facilities to adjust the managed resources and, as a consequence, change their behaviour. For instance, this could be some modification of a configuration file, the instantiation of new objects, the replacement of some outdated elements, etc.

The explicit definition of sensors and effectors is the proper means to encapsulate managed resources. In this manner, the internal structures and states of the managed resources can be kept private and an autonomic manager can only access them via the interfaces that are provided. This is a way for the managed resources to keep some level of control. This is also a way for managed resources to remain directly administrable by a human operator. This is important since it is very hard in practice to foresee all the runtime situations and it is likely that, under some unexpected conditions, an autonomic manager would not able to provide an adequate solution. The autonomic manager may also fail or be deactivated. In such a situation, an expert human administrator has to be able to take over. Note that it is not expected that a 'regular' administrator would take over in such situations, as deep, intimate knowledge of the autonomic system is generally necessary.

The autonomic manager implements the autonomic loop(s). It perceives the current situation, internal state and external context, determines desired management actions and pilots their execution. As previously mentioned, it is driven by administrative goals, generally expressed in rather abstract terms. The purpose of the autonomic manager is then to transform these high-level directives into precise, sometimes obscure actions on the managed resources. A goal can be, for instance, 'be highly secure'. In this case, the autonomic manager has to create the expected security conditions through parameter settings, component creation, specific protocol usage and so on. Usually, the precise security approaches, technologies and techniques used to secure this software element are not known by most software administrators.

As explained previously, the autonomic manager also provides regular feedback to the administrators so that they can remain in the decision loop. Here again, the feedback should be presented in such a way that it remains intelligible by non-expert administrators. It is the duty of the autonomic manager to aggregate data, perform translations of format or vocabulary, build synthesis and transmit the appropriately formatted information to an administration console.

The autonomic manager heavily depends on the touchpoints provided by the managed elements. Touchpoints play a major role in autonomic computing indeed. Without appropriate data representing the system to be administrated and sufficient possibilities to adapt it at runtime, no autonomic management is possible. In new developments, touchpoints can be carefully prepared in order to reach some predefined autonomic properties. In such a situation, autonomic properties are actually part of the system requirements and have to be worked out as any other system requirements. In many cases, however, touchpoints have to be explicitly added to existing, legacy systems. This often demands a reworking of the original system and, generally, limits the autonomic possibilities. This may be caused by many things such as limited support for runtime monitoring, for instance, lack of runtime information, unavailability of appropriate documentation, insufficient understanding of the system and its interactions and limiting runtime modification opportunities.

Ideally, the code of the managed resources and its rationale should be known. This means that the design decisions and the constraints are well understood. This is clearly necessary to be able to take corrective actions. However, it has to be admitted that, in modern developments, such justifications and explanations are rarely documented and/or maintained, for budget reasons, ironically.

4.2.2 Sensors

Sensors are code or components that measure a physical or abstract quantity concerning the managed resource and convert it into a signal for the autonomic manager. Examples of such data would be system performance characteristics, user context or even server temperature. Such data is presented in a timely fashion via the sensor interfaces and contains all the information about a running system that is needed by an autonomic manager. Depending on the target autonomic properties, different types of data and different forms of presentation may be expected. Determining the appropriate data to be collected and implementing the corresponding sensors are a difficult activity in itself. One of the first steps to be achieved when building an autonomic system is therefore to define the data that are needed, their nature and the way they should be collected and presented.

The data of interest may come from the external context (see Chap. 2) and from many parts of the system, including, for instance, components, connections, classes, operations and parameters. Some of these elements are business oriented, while others are more concerned with the supporting infrastructure, like database management systems (DBMS) or middleware. However, many supporting elements take the form of components off the shelf (COTS), and, as such, it is difficult to obtain internal data due to their black box nature.

A distinction has to be made here between desired and accessible data, therefore. In green field situations, this can be a rather straightforward mapping since the interfaces to the desired data are inherently accessible as they are part of the system design. In other words, new systems are built in such a way that autonomic-related data can be naturally provided, granted that no major requirement is violated in doing so. However, dealing with a legacy system or COTS can be a much more complicated a task. The code of the managed artefacts can be partially hidden, unreachable or just not modifiable. It can be the case, for instance, when old, non-instrumented libraries not designed to support monitoring/adaptations are used. Also, some component code may be too large to be completely monitored. In such complicated situations, compromises have to be reached in order to balance the targeted autonomic properties and the complexity of instrumenting the system. In some cases, certain levels of autonomy cannot simply be reached because of lack of sensed data availability, and here clearly the point of an autonomic management solution has to be questioned.

Therefore, given the complexity and cost of instrumenting a system, the goal is not to collect just any information that can be obtained about a system but, rather, get *appropriate* data that can be used to carry out autonomic actions. 'Appropriate' has different meanings here. First, it means that collected data have to be in line with the autonomic properties that are sought. For instance, when it comes to performance management, a number of precise measures are needed to characterise system performance that can include high-level information like memory consumption or disk usage.

Also, more obscure sensor data may be extracted and reasoned about such as the mean execution time of a software component, the time spent in specific parts of the software, the number of threads and recurrent event patterns. Developers of autonomic systems have to realise that presenting useless information to an autonomic manager does not come without impact. It has the effect of degrading the performance of the managed system without improving its autonomic capabilities. Instrumenting a system always has a cost in terms of code size, memory consumption and overall efficiency. This issue is acerbated for embedded systems, for instance, where any addition of code has to be carefully justified due to lack of resources. The trade-off between autonomy and the engendered loss of efficiency, increased code size and memory footprint must always be considered. Finally, collecting data is a dynamic process and the data that is deemed appropriate may change over the managed systems' lifetime.

Likewise, the volumes of data to be collected can be very different: whether it is raw or elaborated, simple or structured and functional or non-functional. Some data is raw in the sense that it corresponds to values directly captured in the managed artefacts. It can be, for instance, the memory consumption at a given time, the available disk space or any business-related value. In this case, there is no difference between what is collected and what is presented to the autonomic manager. Some other data are more elaborate in the sense that they are the result of operations applied to a number of raw data. It can be, for instance, the mean value of memory consumption on a given period. Making up aggregated information is necessary in many situations, for efficiency reasons or because of network contingencies. Again, it is clearly not desirable to communicate a huge number of low-level information to an autonomic manager which would need important computing power to process all the data and deep knowledge to understand and treat the received information.

So, data can be simple in the sense that it takes the form of an integer, a real, a float, an enumeration, etc. It can represent, for instance, the size of a disk or available memory, etc. This favours a decoupling between the autonomic manager and the sensors. In some cases, however, structured data has to be provided in order to group a set of simple values in a dedicated structure. For instance, all memory-related information of a system can be preprocessed into a single rich data structure. This simplifies the work of the autonomic manager and is generally less costly. Building complicated data structures requires computing and time though: it is generally advantageously done at the managed artefact level.

Finally, data can be functional or non-functional. Functional data corresponds to business-oriented values, like intermediary or final outputs of business processes. They are typically used by an autonomic manager to verify how close the current state of the system matches the systems' goals. Some sensor data is concerned with quality of service metrics, such as performance or reliability. They are used by the autonomic manager to evaluate the non-functional properties of the system. Non-functional information is often difficult to quantify and typically is processed and assembled into the aforementioned structured data. An example of this can be where the overarching goal is to ensure that the system is reliable in a power-efficient way. Reliable may equate to a 90 % up-time for the system. CPUs that are underutilised, say, less than 50 %, are switched into sleep mode for power efficiency. These figures may be combined in some ways to provide a metric to represent the overarching goal.

4.2.3 Effectors

Effectors are code or components that effect change and are provided by the managed elements. The purpose of effectors is to allow the autonomic manager, or any other authorised entities, to trigger modifications to the managed artefacts in a synchronised fashion. That is, the timing or order of the changes makes sense and the system's integrity is maintained. Like sensors, it turns out that determining the effectors required and then implementing them can be a challenging task. It demands, in particular, the anticipation of possible changes and the provisioning of the technical means to realise them, especially at the execution platform level.

Management actions can impact on the different architectural elements, including components, connections, classes and operations. Since the autonomic manager may have to act upon several of them, synchronisation mechanisms have to be installed to ensure the change makes sense. As a matter of fact, modifying a software element is always tricky. In our case, it can have impacts on the other managed artefacts and also within the autonomic manager itself. For instance, the way information is collected may be modified when a change is ongoing.

Effectors carry out changes to the managed elements in order to modify their behaviour. Changes can be related to the elements' functionality or to the quality of service it provides. Some functions may have to be added, removed or replaced in order to provide better services or to be adapted to changing runtime conditions. For instance, when a new device appears in a pervasive environment, new functions may be inserted in order to exploit its capabilities. A notion of quality of service has also to be carefully followed in order to constantly satisfy service level agreements (SLA), which are generally specified in the early phases of a project. Adapting the quality of service may have impacts anywhere in the managed artefacts. In particular, it can lead to very low-level actions that change the behaviours of the code (e.g. via parameter changes). Generally speaking, dealing with quality of service often requires a deep knowledge of the code of the managed artefacts and how this impacts the targeted non-functional properties.

Change can be coarse grained, whereby large components are affected, for example, adding or removing servers in a Web server cluster [4], or fine grained where only a single value is changed, for example, changing configuration parameters in a Web server [5, 6]. Technically speaking, the simplest adaptation is the change of configuration parameters. They correspond to programming variables or to symbolic values and are generally specified in specific files, an XML-based language, for instance. Global configuration parameters have to be treated very carefully since several elements can be impacted by a single modification. This is known as external coupling, which is *not* considered good software engineering design practice. This is because it leads to uncontrolled side effects upon modification. Configuration parameters can also be specific to an object, a function, a component, etc. In this case, the scope of change is more tractable. It is, however, good practice to provide an API to manage these parameters. This kind of adaptation has been heavily used in order to self-configure complex middleware such as EJB application servers. Similarly, in autonomic security software, security parameters can be self-adjusted to adapt a system to evolving security conditions. For example, the security system may be monitoring accesses to a Web server from a single user connection. At some point it may notice the number of connections increase above a predefined threshold and the security component then uses connection parameters to throttle the speed at which it allows those connections to be made to the Web server. At a further point the numbers of incoming connections may be increasing at a rate that the security system believes this to be a 'denial of service' attack, and it stops all connections from that client address.

More complex actions relate to changes in the topology of the managed artefacts. As mentioned earlier, managed artefacts are usually made of software modules, objects or components that can be created, suppressed, started, stopped, resumed, replaced and deployed at runtime. The complete life cycle of these modules can be controlled by the autonomic manager. For instance, depending on the available physical resources and their availability, software modules may be moved from a server to another one. This requires creating or modifying code dealing with communication and non-functional aspects like security. New modules may be created in order to deal with context changes. It is common in pervasive environments, for instance, to create or suppress software modules in order to handle dynamic devices or to deal with evolving user goals. Modules can also be replaced to change the behaviour of a system with respect to a given aspect. Finally, connections between modules can also be added or updated. Connections are architectural concepts that represent the flow of control and/or of data through the system and, as such, are also sensitive to context evolutions.

Runtime updates do not happen by magic, however. Software systems cannot be built so as to be fully adaptable, at any time and by any means. In autonomic systems, runtime flexibility is part of the requirements. The types of adaptations that may be demanded by an autonomic manager have to be understood in advance in order to be carefully prepared. This approach can be compared to the product-line philosophy where the variability in products is made explicit at every development stage, including during the requirement and design phase.

The managed elements of an autonomic system have then to be designed with adaptation in mind. As in product lines, flexible architectures clearly defining both variable and inflexible points have to be defined. A variation point can be a configuration file, a component, a connection, etc. The insertion of variation points has, however, a cost. They often rely on indirection mechanisms and, as a consequence, have a cost in terms of execution time and memory consumption. Inserting too many variation points may have disastrous impacts on the overall efficiency of a system. Compromises have to be reached between runtime flexibility and performance all along the software life cycle.

Variability has then to be supported by the execution infrastructure. The best crafted architecture is useless if the execution infrastructure does not allow architectural updates. In some cases, adaptations may only be done after the managed artefacts are allowed to reach a quiescent state and their execution is interrupted. This is especially the case when managed components maintain an internal state that can be rendered incoherent if adaptations are not carefully implemented. Here, specific interfaces are provided to manage the life cycle of the artefacts. Such interfaces may correspond to one or several effectors. Other domains demand the dynamic update of the managed elements. This means that these elements cannot be stopped to be changed and usually require some form of middleware support to transfer the state of the process safely over to the reconfigured process.

4.2.4 Autonomic Manager

The autonomic manager implements the autonomic loops. As explained in Chap. 3, thus, loop is similar to, and probably inspired by, some of the work on control theory, robotics and agent models. However, it targets different goals. Robots collect information on the environment to adapt their behaviour while pursuing their goals. Intelligent agents perceive their environment, interact with other agents and use this to achieve a wide range of goals. Control systems monitor their environment in real time in order to maintain a physical system within acceptable conditions, through the assignment of well-defined state variables. Autonomic managers, however, are completely focused on the administration of software systems. In order to relieve administrators from more and more complex tasks, their purpose is to timely adapt

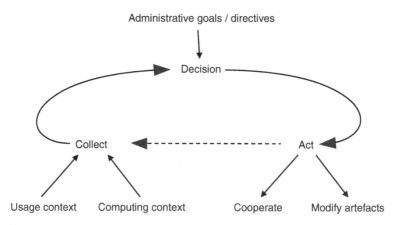

Fig. 4.4 Autonomic manager

the software in order to meet high-level management goals. These tasks, demanding some level of intelligence, therefore seek to assist or replace human administrators in their management tasks.

The purpose of an autonomic manager is to apply domain-specific knowledge in order to gracefully adapt a set of software artefacts at runtime when internal or external changes are detected. It is structured around a collect/decide/act control loop, as summarised by Fig. 4.4. As indicated, the autonomic manager makes use of monitored data and combines this with its internal knowledge of the system to plan and implement management tasks, that is, execute the low-level actions that are necessary to achieve the aforementioned goals. Diverse changes can be triggered on the managed artefacts and, in some limited cases, on the computing context.

The knowledge handled by an autonomic manager concerns the techniques that are used to structure and implement software and the rationale under which these decisions are made. The ontology used by an autonomic manager includes objects like components, data structures, events, files, libraries, operating systems and functions relating these different objects in some points in time. But it also contains concepts like requirements, traceability links and deployment strategies, pertaining to the initial phases of software development. A major challenge when building an autonomic manager is certainly to relate decisions pertaining to different phases of software development and use to make decisions.

The decision part of the autonomic manager has to reason about the present, perhaps the past and possibly even the future. Indeed, in order to correctly comprehend a present situation, an autonomic manager may benefit from being able to reason about previous experiences or historic events, to identify trends and recurring patterns, to better put the current situation into context and to take more appropriate action. A more sophisticated autonomic manager may be able to foresee the consequences of its various actions on the managed resources (e.g. via self-simulation) and accordingly decide on the most appropriate ones to take at any one time. Some level of future prediction may also enable an autonomic manager to take pre-emptive action in order to solve foreseeable problems before they occurred. Finally, an autonomic manager may even understand its own behaviour so it too can adjust its internal logic and future activity. To achieve these capabilities, the decision part makes use of specific knowledge created at design time and possibly evolved during runtime. The more sophisticated the decision logic, the richer the required knowledge needs to be. Enriching and updating acquired knowledge at runtime can be helped with learning techniques. These can be put in place in order to improve the correctness and relevance of the available knowledge and the way it impacts on the decisions that the autonomic manager makes. Generally speaking, the decision part of the autonomic manager can make use of very diverse reasoning techniques, many of which are borrowed from the field of artificial intelligence.

Data that drives autonomicity originates from many sources. The managed arte-facts constitute, of course, a privileged source of data. They are obviously in the best position to provide accurate information about the state of the running systems in terms of internal functions, quality of service, programming structures, etc. These are precisely the entities that the autonomic manager has to administer. Also, this information can be presented in a synthesised way to ease the work of the autonomic manager. This is especially true for new systems where autonomic managers and managed artefacts are conceived jointly. Other relevant data originates from the sur-rounding environment, that is, from the computing context and the usage context. Here, data is not structured to meet the specific needs of a particular autonomic manager. Mediation operations, automatic or not, are generally required to present the information in an appropriate way to the autonomic manager.

As stated before, taking the environment into consideration is important for mod-ern software systems. Many applications are inserted in a dynamic, complex and open world and have to exhibit opportunistic behaviour. That is, they have to take into account the changeable nature of their surroundings in order to correctly self-adapt. The autonomic manager has to be aware of all these evolutions in order to correctly adapt the managed artefacts. Here, its role is to keep some kind of synchronisation between an evolving environment and the code it administers. Let us not forget that contextual information is also getting more and more impor-tant and growing in size. In sensor-stuffed environments, size and complexity of contextual models become increasingly exponential.

The way autonomic managers can be implemented is presented in coming sec-tions and, also, in Chap. 7.

4.2.5 Architectural Properties of Autonomic Managers

At the architectural level, autonomic managers are defined through their capabilities, that is to say their functions, and their properties. Even if the functions provided are approximately the same for all autonomic managers, properties may vary a lot. In particular, an autonomic manager can be optional or mandatory, changeable or fixed, fully or partially autonomic.

As previously mentioned, autonomic management comes at a cost. In systems with stringent resource constraints, one must seriously consider whether an autonomic element is desirable or not. Under certain conditions, it is worth spending some time on advanced autonomic functions, while in others it is an unacceptable waste of time and resources. Autonomic managers may thus be seen as optional software components. In some rare systems [7], autonomic managers can be added and removed dynamically. Such an advanced feature provides a high degree of flexibility that can be used, for instance, to autonomically tune a system at a given moment and leave it alone afterwards. A less ambitious property, but still very useful, is the ability to change some features of an autonomic manager instead of the whole manager. It is advantageous in many situations to update some internal expertise or knowledge of an autonomic manager. This permits control over the life cycle of an autonomic manager. Here again, modifications can be made dynamically—with or without system interruption.

The level of instrumentation of the managed resources may also be dynamically adjusted. This can help reach the best compromise between induced overheads and monitoring accuracy, considering each situation. For example, a limited number of sensors (and corresponding monitoring and analysis functions) may be continuously maintained active to supervise the good functioning of managed resources. When an anomaly is detected, additional sensors can be dynamically injected as necessary to obtain finer-grained information and help better diagnose the anomaly. Once the identified problem is fixed, the additional sensors can be deactivated or completely removed from the managed resources to restore their initial efficiency.

Recently, researchers have been working on *autonomic* autonomic managers. These are autonomic managers that can administrate themselves, changing their internal rules in order to stop or remedy an unsatisfactory situation. One method is to use reinforcement learning and learn policies by trying actions in various system states and reviewing the consequences of each action [8]. The advantage of reinforcement learning is that it does not require an explicit model of the system being managed, hence its use in autonomic computing [9, 10]. However, it suffers from poor scalability in trying to represent large state spaces, which also impacts on its time to train. To this end, a number of hybrid models have been proposed which either speed up training or introduce domain knowledge to reduce the state space, for example, [11, 12].

Autonomic managers can be reactive or proactive. Reactive managers only trigger their decision logic in reaction to some external event, such as new monitoring data becoming available and being sent to it. Conversely, proactive managers may additionally take the initiative of analysing present, past or predicted situations and adjusting the managed resources without being prompted by an external event (e.g. periodically or based on some other internal schedule or mechanism).

Finally, an autonomic manager can be reflex based or deliberative. Reflex-oriented managers are typically stateless managers that react to external events as a reflex, non-deliberative manner. In general, such managers are essentially made of event–condition–action (ECA) rules that directly produce adaptation plans from specific event and condition combinations, taking current goals into account in so far as the ECA rules have been derived from the goals. Stateless means that such managers do not maintain any history about past events and actions. They only consider recent events, occurring in a defined period of time. Stateless approaches minimise complexity, are quite lightweight and, in short, are very effective in uncomplicated situations requiring rapid decisions. They are also very limited, that is, the autonomic manager keeps no information regarding the state of the managed element and relies solely on the current sensor data readings to decide whether to enact an adaptation plan. Some managers may use simple or more complicated learning process to change their reflexes over time. This may be beneficial, for example, for rendering reflexes better suited for the most frequently occurring situations or to temporarily block a reflex after it has just been triggered in order to avoid state oscillations (i.e. switching from state to state and not getting on with the purpose of the system). However, in reflex-based managers, it is not possible to perform advanced reasoning about the situation and, as a consequence, it is hard to deal with complex situations, especially when the nature of these situations is bound to evolve over time. In particular, in reflex-oriented approaches, it is very difficult to realise that past actions have failed.

Alternatively deliberative managers keep and reason about state information regarding the managed element. This information can be updated progressively and dynamically through fresh sensor readings. Accumulated state information allows the manager to improve any existing knowledge it may have, based, for example, on trend analysis, pattern detection and so forth. Better knowledge allows the manager to carry out more complex reasoning and analysis of candidate solutions to identified problems, subsequently increasing its chances of taking the most appropriate action. In addition, recorded state information allows the system to be either more sensitive or less sensitive to the sensor readings, in order to avoid the phenomenon of oscillating forward and backwards between states. This undesirable phenomenon is also known as *state flapping* that occurs particularly in complex systems such as networks (we describe this phenomenon in more detail later on). Such stateful approaches also permit some self-learning, as previously introduced. A deliberative manager can learn from its previous decisions and actions by continuously evaluating and potentially modifying itself. Such capability is, of course, more costly as it requires more resources than reflex-based solutions. This renders deliberative approaches not applicable for certain systems, such as real-time or embedded systems.

Mixed approaches have also been studied, essentially in artificial intelligence. Applied in the autonomic world, such approaches define an autonomic manager as being composed of two complementary parts: a reactive, reflex-based one, in close interaction with the environment, and a proactive, deliberative one, supervising and adjusting the reflex-based functions. The reactive part is in charge of implementing rapid actions in response to some well-defined conditions in the environment. The proactive part, which can be executed on remote, more suitable resources, deals with state conservation and complex reasoning. Based on its findings, this deliberative part can update the reactive part. For instance, it can change some parameters, change reflex rules or even add or remove rules. This approach retains advantages of both worlds but is difficult to realise.

4.3   Autonomic Manager Reference Architecture

4.3.1   The MAPE-K Model

IBM defined a reference architecture to structure autonomic managers [13], usually called the MAPE-K loop. It is a logical architecture, not a blueprint, that defines the different activities to be carried out in order to realise autonomic loops. It is being used more and more to communicate the architectural concepts of autonomic systems and has the added advantage that it is a clear way to identify and classify areas of particular focus. MAPE-K is acronymic for monitor, analyse, plan, execute and knowledge, which are aspects involved within any autonomic loop. This approach is analogous to the clinical practices of observation, diagnostics, solution and treatment.

Depending on the targeted system's complexity and degree of autonomicity, different levels of knowledge and reasoning are required to drive autonomic management. As knowledge about the system and its context is shared among all the phases of the loop, it is shown as a cross-cutting aspect. This architecture, illustrated by Fig. 4.5, can be used to implement both reactive/reflex and proactive/deliberative loops.

The first activity defined in the MAPE-K loop is that of monitoring. Its purpose is to build a model, more or less sophisticated, of the managed artefacts and of the execution context. To do so, it collects or receives information from the sensors provided by the managed artefacts and from the context. The monitoring activity generally has to filter, transform, aggregate and synthesise the collected information in order to build a focused and comprehensive model.

The analysis activity uses the representation of the world built by the monitoring activity in order to assess the situation and determine any anomalies or problems

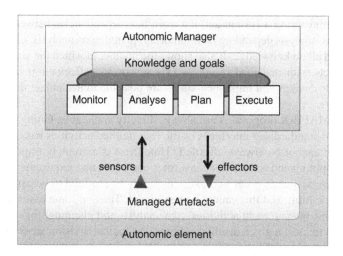

Fig. 4.5 The IMB reference architecture [13]

that would necessitate corrective action. In such a case, it may represent the desired states as a model of the managed artefacts. Once again, as in any model, such a model is a focused, simplified representation of the desired state of the managed artefacts. Detected problems and any associated analysis models are sent to planner, potentially decorated with different attributes, such as the relative importance or the urgency of the problem.

The planning activity logically comes after analysis. Its purpose is to determine a set of management actions allowing the passage from a current state to a desired state, as defined by the monitoring and analysis activities. Action sets are partially ordered and can handle several failures or malfunctions at a time since problems can be intertwined. The planning activity is carried out with some assumptions about the context and the managed artefacts. This has a profound impact on the feasibility of the adaption plans.

The execution activity, finally, has to carry out the plans, instantiating partially ordered management actions. This activity directly interacts with the effectors provided by the managed artefacts.

The MAPE-K logical architecture has profoundly impacted the autonomic field, providing a structuring framework to start with when building an autonomic system. It is a modular architecture making sense for practitioners and combining properties like the separation of concerns or scalability. The different activities, defined in rather abstract terms, take care of focused, well-defined, complementary aspects. Standardising communication interfaces of these activities, as advocated by IBM, would even allow easier integration of various techniques developed by different providers. The architecture is also scalable since activities can be executed on different machines, assuming that this is correlated with network latency and does not affect reactivity.

It is important to note that the MAPE-K loop represents a logical architecture and is not intended to be literally implemented as is in all autonomic systems. Rather, its purpose is to indicate the main functions an autonomic manager must support for administering a system and the main interdependencies between these functions, that is, analysis depending on monitoring, planning on analysis, execution on planning and all on knowledge. It also shows the manner in which the autonomic manager interacts with managed resources (via sensor and effector touchpoints). Various concrete designs and implementations are possible to instantiate this reference architecture.

Indeed, the MAPE-K proposal is not always directly applicable. Going through the well-defined standardised interfaces of the four defined activities has a performance cost that cannot be always afforded. Timeliness is extremely important in autonomic computing and sometimes constitutes one of the first requirements to be met. A corrective action, in order to make sense, may be required to be carried out within some time limit, and this cannot be negotiated. Thus, in some cases, grouping together some management activities, like analysis and planning, for instance, can be required to meet a given deadline. Hence, the logical division advocated by IBM is a high-level model; its merit is to provide high-level guidance facilitating

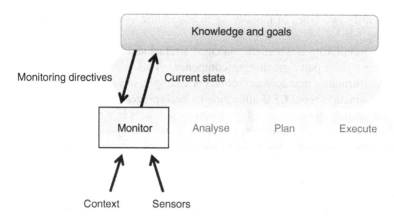

Fig. 4.6 The monitoring activity

the design of an autonomic manager. But, it is only a first step in building a real
autonomic manager for a particular managed system.

Certainly, the major limit of this model is that it does not address the behavioural
dimension of an autonomic manager. Most of the time, an autonomic manager
does not implement a direct, straightforward monitor/analyse/plan/execute loop.
Interactions between the different activities are much more complex than that.
Backtracks are often needed when, for instance, a task needs additional information to
perform its computation. Breaks are also needed when, for instance, a task has to wait
for more data to be obtained or for some effects of adaptation to be measured. Also,
synchronisations are necessary when knowledge is shared by several activities.

4.3.2   Monitoring

We now consider the monitoring component of the MAPE-K loop. Monitoring
involves capturing properties (either physical or virtual) that are of significance to
the self-managing properties of the system. For example, network latency and bandwidth can be used as a measure of the performance of a Web server, while remaining
battery life of a laptop is a measure of its future utility, all of which can be monitored. Information is collected through sensors or gauges, provided by the managed
artefacts or through specific interfaces provided by the computing environment. The
autonomic manager requires appropriate monitored data to be able to recognise the
autonomic artefact's failure or suboptimal performance. It can then decide to make
appropriate changes. The types of monitored properties, and the sensors used, will
often be application specific, just as the mechanisms used to execute changes are
also application, system and programming language specific (Fig. 4.6).

We identify two types of monitoring in autonomic systems: passive and active monitoring.

Passive monitoring is where the managed artefact and its components are monitored using a third party monitoring component. This component may consist of existing performance management tools. For example, in Linux the `top` command returns information about CPU utilisation by each process. Another common command that returns memory and CPU utilisation statistics is `vmstat`. Furthermore, Linux provides the `/proc` directory, which is a pseudo-file system (this directory does not store actual files on a hard disk) containing runtime system information, for example, system memory, CPU information and per-process information including memory utilisation, devices mounted and hardware configuration. Similar passive monitoring tools exist for most operating systems. Armed with the process identifier of the managed element or its components, the autonomic manager is able to establish the element's performance profile in real time. Such situation can be encountered when using COTS components. Some of them actually come with their monitoring tool directly usable by the autonomic manager. This can be an important move in the realm of component-based software engineering since the very nature of software components is to come with non-functional properties and capacities. For instance, components can be delivered with built-in testing capacities. Being packaged with built-in autonomic abilities is certainly one of the very next steps in the evolution of software engineering.

Active monitoring means direct interaction between the monitoring part of the autonomic manager and its surroundings, in particular with the sensors, or probes, provided by the managed artefacts. As said earlier, there is a close relationship between the autonomic manager and the managed artefacts, particularly obvious in the relationship between monitoring and sensors. The autonomic manager may require the ability to add probes, for example, to the managed artefact's software. This may entail modifying and adding code to the implementation of the managed element or its components to capture function or system calls or the times they were initiated and completed. This can also be automated to some extent. For instance, ProbeMeister[2] can insert probes into compiled Java byte code. This information can be combined with passive monitoring solutions to provide the autonomic manager with richer state information.

There is a trade-off where we wish to have as much data to understand the state of the system and make appropriate action, but this data is costly to obtain and moreover store and process. Much work in the autonomic computing research community has focused precisely on how to decide which subset of the many performance metrics collected from a dynamic environment can be obtained from the many performance tools available to it. Interestingly some have observed that a small subset of well-chosen metrics can provide 90 % accuracy in terms of classifying application states [14]. Further, a more dynamic approach to the monitoring of systems to facilitate autonomicity can be taken. For example, Agarwala et al. [15]

---

[2]ProbeMeister home page: http://http://www.objs.com/ProbeMeister/

propose QMON, an autonomic monitor that adapts the monitoring frequency and therefore monitoring data volume to minimise the overhead of continuous monitoring while maximising the utility of the performance data. It could be described as an autonomic monitor for autonomic systems.

Also, data to be collected depend on the goals and on the state of the solving process. Goals set by the administrators clearly affect the way the monitoring should be done. Emphasis evolves as a function of the interest of the human administrators. Similarly, intermediary results about the situation of the managed artefacts regarding the goals can influence data to be monitored and the way to collect them.

The monitoring phase provides information to the other management activities, building a representation, or a model, of the present context and managed artefacts. Once again, this model depends on the current goals and is very application dependent. To create it, the monitoring activity transforms the information collected into an appropriate format, that is, a format that can be manipulated by the other activities. Such transformations can be complicated: they may involve a number of timely operations like filtering, analysing and aggregating. In general, temporal windows will have to be explicitly defined as some information makes sense only when observed during given time periods. Knowing the right period can however be difficult in some situations.

The output model can take different forms: a list of facts or observations, a graph of objects, a state machine, a software architecture, etc. For instance, when handling the battery life of a laptop, a three-state machine can be created and updated on event occurrences. These three distinct states characterise the level of charge: under 1 % of charge, between 1 and 20 % and over 20 % of charge. Changing state can provoke actions from the autonomic manager (analyse/plan/execute loop).

4.3.3 Analysis

We now focus on the analysis component of the MAPE-K loop. Analysing involves evaluating the current state of the context and of the managed artefacts and specifying a target state if problems are identified. To do so, analysis relies on application specific knowledge that can be hard to obtain. Let us remind that problems are defined here as failures in the managed artefacts or suboptimal behaviour. Also, we use the term 'state' in its more general definition, readily acknowledging that various formalisms can be used to define a state.

It is not the purpose of the analysis aspect to provide details about the identified shortcomings but rather to specify the desirable states. It is then the job of the planning phase to come up with the best way to reach a desirable state (Fig. 4.7).

Analysis thus deals with the ability to *understand* the current context and to determine a better state for the managed artefacts.

A wide variety of algorithms and techniques can be used in order to detect misbehaviours and shortcomings, establish correlations, anticipate situations, diagnose problems and define more desirable, and reachable, situations. This can be anything from a model providing an evaluation of the situation to classification

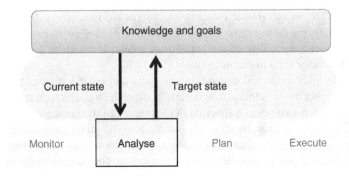

Fig. 4.7 The analysis activity

systems that identify whether or not a constraint or goal has been breached. Prediction systems typically monitor trends and also identify if a constraint or goal will be broken in the near or further future. This can be implemented using anything from simple regression analysis of a window of historical probe data to using hidden Markov models that represent temporal states of the system and can be used to model the outcomes of a plan.

The second purpose of analysis is to determine an improved situation for the managed artefacts. This can be achieved using anything from a set of high-level goals, expressed in a symbolic way, to more sophisticated models such as target software architectures or property graphs. But, whatever the formalism, desired situations have to be expressed in a focused, synthesised way. This is the very purpose of the MAPE-K loop that defines the specialised autonomic components that intercommunicate. In the case of the analysis component, the goal is to feed the planning phase with an abstract situation that is required to be reached from the current situation—this data is also focused and abstracted.

In the autonomic field, three policies have been heavily used to implement the analysis expertise: event–condition–action (ECA) policies, utility function policies and goal policies [16].

Event–condition–action rules are a clear and straightforward way to express domain expertise. ECA policies can take the form:

when *event* occurs and *condition* holds, then execute *action*.

That is, 'when 95 % of a Web servers' response time begins to exceed 3 s and there are available resources, then increase number of communication ports'. In this example, the action is the definition of a state to be reached, that is, a state where the number of communication ports better suits the needs of the managed system. ECA rules and policy driven adaptation have been intensely studied for the autonomic management of distributed systems. However, a difficulty with ECA policies is that when a number of policies are specified, conflicts between policies can arise that are hard to detect. For example, when different tiers of a multi-tier system (e.g. Web and application server tiers) require an increased amount of resources, but the available resources cannot fulfil the requests of all tiers, a conflict arises. In such a case, it is unclear how the system should react, and so in many cases an additional conflict resolution mechanism is necessary, for example, that would give higher priority to the Web server. As a result, a considerable amount of research on conflict resolution has arisen; the real challenge here is that conflict may only become apparent at runtime. A pragmatic conclusion is that ECA rules are very effective when dealing with a small number of policies or when concerns are orthogonal. When too many conflicts arise, other formalisms have to be examined in order to avoid a debugging nightmare.

Utility functions rely on the definition of a quantitative level of desirability of a given system state and any subsequent actions upon that state. This measure of utility is expressed as a function and takes as input a number of parameters and outputs a desirability rating of this state. Thus, as an example, the utility function could take as input the current or predicted response time for a set of Web and application servers available to choose from, thus returning the relative utility of each combination of Web and application server response times. This way, when insufficient resources are available, the most desirable combination of available resources among Web and application servers can be found. The major problem with utility functions is that they can be extremely hard to define, as every aspect that influences the decision must be quantified and combined into a single figure. Nevertheless, utility functions have been found to be very useful and have been used in automatic resource allocation [17], adaptation of data streams to network conditions [18] to name two examples. They are also very useful in very dynamic environments where devices, for instance, come and go. Utility functions are here used in intelligent homes to allow the autonomic manager to decide whether or not to select a given device to run a media stream [19].

Goal policies require planning on the part of autonomic manager and are thus more resource intensive than ECA policies. However, they still suffer from the problem that all states are classified as either desirable or undesirable. Thus, when a desirable state cannot be reached, the system does not know which among the undesirable states is least bad.

4.3.4   Planning

Let us now take a look at the planning aspect of the MAPE-K autonomic loop. In its broadest sense, planning involves making a decision regarding the changes and adaptations to assemble and implement on the managed artefacts in order to move from a current to a desired state. To do so, a planner relies on a set of actions that can be performed on the managed artefacts. Once again, we see the importance of the link between the autonomic manager and the managed artefacts: action plans depend on the effectors and effectors are put in place to carry out some desired action plans. The planner should not consider the implementation details of the actions. It is the purpose of the execution component to implement these actions, which are often realised in dynamic computing environment (Fig. 4.8).

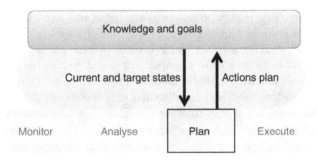

Fig. 4.8 The planning activity

A plan of action can be static or more dynamic. One plan could consist of a static set of steps that must be carried out when a particular condition has occurred. Let us take the example of a large grid system. If the monitoring side of an autonomic manager detects that a node has died, the simple steps may be to inform the user and then automatically reboot the node or if that does not work, then inform the workload dispatcher to reroute the load away from this node. More sophisticated and dynamic solutions may model the behaviour of the components that compose the managed artefact and then choose a plan (from the number of plans that already exist) on the fly or even generate a plan at real time by iterating through the model of different paths or scenarios and choosing the best. To do so, a planner make hypothesis about the effects of the scheduled actions on the managed artefacts.

In autonomic computing, we also often make the assumption that the autonomic manager is the only entity acting on the managed artefacts. This is not always true. In pervasive applications, in particular, many things impacting the managed arte-facts happen in the computing and usage contexts. The autonomic manager has to regularly check its predictions about the effect of its actions and about the state of the managed artefacts in order to verify the adequacy of the plan. In extreme cases, it can be necessary to redo a complete MAPE-K loop in order to determine a new objective and a way to reach it.

In any case, a planner has to anticipate the future and predict the effect of a given course of actions and, furthermore, the data that should be monitored in order to verify its predictions.

We then have two approaches to planning in autonomic computing: domain specific or generic. Domain-specific approaches rely heavily on the administrators' expertise. Typically, the planning module is made of a number of rules taking the form 'when target and condition state holds, then create plan' where the plan is entirely specified, or instantiated, in the rule. An example of such a rule would be 'when the number of communication ports has to be increased and there are avail-able resources, then consume all the available resources and distribute them opti-mally'. In this example, the action is the opening of new communication ports for each of the Web servers. These rules are typically written by system administrators derived from system and business goals. Writing adaptation policies is fairly straightforward but can become a tedious task for larger complex systems, especially when conflicts have to be dealt with.

Generic approaches are much more ambitious. The idea here is to formally express the problem, that is, the notion of state, and to define action operators acting on the states. Operators are generally defined with preconditions and effects on the state. Planning then comes down to determining a sequence of operators allowing the passage from the current state to the target state. It generally takes the form of a graph search, either with or without heuristics.

An architectural model of either a focused part of, or indeed the entire managed system, is often used to formalise the current state. This architectural model reflects the system's behaviour, its requirements and the system states required to reach its goals. The model may also include aspects of the operating environment in which the managed elements are deployed. Here, the model is updated through sensor data and used to reason about the managed system to plan valid and appropriate adaptations. A great advantage of the architectural model-based approach to planning is that under the assumption that the model correctly mirrors the managed system, the architectural model can be used to verify that system integrity is preserved when applying an adaptation. That is, we can guarantee that the system will continue to operate correctly after the planned adaptation has been executed. This is because changes are planned and applied to the model first, which will show the resulting system's state including any violations of system constraints or requirements present in the model. If the new system state is acceptable, the plan can then be executed on the managed system.

Building a model of the system under question is however a non-trivial task. It assumes that the architect understands the components, their interaction and behaviours to ensure accuracy. Further, the model needs to be able to run through the different adaptation scenarios to check that an update is both useful and safe. Given the number of states and each state's interaction, the search of all interactions is a highly complex problem of exponential proportions. This may mean that the model and the system are highly decoupled. For example, the model may run on a different machine so as to not impact the managed systems' operation. This processing can potentially incur heavy execution costs. The timeliness of the solution to the adaptation is important so to speed up the time model takes to reach an optimum solution heuristics may be used, which may or may not add error to the model.

4.3.5 Execution

Let us now examine the fourth and last activity of the MAPE-K loop. The purpose of the execution activity is to implement the management actions determined by the planning activity. Management actions essentially concern the managed artefacts, not the computing context. The purpose of an autonomic element, indeed, is not to modify the environment but to react to its evolutions when they affect its behaviour.

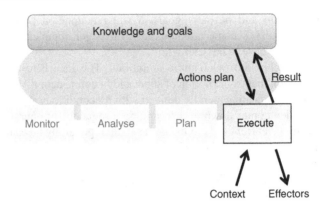

Fig. 4.9 The execution activity

Planning and execution are complementary activities. Planning focuses on high-level actions to be undertaken, on their logical dependencies and, possibly, on their order. Execution is much more concrete; it has to schedule the implementation of the plans as they directly affect the artefacts currently running. It also has to examine in real time the effects of its own actions in order to perform some adjustments if necessary (Fig. 4.9).

Dissociating planning and execution has been heavily investigated in artificial intelligence but also in more traditional domains, like manufacturing execution systems (MES), for instance, in order to deal with complex environments. Separating out these activities is an efficient way to handle dynamic, stochastic or poorly observable computing contexts. The principle adopted here is to work at two complementary levels of abstraction. A plan, for instance, could specify a set of parameters to be changed, with no ordering constraints. The execution activity, then, has to determine how and when the parameters have to be changed. It is a matter of timeliness and synchronisation where a number of functional and non-functional dependencies have to be considered. Usually, a parameter can be changed only if some conditions hold. When several parameters have to be modified, ordering constraints have usually to be respected.

Planning has to make simplifying assumptions about the dynamicity and predictability of the world in order to be able to produce plans at a reasonable cost. It is then the purpose of the execution module to get back to reality and carry out the plans in the real word. That means that it has to transform more or less abstract directives into concrete interventions in the real word. It also may make use of available sensors to get feedback about its actions. In this way, the execution module implements a control loop of its own. Of course, the purpose here is not to replace the global MAPE-K loop but rather to make sure that the management actions decided by the planner are carried out as expected. If not, corrections have to be made perhaps reengaging the planner, or even executing the whole MAPE-K loop again.

Clearly, time management is at the heart of the execution activity. In order to avoid unstable or incorrect situations, management actions have to be undergone at the right time and in the right order. This is made more complicated in dynamic environments where the computing environment has to be constantly surveyed while corrective actions are under execution. For example, in pervasive environments, the way some management actions are realised may have to be changed because of context evolution. Some actions may even have to be cancelled when important changes occur in the environment. One way to deal with this is to use a finite-state machine to orchestrate plan execution in dynamic environments. Such machines allow for explicit and efficient coordination between corrective actions, and also with ongoing operations. This approach has been used successfully for the self-administration of industrial devices.

Another way for the execution module to deal with dynamicity and uncertainty is to demand flexible plans from the planner so that it can recover from unexpected events. Analogy can be drawn here with the field of autonomous robots immersed in uncertain environments. Here, static plans of actions turned out to not be exploitable. Robots are then loaded with related partial plans that are completed at runtime depending on the situations encountered. Reactive plans have also been introduced after the failure of early static approaches like STRIPS [20]. Reactive plans include branches in order to deal with uncertain events or events that can only be known at runtime. Reactive plans can also be combined. Thus, the directives sent to the execution module can take the form of a number of reactive plans, including runtime contingencies.

By definition, the execution module interacts with the effectors of the managed elements and should have no real control over external entities. But, it may also interact with some other accessible entities in the computing environment. The interactions can go from an authorised modification, through a simple setter interface, for instance, to some complex negotiations. Thus, to meet its self-management objectives, the autonomic manager has to request for some modification to other entities. This can include other autonomic managers controlling some other parts of the software at hand. For example, some managed artefacts using threads may need additional threads to improve their performance. Typically, threads are global concerns and are generally managed by the operating system, for example.

A final point is that effectors, like any other computing entities, can fail. This means that the actions requested by the autonomic manager are not carried out. This can happen because of a bug, local to the effectors, or because of the global situation of the managed artefacts. Ironically, such a failure can be very well related to the issue that the manager tries to solve. For example, if the reason the artefact was performing poorly was due to lack of memory resource available to it, perhaps this too will affect the autonomic manager being able to run a new process to effect change.

Thus, the implementation of the execution activity often turns out to be very complex and tricky. For all these reasons, current solutions are essentially domain specific. Of course, they can rely on generic mechanisms, usually provided by the underlying execution machine, in order to control the artefacts life cycle. But, complex timing and synchronisation issues are generally handled case by case.

4.3.6 Summary

The MAPE-K model has had a big impact on the autonomic computing field and is still very relevant. It has to be understood, though, as a *logical* architecture defining the main architectural blocks to be defined when building an autonomic manager. From that, depending on the specifics of each application, different implementations of the MAPE-K model are possible: from a monolithic approach to widely distributed ones.

In any case, the MAPE-K model gives no indication about the way the aforementioned tasks should be implemented nor on the way they should be organised and controlled. Similarly, this model does not address the way the knowledge is represented and shared between the different tasks.

Let us consider knowledge first. The way knowledge is shared among the different activities is not specified in the MAPE-K loop, and it leaves open many solutions, including a global shared database or completely distributed solution based on the exchange of events. So knowledge is essentially represented in the models that correspond to the following: the managed element and its interactions; the classification and feature extraction systems; the effectors or actions that have to be performed (and when they are performed); the plans, etc. Knowledge lies also in recording the changes to the system that occurred when the system is adapted, and some systems may or may wish to close the loop in this respect to allow for further more sophisticated analysis and planning strategies that can improve their operation based on past experiences. Information is required to flow through the system. This means that the managed element must be able to export interfaces to allow the flow of attributes that represent both functional behaviours and control procedures. As can be seen from the examples above, autonomic management operates at many levels of abstraction. Therefore, the MAPE-K loop can be a combination of loops and loops of loops, as we shall see later in this chapter. The knowledge in an autonomic system can come from sources as diverse as the human expert (in static policy-based systems [21]) to logs that accumulate data from probes charting the day-to-day operation of a system to observe its behaviour, which is then used to train predictive models [22, 23].

Control is clearly a hard point. Complex control strategies are often needed to allow the right coordination and an effective synchronisation between the monitor/analyse/plan/execute activities. These strategies depend on the application domain. They can go from a simple state machine controlling the activation of the activities to an AI-based controller allowing opportunistic activation of these activities [24].

As we can see, using the MAPE-K model is a good starting point to define one's autonomic manager. However, its structure and design are not prescriptive, and therefore, the designer may find that they tailor the MAPE-K concepts to best fit the system they are designing; the rest of this chapter gives some examples.

4.4   Architecture with Multiple Autonomic Elements

4.4.1   Introduction

As previously introduced, autonomic systems may form sophisticated architectures made of a number of autonomic elements. The autonomic elements manage parts of the global autonomic system. The decoupling is domain specific: it can be based on functional considerations, on architectural considerations or on both.

The autonomic elements can act independently. In such cases, there is no correlation between their respective management actions. Most of the time, though, the situation is much more complicated and autonomic elements have to cooperate to achieve common goals. Each element is in charge of a given administration aspect and has no rights over the rest of the software. In order to have a global impact, agreements and possibly negotiations have to be initiated in order to produce concerted plans.

For instance, servers in a cluster may optimise the allocation of resources to applications to minimise the overall response time or execution time of the applications they support. Thus, autonomic managers may need to be aware not only of the condition of their own managed artefacts but also of their environment, in particular how they relate to other autonomic elements in the network. This situation is illustrated by Fig. 4.10 hereafter.

This notion of cooperation of individual elements to achieve a common goal is a fundamental aspect of multi-agent systems (see Chap. 3). It is therefore not surprising that considerable research has investigated how multi-agent systems can implement cooperating autonomic elements. Like agents, autonomic elements can be organised in complex architectures based on various collaboration patterns, which can range from hierarchical organisations to fully decentralised structures. These

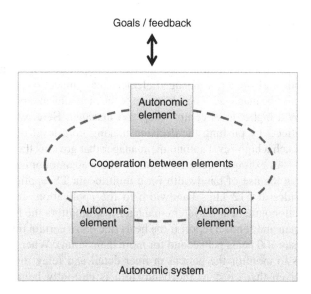

Fig. 4.10 Cooperating autonomic elements

Fig. 4.11 Hierarchical
organisation

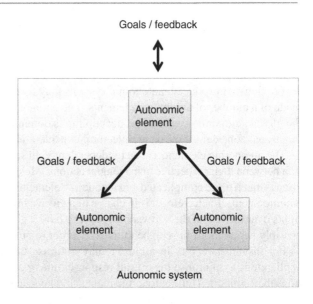

two architectural patterns, heavily studied in the multi-agent field, are presented in
the next sections with examples from the autonomic field.

4.4.2   Hierarchical *Versus* Decentralised Organisation

An approach to multi-agent cooperation is a hierarchical structuring of agents [25].
This organisation can be advantageously applied to the design of autonomic systems,
as illustrated by Fig. 4.11. Autonomic elements are organised into a hierarchy where
elements can set goals to the elements of lesser level, which, in turn, provide feedback about their behaviour.

Hierarchical autonomic management allows the composition of many managed
elements with their intelligent control loops effecting change to that element and no
other. However, a managed element may impact on another element and this too
must be managed. The advantage of the hierarchical model is that this will be handled
by a higher-level control loop and manager. Here, we minimise unexpected side
effects by pushing the decision making up a level of abstraction. Eventually we
reach a high-level autonomic manager that governs the system as a whole.

An example scenario of this is where an autonomic media manager is monitoring the use of bandwidth for a multimedia TV application in the home and provides at 512 kbps bandwidth to the application. In parallel the home has an
autonomic health-system manager that monitors the heart rate of an older gentle-
man and sends a report if the heart rate hits a certain threshold for a given duration
(say 100 beats per second for more than 3 min). When this event occurs, the policy
is to monitor the patient in finer detail and relay this to the hospital. However,
given that most of the bandwidth is currently being used by the TV, the TV

Fig. 4.12 Decentralised
organisation

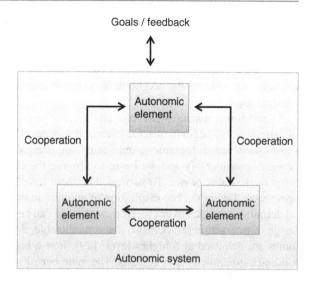

autonomic manager needs to be overridden. Therefore, the next level autonomic manager understands the concept of priority and is able to do this cleanly. In summary, in hierarchical architectures all events travel bottom-up and effectors are triggered from the top-down.

This hierarchical approach has been advocated by a number of authors. In a seminal paper (ref), Magee and Kramer draw an analogy between autonomic computing and robotics arguing that, like robots, autonomic systems can be organised around three types of control loops: one for reflex actions, one for short-term action planning and a third one for deliberative actions. Another work in the domain of home automation makes uses of a hierarchy of autonomic elements to self-manage applications running on Internet gateways and competing for resources (ref).

An alternative to the hierarchical approach is where all autonomic elements in the system can communicate directly, as illustrated by Fig. 4.12. Agent like and emergent autonomic systems tend to have this format whereby each autonomic element is almost autonomous and uses both external data and internal readings to make its decisions. Inter-autonomic element communication is more complex here. The notion of an all-governing solution does not exist, meaning there are no centralised elements in the architecture that may adversely affect scale and robustness, but this is at a cost of the lack of global management.

The particular challenge here lies in guaranteeing that the behaviour emerging from the individual goals of each agent will truly result in the common goal being achieved [13, 26–28].

An example scenario here might be where a number of atmospheric sensing devices are monitoring the environmental conditions of a museum. Each consists of sensing components, processor and transceiver that can relay data to a sink device. Here the main policy is to monitor the environment and send a summarised reading every 5 min. However, some of those sensing devices may have the knowledge to understand that a fire has broken out, and it wishes to relay the message to the appropriate people. This may require it to quickly negotiate a wireless route to the sink (away from the fire) via all the other sensing devices by appropriating their respective transceivers. To do this, they must communicate directly and negotiate with all the neighbourhood autonomic managers and agree to serve this data route.

As autonomic management solutions become more decentralised and less deterministic, we may begin to observe emergent features. That is, even though the interactions between autonomic components are simple, the systems' complexity increases considerably and we begin to observe the evolution of patterns that can either be desirable or not. To harness this, there have been moves to engineer this emergence. Taking the bio-inspiration of autonomic systems further than the original definition, the idea of engineered emergence can be described as the 'purposeful design of interaction protocols so that a predictable, desired outcome or set of outcomes are achieved at a higher level' [29]. It is a highly distributed approach to building autonomicity into systems. The main benefits are that of scale, robustness and stability. This is because there is no central management function; each managed component acts on its own behalf. Therefore, if one managed component dies, then the system should be able to cope gracefully. Likewise if a new, better component arrives, the system should evolve to make use of this. The other benefit of such approaches is that they do not require precise knowledge of lower-level activity or configuration. In such systems the solution emerges at the level of systems or applications, while at lower levels the specific behaviour of individual components is unpredictable.

Here, typically a small set of rules operates on limited amounts of locally available information concerning the components execution context and its local environment. This differs from traditional algorithmic design of distributed applications that typically focuses on strict protocols, message acknowledgments and event ordering. In traditional systems each message and event is considered important and randomness is generally undesirable, imposing sequenced or synchronised behaviour, which is generally deterministic. However, natural biological systems are fundamentally non-deterministic, and there are many examples of large-scale systems that are stable and robust at a global level, the most commonly cited examples being drawn from cellular systems and insect colonies [29]. The main drawback to such systems is that they need regular messaging between components to be able to comprehend their state and adapt if necessary. Furthermore, guarantees are not as solid in such emergent systems, and timely convergence to a desired state may take time.

4.4.3 The ANS Example

An example of engineered emergence is that of the ANS ubiquitous networking protocol. This protocol in itself makes use of both utility functions and decentralised management. As previously introduced, utility is an abstract measure of 'usefulness' or benefit to, for example, a user. Typically a system's operation expresses its utility as a measure of things like the amount of resources available to the user (or user application programs) and the quality, reliability or accuracy of that resource. For example, in an event processing system allocating hardware resources to users wishing to run transactions, the utility will be a function of allocated rate, allowable latency and number of consumers, for example, [30]. Another example is in a resource provisioning system where the utility is derived from the cost of redistribution of workloads once allocated or the power consumption as a portion of operating cost [31, 32].

The (autonomic networked services) ANS protocol was designed to allow fully distributed autonomic decision making where there are more than one alternative state to be able to adapt to. In the ANS a computing system is completely composed as services (not unlike services in service-oriented architectures—see Chap. 6). Each service is called a context and is able to say what it does and to what degree it is able to do this. This ability is termed its quality of context.

The protocol was designed for pervasive computing devices and wireless sensor networks. Constrained resources pose the greatest challenge to the use of such systems. Power availability is severely constrained due to the capacity of current battery technology. Sending and receiving wireless communication is the greatest consumer of power in these systems, and so must be limited as much as possible. The applications also impose other constraints such as robustness, scalability, stability despite configuration change and low communication latency.

So the application may wish to have location information. This can be obtained from a number of devices. The notion of quality of context (QoC) is used by ANS to choose which of these devices will be used when a request is made by a requester node. A process called 'tendering' is used to select the node. The information requester node will broadcast a 'request' command containing the name of a sensing service (like location) and preferences for the QoC attributes (which is essentially the degree of precision the application can tolerate). Every node within range and able to fulfil the service must respond. The nodes use a utility function to calculate its ability to fulfil the request if it matches the requested QoC. The result from the utility function is a signed integer called 'closeness' and is used as the nodes' response to the information request. The sensor node with the QoC closest to that requested wins the tender and becomes the sensor supplying its data to the information requester. Frequent 'retendering' allows the requester nodes to autonomously adapt to the best source available, discover new devices in the network and recover from node failure. Figure 4.13 shows message diagrams illustrating how the protocol fulfils the typical autonomic aspects.

The figure also shows the system that requires a service being turned on and its first task is to tender a message. Any sensors (service providers) that are on and able to service that request reply with a 'can_provide' message; the service with the best utility in terms of quality of context is selected (if there are more than one). For self-healing, we can see that the requestor carries out periodic tenders. If the node that it is currently bound to says that it can no longer carry out the task to the requested level of service, or it dies (i.e. no reply is received from that node), then reconfiguration should happen. This happens by default as all nodes in the system have the

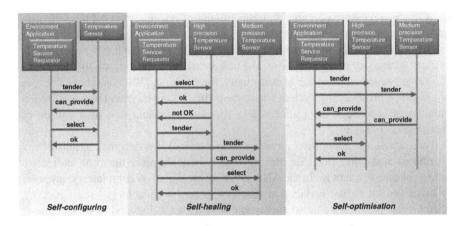

Fig. 4.13 ANS typical autonomic aspects

opportunity to reply to the request indicating their performance levels, then the requestor can just select the next best service. Likewise, if the requestor receives a better offer when carrying out its periodic tender process, it will take it. This sort of protocol is highly decentralised and using lightweight tender messages can ensure autonomic properties.

4.5   Key Points

In this chapter, we have introduced the following important points:

- The architecture of an autonomic system is a dual architecture, comprising a number of autonomic elements managing well-defined software regions. This may include well-delimited functions and some programming artefacts without autonomic capabilities. Non-autonomic parts are typically unaware of the autonomic dimension within the overall architecture.
- Organising a number of autonomic elements is an architectural challenge. A popular approach is to adopt a hierarchical structuring of elements. An alternative is where all autonomic elements in the system can communicate directly. The particular challenge in the latter lies in guaranteeing that the behaviour emerging from the individual goals of each element will result in the common goal being achieved.
- An autonomic element is made of two, intertwined, parts: the autonomic manager and the managed artefacts. Managed artefacts are hardware and software resources that can be manipulated through provided interfaces, called sensors and effectors, more generally known as *touchpoints*. The autonomic manager is in charge of the management of these artefacts through the touchpoints.
- The purpose of an autonomic manager is to apply domain-specific knowledge in order to gracefully adapt a set of software artefacts at runtime when internal or external changes are detected that deviate the operation of the system away from its goals.

- Autonomic managers are structured according to a widely accepted architectural model introduced by IBM, usually called the MAPE-K loop. This is a logical architecture that defines the different activities to be carried out in order to realise autonomic loops. MAPE-K is acronymic for monitor, analyse, plan, execute and knowledge, which are aspects involved within any autonomic loop.
- The MAPE-K model gives no indication about the way the tasks should be implemented nor on the way they should be organised and controlled. Similarly, this model does not address the way the knowledge is represented and shared between the different tasks.
- There is actually often confusion between autonomic managers and autonomic elements. Autonomic managers are certainly central to the approach since they contain most of the knowledge and expertise necessary to exhibit self-* properties. However, an autonomic manager is only one component out of many in an autonomic element. Given the design and implementation of an autonomic manager is a challenging task; however, the difficulty of defining and implementing the sensors and effectors of the managed artefacts should not be underestimated.

References

1. Garlan, D., Perry, D.E.: Introduction to the special issue on software architecture. IEEE Trans. Softw. Eng. **21**(4), 269–274 (1995)
2. Dey, A.K.: Understanding and using context. Pers. Ubiquit. Comput. **5**(1), 4–7 (2001)
3. IBM.: An Architectural Blueprint for Autonomic Computing, 3rd edn. IBM Whitepaper, June 2005
4. Garlan, D., Schmerl, B.: Model-based adaptation for self-healing systems. In: Proceedings of the First Workshop on Self-Healing Systems. ACM Press, Charleston, SC (2002)
5. Sterritt, R., Smyth, B., Bradley, M.: PACT: personal autonomic computing tools. In: Proceedings of the 12th IEEE International Conference and Workshops on the Engineering of Computer-Based Systems (ECBS), pp. 519–527. IEEE Computer Society, Washington, DC, USA (2005)
6. Bigus, J.P., Schlosnagle, D.A., Pilgrim III, J.R., Mills, W.N., Diao, Y.: ABLE: a toolkit for building multiagent autonomic systems. IBM Syst. J. **41**(3), 350–371 (2002)
7. Maurel, Y., Lalanda, P., Diaconescu, A.: Towards a service-oriented component model for autonomic management. In: IEEE International Conference on Services Computing (SCC 2011), 4–9 July2011. IEEE Computer Society, Washington, DC, USA (2011)
8. Sutton, R.S., Barto, A.G.: Reinforcement Learning: An Introduction. MIT Press, Cambridge, MA (1998)
9. Littman, M.L., Ravi, N., Fenson, E., Howard, R.: Reinforcement learning for autonomic network repair. In ICAC: Proceedings of the First International Conference on Autonomic Computing, pp. 284–285, Washington, DC (2004)
10. Dowling, J., Curran, E., Cunningham, R., Cahill, V.: Building autonomic systems using collaborative reinforcement learning. Knowl. Eng. Rev. **21**, 231–238 (2006). Journal Special issue on Autonomic Computing, Cambridge University Press
11. Tesauro, G., Das, R., Jong, N., Bennani, M.: A hybrid reinforcement learning approach to autonomic resource allocation. In: Proceedings of 3rd IEEE International Conference on Autonomic Computing (ICAC), pp. 65–73, Dublin, Ireland (2006)
12. Whiteson, S., Stone, P.: Evolutionary function approximation for reinforcement learning. J. Mach. Learn. Res. **7**, 877–917 (2006)
13. Kephart, J.O., Chess, D.M.: The vision of autonomic computing. Computer **36**(1), 41–50 (2003)

14. Zhang, J., Figueiredo, R.: Autonomic feature selection for application classification. In: Proceedings of the International Conference on Autonomic Computing (ICAC), Dublin (2006)
15. Agarwala, S., Chen, Y., Milojicic, D., Schwan, K.: QMON: QoS- and Utility- aware monitoring in enterprise systems. In: Proceedings of the 3rd IEEE International Conference on Autonomic Computing (ICAC), Dublin, Ireland (2006)
16. Kephart, J.O., Walsh, W.E.: An artificial intelligence perspective on autonomic computing policies. In: Proceedings of the 5th IEEE International Workshop on Policies for Distributed Systems and Networks (POLICY) 2004, 7–9 June 2004, pp. 3–12. IBM Thomas J Watson Research Center, Yorktown Heights, New York (2004). doi: 10.1109/POLICY.2004.1309145. http://ieeexplore.ieee.org/stamp/stamp.jsp?tp=&arnumber=1309145&isnumber=29053
17. Walsh, W.E., Tesauro, G., Kephart, J.O., Das, R.: Utility functions in autonomic systems. In: Proceedings of the First International Conference on Autonomic Computing, 17–19 May 2004, IEEE Computer Society, New York (2004)
18. Bhatti, S.N., Knight, G.: Enabling QoS adaptation decisions for internet applications. Comput. Netw. 31(7), 669–692 (1999)
19. Bourcier, J., Diaconescu, A., Lalanda, P., McCann, J.: AutoHome: an autonomic management framework for pervasive home applications. ACM Trans. Auton. Adapt. Syst. 6(1) (2011)
20. Fikes, R., Nilsson, N.: STRIPS: a new approach to the application of theorem proving to problem solving. Artif. Intell. 2, 189–208 (1971). doi:10.1016/0004-3702(71)90010-5
21. Bougaev, A.A.: Pattern recognition based tools enabling autonomic computing. In: Proceedings of 2nd IEEE International Conference on Autonomic Computing, 13–16 June 2005, pp. 313–314. IEEE Computer Society, Seattle (2005)
22. Manoel, E., Nielsen, M.J., Salahshour, A., Sampath, S.: Problem Determination Using Self-Managing Autonomic Technology. IBM Redbooks, San Jose (2005). ISBN 073849111X
23. Shivam, P., Babu, S., Chase, J.: Learning application models for utility resource planning. In: Proceedings of 3rd IEEE International Conference on Autonomic Computing (ICAC), pp. 255–264, Dublin, Ireland (2006)
24. Maurel, Y., Lalanda, P., Diaconescu, A.: Towards a Service-Oriented Component Model for Autonomic Management. IEEE SCC, Washington, DC, USA (2011)
25. Wise, A., Cass, A.G., Lerner, B.S., Call, E.K.M., Osterweil, L.J., Sutton, Jr, S.M.: Using Little-JIL to coordinate agents in software engineering. In: Automated Software Engineering Conference, 11–15 September 2000. IEEE Computer Society, Grenoble (2000)
26. Jennings, N.R.: On agent-based software engineering. Artif. Intell. 117(2), 277–296 (2000)
27. Gleizes, M.-P., Link-Pezet, J., Glize, P.: An adaptive multi-agent tool for electronic commerce. In: Proceedings of the IEEE 9th International Workshops on Enabling Technologies: Infrastructure for Collaborative Enterprises, 14–16 June 2000. NIST, USA, IEEE Computer Society (2000)
28. Kumar, S., Cohen, P.R.: Towards a fault-tolerant multi-agent system architecture. In: Proceedings of the Fourth International Conference on Autonomous Agents. ACM Press, Barcelona (2000)
29. Anthony, R.: Emergent graph colouring. In: Engineering Emergence for Autonomic Systems (EEAS), First Annual International Workshop at the Third International Conference on Autonomic Computing (ICAC), June 2006, pp. 2–13. IEEE Computer Society, Dublin (2006)
30. Bhola, S., Astley, M., Saccone, R., Ward, M.: Utility-aware resource allocation in an event processing system. In: Proceedings of 3rd IEEE International Conference on Autonomic Computing (ICAC), pp. 55–64, Dublin, Ireland (2006)
31. Osogami, T., Harchol-Balter, M., Scheller-Wolf, A.: Analysis of cycle stealing with switching times and thresholds. Perform. Eval. 61(4), 347–369 (2005)
32. Sharma, V., Thomas, A., Abdelzaher, T., Skadron, K., Lu, Z.: Power-aware qos management in web servers. In: RTSS'03: Proceedings of the 24th IEEE International Real-Time Systems Symposium, p. 63. IEEE Computer Society, Washington, DC, USA (2003)

The Monitoring Function

5

Monitoring can be seen as putting the *self* into self-management. Just as in psychology, the self is the representation of one's experience or one's identity; in autonomic computing, the data obtained from monitoring contributes to the representation of the system's experience or current state, self-knowledge if you like. Knowing the system state both from a functional and non-functional perspective is fundamental to being able to perform the operations necessary to achieve system goals at the desired level.

To maintain the analogy, just as a human can become self-conscious, that is, excessively conscious of one's appearance or manner leading to suboptimal functioning, so too can an autonomic system. Here where there is too much monitored data or the understanding of that data is erroneous or unclear which means the system is trying to change but does not know how to. Therefore, there have been a number of approaches to the monitoring of autonomic computing systems, the aim being to minimise the intrusiveness of the monitoring function while ensuring sufficient system self-awareness to optimise decision-making.

This section will focus on the monitoring function. To this end, we focus on the establishment of absolute measureable technical metrics that represent the performance or state of the system. This data can then be processed and these conclusions used to derive whether or not a system is meeting its quality levels or fulfilling a contractual obligation at the much higher levels of abstraction.

P. Lalanda et al., *Autonomic Computing: Principles, Design and Implementation*,
Undergraduate Topics in Computer Science, DOI 10.1007/978-1-4471-5007-7_5,
© Springer-Verlag London 2013

5.1   Introduction to Monitoring

Monitoring[1] generally refers to the systematic collection of relevant information with the purpose of understanding, evaluating and/or controlling a targeted system. Within the autonomic computing context, monitoring represents an essential initial activity in the self-management cycle of any autonomic system. Here, monitoring ensures the runtime acquisition of information that is relevant to autonomic administration processes. This information can represent either data related to the autonomic system's context (or external environment) or data related to the internal state of its managed resources. The former is essential to the autonomic system's context awareness and the latter to its self-awareness characteristics (as defined in Chap. 2). Finally, to close the self-management loop, the system's self-adjusting capability enables it to adapt to changing conditions (developed in Chap. 6).

Monitoring data collected over a longer term helps develop various models of the managed artefacts and of their execution context. Additionally, monitoring data collected at a certain instant indicates the present state of such entities. Basic autonomic managers can simply react in response to currently reported system states. More sophisticated ones can compare current states with desirable states and accordingly determine and execute self-adjusting plans. Moreover, they can rely on models and historical information to predict future states considering the current situation and the envisaged effects of possible actions; this renders system adaptation more viable and efficient.

Let us now take a few concrete examples that illustrate how different forms of monitoring can actually contribute to achieving the most important self-capabilities of autonomic systems. First, monitors for software component instances and their interconnections can be introduced to determine the runtime architecture of an administered application. Such architectural model can be subsequently used for self-repair, when the current state indicates, for example, a missing component or connection. It can also be used for self-optimisation, where the current architecture can be replaced with a better performing one. Similarly monitoring can be implemented to model the hardware system topology and detect, via 'heartbeat' or 'keep-alive' messages or pulses, when a machine or connection becomes defective and needs self-repair. More fine-grained monitors can dynamically trace functional calls through interconnected computing entities, determining frequent execution paths and detecting potential performance bottlenecks or design anti-patterns that require self-optimisation. Various performance parameters such as response time and resource consumption can be monitored to evaluate the system's current performance and whether consequent self-optimisation is a necessity. Finally, autonomic managers themselves can be monitored by higher-level meta-management processes, to adapt their structures and behaviours.

---

[1] To monitor (vb): "to watch, keep track of, or check usually for a special purpose" (Merriam-Webster online dictionary—http://www.merriam-webster.com/dictionary/monitoring); "to watch and check a situation carefully for a period of time in order to discover something about it" (Cambridge Advanced Learner's dictionary—http://dictionary.cambridge.org/dictionary/british/monitor_5).

Considering the actual architecture of an autonomic manager, the monitoring function requires at least two types of components: sensor touchpoints for extracting the actual data and monitor components for integrating the data into self-management control loops. Chapter 4 introduced essential sensing and monitoring concepts and showed how these functionalities integrate into the logical MAPE-K architecture.

An important remaining question relates to the manner in which raw monitoring data is actually transformed into information and knowledge that are relevant to the manager's reasoning processes. Depending on the constructed model types and the reasoning processes that use them, information may be required from the monitoring function in different formats or levels of abstraction. For example, managing the performance of a computer cluster may require fine-grained measurements of each server's resource consumption as well as aggregated measurements of the cluster's overall load. Moreover, such information may be provided either in a system-specific format, such as the concrete CPU consumption, or as a domain-specific indicator, like a critical state signal. In such cases, the monitoring function must additionally process collected data so as to deliver it to the decision processes with the expected format and semantics. Similarly, correlating causes and effects in order to form an efficient feedback loop may require the monitoring function to associate data of different natures and over various periods, for example, it could confirm that an action has been successfully executed at a certain instant and observe the outcome effects at a later time.

Hence, in addition to collecting and delivering raw information, the monitoring function may initiate various data-processing and scheduling operations, including aggregation, filtering and synchronisation, for obtaining more abstract, domain specific indicators. Here, the boundaries between the monitoring and analysis components of the logical MAPE-K architecture may become blurred, depending on the concrete architectural solution for each particular system. In some cases, monitoring and analysis can remain as clearly separated as indicated in the MAPE-K design. Other systems may employ data-mediation solutions to simultaneously perform monitoring and analysis operations and provide state information from different perspectives and at various abstraction levels. Chapter 9 provides an example data mediation framework—Cilia mediation—that can be employed for such purposes. Finally, certain solutions may prefer to use external analysis services [1],[2] for processing large amounts of collected information. Indeed, efficiently extracting and managing logging information can represent a research topic in itself [2].

Monitoring represents a vast topic encapsulating various subjects and raising requirements that differ quite significantly depending on the administered system and targeted objectives. In this chapter, we generally concentrate on performance monitoring, as an important QoS concern commonly specified in Service-Level Agreements (SLAs). This provides an illustrative example of the main concerns raised by system monitoring.

---

[2] An increasing number of log management services are becoming available to deal with the progressively high amount of system monitoring data. These include open-source solutions, such as GrayLog2 (http://graylog2.org), LogStash (http://logstash.net) or Sentry (http://sentry. readthedocs.org/en/latest), and commercial services, including LogEntries (https://logentries.com), Sumologic (http://www.sumologic.com), Loggly (http://loggly.com) or Splunk Storm (https:// www.splunkstorm.com).

5.2   Performance Monitoring

Computer performance monitoring is an activity that has been carried out since the invention of computing and, put simply, is the measurement of how well the system is doing what it was designed to do. Traditionally performance data was available to those interested via system performance logs, and a large range of performance analysis tools were developed to allow the user to make sense of those logs, mostly using statistical analysis techniques. In the early days of autonomic computing, these logs were also used to help drive autonomic management, for example, IBMs Log Trace Analyzer (LTA) that was part of the autonomic computing toolkit [3].

Many computer performance metrics have been established to allow us to communicate the system's non-functional state, and benchmarks have been developed to allow us to compare different systems or versions of a given system or algorithms. Initially the processing speed was deemed as the most important performance metric, but as more components were added to the computing infrastructure, new metrics that better represent their performance, or some notion of end-to-end performance, have since been derived. The major metrics are those that provide a notion of throughput (work done over time), component utilisation, or the time to carry out a particular task (response time is one example). The most popular general performance metrics are:

- *Instructions per second (IPS)*—This is essentially a measure of processing speeds; this metric represents the number of predefined (usually artificial) instruction sequences that can be run over a given unit of time for a particular CPU. This metric is useful to compare CPUs; however, it has been criticised because the instruction sequences may not be representative of the work load that that CPU will undertake. Further, other components that interact with the processor may have a large impact on that processor's performance, and therefore this decoupling of CPU measurements of performance and performance metrics relating to other components may mean IPS becomes meaningless. Perhaps the most used metric in this class is MIPS, millions of instructions per second, which has been used to describe the capacity of a machine since its inception in the 1970s.

- *Floating-point operations per second (FLOPS)*—This metric is similar to the IPS, above, as it also represents a notion of processing throughput. It was primarily designed to make comparisons between machines designed to carry out the heavy mathematics required by scientific applications, hence the focus on floating-point operations in particular. Like with IPS, a predefined set of instructions compose a benchmark that, in some cases, have been standardised, to permit fair comparisons. Interestingly, this metric is used to compare supercomputers in the yearly Top500 competition. Currently the top machines are running in the petaFLOPS (1015 FLOPS) region of performance.

- *Response time*—This metric represents the length of time a system takes in carrying out a functional unit of processing. It is a measurement of the time duration taken to react to a given input and is predominately used in interactive systems. Therefore, one example would be the time instant at which the first character of the response is received on the computer screen when the user hit 'return' to initiate some processing; a computer game would become unplayable if the user were to experience response time lag. Responsiveness is also a metric used in measuring real-time systems. Here the elapsed time between the moment the real-time task (or thread) is ready to execute until the moment it finished is measured.

- *Latency*—This is a measure of time delay experienced in a system and is generally used when describing the elements of the computer that concern communication. For example, to establish an idea of network performance, one could measure round-trip delay whereby the time for a packet to be sent until it is received back at the same machine is measured, for example. Latency takes into account not only the CPU (or CPUs) that processes that packet but, more importantly, the queuing delays that incur during the trip that the packet took.
- *Utilisation and load*—These metrics are intertwined and primarily used to understand the resource management function. Utilisation metrics provide a notion of how well a given system component is being used and is described as a percentage utility. For example, a CPU running at 90 % utilisation means that over a given Window of time, the CPU was used for 90 % of that time. Load too is a measure of work performed by the system and is usually reported as a load average for a given period of time. The load metric is typically calculated as a weighted average of the processes in the operating system's run queue over time; so it does not only measure the work carried out by the CPU but gives an indicator of how well that CPU is serving the jobs scheduled for it. For example, one could have a CPU that is 99 % utilised but no tasks ready and waiting to run; however another could also be 99 % utilised but have a large number of tasks in the run queue, which represents a much heavier load.

There are many more performance metrics that can be used. Some may focus on costs, such as transactions per unit cost or a function of reliability (length of time the system has been in operation without crashing) or a function of availability to indicate that the system is ready to be used when needed. Others may focus on size or the weight of the system; this indicates how portable the device is; smart phones or laptops are compared using such metrics.

With the recent interest in green computing, other cost metrics are coming to the fore in the form of measures of energy efficiency. In particular, performance per watt is being measured and represents the rate of computation delivered by a machine for each watt of power consumed. The computation rate is typically the number of FLOPS or MIPS achievable for each watt. However, given the cost of cooling larger systems, the total energy cost may also be included. Correspondingly the heat generated by machine components is also being used as a performance metric. Like with other performance indices, a benchmark may be developed for comparative purposes. One such benchmark is the GCPI (Green Computing Performance Index) that has evolved from the high-performance computing community's industry standard performance benchmarks. These performance metrics mostly focus on the performance of larger server systems and systems housed in data centres; however, at the mobile and laptop end of the computing field energy, consumption has been a focus for some time due to such devices being battery powered.

There are many raw performance metrics that enable us to better understand the non-functional state of the system, or provide a measurable means to allow us to detect an event that has occurred in the system that has changed its non-functional behaviours. However single metrics measured in isolation may not be enough to understand the system, instead performance may be required to be derived from combinations of such metrics. An example would be where an autonomic system is required to balance the conflicting goals of maximising performance while minimising energy consumption. This system may have a rule that says if the CPU is saturated (exhibits a high utilisation), start a new virtual machine by bringing up a new physical machine, move some of the jobs to the new machine and then carry out load balancing between the two. If the system sees that its CPU is 99 % utilised, it may think that the CPU is saturated. However on examining the load average where it was found to be low, bringing up a new physical machine in this instance would be costly in terms of energy consumption (and performance), so CPU saturation in isolation is not a good indication of current performance. Therefore combinations of metrics are required to be used to better understand what is going on in the system and to make more informed decisions.

5.3   Knowing What to Monitor and Monitoring Overheads

One of the main challenges in building an autonomic system is to determine which information best represents the system's behaviour and when and how it should be obtained. This section concentrates on how one decides on what to monitor. Subsequent sections focus on how to obtain that data.

In most autonomic systems, we monitor both changes in state and/or event occurrences, and these may be measured for different system components at differing levels of abstraction. The monitoring cycles of each of these two may be heterogeneous in that one state may be measured once per hour and another every second; typically reflecting the granularity of each feedback cycle designed into the autonomic monitor.

Approaches to understanding what to monitor very much depend on the system in question. A legacy system may have performance monitoring tools readily available that have been monitoring and reporting performance for many years. In this scenario, a performance analyst may have a great deal of experience in what exactly to look for in the usually large amounts of performance statistics and how to process this to recommend meaningful actions. Harnessing this knowledge and experience is key to being able to evolve a legacy system into an autonomic system. Here we are essentially automating the performance analyst and technical support roles, replacing their functions with the automatic manager. Mapping the logic of these roles, though not straightforward, is relatively tractable. However, for a system that is being designed from scratch, we may not have this experience and knowledge readily. Of course, one may have access to performance and technical experts who can help the development of the autonomic manager's logic. Here, such domain experts, specialists in running banking systems or Web services are able to apply their knowledge to the new autonomic system.

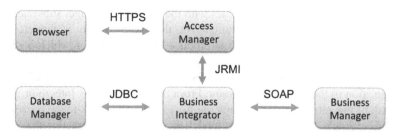

Fig. 5.1   Autonomic element

One starting point is to understand the goals of the autonomic manager. If its job is to ensure the system will be running with a 90 % uptime, then one would start by identifying the possible causes of failure. This means that we need detailed understanding of the system's components and their interaction. Some of those components may indeed be legacy systems themselves, and some may be under the jurisdiction of another business concern and provide a service to the system under focus. Therefore the software that has the potential to fail is embedded throughout potentially many subsystems.

Therefore it is paramount that some form of model of the system is established so that this problem can be tackled through a divide and conquer approach. Hierarchical-based performance monitoring and diagnoses are a concept that has been around for some time [4, 5], as far back as 1991 architectural models were being used to simplify this process. Some hierarchical models that can be used today are state transition or other architecture models [6, 7] or use cases [8]. Both represent the flow of logic, data and process activations. They represent both the structure and behaviour of the system. From this, one can identify where potential failures may occur. However, in larger systems, it is a more difficult task to identify the source(s) of error even when using such modelling tools. However, it is valuable to be able to identify failure early so that amends can be made.

An example of a hierarchical approach comes from Haydarlou et al. (see Fig. 5.1). Here they use a combination of abstraction and use cases to establish what to monitor and when [8]. They divide the system into levels, which helps with large and/or complex systems. At the highest level, the application is described as being composed of a number of communicating subsystems, which they call runnables. At the next, lower level, each subsystem is composed of a number of components, and finally, each component is composed of a number of classes and methods. The use cases then represent the flow of logic or interactions between runnables. An example [8] is a secure portal authentication request, and this is described at the application level of abstraction below.

In the example in Fig. 5.1, a portal application is accessed by business users via a Web browser who provide their certificates to the Access Manager subsystem using HTTPS negotiation. When the certificate has been received, the Access Manager verifies it and passes it to the Business Integrator subsystem over a JRMI connection which in turn communicates with the Database Manager subsystem via JDBC. In the Business Integrator component, the user's identity is extracted and matched against the user's password to produce login information which is sent to the Business Manager subsystem (a legacy back-end system using a SOAP connection). The Business Manager authenticates the user and returns the result of the authentication to the Business Integrator. From this, the Business Integrator passes the result of the authentication through the Access Manager back to the browser.

In this example, the architecture is modelled, at a level of abstraction that shows the interactions between components; see Fig. 5.1. They then move down a level of abstraction in the hierarchy to focus on these interactions because this is where the potential for failure resides, for example, a broken connection, an incorrect start-up sequence of runnables or excessive heap usage. Therefore in this example, the monitoring task will be positioned to report connections between these runnables, for example, in this case sensor code is automatically generated to monitor the output state of the invocation between the components. Another example that is supported by this approach is at a further lower level of abstraction. Here the occurrence of a given event (e.g. a NullPointerException) can be monitored, in a similar way to how we carry out exception handling. Here the self-monitoring engine again generates sensor code that gathers information (such as time-stamp, stack trace, name and line number) about the exception which in turn is passed to the analysis element of the MAPE-K loop. To monitor state changes, the system may choose to sense a value before and after the instantiation of a component for comparative purposes. The system that Haydarlou et al. propose is one that automatically places sensors within the managed element's (i.e. the runnables) code; they also permit complementary user-specified sensor placement.

In addition to varying the level of abstraction, the reporting period and amount of sensor data measured can vary. As mentioned previously, the amount of data monitored can not only directly affect the autonomic manager's ability to understand what is going on in the system but also affect the autonomic manager's ability to compute conclusions and take action in a timely manner. To improve this, one could reduce the amount of data measured; however, this may increase the likelihood of missing an event or cause the adaptivity to lag—meaning the system is not agile enough to adapt quickly to change. Moreover, given that sensors are lines of code that run with the system components (usually within the system components), they too consume system resources, thus directly affecting the performance of managed elements. This is in terms of the resources being used to run the sensing code but also in terms of the dynamic scheduling decisions the operating system may make when deciding to run that code. This situation can be overcome through adapting the monitoring function to the context, that is, depending on the situation, more monitoring data may be gathered and in other cases less—further the number of components monitored can be likewise adapted.

The data values read from a sensor obviously must be augmented with a mechanism to identify that sensor. Also data regarding the moment that the observation occurred is also required therefore quantitative temporal information, usually in the form of a time-stamp, is added to the message communicating the sensed value.

In a distributed system, this method of identifying the time of the observation may be problematic due to different hardware clocks not being synchronised resulting in the observation moment being represented by different times.

5.4 Profiling

There are a number of self-awareness data gathering techniques that can be combined to obtain a view or profile of the system. These we call profiling tools, and their primary aim is to obtain runtime information to characterise the behaviour of the system. There are a number of approaches to this summarised below, from [13]:

- *Manual instrumentation*—One of the most direct ways to obtain information about the runtime behaviour of a program is to manually inject monitoring code into a program. However, this can be a complex approach and potentially error-prone, intrusive and impractical in complex applications. This is not only because both knowledge of the managed element and its interfaces are required, but there may be side effects due to altering code that can affect both the monitored element and other elements that rely on it.

- *Compiler-based instrumentation*—Profile code may be introduced automatically by some compilers. This obviously occurs at compile time which assumes one has access to the source code to be able to compile it. Nevertheless this approach has the potential to be less error-prone than manual injection of profile points; assuming the complier's profiling action has been well reasoned in advance by those who supply the compiler. Though compiler-based instrumentation can ensure that the profiling code is syntactically correct, one is limited to only the features that come with that compiler. Furthermore, semantic errors can occur even here, or temporal side effects as, again, extra code are being added to the managed element. Once the program has been compiled with profiling features enabled, extraction tools can be used to capture the profiled data for analysis. This is the approach used by GNU gprof.[3]

- *Interception-based instrumentation*—Languages, like Java or Python, that can be interpreted or executed in virtual environments, can also provide instrumentation at the virtual machine level. In many cases, hooks are used, that is, predefined points in the execution where monitoring code can be attached to report performance data or generate event notifications. This technique is dynamic and minimises intrusiveness in that it does not require changes to the managed element's code. It also permits the development of the monitored program code to be decoupled and abstracted from the monitoring code. For many of these systems, the types of hooks are predefined by the virtual environment, for example, JVMTI[4] (JVM Tools Interface), .NET and the Python profiling module. More recently aspect-oriented approaches have been deployed [9]. Here the programmer can

---

[3]GNU gprof profiler: http://www.cs.utah.edu/dept/old/texinfo/as/gprof.html

[4]JVM Tool Interface: http://docs.oracle.com/javase/7/docs/platform/jvmti/jvmti.html

define *pointcuts* as points where the execution flow can be intercepted by an aspect code and the aspect is programmed separately and weaved into the application code at compile time. This approach is flexible in that custom monitoring code can be developed in an independent way.

- *Statistical profiling*—Statistical profilers use regular sampling at the hardware and/or operating system level while leaving the code binaries untouched. The hardware or operating system kernel is probed to provide an approximate view of the behaviour of the application. The precision of the data gathered may depend on the frequency of the sampling, though intrusiveness is still relatively low. The flexibility of this technique is limited, however, as the information obtained is mostly general and not easily associated with specific parts of a given monitored element. Examples of such tools are Intel VTune,[5] AMD CodeAnalyst [10] and Apple's Shark.[6]

In the next section, we discuss the advantages of profiling in terms of monitoring costs.

5.5   Monitoring Overheads

The cost of adding autonomic capabilities must be outweighed by the benefits of either a self-optimising system that performs better or a self-healing system that runs reliably for a considerable lifetime.[7] The cost of the analysis components of the MAPE-K loop and the reconfiguration or adaptation mechanisms obviously contribute to the overheads of an autonomic system. However, as we have seen, monitoring alone can have a large impact on this overhead also.

Let's illustrate how this cost can escalate. Take a simple measurement of system load as defined by the UNIX operating system for a single-processor machine. Load is a metric generated by the operating system; in fact it generates three load average numbers in the kernel. By issuing the `uptime` command in the shell, one can access these numbers. The following example was taken from one of this book's author's machines while typing this page:

```
vm-shell1% uptime
  17:35:51 up 11 days, 22:38, 9 users, load average:
    0.08, 0.03, 0.05
```

The exact meaning of load varies between UNIX-like systems; however, traditionally if a computer is idle, it has a load number of 0. Each process, whether it is

---

[5]Intel(R) VTune™ Amplifier—Performance Profiling Tools: http://software.intel.com/en-us/intel-vtune-amplifier-xe

[6]Shark User Guide: https://developer.apple.com/legacy/mac/library/documentation/Developer Tools/Conceptual/SharkUserGuide/SharkUserGuide.pdf

[7]Or a self-protecting system that can react to detected threats or a self-configuring system that can dynamically integrate new components, etc.

using the CPU (i.e. it is in the run queue) or is waiting for the CPU (in the ready queue), increases the load number by 1. The average load itself is calculated using an exponentially *damped/weighted moving average* of this load number. Therefore the load averages reflect the system utilisation that occurred over the past 1, 5 and 15 min of system operation.

The load figure is usually obtained by periodically sampling the state of the scheduler. An alternative would be to carry out calculations at a finer grain, that is, when the scheduler enforces a change of state. However, this would be impossible to realise as the scheduler is central to the operating system function, and so its efficiency impacts significantly on the overall system's performance. Note that in the scheduler, events are plentiful and frequent, processes can move from run to ready or wait states, etc. every 100 ms. There is a slight disadvantage to the periodic sampling approach—it may not exactly reflect actual system behaviour. Let's drill down a little further as an example. The clock tick that determines how Linux systems run the load calculation function is based on the clock frequency at 5 Hz, which equates to the load code running every 5 s [11].

As the reader can hopefully see, to just understand the load of a single CPU, albeit not even a 100 % accurate representation of load, will cost the system at least in terms of reading the current load (active_tasks), reading the older averages from the three time period arrays (EXP_n), then carrying out the updating calculations of the three moving averages (avenrun) and then writing out the updated values back to the three time period arrays. This has to happen every 5 s! This is a trivial example; imagine how much the monitoring functions alone would cost in terms of a full autonomic system's overheads.

5.6 Monitoring for *Free*

The monitoring function can be seen as active or passive. Here, active monitoring involves the placement of probes into the system to monitor its function. We discuss this more in the next section. Alternatively passive monitoring is where state information is captured by an external monitoring element or service and this data is provided to the autonomic manager. The code to do this can be developed as part of the autonomic system architecture. However, there exist a number of tools that carry out this function, and some of these come with the operating system—for free.

We describe the monitoring function as being for 'free' in this example because typically the autonomic system is placed on one or many machines that run an operating system and all modern operating systems (bar some embedded systems) come fully instrumented and very able to provide performance statistics concerning system operation. The load average example presented in the last section is an example of some of the statistics being recorded automatically. Since the operating system has to constantly probe its performance anyway, the autonomic manager may as well make use of that information.

Typically the autonomic manager will wish to monitor the 'health' of the system. Runtime information such as CPU utilisation, memory and network usage can be

Table 5.1 vmstat and top performance reporting tools that report operating system and virtual memory statistics; it obtains its data from the UNIX virtual file system /proc

Sample UNIX performance statistics	
Vmstat: memory statistics	Top: process statistics
The number of processes waiting for runtime or in uninterruptible sleep	Process priority
Memory: the amount of virtual memory used or idle memory left and of memory used as buffers or cache. Amount of inactive and active memory	Last used processor
Swap: the mount of memory swapped in from disk or to disk	%CPU usage and % memory usage
IO: the rate of data blocks received and sent to/from the block device	CPU time the task has used since it started
System: the number of interrupts per second (which includes the clock) and the number of context switches per second	Virtual image used by the task
CPU percentage of the CPU spend running non-kernal code, kernel code, idle, waiting for IO and stolen from a virtual machine	The swapped out portion of a task's total virtual memory image
Successful reads/writes, time spend reading/writing	Code size, Data+Stack size
	Page fault count
	Dirty pages count
	Process status

Table 5.2 Sample of Windows statistics, originating from the WMI

Sample of Windows performance statistics	
Win32_PerfFormattedData_OS_System: operating system statistics	Win32_PerfFormattedData_PerfOS_Memory Class: memory statistics
ContextSwitchesPerSec;	AvailableMBytes;
FileControlBytesPerSec;	CacheBytes;
FileDataOperationsPerSec;	CacheBytesPeak;
FileReadBytesPerSec; FileWriteBytesPerSec;	CacheFaultsPerSec;
PercentRegistryQuotaInUse;	PageFaultsPerSec
Processes;	PageReadsPerSec;
ProcessorQueueLength;	PagesInputPerSec; PagesOutputPerSec;
SystemCallsPerSec;	
SystemUpTime;	

obtained directly from the operating system. The length of time the system has been running is useful to understand how reliable the system is and is also a metric that can be obtained from the operating system.

Not only can runtime and accumulative information be obtained for 'free' but other relatively more static data such as the names of the nodes in the system, the processor capacity of each, memory sizes, communications bandwidth and disk meantime before failures may be available. Tables 5.1 and 5.2 show a very brief overview of the sorts of performance information provided by the two major flavours of operating system used in enterprises today: UNIX-like systems and Windows.

As described by Table 5.1, many of the statistics used by UNIX-like systems' management tools come from /proc. This virtual file system presents performance information about the machine components such as memory and processes as a hierarchical file directory-like structure and is mounted at boot time. Likewise, as depicted in Table 5.2, the Windows-like operating systems also provide such services. Windows Management Instrumentation (WMI) provides an operating system interface that permits the ability to instrument the system.

Essentially the ultimate aim is to design an autonomic architecture such that the autonomic function itself has as low an impact on the system that is being monitored. Some approaches use third-party monitors; however, if those monitors are using the same computing resource as the monitored element, then the aforementioned goal is unattainable as the probes and data messages will consume the same CPU, memory and communications channels as the monitored element. On the other hand, there is an advantage to decoupling the autonomic functionality, in terms of reaping the benefits of abstraction in software engineering terms. That is, an autonomic system is less difficult to develop, debug and maintain if it is less complex; as a result, the separation of the monitoring concern from the main function of the monitored system is therefore advantageous.

5.7 Building Probes

So far we have described the trade-off between information richness and accurate autonomic problem determination. Essentially the ideal is an optimisation that minimises the number of sensors or probes that are required to sample system state and report it somewhere (a task that perhaps includes expensive disk saves) and yet maximises the autonomic manager's notion of current system operation. To this end, the developer must establish what sensor types are required and the scope that they cover. Some of these come from the 'free' monitoring systems described in the last section. At the other extreme is the purposeful placement of code that records system state values or sets a trace on values that compose a set of operations. For example, while system load can be obtained from the operating system, the response time of a particular transaction or complex task within the system will require some code embedded at the start and end of that transaction to establish time differences. This not only impacts on the performance of the system in terms of the overheads that are now attributed to the monitoring process but also contributes to the complexity of the system. Intuitively one would wish to develop simple sensors that cover a well-defined minimal scope so that debugging the autonomic system's interface to the managed system and the autonomic system's function is less complex. However to establish a richer understanding of the managed system, we would require a larger number of sensors, and this means that the system is required to have more probes or to carry out more probing of the managed system. As stated before, a balance is required.

Once we have established the sensors that are required, the observation points need to be identified, and obviously both are closely coupled. From this, the probes can be placed.

At this point, raw data extracted by probes must be integrated into the autonomic management process. Two main functions are generally required in this regard: information communication and, potentially, information preprocessing. Communication is compulsory as data extracted by sensors must be sooner or later transmitted to the autonomic managers' monitor components. Preprocessing is optional and may be executed either by sensors (before communication), by monitors (after communication) or by both. On the sensor side, some analysis code can be added to enable the preprocessing of the information gathered by the probes to reduce sensing communication costs. For example, the sensing function may obtain response times every 5 s but only report the average response time per minute to the autonomic manager. This is essentially trading-off processing time against the volume of data that is sensed, where some form of preprocessing of sensed data can be carried out and only the result of this sent to the autonomic manager. On the autonomic manager's monitor side, similar analysis code can be introduced for preprocessing raw data into more relevant information, such as higher-level domain-specific indicators. As previously indicated (in Sect. 5.1), preprocessing functions on the autonomic manager's side can be attributed to both monitoring and/or analysis components, with respect to the generic MAPE-K architecture.

So probes generally consist of code that instruments the managed software system and its execution environment to provide information about system and context state. In addition, physical probes can be introduced to monitor hardware resources or environmental parameters, such as temperature sensors in enterprise clusters or pervasive systems. Collected state data may be periodically communicated to the autonomic manager's reasoning processes, which then make decisions about how to change the system and implement self-properties (improve system performance for example). Certainly, in addition to input for the managers' decision-making logic, monitoring information can be used for knowledge-acquisition purposes. In all cases, when data aggregation or filtering is enabled, only preprocessed data or events are sent to the autonomic manager's information processing logic. That is, the probe touchpoints, monitoring and analysis components of the MAPE-K loop may be more closely coupled.

Alternatively, the monitoring functions may contain event-reaction rules or policies, for example, that not only trigger an event interesting to the autonomic manager but also indicate when to send the monitored data. The decision of when to communicate this data is important, however. One example could be where the state value may reach (or exceed) a threshold, and this triggers an action to pass on this information to the autonomic manager; this would be like the autonomic manager saying I only want performance data when the average response time is less than 10 ms for the last minute, for example. This communication may or may not contain the raw data that caused the event to be triggered. However, for most cases, it will contain temporal data to say either what time the event was triggered or after which instructions within a sequence the event occurred. Also, the time lag between the probe's measurement and its subsequent communication may also be important; if the lag is large, there could be a situation whereby the autonomic manager is acting on out-of-date information. Further, it is important to know where the event was triggered within the architecture of the system, both in terms of the software architecture and the hardware itself. For example, it might report a response time violation event if a probe read and calculated that response time for a given task was greater than a given threshold. It would report this violation to the autonomic manager with information about degree of violation in terms of time, what time it occurred information about what task (or tasks) was involved and on what node in the system this was running, etc.

The monitoring infrastructure, both at the probe and the monitor component levels, may be hierarchical in that data probed from lower layers in the system are passed to higher-level layers for correlation and analysis. This is typically the case when the autonomic manager system is also organised in a hierarchical fashion. As discussed in previously, the intermediate layers analyse and, perhaps, filter data which is then passed to the autonomic manager functions at each layer of the hierarchy. It may be sent to the layer above to take action upon the managed element. Correlation or corroboration is an important part of this process. This may compare readings from probes to ensure that the reading is accurate or reasonable within bounds. To do this, either moving Windows of historical readings are maintained and trends observed, or probe readings from similar processes running in the same environment may be compared to see if the current value is an outlier. The system then may decide to ignore the erroneous result or store it for later. Perhaps here, higher levels will be informed when a number of these unusual results occur. Beyond error detection, correlation and corroboration can be used to reduce the amount of data communicated from probes to monitoring and analysis functions and finally to the autonomic manager's decision logic.

The movement of monitoring data may not necessarily be in a hierarchical fashion. In more complicated systems where raw probe data is aggregated and passed around the system, a publish–subscribe mechanism may be used. Here, sensors supply or publish their results to a pool of such data. Then the autonomic managers that are interested in this data subscribe to receive notifications of changes in this data. Other sensors or monitoring components that have analytical capabilities may also subscribe to this to use for comparative or correlation purposes. An example of this is where some autonomic managers in the system react to specific aspects of system performance (e.g. transaction throughput) values, and therefore they subscribe to be notified regarding the throughput of a particular component. Therefore it will publish its interest as say 'current throughput of Web server 4 on node 9'. As one can imagine in a large enterprise-wide autonomic system, the amount of raw probe data can be immense. Therefore abstraction may be used to categorise notifications into themes, and the autonomic manager can then narrow the field of performance data

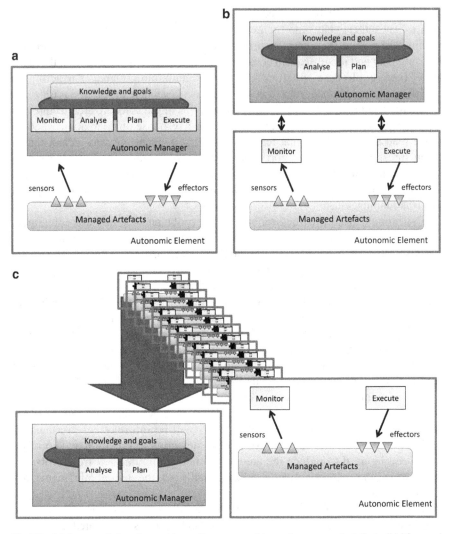

Fig. 5.2 (**a**) Autonomic function resides on the same machine as the managed artefacts. (**b**) Managed artefacts and autonomic functions reside on different physical machines. (**c**) A large-scale autonomic system consisting of many managed artefacts residing on numerous computers or devices

that it is interested in to be of a particular theme, for example, throughput problems or responsiveness problems. Data from a number of probes may have combined their knowledge to produce the data that feeds the published stream of notifications, in this instance.

The assumption thus far has been that the code to monitor the autonomic system is placed on the same hardware as the autonomic system itself (Fig. 5.2a).

However if economic costs are not prohibitive, there is nothing to prevent the system's architecture being composed of nodes dedicated solely to the monitoring and management of the system, while the remaining nodes are the nodes that run the monitored system (Fig. 5.2b). In such systems, a separate CPU and associated memory hierarchy is essentially carrying out the autonomic function. This kind of architecture is more common in systems that require either very complex analysis of the monitored data, and so a dedicated CPU is required, or they require the complex monitoring of very large-scale systems (1,000's of nodes).

An example of the former case, where the analysis is complex, is where Kalman filters are used to establish a model of the monitored system's state. This technique produces estimates of monitored values based on a series of measurements observed in the past, ensuring that noise, for example, has been filtered out. From this, the planning phase can better understand potential future state and better make decisions regarding how and when to adapt the system. Such an approach can require a large number of inputs, depending on the monitored system size, and as the processing consists of recursively iterating on this potentially noisy data, its processing is correspondingly complex, possibly consuming more CPU and other resources than the actual managed system could tolerate. Hence, it is best to place this analysis on another machine, perhaps even a supercomputer!

An example of the latter, the large-scale system, is InfoScope,[8] which continuously monitors planet-wide systems and consists of distributed monitoring facilities for thousands of nodes. Here mechanisms are used that improve the performance of the monitoring system through both tailoring and compressing the monitored data to best suit the current states of the system and the requirements of the autonomic function at that a given time. The probes remain with the managed system and communicate state and performance data to the separate computing entities that analyse the data. However, in an extremely large system, this too impacts on the performance of the system as the bottleneck becomes the communications infrastructure and the machine, or set of machines, that carry out the analysis; see Fig. 5.2c. Schemes to reduce the amount of monitored data that is communicated are favoured therefore.

5.8   Examples of Monitoring Tools, Frameworks and Platforms

In the previous sections, we saw that the monitoring functions of autonomic systems rely both on sensors embedded into relevant artefacts and on monitor components included in the autonomic managers' MAPE-K loops. Communication functions

---

[8]NCSU's InfoScope: Continuous Information Monitoring for Large-Scale Distributed Systems: http://dance.csc.ncsu.edu/projects/infoscope

are required to feed necessary information into the autonomic management process. Additionally, analysis functions, such as aggregation, filtering and scheduling, can be mixed with monitoring functions and placed within either sensors or monitors to provide preprocessed data into the autonomic managers' reasoning logic. Various architectural and technological solutions are possible for achieving such monitoring and analysis functions, depending on the specific requirements of each autonomic system. In this section, we illustrate a few examples of available solutions in order to provide an overall flavour of this vast domain.

First, numerous monitoring utilities are available for collecting different data types from various managed resources and context artefacts. For instance, for monitoring Java applications, the JVM™ Tool Interface[9] (JVMTI) provides a means for both extracting information and controlling applications running in a Java virtual machine (JVM). Targeting the performance management of component-based applications based on Java EE, the COMPAS[10] open-source framework was developed to support portable, extensible and adaptable EJB component instrumentation and monitoring. Also for enterprise systems, QMON [12] provides utility-aware QoS monitoring, for different Service-Level Agreement (SLA) classes. For the performance management of distributed systems at the resource level, the CLIF[11] open-source project provides a testing platform which includes both load-injection facilities and a wide range of resource monitoring probes (including CPU, memory and network bandwidth). For larger-scale systems like cloud and grid applications, the ganglia[12] open-source project relies on a hierarchical design for offering a scalable distributed monitoring system. Additional freeware monitoring facilities providing support for hierarchical organisation in grid and cloud environments include the Clomon[13] and Supermon[14]systems. On the industrial side, similar examples include the Paramon cluster monitoring, the Big Brother[15] Web-based network monitoring or IBM's Tivoli® Monitoring software[16] for managing operating systems, databases and servers.

Most of these tools represent mature, scalable and efficient monitoring solutions for the specific system types they were designed for. In addition, they are often bundled with complementary visualisation, analysis and control facilities providing a rich support for domain-specific system management.

---

[9]JVMTI homepage: http://docs.oracle.com/javase/1.5.0/docs/guide/jvmti; JVMTI replaces previous utilities that provided similar functions, namely, the Java Virtual Machine Profiler Interface (JVMPI) and the Java Virtual Machine Debug Interface (JVMDI).

[10]COMPAS project: http://compas.sourceforge.net

[11]CLIF project : http://clif.ow2.org

[12]Ganglia project: http://ganglia.sourceforge.net

[13]Clumon project: http://clumon.ncsa.illinois.edu

[14]Supermon project: http://supermon.sourceforge.net

[15]Big Brother® Software homepage: http://bb4.com

[16]Tivoli Monitoring software: http://www-01.ibm.com/software/tivoli/products/monitor

Increased demand for customisation and flexibility in certain managed systems fuelled the provisioning of reusable platforms and frameworks that facilitate the in-house construction of monitoring and analysis solutions. Notably, the concepts and architectures featured by data-mediation approaches appear as particularly suited for developing highly flexible and extensible applications for data collection, processing and delivery. Generally, data-mediation frameworks can be employed to develop directed graph-like structures, taking as input monitoring data from multiple heterogeneous sources and providing as output various domain-specific indicators, for multiple heterogeneous destinations or information consumers.

For example, within the application management realm, the Composite Probes framework prototype was developed to help handle the massive amounts of data extracted via CLIF monitoring[17] from distributed platforms. Composite Probes provided reusable support for the construction of flexible data-analysis hierarchies, similar to data-mediation graphs, capable of preprocessing information via customisable functions and at different abstraction levels. Subsequently, Cilia mediation[18] (or Cilia) was developed as a general-purpose data-mediation framework, highly adaptable to different application domains. Cilia can integrate an extensible set of probing and communication technologies and include diverse data-processing, scheduling and content-based routing functions. These features enabled Cilia-based data-mediation graphs to be developed for applications as diverse as pervasive monitoring and analysis, highly adaptable decision-making processes [13] and adaptive human-computer interaction solutions [14] [15].

Finally, another noteworthy development platform for monitoring and analysis solutions is provided by the Eclipse Test and Performance Tools Platform (TPTP) Project.[19] TPTP offers an open platform with several frameworks and services for enabling developers to build customised testing and performance tools. Existing tools include runtime application monitoring, tracing, profiling, log analysis, correlation and evaluation support.

As previously indicated, monitoring and analysis are vast subjects, and a myriad of open and commercial tools, frameworks and platforms are available to suit diverse systems and management requirements. Here, we have merely provided a few illustrative examples aiming to cover some of the most important categories of available utilities and solutions.

---

[17]Composite Probes and CLIF (http://clif.ow2.org) projects were developed at Orange Labs, France, and based on the Fractal component technology (http://fractal.ow2.org)

[18]CiliaMediation project (https://github.com/AdeleResearchGroup/Cilia) was developed by the Adèle team at University of Grenoble in collaboration with Orange Labs, France, and based on based on a dynamic service-oriented component technology—iPOJO/OSGi (www.ipojo.org) (discussed in Chap. 9).

[19]The Eclipse Test and Performance Tools Platform (TPTP) Project: http://www.eclipse.org/tptp

5.9   Monitoring the Monitors: Adaptive Monitoring

Balancing the amount of information required to understand a monitored system is non-trivial and can change as the system or its environment changes. Therefore to overcome this complexity, adaptive automatic monitoring systems have been proposed. These essentially adapt their monitoring frequency and data volumes and adjust the number and placement of probes/sensors to minimise the overhead of continuous monitoring while maximising the utility of the performance data.

There have been a number of schemes that aim to dynamically adjust the amount of monitored data being communicated around the system. For example, they may prioritise the events therefore ensuring that the autonomic manager is able to handle the important notifications first. This may also have the advantage that some of the other events triggered by the probes may disappear due the more important problem being solved. Alternatively, compression mechanisms have been used; monitored values are averaged to represent a given scope of the system's performance. In the aforementioned InfoScope approach, the monitoring system exploits knowledge on node's temporal correlations and distributed spatial correlations to reduce the amount of monitoring data required to be communicated to the autonomic manager. That is, if the system understands the relationship between the expected performance of a number of nodes (whose values correlate), then the monitored data value can be predicted; therefore, the communication of all the raw node data can be suppressed. Further, in a cluster of nodes, only one node may be required to send its raw monitored data where the data from the other nodes in the cluster can be inferred from that value. The approach is also adaptive in that both the monitored value predictors and the clusters can be adapted to match the variations in correlation patterns. As mentioned earlier, a further advantage of using correlations to reduce the communications overheads of monitoring systems is that correlations can also highlight where perhaps there is an error in the reported performance value(s) and if an error is detected, a message can flag this to the user (system manager) or it can be suppressed and not used by the autonomic manager. Alternatively, an adaptive monitor can adapt the sampling function when it sees potential problems with the samples to better understand if there is an error or a system glitch that requires the autonomic system to adapt to. Here the sample rate can increase, producing more performance data to enable the autonomic manager to receive more detailed performance data to better understand the anomaly. Some such systems focus on understanding the root cause of the problem through machine learning and data mining techniques. Here, the monitoring function can be adjusted to feed these techniques. The volume of monitored data can then be reduced when it is no longer needed.

For many autonomic systems, condition-action rules or policies have predefined triggers. These thresholds are, for many systems, hardwired. That is, their values have been defined at the time the autonomic system was architected and remain constant until they are discovered to be not so useful. Here they may well be updated manually. This approach is clean and simple but has obvious implications for the autonomic manager's ability to react to the system as it changes over time, that is, its environment changes or its purpose changes. To better 'future proof' the system, alternatives to the hardwiring approach are coming to the fore. Here, a feedback loop, dedicated to understanding how useful the parameters to measure and adapt in the autonomic system, is added. The autonomic manager too can change the parameters to ensure that the autonomic system as a whole better meats its goals.

Other more abstract approaches do not require the understanding of the monitored system but view the autonomic system in terms of its feedback loops—the aim being to maintain stability in the system via the adjustment of these feedback loops. One example of this is in AdaptGuard [16]. This system builds adaptation graphs by essentially 'sniffing' the monitored values coming from the probes to the autonomic manager. It is able to use this data to detect whether or not the system is likely to remain stable or not. If not, then stability recovery policies are put into action which may involve the user to intervene. These, like many of the systems presented in this subsection, are essentially autonomic, autonomic monitors!

5.10   Key Points

- This chapter has presented the many different methods and techniques that can be used to achieve the monitoring function in autonomic computing.
- Here we see that the monitoring function can have an important impact on the autonomic system's ability to understand its non-functional behaviours, its ability to perform, as well as impacting on the monitored element's performance. This can be in terms of probe code and perhaps even analysis code competing for the same resources as the monitored element itself!
- The numbers of, and the placement of, probes is an important issue therefore.
- We learned that the monitoring function of the autonomic system may double up as the performance reporting function for some systems. More commonly, operating system produced statistics are used to report performance and feed the autonomic monitoring function.
- Non-performance data that measures aspects such as the numbers of times a piece of code runs or uses specialist probes that determine some form of qualitative measure of the managed element's behaviour may also be used.
- We learned that there may be large volumes of such data produced and, depending on the kind of data gathered performance data, may be relayed to users in different ways. This may take the form of a call graph, detailing dependencies between method calls; statistical summaries, detailing resource consumption per method or unit of computation; or an execution trace, detailing sequence of method calls and performance related information, for example.

- We reiterated that the monitoring function is another component that adds complexity to the autonomic system. This function can also be adaptive in its own right by either adapting the focus of what is being monitored—deciding on which components are monitored and when or adapting the amount of times or numbers of samples that are required.
- We also discussed the irony that in situations where finer-grained monitoring is required during an 'interesting situation' to better understand the performance of what is going on at that time that extra monitoring has the potential to exacerbate the performance problem!

References

1. Biyani, V.: Log management as a service. What & why: Log management in cloud. Cloudspring, Nov. 2012. http://cloudspring.com/log-management-as-a-service
2. Chuvakin, A.A., Schmidt, K.J.: Logging and Log Management: The Authoritative Guide to Understanding the Concepts Surrounding Logging and Log Management, 1st edn. Syngress, Waltham (2012). 460 p. ISBN 1597496359
3. IBM.: Autonomic computing toolkit: Developer's guide. Technical Report SC30-4083-02, IBM. Available at http://www-128.ibm.com/developerworks/autonomic/books/fpy0mst.htm. Aug 2004
4. Mozetic, I.: Hierarchical model-based diagnosis. Int. J. Man-Mach. Stud. **35**(3), 329–362 (1991)
5. Garlan, D., Schmerl, B.: Model-based adaptation for self-healing systems. In: WOSS '02: Proceedings of the 1st Workshop on Self-Healing Systems, pp. 27–32, New York, 2002
6. Cheng, S.-W., Huang, A.-C., Garlan, D., Schmerl, B.R., Steenkiste, P.: Rainbow: architecture-based self-adaptation with reusable infrastructure. In: Proceedings of the 1st IEEE International Conference on Autonomic Computing ICAC, pp. 276–277, New York, 2004
7. Foster, H., Uchitel, S., Magee, J., Kramer, J.: LTSA-WS: a tool for model-based verification of web service compositions and choreography. In: ICSE 2006, pp. 771–774, Shanghai, China (2006)
8. Haydarlou, A.R., Oey, M.A., Overeinder, B.J., Brazier, F.M.T.: Use case driven approach to self-monitoring in autonomic systems. In: Proceedings of the Third International Conference on Autonomic and Autonomous Systems (ICAS07), IEEE Computer Society Press, Athens, Greece 2007
9. Kiczales, G., Lamping, J., Mendhekar, A., Maeda, C., Lopes, C., Loingtier, J.M., Irwin, J.: Aspect-oriented programming. In: ECOOP'97—Object-Oriented Programming, pp. 220-242. Springer, Jyväskylä (1997)
10. Drongowski, P.J., AMD CodeAnalyst Team, Boston Design Center.: An introduction to analysis and optimization with AMD CodeAnalyst Performance Analyzer. Advanced Micro Devices, Inc, Sunnyvale (2008)
11. Hughes, P., Navratilova, V.: Linux for Dummies Quick Reference, 3rd edn. IDG Books Worldwide, Foster City (2000). 256 p. ISBN 0764507605
12. Agarwala, S., Chen, Y., Milojicic, D.S., Schwan, K.: QMON: Qos- and utility-aware monitoring in enterprise systems. In: Proceedings of the 3rd IEEE International Conference on Autonomic Computing (ICAC'06), Dublin, Ireland, June 2006
13. Maurel, Y.: PhD thesis, CEYLON: a framework for creating extensible autonomic managers and dynamics or CEYLAN: Un canevas pour la creation de guestionnaires autonomiques extensibles et dynamiques', University of Grenoble (2010)
14. Avouac, P.A., Lalanda, P., Nigay, L.: Autonomic management of multimodal interaction: DynaMo in action. In: Proceedings of the 4th International Conference on Engineering Interactive Computing Systems, EICS'2012, June 25–28, pp. 35–44. ACM, Copenhagen (2012)

15. Avouac, P.A., Lalanda, P., Nigay, L.: Service-oriented autonomic multimodal interaction in a pervasive environment. In: Proceedings of the 13th International Conference on Multimodal Interfaces, ICMI'2011, 14–18 November 2011, Alicante, Spain, ACM, pp. 369–376 (2011)
16. Heo, J., Abdelzaher, T.: AdaptGuard: guarding adaptive systems from instability. In: The 6th International Conference on Autonomic Computing and Communications (ICAC '09), Barcelona, Spain, 15–19 June 2009

The Adaptation Function

6

Software adaptation is at the heart of autonomic computing. Indeed self-management cannot be reached without the ability to modify the structure and behaviour of a system. Unfortunately, software adaptation remains a particularly complex task. It requires changing low-level code, an act that is often complicated and intricate. Side effects that succeed an update are difficult to anticipate and to fix. An additional challenge specific to autonomic computing is that the code to be modified has already been run or is currently executing, meaning that computational state has to be identified and preserved.

The purpose of this chapter is to define precisely the notion of software adaptation and discuss the related challenges. It is also to present a set of techniques that can be used to implement self-managed software systems. As we will see, adaptation can be realised at different levels of abstraction, and very diverse approaches can be implemented. This diversity of technique is welcome. As said in previous chapters, a self-managed system is made of a number of collaborating autonomic elements with different requirements in terms of reactivity, scope, precision, etc. Different, complementary approaches are needed to meet these demands.

In this chapter, we will focus on techniques allowing dynamic updates. Indeed, more and more, users require updates to be dynamic, at runtime, as downtime is not an option; service interruption can be very costly and has to be avoided as much as possible. This is especially true for critical systems that may have to be updated tens or hundreds of times every year and that cannot be stopped that often.

P. Lalanda et al., *Autonomic Computing: Principles, Design and Implementation*, Undergraduate Topics in Computer Science, DOI 10.1007/978-1-4471-5007-7_6, © Springer-Verlag London 2013

6.1   Software Adaptation

In the context of autonomic computing, software adaptation is a discrete process allowing a software system to continuously meet its goals in a changing environment. As explained in Chap. 4 about architecture, this process is conducted by a set of collaborating autonomic managers.

Specifically, autonomic managers have to modify the structure or behaviour of a system. These notions of structure and behaviour take on many forms in software, and this has nourished a number of endless debates in the software engineering community. This is due to the fact that a software system can be perceived and manipulated at different levels of abstraction, which is a necessary instrument to allow us to handle complexity. As we will see later on, this allows software engineers (and autonomic managers!) to adapt a software system in many ways, using different techniques and levels of abstraction.

In concrete terms, the structure and behaviour of a software system resides in its binary code, its configuration data and the resources it uses (Fig. 6.1). Resources can be internal or external. Internal resources refer to services and facilities provided by the supporting execution infrastructure, like an operating system (OS), a virtual machine (VM) or more sophisticated middleware. External resources include services and data provided by remote facilities. Using such remote resources, like Web services for instance, is becoming increasingly popular in software engineering. This of course decreases the cost of code ownership and can improve performance, availability, etc.

So, for an autonomic manager, adapting a software system comes down to:
- Modifying the binary code
- Modifying data, local or remote
- Modifying resources, local or remote

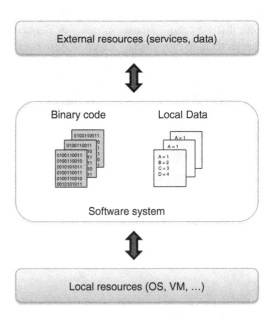

Fig. 6.1 Software structure

If the binary code is under your jurisdiction, you can change it (if you are the initial developer) or update it when new versions or patches are available and whenever you decide to; this is a bit different with external resources. At best, you can change some configuration parameters or switch to different services. But there is usually no way to change the internals of a service or the pace of its evolution since a third party controls it.

Adaptability is an essential requirement of software systems. This is not only due to the evolving nature of both the requirements and the execution environments but also due to the difficulties we encounter to build correct software systems. By correct, we mean software systems providing the services or capabilities demanded by users along with expected qualities like performance, resilience and availability. Since many systems are not perfectly correct in this sense at installation time, adaptations are obviously necessary.

By nature, an adaptation is carried out while the system is under operation. This means that the software system already has been running for some time when *something* is required to adapt. Let us refine that *something*. First, it can refer to a change in the computing environment. In this case, the software system has to be updated in order to integrate changes regarding its resources. The purpose is to maintain the systems' functionality while remaining in sync with its environment. Also, adaptation may be needed because the context *decides* it is time to do so. For instance, for an embedded system when the battery is low, it may be necessary to operate in a low-power mode that might, in turn, decrease computational precision.

Adaptation can also be triggered to provide functional evolutions. The goal here is to bring new services or capabilities or to modify the existing ones in order to better satisfy users or to take into account new running conditions (and related opportunities). Similarly, adaptation can bring non-functional evolutions. The purpose here is to modify the properties attached to the provided services or capabilities (again, to better satisfy users or to exploit new possibilities). For instance, changes can be brought to improve performance or security.

Last, but not least, fixing a bug is a good reason to perform an adaptation.

Software adaptation is a real challenge. As a subject, it has been studied for decades in the realms of software engineering, but for the most part, it still relies too often on ad hoc solutions. The bottom line is that most systems are not conceived to be easily adaptable. They are merely designed and coded to meet the requirements at hand, with little projection into the future. Some development methodologies, like agile approaches, even argue that explicitly preparing a software system for evolution is counterproductive, resulting in fat and slow code for uncertain, illusive gains. The consequence, and problem, is that adapting a software system can turn into a scary, uncontrolled process, requiring much expertise and huge effort.

Software adaptation is thus an open issue in many regards. It is however at the heart of autonomic computing. And the requirements here are very high! Adaptations have to be carried out on software that is already in operation, and well-defined support has to be explicitly provided so that autonomic managers can trigger safe and controlled adaptations in programmatic ways.

6.2   Code Adaptation

6.2.1   Upgrading Code

As explained before, adapting a software system comes down to modifying code, data or resources. Many of the current autonomic systems focus on data and resources. Technically speaking, it is much easier to change these elements, even if side effects still must be controlled, as for any modification. More and more, however, autonomic managers are used to carry out changes in the code structure.

The focus of this chapter is primarily on code adaptation, which is arguably a very complex activity. It generally takes the form of a two-phase process: first, the updated code is produced and then injected into the code under execution.

Code adaptations can intervene anywhere. They can affect any programming structure, whatever its level of abstraction, its role, its granularity, etc. In a component-based system, for instance, an adaptation may concern a complete component, some encapsulated data, a method of an encapsulated object, a connection between encapsulated objects, etc. Also, an adaptation can take any form. Returning to our component-based example, a new component can be created; an existing component can be modified, suppressed, duplicated and moved to another machine, and connections between components can be rebound.

An adaptation is generally not limited to a single, well-identified programming structure. It often affects a number of coupled structures that cannot be changed independently. In this context, controlling side effects becomes a major challenge. The impact of an adaptation is actually not directly related to software granularity or size but to its *coupling*. Coupling is a qualitative property measuring the dependencies between software elements. It is based on the number of links between elements and the complexity of these links. Thus, changing a configuration parameter, such as a simple integer, can potentially have a tremendous effect on a system. On the other hand, upgrading the supporting DBMS of a database can be almost transparent due when decoupling is well implemented (this is unfortunately not always the case [1]).

To understand how an autonomic manager can upgrade code, it is useful to know how this code is produced. As illustrated by Fig. 6.2, binary code is generally obtained through a number of transformations. The goal of this transformational approach is to break down complexity through decomposition into 'simple' structures that are manageable by human developers.

Thus, software systems are developed with programming languages providing notations and semantics. High-level structures are thus defined and composed to make up programs. The result, the source code, is then transformed into executable code by a compiler (and a linker) or by an interpreter. The code thus obtained is then deployed, loaded and launched on the target machine (see Chap. 1). Only then is the software system up and running!

There are actually many ways for an autonomic manager to modify binary code that has been already developed. First, when the software system to be modified has

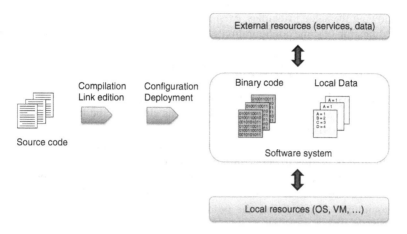

Fig. 6.2 Binary code modification

been developed in-house, a natural approach is to go back to source code, modify it and regenerate the binary code. This strategy best fits current software engineering practices. It is convenient in the sense that programmers in charge of adaptations can use a high-level programming language and generally benefit from advanced development environments. To be handled by an autonomic manager, the new code has to be placed on some facility (a repository for instance) from where it can be uploaded and integrated into the existing code.

However, existing binary code can be modified without returning to source files. Specifically, a way to obtain upgraded binary code is to recompile, or re-link, existing source code. This approach relies on conditional directives included in the source code. A preprocessor is then used to insert instructions or calls to specific libraries. For instance, the source code may have the following instructions that allow a piece of code to be tailored to a particular operating system (MSDOS in this example):

```
# if SYSTEM == MSDOS
        # include <msdos.h>
# else
        # include <default.h>
# endif
```

This approach is very convenient since upgraded code is obtained through 'simple' compilation. It is to be noted, however, that all possible runtime conditions have to be anticipated in the source code through conditional directives. The range of possible adaptations is de facto limited to expected situations therefore. Also, the source code has to be accessible by the autonomic managers so that they can recompile it.

Following the same principles, existing binary code can be customised through the modification of some configuration parameters. Those parameters can be defined and assigned in a text file. They can also be specified (and evaluated) when launching an application. In this latter case, restarting some modules is necessary in order to update binary code. This approach is often used today, notably in pervasive computing applications, for instance, where a process is being transferred between devices (e.g. a phone to a PC with a TV screen). In this situation, the binary code is not really impacted (where programming languages and CPUs permit). It remains the same; only a few variables impacting the behaviour are changed, for example, to adjust the text rendering to better suit the output device.

In order to ease adaptation and avoid side-effect issues, the source code can be prepared for evolution in advance. It is an approach advocated by the software product lines community that promote the production of collections of similar software systems from shared assets where software reuse is proactively engineered for.[1] Here, software artefacts that are likely to be context aware (i.e. able to adjust to their environment) are designed and implemented with adaptation in mind. Specifically, variation points are explicitly introduced in the source code in order to make room for late modifications. Variability is a property of software artefacts allowing them to be extended, modified, personalised or customised in order to meet some specific needs. A variation point embodies a delayed design decision. It can be complemented by possible choices, called variants. In the product-line approach, development is seen as a two-phase process. The purpose of the first phase is to develop the software architecture and a number of software artefacts with reuse and adaptation in mind. Facilities can be provided in order to ease the creation of adaptable artefacts. The purpose of the second phase is to reuse and adapt the artefacts produced during the first phase in order to obtain a software system in line with the requirements at hand. Here also, tools are generally provided to bring adaptations based on the variation points.

This approach can be used advantageously in autonomic computing. That is, it can be useful to determine and implement variation points in the code and let autonomic managers act on them when necessary. If variants are associated with variation points, modifications triggered by autonomic managers are safer and more controlled. Also, relationships between variation points can be established, meaning that a modification on a given point has to be followed by modifications on other points in order to leave the system in a coherent state.

As explained, autonomic managers can change configuration parameters, recompile some or modify source code. In any case, however, programmatic interfaces have to be provided and some variability has to be integrated, like options in a compilation for instance. This is especially true for modifications in the source code; an autonomic manager needs tools and interfaces to adapt the variation points. The bottom line here is that, whatever the approach, adaptations have to be prepared during the initial development phase. Otherwise, only the (human) developer can go through the code, at whatever abstraction level, and introduce the necessary modifications.

---

[1] http://www.sei.cmu.edu/productlines

6.2.2   Integrating Code

Once the new binary code that is better suited to the current runtime conditions has been produced by an autonomic manager or released by the maintenance organisation, it has to be installed and activated in the computing environment. To do so, it has to be integrated with the existing code: this means that 'new' and 'old' code must interact safely, preserving correctness.

Updates can be static or dynamic. Static update means that the software to be adapted is stopped and then restarted after modification. This is the simplest and most traditional method of integration. Here, the autonomic manager has to decide on the best moment to stop and restart the software. This is exactly what happens when your computer downloads the latest version of your preferred Internet browser. In some cases, however, the software system can decide by itself to reboot. This is for instance the case for major operating system upgrades. Static update is rather easy to implement, but it can be costly since it decreases the availability of the software. This can have very negative impacts in domains, such as in pervasive computing, where continuous services are needed. In addition, we are moving to a world where updates, easily made available on a Website, are more and more frequent. It is unacceptable that the system would halt for every update.

When interruptions are not permitted, the adaptation is said to be dynamic. A dynamic adaptation is always a delicate operation and must be conducted with care. The operation is complex for the simple reason that the software system to be modified is still running! This raises a number of specific issues related to code integration per se but also to software correctness and to the preservation of data and control flows, that is, state.

Indeed, the fact that the software has already been running before, this new activation completely changes the situation. A major issue is that internal computational states are often lost between two activations. In addition to that, the mere definition of state between two activations may be different, even incompatible (e.g. perhaps due to the use of new programming structures). Similarly, advanced transactions and isolation mechanisms may be needed to maintain state with regard to consistent interaction with other external software that has a dependency relationship with the software that is being integrated. However, this does not prevent these other software systems being placed in a pending state, which may imply that they suffer downtime or loss of quality in some way as a result.

Thus, for technical and business reasons, a number of software systems today require dynamic upgrades and without service interruption. However, dynamic updates should not endanger the correctness and robustness of software [2].

Correctness is an absolute. An updated software system often has to meet new or modified requirements. Regression tests and tests accounting for new features must then be somehow combined to make sure that the newly specified requirements are met. Test strategies are clearly impacted by the fact that the system continues to run. Verifications have to be conducted while the system is active and executing and, in general, cannot be performed as in traditional design-time testing.

Further, the ability to carry out dynamic updates should not alter the quality of a software system. Crashes, loss of data, inefficiency and so on are obviously not acceptable during the course of an update. The problem is that such bugs are very likely to occur if dynamic modifications are not perfectly controlled. A number of recurrent issues must be handled with care, especially those related to the preservation of the computational state (once again!). In particular, data and control flows must not be lost or altered after an update. Taking the classic example of a merchant Website, the active carts have to remain unchanged when a software update is carried out. Regarding control flows, connections between structures (e.g. class instances) must remain valid. That means, in particular, that a structure cannot be suppressed if another is using it (i.e. connections in an active control thread must not be invalidated). On the other hand, a structure not involved in the main control flow is said to be in a *quiescent* state and can be safely updated.

In general, it is not possible to upgrade active code. Active code corresponds to code being run or referenced in the execution stack. At best, the system can wait for the code to become inactive, which unfortunately is not always possible. For instance, some parts of code may always be referenced and the window to allow an update may never open. A common technique is to implement a *quiescence* protocol. The principle here is to intercept calls to the code to be changed and to wait for the code to become inactive. When this happens, the object is upgraded and the blocked callers are then resumed. The main issue here is that dependencies between the updated objects could result in very complex situations (such as deadlock, livelock and starvation).

If possible, a safe way to proceed is to carry out non-destructive updates, meaning that the structure of the software that existed before adaptation is not lost or, worse, unrecoverable. For instance, some programming languages allow the cohabitation of different versions of the same structure and provide an elegant solution to this so-called versioning problem. Destructive updates are easier to implement but, of course, can be rather hazardous. Let us take the example of Web services. Here, services provided by the system are regularly updated, including at the interface level. A non-destructive approach is to maintain the old interface for some time when creating new versions. Thus, clients can progressively adopt the new interfaces. In a more destructive philosophy, old interfaces would be immediately suppressed! This is easier to manage, of course, but the risk of compatibility problems at the client side is higher.

A very popular approach to implement dynamic updates, known as *rolling upgrades*, is to use hardware redundancy, especially in mission-critical, software intensive or enterprise systems. Essentially, the principle is to deploy the upgraded version of a software system on a new or alternative machine and to activate it. In the meantime, the software to be updated continues to run and to provide full services. A load balancer is used to redirect all the requests that were sent to the original software to its new version. At some point in time, the original software becomes idle and the swap between old and new versions can be made. This approach is costly since additional hardware has to be used and maintained. In addition, it demands the synchronisation of states between old and new versions of the software. This is however an approach used today in cloud computing (coupled with virtualisation techniques) where resources are added on demand or the load gets too high.

An alternative approach is to use redundant software, at the operating system or virtual machine levels. Here, when an application has to be updated, a second OS or VM is started on the same machine and an upgraded version of the application is installed and activated. As before, requests are redirected to the new software version as long as necessary. The replacement is made when the software to be changed becomes idle.

This approach is popular and effective but...not so simple! First, state transfer remains a potentially complex operation. It requires defining the notion of state on both sides and synchronising states. In some cases, the alignment is not direct and transformations between the two forms of state have to be made, using mapping proxies for instance. Second, the time the swap occurs is often hard to define. Simply waiting for everything to be released from the old version can be insufficient since dependencies between updated objects have to be considered. Finally, fine-grained control may be needed when new and old systems use the same resources; otherwise, some incoherent situations may occur. For instance, in the pervasive domain, old and new software systems must not modify the same effectors in incompatible ways.

6.3   Code Adaptation Techniques

Due to its complexity, it has become necessary to provide some support that controls the dynamic adaptation of software applications. Too many parameters have to be considered (coupling, side effects, timeliness, etc.), and requirements are just too high to adapt a system in a dynamic fashion without tools that abstract away some of the complexity.

In this section, we give an overview of approaches that are commonly used in particular domains and that make sense in the context of autonomic computing. To do so, we consider three different levels of abstraction:

- The operating system level where resources and services used by a software system can be adjusted
- The programs level where algorithms or quality of service can be modified
- The component level where the high-level structure of software systems can be changed

The bottom line is that, in most autonomic systems, adaptations have to be made at different levels. Complementary techniques are needed to intervene at different levels of abstraction and at different places. Thus, some modifications are to be done at the operating system level, other changes have to change an instruction in a program and, in other cases, it is more appropriate to update a whole chunk of code (a component).

6.3.1   OS-Level Adaptation

The operating system (OS) community has studied the issue of dynamic adaptation for a long time. Robust and relevant techniques have been developed and can be

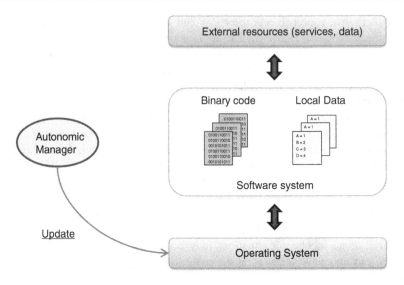

Fig. 6.3 OS-level autonomic manager

advantageously used by autonomic systems. These techniques are not intrusive in the sense that they do not change the internals of the programs being run. They change the resources and services provided by the operating system.

Specifically, the purpose of an operating system is to abstract away hardware resources and provide a set of common services to ease the development and execution of software applications. Much research has been conducted in order to allow the dynamic integration of resources and services. This is a major requirement that aims at improving the stability and availability of applications. Obviously, you do not want your laptop to reboot, stopping all applications every time you plug in a USB key!

Most operating systems are thus capable of integrating new resources on the fly, that is, without interruption of services. A number of successful techniques have been developed to do so, for instance many of the plug and play technologies used in pervasive networks today come from operating systems. This is the case of the UPnP standard (www.upnp.org), originally developed by Microsoft.

Similarly, operating systems also allow the dynamic deployment of new services. Deployment, here, has to be taken in its broadest sense (see Chap. 1) including activities like installation, activation and deactivation. In order to install a new shell command on Linux, for instance, one simply copies the executable (binary file or script) into the '/bin' directory. The service is launched by typing its name, and it is then dynamically made available to the OS computing environment.

Operating systems can thus constitute a supporting infrastructure in autonomic computing in order to dynamically adapt software systems. As illustrated by Fig. 6.3, new resources and new code can be added in a relatively easy way by an autonomic manager. New code, however, is not finely integrated into the existing code. In fact, it is packaged and deployed as a stand-alone service in the OS file system and made available. Some running code can then call this new service and thus be upgraded.

However, in spite of this valuable ability to dynamically integrate new code, building a dynamic application on top of an operating system is complex and often based on ad hoc mechanisms set up by the application itself. The example of the shell command cited above is based on the introspection of directories specified in a global environment variable. In addition, it is extremely difficult to establish an infrastructure for the interception and redirection of messages exchanged between two internal structures of the application code (two objects for instance). As seen before, such infrastructures are often necessary for the management of application dynamism.

To sum up, OS-based techniques can be very useful to implement autonomic properties. They however remain very technical and complex. They have to be complemented with other, certainly more abstract, approaches to deal with a range of self-management properties.

6.3.2 Program-Level Adaptation

6.3.2.1 Programming Languages

Programming languages provide notations to form programs, which are specifications of a computation. Programming languages rely on the notion of building blocks, often called modules. Over the years, many forms of modules have been proposed such as functions or classes. A module defines a set of symbols associated with code fragments. For instance, a class defines a set of methods, where each of them has a symbolic name (called its signature or profile) and some associated code. Modules can be compiled and assembled to form executable code (binary code). A special program, called a 'linker', builds this assembly. A link editor combines the code of different modules and resolves references to external symbols. Resolving references simply means that symbols are associated with an address in the code.

Programming languages provide a number of techniques allowing dynamic adaptation that can be leveraged to build autonomic systems. This is illustrated by Fig. 6.4 where it appears that an autonomic manager can bring adaptation directly in the binary code of a software system. This is a complex but very powerful approach.

Some techniques, like reflection, can be quite complex and are very tricky to employ in practice. Others, like dynamic linking, are much more popular and simpler to use.

In this section, we focus on two very useful techniques, dynamic linking and code interception, that are regularly put into practice today.

6.3.2.2 Dynamic Linking

Putting together the code of different modules and resolving references to external symbols are an essential phase when building a program. This can be done statically or dynamically. Static linking is the traditional approach. Its purpose is to assemble modules and to allow the modular development of applications. All external references are to be resolved before the execution of a program.

Many programming languages support dynamic linking. This means that external references are not completely resolved before execution and that some of them can be changed at runtime. It is then possible to bring in new code at runtime, therefore dynamically adapting the software system.

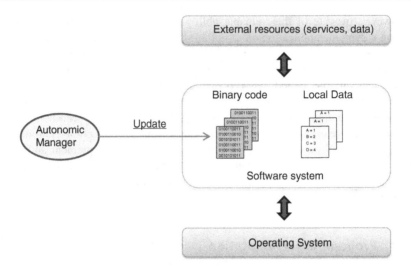

Fig. 6.4 Programme-level autonomic manager

Dynamic linking usually relies on indirection and 'plug-in' mechanisms. Let us look at indirection first. Two approaches are employed generally. The first one consists of compiling all the external references of a module in a table that can be progressively filled in and even updated at runtime. This allows client code to transparently call a new piece of code. The second approach is based on 'code rewriting' in the sense that specific instructions are introduced into the binary code to allow runtime adaptation. Specifically, variation points are introduced at places where external symbols are referenced. The precise calls, which employ the address of the code to be triggered, can then be changed at runtime. Erlang and C use this table-based approach to implement dynamic linking. Linux employs the rewriting option to dynamically load modules in the kernel.

A plug-in can be defined as an extension module bringing additional functionality to an existing software system. Plug-in mechanisms impose typing constraints. Modules that are loaded dynamically must conform to predefined signatures that are expected by the running code. Of course, some flexibility in the signature definition can be accepted. But, the bottom line is that extensions are prepared and must conform to a predefined shape. Such an approach requires the code to be adapted to have the appropriate structures explicitly in place accordingly: for instance, abstract interfaces should be defined to allow flexibility in the plug-in-based extensions.

6.3.2.3 C Language

In the C language, modules that can be linked dynamically are packaged in specific libraries. Their implementation depends on the operating system. These specific libraries are called *dynamic-link libraries* (.dll) in Windows and *shared libraries* (.so) in Linux.

The following example shows how to load a library with the *dlopen*() function, how to get the address of a symbol defined in a shared (dynamic) library with the *dlsym()* function and, finally, how to unload the shared library with the *dlclose()* function:

```
void   *handle;
int    *iptr, (*fptr)(int);

/* loading the expected library */
handle = dlopen("/usr/home/me/mylib.so", RTLD_LOCAL | RTLD_LAZY);

/* getting the address of « my_function » and « my_data »*/
*(void **)(&fptr) = dlsym(handle, "my_function");
iptr = (int *)dlsym(handle, "my_data");
/* Call to « my_function » with « my_data » as parameter*/
(*fptr)(*iptr);
```

As illustrated by this example, managing dynamism in C is complex. It can also be risky in the sense that there is almost no supporting mechanism to limit programming errors. In particular, dynamic libraries are loaded with no verification about the correctness of the new code, regarding the typing system for instance. Also, there is no notion of scope in the libraries. Thus, one cannot define explicitly what is shared and what is not shared with other modules. This limitation rapidly raises security issues. Finally, there is no preventive verification when a module is unloaded. This frequently results in so-called dangling pointer issues. References to nonexisting objects are one of the major causes of system crashes.

Also, replacing a function is extremely complex since it demands the unloading of the 'old' function. There is no easy way to do that in C. A common technique to implement this is to always reference functions that are likely to be replaced via pointers. Thus, changing a function amounts to change a pointer (if the interfaces are compatible of course) [2].

6.3.2.4 Java Language

The Java language presents a very different picture. In Java, source code is always transformed into some intermediary code, called byte code, in order to be executed by a virtual machine. A virtual machine is a software framework that isolates applications from computer specifics such as the operating system or the physical hardware architecture. This abstraction layer allows application developers to ignore low-level aspects and permits applications to be run on different computers, minimising the effort involved in porting software between different systems. Virtual machines are today rather common. The Java virtual machine and Microsoft. NET virtual machine are the best-known examples. They are not alone, though. Virtual machines like Parrot, supporting dynamic languages including JavaScript, PHP and Perl 6, are becoming increasingly popular.

In Java, thus, there is no static linking. Loading a class is done on demand when the class is needed for execution when a running class has referenced it. Specifically, the action of loading classes in a virtual machine at runtime is done by specific

entities called 'class loaders'. The purpose of a class loader is to resolve external references. To do so, it has to locate libraries containing the appropriate classes in the system resources and load them into the virtual machine. Several class loaders can be used in the same virtual machine. Their use is based on the following rules:
- Every class loader but the initial one (bootstrap) has a parent.
- Every class loader delegates the task of class loading to its parent before doing so itself.
By default, a Java virtual machine possesses three hierarchical class loaders:
- The *initial class loader* whose purpose is to load standard Java classes (rt.jar)
- The *extension class loader* which loads classes of the extension directory (jre/lib/ext)
- The *application class loader* that loads archives defined by the *CLASSPATH*

More class loaders can be added to load specific aspects in a modular way. Each class loader then has its own name scope. This is a powerful approach applying the separation of concerns principle to dynamic class loading. In particular, it allows the loading of two implementations of the same class as soon as they are loaded by two different class loaders. Such an approach brings flexibility since two versions of a class can be used by different parts of a system. In addition, backtracking to a previous state is made possible. However, the class loader concept is not one that is always mastered by programmers. This results in tricky, buggy situations where unexpected classes are used in a programme.

In contrast to the C approach, verification is done before loading a Java library. In particular, type system compatibility is checked. The following example shows how to dynamically load a Java class:

```
Class type = ClassLoader.getSystemClassLoader().loadClass(name);

Class type = this.getClass().getClassloader().loadClass(name);
Object obj = type.newInstance();
```

As in C, unloading modules raises an issue. A class loader cannot unload a class. Unloading a class requires unloading the class loader itself! This is why programmers, even experienced ones, tend to define several class loaders (with all the potential problems mentioned previously).

Dynamic adaptation is at the core of many programming languages. A number of techniques have been proposed to allow code evolution at runtime. Dynamic linking that has been presented here is one of them. Many others do exist. For instance, programming languages like Smalltalk are dynamically typed and reflective. Some script languages like JavaScript are weakly typed and dynamic in the sense that programming variables can change types. A language like Erlang allows developers to dynamically load new code and to explicitly manage code replacement.

These are all powerful techniques that can be used by autonomic managers to bring dynamic code adaptation. The essential issue, though, is that it is often hard to master and control these techniques. An excessive use of programming-level techniques may result in buggy code, extremely hard to test and maintain. Another thing is that employing such programming-level techniques has often a strong impact of the code itself. For instance, in order to dynamically load C libraries, extension points (variation points) have to be introduced. This results in complex code and requires limiting the possible dynamic extensions. Variation points cannot be introduced everywhere in the code; otherwise, it just gets unmaintainable!

As a conclusion, dynamic code loading is an essential feature allowing the introduction of new code in the scope (name space) of some code already running without interrupting it. The ability to discharge code, though, is not as well supported and generally requires one to develop additional code on top of the virtual machine. Unloading code becomes necessary when one wants to replace a programming structure like a class for instance. In this case, it is necessary to be able to deploy, load and instantiate the new structure. Also, the structure to be replaced is then required to vanish. It has to be unloaded from the virtual memory, and clients of the old structure are routed to the new one.

6.3.2.5 Interception Mechanisms

Interception is an essential mechanism in many programming languages that can be leveraged to implement self-management. The purpose of this technique is the explicit manipulation of connections between programming structures (functions, methods, messages, etc.) by intercepting their communication. It is thus possible to block and reroute messages during dynamic adaptation or to modify the content of a message. It is also possible to add some code that modifies the behaviour or QoS of the software system.

Several approaches can be used to implement interception; many are based on meta-object protocols [3]. The principle of such a protocol is to provide some means to observe and manipulate the structures of a running program. For instance, some virtual machines provide interfaces to observe running code and to dynamically create proxies designed to intercept messages exchanged between two structures. Such facility is very useful since low-level; complex code is required to provide reflection (to observe running code and react to changes).

Indeed, interception mechanisms can be implemented without a virtual machine, but it rapidly gets extremely complex. In C for instance, interception points can be inserted in the code. Most techniques rely on the manipulation of the function's entry points. That is, the entry point of a function can be altered (rerouted) so that some additional code is called before the execution of the function. In some cases, the original function can be merely ignored. The function is not unloaded but not called anymore or called by other structures.

Interception can be implemented at design time or at runtime. In the first case, the executable code is usually modified by an extended compiler (or some sort of post-compiler). In the second case, a software system has to provide means to change the very first few code instructions of a target function to jump to an injected code.

This approach somehow continues the idea of variation point (see Sect. 6.2.2) in applying it to the code and not only to an abstract design. Its main limit is its complexity since it requires to physically modify some binary code. It relies then on tools producing non-standard code, that is, code different from the one produced by

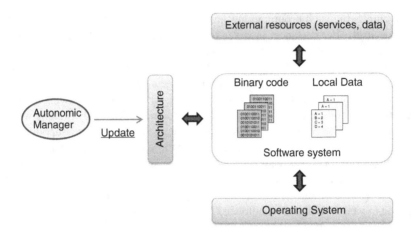

Fig. 6.5 Component-level autonomic manager

a 'regular' compiler. This raises the usual issue of conformity and maintenance of these often ad hoc tools.

6.3.3 Component-Level Adaptation

The introduction of software components in the late 1990s aimed at providing a new level of abstraction and new facilities to software developers [4]. Developing large software systems solely using fine-grained programming concepts like objects or functions does not scale very well. This is because the granularity is too fine and a number of global aids to development and maintenance are not supported. In most programming languages, for instance, there is no provision that supports non-functional qualities or code dependency management for instance. That is, there is no global view of applications, which is a sticking point to implementing adaptations. In many cases, code upgrade is limited to small sets of instructions because of this lack of global perspective [5].

Components provide a very useful level of abstraction for self-managed systems [6]. As a matter of fact, a number of self-managed systems are today based on the component granularity for adaptation. As illustrated by Fig. 6.5, autonomic managers directly manipulate components to adapt the system and are not aware of low-level details. This leads of course to coarse-grained adaptations.

A software component is a unit of composition that can be independently deployed and executed. A component model defines a common structure for components and rules to assemble them. Many component models are based on the notion of provided and required interfaces expressing what a component can do and what it needs in order to be executed. Many component models also introduce a set of non-functional properties that are used to characterise the overall behaviour of a

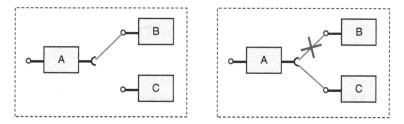

Fig. 6.6   Example of architectural reconfiguration

component. These properties are usually specified in a descriptive metadata file that can be used during deployment, instantiation or composition.

Components usually come with development environments and execution environments. Development environments provide facilities to produce (source and binary) code. A framework then provides online support services that allow the deployment, composition, execution and administration of software components. Programmers and administrators manipulate an application through its architecture, not through low-level programming structures. Generally, the framework allows the management of two artefacts: component implementations and component instances.

Adaptation, here, is usually termed 'architecture reconfiguration'. The architecture of an application, consisting of a number of components in interaction, can be modified (or reconfigured) at runtime. This is made possible since the constituents of an architecture, components and bindings, can be explicitly manipulated through the execution framework. Reconfiguration may take various forms: modifying the interface of components, modifying the bindings between components, replacing a component by another one, adding and removing components, etc. This is illustrated by Fig. 6.6 where the binding between components A and B is suppressed and replaced by a binding between components A and C.

Binding modification is often implemented with proxies placed between components in interaction. This is of course the implementation of the interception mechanism presented in Sect. 6.3.2 in the component world. A proxy is a variation point: it is changed in order to update the communication QoS or to replace one component involved in the communication.

Bear in mind, however, that such proxies cost as they are an indirect requiring more messages and processing and are therefore generally avoided when performance is important!

Generic component models supporting adaptations generally require important work from programmers to preserve state, perform reconfiguration at the right time, maintain control flows and so on. In contrast, domain-specific component models can provide a much higher level of support. Domain-specific component models focus on well-defined and limited domains. They bring high-level compositional capabilities and may provide advanced dynamic features. For instance, replacing a component can be simply made through an API. The associated runtime is then able to save and restore states that are explicitly defined in the domain, to block client calls, to synchronise updating actions, etc.

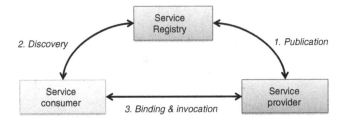

Fig. 6.7   SOC base pattern

6.3.4   Software Services

Service-oriented computing (SOC) is a relatively new trend in software engineering [7]. It is a compositional approach where applications are built through the late composition of independent software elements, called services. A service is characterised by the functions it provides. Services are not software components, but they can be implemented as one or several components.

The service-oriented approach offers excellent opportunities to achieve software application dynamism and is used more and more to build autonomic software systems.

A service is a software resource that is described and published by a provider in a *service registry*, sometimes called a service broker. The registry acts as an intermediary between service providers and consumers. More precisely, service providers publish service descriptions in the registry. Then, service consumers can send queries to the registry to get the available services meeting their requirements. Once a service has been selected, consumer and provider can in some cases negotiate a contract specifying how the service is to be used. Today, there are very few automated methods to verify that a contract is actually respected. The next step, of course, is the service invocation. Here, the consumer can use (call) the selected service. The SOC base pattern is illustrated in Fig. 6.7.

The overall approach is made possible by a supporting infrastructure, called a service-oriented architecture (SOA). An SOA provides all the necessary mechanisms to describe, publish, discover and invoke services. It can also provide additional features related to non-functional requirements like security, transaction and quality of service. In particular, mechanisms related to contract definition, establishment and verification belong to these additional (and optional) features.

Dynamic SOAs are architectures that have been extended with specific features allowing the dynamic management of services. Essentially, this means that a service provider can un-register a service if it is no longer able to deliver it. In addition, notifications are sent to inform consumers when new services arrive and when a service is removed from the registry.

Depending on runtime conditions, a consumer has then the ability to release a service currently selected and choose (and invoke) a new one. This can be triggered

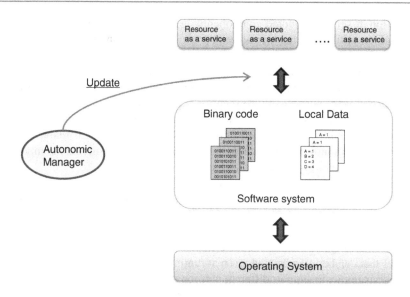

Fig. 6.8 Service-level autonomic manager

by the appearance of a new, perhaps better, service in the architecture (in the registry) or because the current service does not provide the expected functionality or functions rated at the quality level required (this quality-level requirement can be expressed in a service contract).

A number of implementations of the SOA concept have been proposed, sometimes for different purposes. Web services,[2] for instance, represent a solution of choice for software integration. UPnP[3] and DPWS (Devices Profile for Web Services) are heavily used in pervasive applications in order to expose volatile devices.

As illustrated by Fig. 6.8, these technologies are very useful to implement and dynamically integrate resources. Service orientation is therefore of great interest for autonomic computing. The loose coupling between service providers and consumers facilitates architectural evolutions. Architecture is an important word here: services are large-grained artefacts, and they target large-grained evolutions. Changing services means changing big chunks of code. It is then perfectly adapted to adaptations at the architecture level, not at the instruction level.

Service orientation is so promising that it has been extended to handle more than resources. Cervantes and Hall introduced the notion of service-oriented component in 2004 [8]. Their main motivation was to combine the advantages of two different paradigms into a single programming model, that is, the architectural dimension of software components and the inherent flexibility of services. The essential

---

[2] www.w3c.org

[3] www.upnp.org

innovation of service-oriented components resides in the way bindings are established. In traditional component-oriented composition, components are selected and bound at design time. Afterwards, reconfiguration is driven by an administrator or by a global autonomic manager in a centralised fashion. By contrast, the selection process for a service-oriented composition occurs at runtime as component instances are created. It is the purpose of the execution framework to bind the service-oriented components together. To do so, service-oriented components come with a description of their provided and required functions. Depending on the available components, the execution framework binds the appropriate service-oriented components together (i.e. it binds provided services to required services).

Building a software system using a service-oriented component approach comes down to decomposing the system into a collection of modular interacting services. These services are described in a specific file, separately of any implementation. By doing so, it is possible to develop service-oriented components independently of each other. It is also possible of course to provide variant implementations for the services that can be interchanged, even at runtime. Variant implementations can be used, for example, to support different non-functional requirements.

The execution of the software system based on service-oriented components starts when all the dependencies are satisfied. The final topology of a system depends of course on the available components. Components can be pushed down in the execution platform or pulled from repositories by the platform. A composition can be seen as an abstract architectural description that could be used by an autonomic manager to deploy components that satisfy the service specifications required by the composition. The resulting system may vary dynamically at runtime.

A service-oriented component is characterised by the following information:
– A set of provided service interfaces.
– A set of required service interfaces, declared by the component and handled by the execution platform (i.e. the dependencies are resolved by the execution platform).
– Management interfaces. They allow direct management of the service-oriented component and are of major importance when it comes to dynamism.
– Required and exported resources. These are references to (code) resources that have to be provided by other components or used by other components.

This approach facilitates the work of programmers in many aspects, especially the management of dynamism. Somehow, service-oriented components infuse autonomic computing concepts into traditional component model. Reconfiguration is not decided by a global manager but, locally, by autonomic managers attached to components. That is, depending on the available components, bindings can be regularly evaluated and possibly changed.

Several implementations of service-oriented components have been proposed, including OSGi (www.osgi.org) and iPOJO (http://felix.apache.org/site/apache-felix-ipojo.html) which is built on top of OSGi. These two technologies are today used to aid the building of dynamic (sometimes autonomic) systems through their ability to support dynamism at the architecture level and are therefore presented in more detail in the latter sections of this chapter.

6.4   OSGi

OSGi (Open Services Gateway initiative) is an execution framework developed on top of Java [9]. It was initially employed in pervasive environments to build home automation boxes or energy management boxes capable of hosting dynamic and sometimes autonomic applications. It builds on Java's dynamic features (on demand class loading, multiple class loaders, typing verification before loading, etc.) to provide a coarse-grained level of modularity. Today OSGi is the solution of choice when building dynamically adaptable applications in the Java world. It is used in Eclipse (www.eclipse.org) and a number of J2EE application servers like Jonas (www.jonas.org) in order to allow the dynamic integration of new modules or services.

OSGi is very useful regarding autonomic computing in the sense that it both supports the notions of modularity and services. In other words, it provides means to dynamically load new code on a platform and to integrate it with existing code.

6.4.1   Modularity

Firstly, OSGi defines a form of modularity for Java, beyond the modularity provided by classes and objects. It allows developers to modularise their applications. Modules are called *bundles* in OSGi (the two terms, modules and bundles, are often used without distinctions by practitioners).

The notion of a bundle is pivotal to OSGi; specifically, a bundle is a Java archive. It can contain, in addition to Java classes, a number of resources including *.gif* and *.png* files, properties files, containers like *.jar* or *.zip* files and libraries of native code such as *.dll* or *.so* files. In other words, all the files that are required to implement a module. A module can be defined as a set of coherent, collaborating classes grouped together. The purpose is to organise Java applications into a set of loosely coupled, highly coherent interacting modules.

A bundle is both a deployment unit and a composition unit. Regarding deployment, bundles are used to package classes and resources so that they can be deployed on one or more execution platforms. Bundles are thus tangible artefacts that can be copied or transferred by software administrators.

But bundles are also used as composition units at the application level. That means that they are used as building blocks to form modular Java applications. Note that this double role played by bundles often leads to confusion since differences between the notions of deployment and composition are not always well understood by programmers. Regarding the compositional aspect, bundles allow the definition

Fig. 6.9 Bundle structure

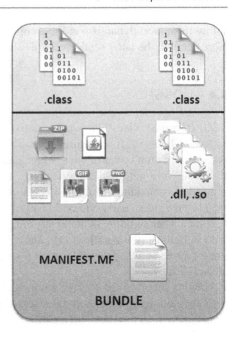

of what can be shared and what is private to the bundle. This aspect is defined in a metadata file included in a bundle.

OSGi uses the Java manifest facility to specify metadata (manifest.mf in Fig. 6.9). A manifest is a file defining high-level properties called metadata. By default, Java defines a set of metadata, such as the vendor name and the version of the associated archive. Most metadata depends on the execution context or on the nature of the archive. However, the OSGi standard defines a complete list of metadata.[4] Two of them are especially important:

– *Export-Package* defines packages of the bundle that are exported (made available to the other parts of an application).
– *Import-Package* defines packages required by the bundle for its execution.

One of the main assets of OSGi is related to modularity management, which allows the installation and deinstallation of Java modules without the interruption of services. This capability is made possible by the advanced use of Java class loaders.

Specifically, a class loader is defined for each bundle. Then, OSGi introduces visibility between bundles via the notions of public and private packages. Public packages can be imported or exported, specified through the use of metadata. A bundle then has access to the classes of its own packages and to the classes of the imported public packages belonging to other bundles. This defines the bundle *Class Space*. Having a class loader per bundle allows several versions of a class to coexist

---

[4]http://www.osgi.org/download/r4v43/r4.core.pdf

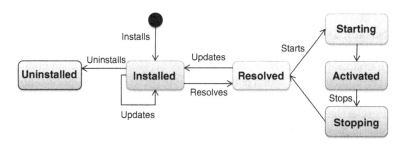

Fig. 6.10 Bundle states

in the same program. The only constraint is that a given bundle can only access a single version.

Bundles have a life cycle of their own. Specifically, a bundle can be:

- *Installed*. The bundle is said to be valid, and it is assigned with a unique identifier by the running platform. Installation is an atomic and persistent operation. A bundle object is created and is used for every upcoming administration operation.
- *Uninstalled*. The physical representation of a bundle has been deleted, and its different resources have been correctly released or discharged from the platform.
- Resolved. All the dependencies of the bundle (packages, capacities, etc.) have been satisfied.
- *Starting*. The bundle is initialized through a call to its *start* method. A notification is sent upon bundle activation.
- *Activated*. The bundle has been successfully activated and is running.
- *Stopping*. When a bundle is deactivated, all services and resources being used have to be released, all the threads of the bundle are stopped and all services provided by the bundle are deleted from the platform.

Thus a bundle goes through different states from its installation up to its retirement. This is illustrated by Fig. 6.10 which summarises the different states and transitions.

6.4.2   Service

OSGi allows the dynamic management of deployment and composition units, also known as bundles, meaning that the execution platform does not have to be rebooted to instantiate the change to its architecture. However, this dynamicity only concerns classes. However, the dynamic management of bundles does not imply the dynamic management of applications. To do so, a bundle exposes its functions (services) to the other bundles and, conversely, is able to use functions (services) offered by the other bundles. These functions are concerned with the instance level: they correspond to running classes.

As introduced previously, a major aspect of service-oriented computing is the notion of a contract. This notion defines what is expected (service specification) and what is effectively used (concrete service). Clients use service specifications in order to select a service provider and invoke a concrete service. This two-phase protocol also gives clients the ability to change concrete services when the currently used ones are not satisfactory (for whatever reason).

OSGi relies on the definition of a service *register* containing the services available on the platform at a given time. Services correspond to running classes that belong to a bundle and are where their interfaces are explicitly exported. Bundles are then concerned with instances of classes that can be shared by all other bundles. A bundle therefore contains a number of service consumers and providers.

Regarding service provision, a bundle has to provide the following elements to the registry:
– A description of the provided service (Java interface)
– The invocation point of the provided services (a reference to the implementation class)
– The non-functional properties

When a bundle registers a service, the register gets a reference to the record (*ServiceRegistration*) which is used to administer the service, which is also used for its deregistration. In particular, a bundle has to deregister its declared services when it is deactivated. Some OSGi implementations automate this aspect, however.

To use a service, a consumer has to look for it. Two modes are available to do this: *active* mode and the *passive* one. In active mode, the potential consumer explicitly accesses the register to get one or several references to services running at that moment, using the following:

ServiceReference[] refs = context.getServiceReferences(NeededInterface.class.getName(), null);

In passive mode, the consumer subscribes to events corresponding to the arrival, departure or modification of specific services. Thus, a consumer can discover, select and invoke a service when it becomes available. It can also select and use a new service when the previous one becomes unavailable. Here is a code example illustrating this:

```
context.addServiceListener(this);
    //...
public void serviceChanged(ServiceEvent event) {
    //...
    switch (event.getType()) {
    case ServiceEvent.REGISTERED:
        ServiceReference serviceRef = event.getServiceReference();
        //...
```

6.4.3   Conclusion

OSGi is one of the few industrial-strength platforms explicitly designed to run dynamic applications. It is based on the notions of bundles (modules) and services. An exciting point is that OSGi tackles the two main challenges of dynamic applications, that is, the integration of code in both the execution environment and in the running application. More precisely, bundles are used to dynamically integrate code on the platform through the advanced use of class loaders, while services are used to dynamically upgrade applications.

However, while class sharing is managed by the platform itself, this is not the case for function sharing. That is, managing service-level dependencies within a bundle is left to the developer. It is necessary to capture the different events emitted by the platform in order to discover, select, use, and change services. This turns out to be an error-prone approach that can endanger the dynamic nature of the application. For instance, references can become stale, events can be missed, incompatible class versions can be called, etc.

Several approaches have been investigated to improve OSGi in terms of dependency management. In the section, we will focus on the iPOJO component model approach. One of the main goals of iPOJO is to simplify the creation of dynamic, service-oriented applications in OSGi.

6.5   iPOJO

Very early, OSGi appeared to be a powerful but complex framework. In particular, one of the major concerns in OSGi is that service management is entirely left to applications programmers. That is, programmers have to insert specific instructions in their code in order to follow the arrival and departure of services of interest and to react accordingly. This code is complex and highly error-prone.

Several approaches have then been investigated in order to make dependency management easier and more automated. Service Binder was one of the earliest works in that direction. A similar approach, called Declarative Services, appeared in the fourth release of the OSGi compendium. This specification defines how a framework can manage service publications and service dependencies in order to significantly lower *business* code complexity. Other component-based approaches have been proposed on top of OSGi, including Google Guice peaberry,[5] Scala[6] and iPOJO.[7] In this section, we focus on the latter for it is today more and more used in order to implement autonomic software systems.

iPOJO is a service-oriented component model complemented with a supporting execution framework [10]. One of the main goals of iPOJO is to make the

---

[5]http://code.google.com/p/peaberry/

[6]http://wiki.github.com/weiglewilczek/scalamodules/

[7]http://felix.apache.org/site/apache-felix-ipojo.html

Fig. 6.11 iPOJO extensible
container

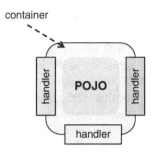

development of dynamic applications as simple as possible. To this end, the overall
approach is to keep a component as close to a 'plain old Java object' (POJO) as
possible. The code of a component should focus on business logic, not on mechanisms for dynamism or other non-functional requirements.

iPOJO relies on the 'inversion of control' pattern and provides an extensible
component container that manages all issues regarding dynamism. In particular, it
manages all the service-oriented interactions: service publication, service instantiation, service selection and service discovery. The container can be extended in order
to support other non-functional concerns such as configuration, persistence and
security.

As illustrated by Fig. 6.11, each aspect is managed by a special element called a
handler. Thus, containers are not monolithic constructions but are made of a number of handlers. Some handlers like the 'service dependency handler' are mandatory
and always part of a container, whereas others are optional. The 'service dependency handler' and the 'life-cycle management handler' are examples of mandatory
handlers. The latter is called when an iPOJO instance changes state (as explained
further in more details).

The most commonly used handlers are available on Apache. Custom handlers
can be developed for iPOJO, using framework facilities, allowing developers to
handle other more specific non-functional concerns.

The purpose of the container is thus to wrap a plain Java object and provide non-
functional features. The link between the 'POJO' and its container (and the handlers
in fact) is transparently created by the supporting framework through analysis and
manipulation of the POJO byte code. Code injection is done at compilation time by
the framework. At that time, the framework also creates bundles (essentially the
manifest part of the bundle) containing iPOJO components and related metadata.
Bundles are used as the deployment unit to resolve package dependencies, as it is
normally carried out by OSGi.

Concretely, a component is connected to the iPOJO supporting framework by
configuring the component instance container, which consists of declaring metadata
that will be used by the container for runtime management. Handlers are plugged
into the component instance container at runtime. Only the required handlers are
plugged into the container. The resulting container manages the interaction between
the POJO and the external world.

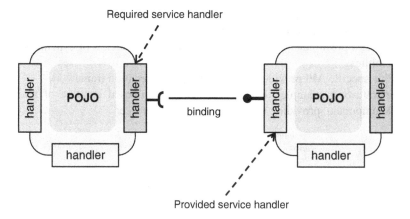

Fig. 6.12 Service-based interaction between two iPOJO instances

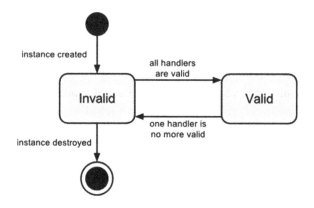

Fig. 6.13 State diagram of an iPOJO instance

First thing when an 'iPOJO bundle' is deployed is to create iPOJO instances. Instances life cycle is very simple: an instance is valid or invalid. That is, once created, an instance is valid if and only if all dependencies (expressed by the handlers) are satisfied. In particular, all the service dependencies must be resolved (see Fig. 6.12). Life-cycle handlers are called when an instance becomes valid (validate callback) and when it becomes invalid (invalidate callback). States and associated transitions are illustrated by Fig. 6.13.

The complete specification of an iPOJO component includes the declaration of provided services, required services, callback functions related to the life-cycle management (upon activation and deactivation of instances) and all non-functional aspects implemented by specific handlers.

An iPOJO component can be created in three different ways:

- With specific annotations added in the Java source code
- With a compositional model to describe an architectural view of dynamic service assemblies
- With a specific API provided by the supporting execution framework

The following example illustrates the annotation-based creation of a simple iPOJO component, providing the « HelloService » service:

```
@Component ( name=" acme.hello.component " )
@Instanciate ( name="helloService " ) //defaultInstance
@Provides
public class MyComponent implements HelloService {
@Requires (optional=true) // require a Log service
private LogService logger;
public String hello (String name) {
return "Hello "+name+";
}
@Validate // on validation callback
private void start () {
logger.log (INFO, "Hello Service started");
}
@Invalidate // on invalidation callback
private void stop (){
logger.log (INFO, "Hello Service stopped");
}
```

The same result can be obtained through the use of a metadata file:

```
<ipojo>
<component classname= "acme.MyComponent" name="acme.hello.component">
<provides/>
<requires field="logger" optional="true"/>
<callback transition="validate" method="start"/>
<callback transition="invalidate" method="stop"/>
</component>
<instance component="acme.hello.component" name ="helloService"/>
</ipojo>
```

As said earlier, the specification includes the required services (@requires), the provided services (@Provides) and optional life-cycle-related callbacks (@Validate, @InValidate). These elements are then interpreted during execution: component instances are created, service dependencies are dynamically injected and callbacks are called depending on the instance state.

Finally, a useful aspect of iPOJO is the possibility to define hierarchical compositions. Here, instances can be regrouped into separate name spaces called *composites*. This notion of composite allows the isolation of services in an execution platform.

iPOJO composites can be created in a declarative way in a description file, just like iPOJO instances. The following example illustrates the creation of such a composite:

```
<ipojo>
< !—Declare a composition -->
<composite name= "compositionLambda" >
< !—Instanciate a component implementing the contract acme.HelloService -->
<subservice action="instanciate" specification="acme.HelloService"/>

< !—Create an instance of the component acme.componentLambda -->
<instance component="acme.componentLambda" />
</composite>
< !—Create an instance of compositionLamba -->
<instance component=" compositionLambda " />
</ipojo>
```

6.6 Conclusion

The ability to update a running software system is at the heart of autonomic computing. We believe that a self-managed system has to be designed with this in mind. That is, the supporting running platform has to be conceived with the adaptation in mind, and the autonomic properties have to be defined with the platform possibilities in mind.

An important output of this chapter is that there is no generic method guaranteeing correct and consistent dynamic updates. The techniques that are used today are mainly application specific. Implementing them can be a real challenge, especially when carried out by the programmers that were not involved in the initial software development. Fortunately, there are some favourable situations. For instance, stateless and loosely coupled software systems are much easier to adapt. There may be no state to preserve and very few internal connections to maintain. Otherwise, it is up to programmers to do the tedious, error-prone tasks like state encoding and decoding, state alignment and state synchronisation.

The good news is that autonomic computing can take advantage of the different techniques investigated so far. Indeed, as explained in Chap. 3, autonomic systems are made of a number of autonomic elements acting at different levels of abstraction. Some autonomic elements are close to the execution machine (OS, VM), while others are more concerned with high-level, business-related code (classes, components, services). Adaptation techniques required by these different elements are of course different, with various requirements in terms of granularity and QoS. For instance, a 'low-level' autonomic element can rely, for instance, on a 'meta-object protocol' to manage the configuration of the virtual machine at runtime. Service-level approaches, on the other hand, can be used to deal with the dynamic integration of new business algorithms.

The bad news is that autonomic systems tend to be complex, more complex than traditional systems. The point is that they have to use sophisticated techniques to self-manage some of their parts. Of course, this additional complexity is the price to pay to reach the desired level of autonomy.

Good sense (and the use of strong software engineering principles!) can hide this additional complexity as much as possible. The adaptation code, whatever the technique it uses, should be encapsulated and only changed when required by an expert.

6.7   Key Points

In this chapter, we have introduced the following important points:

- Software adaptation is key to modern computing. It remains however very complex and is often based on *ad hoc* techniques. A major reason for this is that software systems are not built so that they can be easily evolved, due to the difficulties and costs in being able to anticipate a wide enough range of evolutions that would be required in advance.
- Two activities constitute the core of software adaptation process—providing new code, possibly based on existing code, and integrating this new code into the existing, running code. Providing a new piece of code requires the code to be (re-) written or modified via directives related to the code's compilation or linkage. This is much easier when extension points (variation points) have been explicitly inserted into the original code. To reiterate, the latter requires anticipation of possible changes, which is extremely difficult. Domain-specific approaches, like software product lines, can provide such a level of support.
- Integrating new pieces of code into an existing one is a challenging task, especially when the existing code has already been executed. A major issue in this situation is to preserve the internal computational states.
- Integration can be performed statically or dynamically. Static integration is simpler (relatively!). Dynamic integration is very complex but more and more in demand in order to avoid costly service interruptions.
- Many techniques have been proposed to handle dynamic integration. They operate at different levels of abstraction and are complementary. We believe that service orientation is particularly useful. This is why we have presented the OSGi technology in some detail. OSGi is a dynamic execution framework developed on top of Java. It improves modularity and facilitates flexibility.
- iPOJO is a service-oriented component model facilitating the use of OSGi, automating a number of features. iPOJO already presents some autonomic properties that turn it into a candidate to build modular, component-based autonomic software systems. It is for this reason that we use it to illustrate the practicalities of building autonomic systems in this book.

References

1. Lin, D.-L., Neamtiu, L.: Collateral evolution of applications and databases. In: ERCIM Workshop on Software Evolution/International Workshop on Principles of Software Evolution (IWPSE-Evol'09), Amsterdam, Aug 2009

2. Neamtiu, I.: Practical dynamic software updating. Ph.D. dissertation, University of Maryland, Aug 2008
3. Kiczales, G.: The Art of Meta-Object Protocol. MIT Press, Cambridge, MA (1991)
4. Szyperski, C.: Component Software: Beyond Object-Oriented Programming. Addison Wesley/ Longman Publishing Co., Inc., Boston (1997)
5. Krakowiak, S.: Middleware architecture with patterns and frameworks http://sardes.inrialpes. fr/~krakowia/MW-Book/ (2007)
6. Kramer, J., Magee, J.: Self-managed systems: an architectural challenge. In: Future of Software Engineering, pp. 259–268. IEEE Computer Society, Washington, DC (2007)
7. Papazoglou, M.: Service-oriented computing: concepts, characteristics and directions. In: Proceedings of Web Information Systems Engineering, Los Alamitos, CA, 2003
8. Cervantes, H., Hall, R.: Autonomous adaptation to dynamic availability in service-oriented component model. In: Proceedings of the 26th International Conference on Software Engineering, pp. 614–623. IEEE Computer Society, Washington, DC (2004)
9. Hall, R., Pauls, K., McCulloch, S., Savage, D.: OSGi in Action: Creating Modular Applications in Java. Manning Publications, Greenwich (2011)
10. Escoffier, C.: iPOJO: a flexible service-oriented component model. Ph.D. dissertation, University Joseph Fourier. http://defense.pdf. Dec 2008

The Decision Function

In the previous chapters, we saw how self-managed systems could accumulate information about their execution context and how they could adapt their own internal structures. We now focus on the decision function that links sensory inputs to actuating outputs. This function heavily relies on the notion of knowledge (knowledge about the system internals, knowledge about the computing environment, knowledge about ways to solve problems) and as well as the ability to reason about this knowledge. There are many different ways to represent knowledge in computing science, and a wide range of reasoning techniques have been proposed, in particular in the artificial intelligence community.

The purpose of this section is to present different knowledge representations and associated reasoning techniques well suited to autonomic systems. It is not meant to be exhaustive. In fact, there is no such thing as a general knowledge representation of reasoning approach for autonomic management. Depending on the requirements, different formalisms and techniques with different properties can be selected.

P. Lalanda et al., *Autonomic Computing: Principles, Design and Implementation*,
Undergraduate Topics in Computer Science, DOI 10.1007/978-1-4471-5007-7_7,
© Springer-Verlag London 2013

7.1   Introduction to Knowledge

7.1.1   Definition

Knowledge is a central notion in autonomic computing. Indeed, in order to exhibit
self-administration properties, autonomic systems must rely on some form of knowledge about themselves, about the computing environment and about ways to solve
problems. The more sophisticated the autonomic capacities required, the more
advanced the knowledge.

We have seen that autonomic systems are made of a number of interacting autonomic managers. From a logical point of view, these managers are organised around
administrative tasks, the MAPE tasks, which are used to monitor the managed artefacts, analyse the situation, plan countermeasures when necessary and eventually
execute courses of action. As illustrated by Fig. 7.1, the MAPE tasks strongly rely
on knowledge, for example, the K in the MAPE-K pattern.

The general notion of knowledge is very complex, to such an extent that its study
gave birth to a philosophical domain of its own called epistemology.[1] The mere definition of knowledge is still a matter of intense debate, and, in fact, there is no single
agreed definition today. The classical definition of knowledge traces back to antiquity: Socrates[2] stated that knowledge is *true belief* that has been *justified*.[3] This
theory means that someone *knows* something if:

- He/she believes it.
- This *something* is true.
- It is explained in some way.

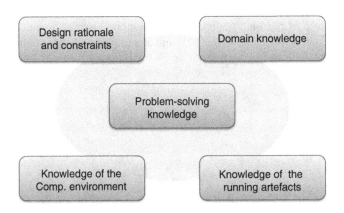

Fig. 7.1   Type of knowledge needed to perform autonomic tasks

---

[1] From the Greek *epistēmē* meaning 'knowledge' and *logos* for 'study of'.

[2] Socrates (469 BC–399 BC) was one of the classical Greek philosophers who laid the foundation
of western philosophy. His work was transcribed by Plato, his student (428–427 BC–348
347 BC).

[3] In the *Theaetetus*, one of Plato's dialogues about the nature of knowledge.

This classical definition is sufficient for this book. In our scope, it puts forward the fact that an autonomic system must rely on justified beliefs about itself, its environments and the effects of its actions. These beliefs have to be true; otherwise, autonomic actions may be inappropriate.

The notion of truth has also been the subject of intense debates and numerous research works. Once again, for the purpose of this book, we retain the classical definition, also tracing back to the Greek philosophers, which defines truth as the real states of things. A statement about something is true if it reflects the state of *this* something at some level of abstraction.

7.1.2 Forms of Knowledge

Since the time of Aristotle,[4] it is understood that there are different forms of knowledge and different ways to acquire knowledge. It is noteworthy to mention here the distinction between 'knowledge by acquaintance' and 'knowledge by description'. Knowledge by acquaintance is the result of a direct interaction with a person or with an object. For instance, knowledge about snow can be obtained by touching it and throwing snowballs. Knowledge by description is not based upon direct experience. It is a familiarity with someone or something that is acquired indirectly, by education, for instance. Knowledge about snow can thus be obtained through discussions with people living in cold countries.

Knowledge can also be *a priori*. We say here that this knowledge is 'innate'. Simply put, the idea here is that someone possesses knowledge before acquiring knowledge by acquaintance or by description. Again, this statement traces back to Socrates who believed in the reminiscence of souls and in the transmission of knowledge. The notion of category, introduced by Aristotle and formalised by Kant, can also be mentioned here. According to Emmanuel Kant,[5] in the *Critique of Pure Reason*, we naturally see the world through existing schemas and we use them to reason. Categories allow us to organise the world and create objects.

These different forms of knowledge are encountered when building autonomic systems. Typically, knowledge related to the running managed artefacts can be seen as knowledge by acquaintance. Such knowledge is acquired through direct interaction with *touchpoints* provided by the artefacts or by the computing environment. By contrast, knowledge about the initial design objectives and about the way problems should be solved can be seen as innate knowledge. Indeed, this knowledge is specified by a number of persons (designers, architects, developers, domain experts, etc.) when the autonomic system is yet to be built. This knowledge is engraved in the system during its implementation and already exists when the system is run for the first time.

There is also a more recent distinction between descriptive and prescriptive knowledge. Descriptive knowledge, also called *declarative* knowledge, is general, theoretical knowledge about a domain or about a given software system. It is often

---

[4] Aristotle (384 BC–322 BC) was a classical Greek philosopher. He was a student of Plato.
[5] Emmanuel Kant (1724, 1804) was a German philosopher.

expressed with propositions. By contrast, prescriptive knowledge focuses on the way some tasks are to be performed. This form of knowledge is also known as imperative knowledge or 'know-how', for example, it can take the form of details of how some goals or behaviours can be achieved. Where descriptive knowledge would relate to problem solving, procedural knowledge is used to direct the solving of problems. Procedural knowledge is practical, domain or even task specific and generally less general than descriptive knowledge. Problem solving is of course at the heart of autonomic computing and these two forms of knowledge are often used in autonomic systems (in the different MAPE tasks).

Knowledge can be augmented by different forms of reasoning. Deductive reasoning allows knowledge to be obtained from a set of findings or observations and prior or acquired knowledge. *Deduction* is an inference from general observations to specific arguments. Inductive reasoning is similar to deductive reasoning in the sense that it also starts from observations but it aims at reaching more general conclusions. Induction is then an inference from observations to general statements. The truth of the conclusion is not certain and is generally associated with a probability. *Abduction* is a form of inductive reasoning whose purpose is to explain or justify an observation rather than generation of new concepts through generalisation. Abduction is not guaranteed to be true and can also be associated with a probability. Finally, let us mention *analogical* reasoning which is an inference from a specific observation to some specific finding.

The acquaintance theorists argue that knowledge based on reasoning, whatever its nature, cannot be certain, even if generally valid and much used in practice. That goes back to the notion of belief introduced in the previous section. We will see later on that the use of probabilities to qualify statements obtained through reasoning is an interesting way to take this observation into account.

Another important source of debate in epistemology deals with the notion of partial knowledge. Some philosophers argue that we never truly know a person or an object. We only have a partial understanding for a number of reasons. First, in order to deal with complexity, the human mind abstracts, simplifies and selects information. Second, we have no direct access to the inner parts of someone or something. The only knowledge we can acquire is the one that is presented by the subject itself, consciously or not. Children, for instance, have often a hard time to express and localise the notion of pain. Thus, in order to solve real problems, we generally dispose of partial knowledge and make decisions accordingly. Some knowledge, of course, is non-required to solve a problem but some non-available knowledge would be useful in some cases.

This applies to autonomic systems. Self-management decisions have to often be made with incomplete knowledge, and, in some cases, probabilities have to be used to handle this aspect. Managed artefacts are complex software constructions that cannot be completely known. They are apprehended through the *touchpoints* they offer, and only a limited amount of information can be collected. This is clearly the very same for the computing environment, which is often only partially known. This brings us back to the epistemological relationship between managed artefacts and autonomic managers presented in Chap. 4, autonomic system architecture.

It is then of utter importance for the autonomic managers to align the problems to be solved with the knowledge at their disposal (see Chap. 5 about dynamic monitoring). An autonomic manager has to be proactive and fetch the information that is necessary to solve the problems at hand. It is also necessary to evaluate autonomic actions to make sure of their appropriateness. Chapter 8 is dedicated to this thorny problem, which requires that the system has knowledge about the possible effects of an action and is able to log the different actions taken so far.

7.1.3 Knowledge Representation

An essential matter regarding knowledge is the way it is represented and communicated. There are several ways to transfer knowledge, including verbal exchanges, audio and video recordings and symbolic representations. The latter, of course, is the preferred form of representation used in computer science. In autonomic computing, specifically, it is necessary to devise languages in order to represent such things as objects, components, services, properties, relationships, events, states, time, causes and effects and many more.

In philosophy, the study of things and their interrelationships is called *ontology*. Categories, as introduced before, are also called ontological predicates by Kant. The term ontology has been borrowed by computer science to refer to the definition of a domain in terms of concepts and relationships between those concepts. In order to build an autonomic system, it is then necessary to build an ontology defining the concepts that have to be reified, manipulated, tracked, reasoned about, etc. It is even one of the first tasks to be achieved since it determines the touchpoints to be implemented and the possible forms of reasoning associated with the entities.

In fact, knowledge representation and reasoning are deeply related. Reasoning can be made easier and more relevant by an appropriate choice of knowledge representation. Depending on how knowledge is represented, certain problems are easier to solve and others more complicated. The problem in our case (and in many others) is that autonomic managers are very diverse in scope and, also, in terms of abstraction, types of actions to be undergone, timing constraints to be met, etc.

There is no single way to represent knowledge. However, there are some driving characteristics to be considered when devising a knowledge representation. Generally speaking, a 'good' knowledge representation should exhibit the following properties:

– *Appropriate expressiveness*. Knowledge representation should allow expression of all the concepts and relationships of interest in the domain.
– *Computationally tractable*. The knowledge representation format can be read and used by a machine.
– *Suitable reasoning support*. Knowledge representation should allow the system to reason about concepts and relationships without ambiguity. A representation is said to be consistent when all the inferences are true and complete when all the possible deductions can be made. Reasoning should be doable with the processing capabilities available today.

– *Structured*. A knowledge representation should support modularity and abstraction appropriate for its usage and evolution.

A key feature of knowledge representation is its expressivity. A highly expressive representation technique allows rich information to be defined and manipulated. But, at the same time, such expressive knowledge representations tend to be difficult and give rise to complex reasoning algorithms, not always doable by computers within an appropriate time. Conversely, less expressive knowledge representations may be simpler in terms of how they are manipulated and controlled, even if some concepts are hard, or impossible, to express.

The matter of knowledge representation has been intensively discussed in the early days of artificial intelligence. John McCarthy, at Stanford University, focused on descriptive knowledge and investigated formal logic to express and solve general problems. In contrast, researchers at the MIT like Marvin Minsky concentrated on prescriptive knowledge, arguing that there was no single principle for knowledge representation and reasoning.

This scientific and philosophical debate seems to be over, and it is today admitted that both forms of knowledge are needed (see Chap. 3). Let us quote Marvin Minsky:

> In the 1960s and 1970s, students frequently asked, "Which kind of representation is best?" and I usually replied that we'd need more research. … But now I would reply: To solve really hard problems, we'll have to use several different representations. This is because each particular kind of data structure has its own virtues and deficiencies, and none by itself would seem adequate for all the different functions involved with what we call common sense.

This of course also holds for autonomic systems. A major issue when building a self-managed system is then to find out how to represent the different forms of knowledge (and how to acquire them). In most cases, different formalisms are needed to represent the different pieces of information to be expressed. Intuitively, it may seem natural that prescriptive knowledge will often be at the heart of the MAPE tasks and that, by contrast, descriptive knowledge will often be used to express information related to design and domain constraints. But it is not so simple. For instance, propositional knowledge can be used to 'automate' analysis or planning, and, by contrast, procedural knowledge can be needed to express complex constraints verifications.

7.2 Knowledge in Autonomic Managers

7.2.1 Introduction

As said earlier, knowledge and reasoning are very much related. Depending on the expected adaptations, different forms of knowledge will be required in autonomic systems. Various representations, used to handle different aspects, can coexist in a same system. For instance, different knowledge representations may be used to reason about and implement self-reparation and self-configuration.

The issue, for each self-property targeted by a system, is then to identify and represent the different forms of knowledge that are needed: the acquaintance knowledge that is captured via *touchpoints* on the managed artefacts, the innate knowledge that is engraved in the heart of autonomic managers and that captures the domain expertise and, in some case, the description knowledge collected by tier parties.

Many knowledge representations used in current autonomic systems found their inspiration in artificial intelligence (see Chap. 3). Indeed, knowledge representation has always been central to AI. In order to act as a person, and incidentally to pass the Turing test [1], an intelligent machine has to be able to interact with its environment, to acquire and store knowledge, to conduct reasoning based on that knowledge and to learn.

There have been numerous debates in the AI community about the way knowledge and reasoning should be implemented. In short, the question is: should a machine have to think *like* a human or not? (Granted, this would depend on what that we know how a human thinks, another source of debate.) Answering this question leads to different ways to represent knowledge. As explained in Chap. 3, the 'thinking has a human' theorists explored domains as diverse as step-by-step logical inferences, neural networks, psychology, etc. Opponents of this theory sought to leverage the machines outstanding processing power and proposed solutions based, for instance, on space searches. In all the cases, the division between reasoning and knowledge is quite fuzzy, as one would expect. This is the very same when it comes to the division between planning (reasoning) and knowledge used to effect adaptation in the autonomic MAPE-K loop.

In this section, we use a classification commonly adopted in AI to distinguish between intelligent systems [2] depending on the adopted knowledge representation and associated reasoning:

- Rule-based systems implement knowledge through simple event–condition–action rules and are capable of quick, simple reflex adaptations.
- Model-based systems maintain models of the managed artefacts and of the computing environment in order to produce more thoughtful actions.
- Goal-based systems introduce and use an explicit definition of goals in order to guide reasoning.
- Utility-based systems introduce utility functions in order to compare and rank states satisfying goals.

7.2.2 Rule-Based Autonomic Systems

The simplest way to build an autonomic system is certainly to define reflex actions, which are essentially sets of event–condition–action (ECA) rules. In general, such systems determine plans of actions on the basis of their current perceptions and some internal policies. These rules, typically written by system administrators, are derived from system and business goals and describe the adaptation plans of the system. Knowledge acquired from the touchpoints is expressed as statements modelling the current state of the managed artefacts. The expertise to solve problems, the *know-how*, is entirely encoded in the production rules.

Rule-based autonomic systems are not *that* smart but can be very effective in many situations. For instance, ignoring the past considerably reduces the amount of

Fig. 7.2 Rule-based
autonomic systems

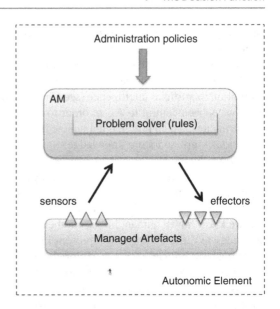

knowledge to be expressed and maintained. It also allows very quick reactions to be implemented on the managed artefacts (at least, the decision part is taken very rapidly). This approach is illustrated by Fig. 7.2. Let us note, however, that there is work in ECA rules that are dependent on historical data or past state, which allows more complex reasoning.

Writing adaptation policies is fairly straightforward but can become a tedious task for larger complex systems. Yet its simplicity remains its biggest strength. However, an issue with ECA rules is the problem of conflicts: an event might satisfy the conditions of two different ECA rules, yet each rule may dictate an action that conflicts with the other. Worse, these conflicts cannot always be detected at the time of writing the policies; some are only detected at runtime. This means that a human may remain in the loop to solve policy conflicts when they arise. There is however promising work on analysis of ECA rules to minimise conflicts and, then, reduce human intervention.

Here is a simple example of such rules:

```
<policy>disaster prediction - Client code
<condition> When disaster horizon is < buffer disaster
   threshold
<action>   Reduce QoS
</policy>

<policy>throughput prediction - Server Code
<condition> When average throughput peak is > throughput
   required for next QoS upgrade
<action>   Increase QoS
</policy>
```

Here we have a system that delivers audio data to differing quality of service levels. When the perceived network bandwidth is plentiful, the quality of the data can be increased. Conversely, when the bandwidth is less, the data is compressed and sent at a lower quality. The aim is to constantly deliver audio at the highest quality possible. This example shows two policies. The first one calculates the time that the client data buffer will be empty—meaning it cannot play the audio clip, something the system wants to avoid—and, if the threshold indicates this, tell the server to compress the data. The second one takes a bandwidth measurement from the server's point of view, and if it sees that the bandwidth is getting better, it increases the quality of the audio file. The conflict here is that networks are somewhat asymmetrical, and therefore the bandwidth available at either the client or server could be different resulting in the client wanting compressed data and the server wanting to increase the quality at the same time.

In the broadest sense, reasoning in autonomic systems involves making a decision regarding the changes and adaptations to assemble and implement on the managed element taking monitoring data as input. In the simplest case, we could define event–condition–action (ECA) rules that directly produce adaptation plans from specific event combinations. However, while applying this approach in a stateless manner minimises complexity and is quite lightweight, it is also very limiting. That is, the autonomic manager does not have to keep any information regarding the state of the managed element but relies solely on the current sensor data readings to decide whether to trigger an adaptation plan.

7.2.3 Model-Based Autonomic Systems

Alternatively the autonomic manager may keep information on the state of the managed element that can be updated progressively through fresh sensor readings and then reasoned about. This allows the manager to carry out predictions of what is coming next through trend analysis; it allows complex reasoning and analysis of the candidate solutions to the problem and then takes appropriate action. It also allows the system to be either more sensitive or less sensitive to the readings to avoid the phenomenon of oscillating forward and backwards between states and is also known as *state flapping*, in complex systems such as networks (we describe this phenomena in more detail in Chap. 8).

The information about a managed element is called a model. A model is a simplified, biased view of some reality or some intention. It is made of related concepts, devised by human beings in an attempt to intellectualise existing or possible things. Concepts must come with clear semantics that, in addition, has to be unique in order to avoid misunderstandings and confusion. Models are built with a specific purpose in mind. They are generally established in order to simplify as much as possible some sort of problem solving. That is, a model is created so that someone or something (*i.e.* a machine) can solve a certain problem or perform a specific task.

Many different models can be built to express the same reality or the same intention. For instance, a huge number of models of the world have been built in order to serve different purposes (estimate the time of a trip, forecast the weather, predict long-time climate evolution, etc.). And no single model can capture all the information needed to solve all sorts of problems. The variety of goals then lead to the variety of models.

Several models of the same thing, but handling different aspects, can be used jointly to support problem solving. This is a way to separate out concerns and get simpler and more focalised models based on different representation ontologies. Synchronising the different models at runtime may be an issue. One way to do so is to use a central model and to relate all the other models to it.

Models have always played a major role in science. They are in fact an essential means (if not the only one in certain cases) to reason about complex phenomenon that cannot be observed in detail or totally embraced by the human mind. In spite of considerable computing power, the situation is the same in computer science. Software systems have to use models in many situations because the domain problem is too complex or impossible to catch completely. For instance, models have been heavily used to represent the different structures of software systems (see Chap. 1) like their topology, behaviour and deployment units.

Numerous model representation languages have been devised in AI but also in software engineering. This is still a subject of intense research. Today, there is no agreement on a single general representation. Current research efforts concentrate on the definition of domain or aspect-specific modelling languages (DSL). Later, we will illustrate representations currently used to model pervasive applications and their associated environment.

In autonomic computing, models can be used to represent knowledge by acquaintance, which is acquired from the touchpoints, but also innate knowledge like reference architecture, devised at design time, for the managed artefacts. The expertise to solve problems, on the other hand, is encoded in a dedicated module, called problem solver in Fig. 7.3, which is kept separated from the models. Of course, the reasoning techniques employed by the problem solver heavily depend on the nature of models.

Although very useful, it should always be remembered that models are incomplete knowledge. Regardless of the representation language, the very purpose of models is to present a partial or abstract (or both) view of the managed artefacts because they are partially observable or because more advanced views would not be usable. Decisions based on such models have to be backed up by human beings, as it is anticipated in all definitions of autonomic computing.

7.2.4 Goal-Based Autonomic Systems

The model-based approach allows an autonomic manager to reason about the past and possibly about the future. That means that an action can be justified by the current state of the managed artefacts but also by trend analysis, by anterior events, by observed patterns, etc. This, of course, is not the case with reflex-based systems that only react to a given sequence of events (Fig. 7.4).

Like the rule-based approach, the model-based approach is driven by administration policies set by the administrators. These high-level goals are business or domain

Fig. 7.3 Model-based
autonomic systems

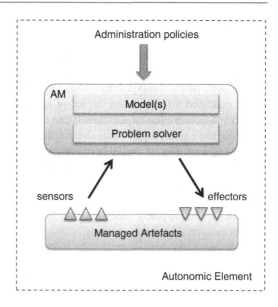

Fig. 7.4 Goal-based
autonomic systems

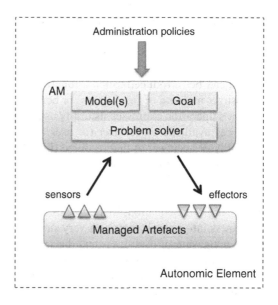

oriented and remain rather abstract. Detailed goals pursued by the system, in terms of expected states of the managed artefacts, are not made explicit. They are in fact embedded in the problem solver, and, as a consequence, they cannot be explicitly manipulated. Changing such detailed goals requires changing the code of the problem solver, which is always a daring task.

In goal-based autonomic systems, some part of the knowledge supporting management decisions is made explicit. Goals that are pursued by the system are represented separately from the problem solver. As said earlier, the notion of a goal has to be understood as the expected state of the managed artefacts, not like high-level administrative directives.

Making explicit this notion of a goal allows the definition of more flexible and more generic problem solvers. In this approach, a problem solver takes as inputs the current state of the managed artefacts, a goal (that can be expressed as target state of the managed artefacts) and the set of actions that can be triggered through the effectors to achieve the target state. It can then rely on generic, reusable algorithms to handle the current issue since the problem is now to align two state representations using a number of available operations. Search-based algorithms, forward and backward, have been very much used in this context.

Flexibility is a major advantage. We have seen throughout this book how dynamism is important in modern computing. This of course applies to autonomic systems. Being able to finely tune the target system states in a dynamic way is certainly a major property for many systems.

7.2.5   Utility-Based Autonomic Systems

In goal-based autonomic systems, the desirable states of the managed artefacts are made explicit. Such information is not always enough to decide on the right course of actions to solve a problem. Indeed, several states may be satisfactory and the problem solver has to choose between them.

In order to compare alternative states, a specific function allowing states to be ranked can be introduced. Such a function is called a *utility function*. Utility is an abstract measure of 'usefulness' or benefit to, for example, a user. Typically a system's operation expresses its utility as a measure of things, like the amount of resources available to the user (or user application programs), and the quality, reliability or accuracy of that resource (Fig. 7.5).

The notion of utility, or how useful something is, is indeed key to many autonomic systems. This drives the decision-making components of the system to allow it to decide between alternatives or to plan future configurations. Utility functions are the equations that allow us to combine the parameters that represent usefulness into a single metric. A very simple example is where we have throughput as a measure of usefulness and the server energy consumed as something we wish to minimise; then our utility function could be the throughput metric minus the cost of energy. Techniques, such as in decision networks, can then use utility functions to decide between choices. They can also be used in game theory whereby an agent representing some part of the system wants to maximise their utility but not at the cost of the other agents in the system, for example, and they trade off strategies to reach that state where a significant number of (or all) participants are happy (they reach a Nash equilibrium, e.g. see Chap. 2). Another example is in a resource provisioning system where the utility is derived from the cost of redistribution of workloads once allocated or the power consumption as a portion of operating cost [3, 4].

Fig. 7.5 Utility-based autonomic systems

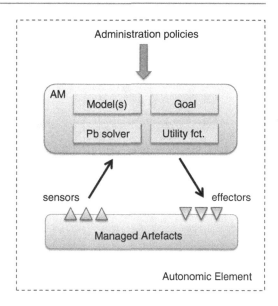

7.2.6 Autonomic Systems That Learn

The most ambitious autonomic systems are those that comprise learning capabilities. The purpose of such systems is to learn about their actions and to change the knowledge supporting the reasoning accordingly and, in some cases, the reasoning itself. That means that models can be changed, as well as utility functions used to compare desirable states.

A learning system relies on the ability to evaluate the usefulness of an action and to modify its knowledge based on that evaluation. Learning can take many different forms depending on the goals pursued by the autonomic systems and on the knowledge that needs to be updated as a function of the action's usefulness. Many methods have been defined in the AI community to better support learning, including neural networks. Most of them remain extremely complex. Another interesting approach is to use domain-specific algorithms to implement less ambitious but more focused learning capabilities (Fig. 7.6).

Many autonomic computing systems make use of reinforcement as a learning mechanism. Essentially, if the autonomic system is modelled as sets of agents, each agent's aim is to maximise its accumulative reward. These awards are given in response to the decisions made by the agent. Reinforcement learning crosscuts the AI techniques. It has been used to learn from expert domain knowledge and then derive the policies that would then be acted upon by the autonomic system. Its main usefulness is in its ability to carry out unsupervised learning. That is, its ability to derive relationships or structures between agents or components that hitherto were unknown and to do so where there is an absence of explicit system models or domain-specific knowledge.

Fig. 7.6 Learning autonomic systems

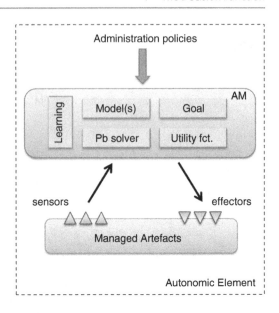

A very simple example is where we have an autonomic system supporting a mobile application that sends its output to the 'best' screen in the space where the user currently is. This makes use of data concerning the user's location and information about the screens that exist in that location. Such information can be the size of the screen or its frame rates or the colour encoding, etc. Some form of utility function can be derived that represents the best fit of data for a given screen (e.g. a movie would prefer a large high-definition screen, whereas text might want the closest screen to the use at this time). The system would need to trade off between the different utilities, and this may be difficult when all things are even. Therefore the system might decide to ask the user if it is doing a good job. It will send a message to ask if the decision was good and take tally of the times when it made a good decision and use this to reinforce that decision. That reinforcement will add weight to the decision process, influencing how it carries out the trade-offs in future.

Closely related to reinforcement is the use of stigmergy. Stigmergy is the trace left in the environment to allow two agents to help them make decisions. It comes from the study of how insects self-organise. Specifically ant colonies lay down a pheromone (scent) trace when they are returning to the next from gathering food. The routes taken by the ants may vary, but the 'best' route (which may be a function of distance and safety) is the one that the majority of ants travelled and therefore placed the largest scent on. This way, when they leave the nest, they pick the strongest route. In computing systems, we can increment (decrement) a value that increases (decreases) when something good (or bad) happens to represent the value of a decision biasing that decision for the future. Ant colony optimisation is an example of a decentralised self-organising technique that uses stigmergy to find solutions to complex problems [5].

7.3 Model-Driven Autonomicity

7.3.1 Introduction

Let us now focus on the notion of model, which is arguably central to advanced autonomic systems (i.e. those not solely based on reflex rules). An important question arises when it comes to models: what should be explicitly represented with models? (And, conversely, what should be kept in the problem solver?)

Potentially, all the knowledge obtained by acquaintance and part of the innate knowledge could be made available in explicit models. Concretely, the currently preferred strategy of researchers and practitioners is to build a number of separate models, including a model of the running software architecture, a model of the computing environment and models focusing on relevant non-functional properties like security and performance. To properly implement the principle of separation of concern, these models are kept distinct, but they are often closely linked. For instance, security concerns can be traced to architectural elements [6]. The explicit separation of models favours their independent evolution. Depending on the situation and the problems to be solved, some models can be refined more than others. However, the models to be represented, their level of abstraction, their formalisation, etc. are still defined on a case-by-case basis today.

Generally speaking, the more information is made explicit in models, the better for autonomic software evolution. This allows the MAPE tasks to focus on the computation (the know-how) and not on the data representation and collection. Furthermore, several tasks can use the same data representation. This makes the code leaner, more focused and easier to change.

Making models a key concern in autonomic computing is today a strong tendency. This is also a major trend in software engineering where an ambitious research field exclusively dedicated to the study of models has been recently established. Specifically, the model-driven engineering (MDE) community advocates the creation and exploitation of models to entirely drive the development and maintenance of software systems. Initially, models were essentially used to drive software development. The main principle was to bridge the gap between the specification of a problem and its solution through successive model transformations (representing a same system at different levels of abstraction). This was to hide the technological complexity of the implementation and allow a better communication between the different actors involved in software development.

Models used in MDE are said to be productive in the sense that they lead to an implementation in a programming language after a certain number of transformations. Otherwise, models are said to be contemplative and are solely used to improve communication between stakeholders and drive development informally.

Models are now seen as strategic artefacts that can be used all along software life cycle and not only at design time. France and Rumpe [7] introduced the idea of model at runtime (*model@runtime*) to abstractly capture runtime phenomenon. Such model is in synchronisation with an operational system and can be used to get synthetic information about the system operations. This is clearly in line with the

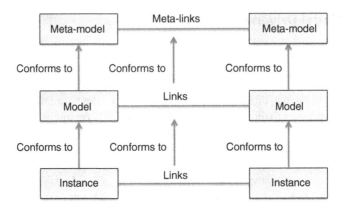

Fig. 7.7 Models and meta-models

autonomic purposes, and it is no surprise that the model orientation brings together scientific communities working on autonomic computing and software engineering at runtime (as outlined in the introductory chapter).

7.3.2 Model Representation

In the MDE community, models are often presented as graphs. A node is a concept (a file, a programming structure, a property, etc.), and a link is a relationship between concepts. Cardinalities can be added to represent the number of concept instances than can be implied in a relationship. UML is an example of language for graph-based representation of models [8].

In order to be productive, a model has to be usable by a machine. To do so, models must be formalised in a specification language that has to be clear, precise and non-ambiguous. Since all the aspects of such a specification language have to be modelled, the language itself can be seen as a model. This introduces the notion of meta-model, which is a model that defines the language for expressing a model [9]. Just like a model, a meta-model can be expressed as a graph. In the specific case of UML, a meta-model is represented as a class diagram (Fig. 7.7).

A meta-model is used to define a grammar and a vocabulary allowing the creation of models that are conformed and coherent. To ensure conformity, models are created through instantiation of the meta-model.

As said earlier, a system can be represented by several models focusing on different aspects, possibly at different levels of abstraction. For these models to be productive, it is necessary to compose them in order to have a global view of a system. Model composition can be defined as the mechanism of combining two models into a new one [10].

Model composition can be expressed at a meta-level, since meta-models are models. Specifically, a composition of meta-models is the union of several meta-models, which sometimes requires integrating, bridging rules. Links between meta-models are called meta-links. Model composition is difficult and is still the subject of numerous research initiatives. Yet nevertheless it constitutes a great technique to express knowledge in autonomic systems. As said earlier, there are different aspects to be represented in self-managed systems: design models, domain models, models abstracting away runtime phenomenon, etc. It is good practice to separate these different aspects. It allows a better understanding and better testing and leads to better evolution. In addition, all the pieces of information are not needed all the time. If models are separated, they can be loaded or updated at different moments in a context-aware fashion.

7.3.3 Architectural Models

In the architectural model-driven approach, a model of either a focused part of or indeed the entire managed system is understood by the autonomic manager. This architectural model reflects the system's structure and behaviour, its requirements and the system states required to match its goals. The model may also represent some aspect of the operating environment in which the managed elements are deployed. The operating environment can be understood as any observable property (detected by the sensors) that can impact the managed element's execution, for example, end-user input, hardware devices and network connection properties (see discussion about context in Chap. 2). The model is updated through sensor data and used to reason about the managed system to plan valid and appropriate adaptations. A great advantage of the architectural model-based approach to planning is that, under the assumption that the model correctly mirrors the managed system, the architectural model can be used to verify that system integrity is preserved when applying an adaptation, that is, we can guarantee that the system will continue to operate correctly after the planned adaptation has been executed. This is because changes are planned and applied to the model first, which will show the resulting system state including any violations of constraints or requirements of the system present in the model. If the new state of the system is acceptable, the plan can then be executed on the actual managed system, thus ensuring that the model and imple-mentation are consistent with respect to each other.

Building a model of the system under question is a non-trivial task. It assumes that the architect understands the components, their interaction and behaviours to ensure accuracy. Further, the model needs to be able to run through the different adaptation scenarios to check that an update is both useful and safe. Given the number of states and each state's interaction, the search of all interactions is a highly complex problem of exponential proportions. This may mean that the model and the system are highly decoupled. For example, the model may run on a different machine so as to not impact the managed systems' operation. Also to improve on the time the model reaches an optimum solution, heuristics may be used, which may or may not add error to the model. Either way, this processing may incur heavy execution costs.

Repair strategies of the architecture model may be specified as ECA rules, for example, where an event is generated when the model is invalidated by sensor updates, and an appropriate rule specifies the actions necessary to return the model to a valid state. In practice, however, there is always a delay between the time when a change occurs in the managed system and this change is applied to the model. Indeed, if the delay is sufficiently high and the system changes frequently, an adaptation plan may be created and sent for execution under the belief that the actual system was in a particular state, for example, a Web server overloaded, when in fact the environment has already changed in the meantime and the system no longer requires this adaptation anymore (or it requires a different adaptation plan) [11]. To overcome this, in many of the model-driven adaption systems, the model is stored and executed on a separate machine from the computers that host the managed elements and the resulting parallelism improves the processing of the model.

Architectural models tend to share the same basic idea of the model being a graph of components and connectors. The components represent some unit of concurrent computing task, whereas the connectors represent the communication between components. Usually, there is no restriction as to the level of granularity of a component: it could be a complete Web server, an application on a Web server or a component of an application. The architectural model does not describe a precise configuration of components and connectors that the managed element must conform to. Instead, it sets a number of constraints and properties on the component and connectors, so that it can be determined when the managed element violates the model and needs adaptation. Let us now continue our description of architectural model-based planning in the MAPE-K loop by taking a look at some of the most notable architectural description languages (ADLs), which can be used to specify an architectural model of a managed system.

Let us start with Darwin, one of the first ADLs that was the result of seminal work by Magee et al. [12]. In Darwin, the architectural model is a directed graph in which nodes represent component instances and arcs specify bindings between a service required by one component and the service provided by another. Further, the allow object modelling notation [13] has been applied to Darwin components to be able to specify constraints on the components [14]. For instance, consider the scenario where there are a number of server components offering services and a number of client components requiring services. Each service of a component is typed so that different services offered by a server or requested by a client can be distinguished and properly matched. In this scenario, the architectural model can guarantee that there are enough servers to service the clients. Should that not be the case, new server components must be started that offer the unavailable service types in order to return the model to a valid state. In this approach, each component keeps a copy of the architectural model. In other words, each component in the architectural model is an autonomic element with a managed element and an autonomic manager that holds the architectural model to the entire system. This approach avoids the presence of a central architectural model management service,

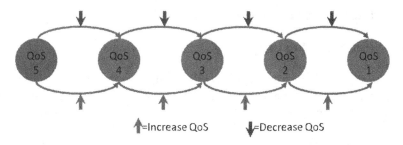

Fig. 7.8 Darwin component model

which would otherwise introduce the problem of detecting and handling the failure of this central component. Where such a decentralised approach is taken, there is however the problem of keeping the architectural model up to date and consistent across all copies in the autonomic managers. This can be achieved with fully ordered atomic broadcasts, which work as long as no communication partitions occur between the components.

Figure 7.8 shows how to represent a component in Darwin. To initially construct and subsequently change systems, we need a set of operations on components. These are typically to create, delete, bind components to a port, unbind, and set mode to a value. A system constructed in this way will have a configuration or management state consisting precisely of the set of components instances, the set of connections between components and the set component mode values.

Other architectural models have since been developed, we show only two of the many as they summarise many of the styles that are available. The Acme adaptation framework [11, 15, 16] is a software architecture that uses an architectural model for monitoring and detecting the need for adaptation in a system. The components and connectors of their architectural model can be annotated with a property list and constraints for detecting the need for adaptation. A first-order predicate language (called Armani) is used in Acme to analyse the architectural model and detect violations in the executing system. An imperative language is then used to describe repair strategies, much like the policy-based approach. The difference lies in how the need for adaptation is detected and the appropriate adaptation rule selected. Whereas in policies it is explicitly described in the rules, with an architectural model, the need for adaptation implicitly emerges when the running system violates constraints imposed by the architectural model.

Similarly in C2/xADL [17, 18], an important contribution lies in starting with an old architectural model and a new one based on recent monitoring data and then computing the difference between the two in order to create a repair plan. Given the architecture model of the system, the repair plan is analysed to ascertain that the change is valid (at least at the architectural description level). The repair plan is then executed on the running system without restarting it.

7.4   Reasoning Techniques

7.4.1   Programming Languages

Models are built to support reasoning. Simply put, they have to enable administration task to analyse the situation and plan eventual courses of actions. The information they contain is a necessary element to make the right decisions with the available resources (time and computation power).

As said many times, models and associated reasoning are however closely tied. This is illustrated by Fig. 7.9. In fact, models representation and reasoning techniques are designed jointly. These complex design decisions are driven by the complexity of the problems to be tackled, the needed forms of reasoning, the available data, the time and computing resources available, the expected software qualities like reusability or flexibility, etc.

The purpose of this section is to present reasoning techniques well suited to autonomic systems. It is not meant to be exhaustive. In fact, there is not such a thing as a general reasoning approach for autonomic management. Depending on the requirements, different techniques with different properties can be selected.

In computer science, a natural way to reason about a model (or more generally speaking a knowledge base) is certainly to write a program with a classic programming language like C or Java, for instance. Although this is not always the easiest way, it is certainly the most widely applicable approach implemented so far. Programming languages provide rich notations for the specification of computations (algorithms) manipulating complex data structures. Data can be the result of the computation or be acquired from a database, a model, etc. Programming languages are also complemented with supporting tools facilitating program specification, compiling, debugging, execution tracing, etc.

The AI community, however, pointed out some limitations of general-purpose programming languages. First, programs are essentially domain specific. That is, they are written by programmers to deal with a specific problem. Programs can be extremely effective and relevant to the problem at hand, but they are hardly reusable and often lack flexibility. Also, programming languages do not possess automatic inference capabilities, allowing the on-the-fly creation of new knowledge. Obviously, this constraint is not an issue for most systems. It can be seen as a limitation when creating general problem-solving techniques, which is precisely an important goal in AI.

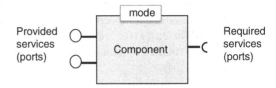

Fig. 7.9 Epistemological relationships between models and reasoning

7.4.2 Search-Based Reasoning

Some approaches, often originating from AI, thus put forward general-purpose algorithms that can be used to solve classes of problems. This is the case, in particular, of search-based techniques that can be applied to deal with some autonomic management issues.

Indeed, knowledge in autonomic computing systems can be described as a problem space where we want to find either a good or the best solution. That is, the system is characterised by a current state, captured via touchpoints, and one or several possible target states. The problem is then to find out a path from the current state to a satisfactory state.

In the context of autonomic computing, a search problem can be defined by:

- The description of the initial state, corresponding to the current situation of the managed artefacts.
- The description of the acceptable target states (the goals), also in terms of the managed artefacts.
- The set of actions that can be realised on the managed artefacts. These actions correspond to the effectors provided by the managed artefacts.
- A transition model defining the actions to be realised to change states.

Historically, search-based problem solving has been one of the first fields heavily explored in AI. Many algorithms have been devised and successfully used in many domains. The most successful algorithms are known under the names of breadth-first, depth-first or iterative deepening. These algorithms defer on the space exploration strategy that is implemented: depth-first algorithms expand the node further away first, breadth-first algorithms expand the closest node first, and iterative deepening uses depth-first strategy but with a depth limit that can be augmented if no solution is found. These general-purpose algorithms can be extremely costly, depending on the number of nodes and the branching factor. They can be complemented with domain-specific heuristics to improve their performance.

Let us note that abstraction is key here. States and actions are described abstractly. As already emphasised, it is not possible to describe in detail every aspect of the managed artefacts. A model focusing on the necessary information is then built to support reasoning (search based in this case). Similarly, actions are also described abstractly. The details are kept in the touchpoints (effectors) and not explicitly manipulated by the problem solver.

An example of a search-based autonomic system may be one that has to maximise the processing throughput of a mobile computing device, say, but at the same time has to save energy (see Fig. 7.10). The problem space that is searched to find an optimum solution covers the parameters or settings that affect throughput, and this is conjoined to a further space that covers how those parameters affect energy usage.

Therefore we need to search through both those spaces to find possible solutions where the optimal of one does not impact negatively of the other. This may involve searching through trees of goals or bounded areas to find localised solutions; the search also may be the result of logical step-by-step analysis of rules that deduce the solution. Some approaches start with an initial idea of where in the search space a

Fig. 7.10 Example of search
space

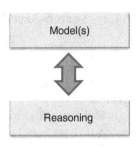

potential solution to the problem lies, and then this initial idea is iteratively refined until no better solution can be found. Where the search space is large or unwieldy, or worse impossible to cover, heuristics are used to reduce the amount of area that is required to be searched. Heuristics are methods and rules that help us to guide the search, and these can originate from human knowledge about the problem. The ultimate aim is to reduce the search space, to reach the solution quickly, but with techniques that cause minimal impact on the solution optimality.

Evolutionary approaches to optimisation, which can sometimes be described as bio-inspired, carry out the search for the optimal solution by representing the space of potential solutions as organisms. In, for example, genetic algorithms, the organisms mutate and recombine, and only those organisms that are described as 'fit', that is, they are part of the algorithm parameters that bring the search closer to the solution, survive to the next round or iteration of the algorithm. Another example of a bio-inspired approach is those one that exploits swarm intelligence (e.g. network routing with stigmergy, as mentioned earlier). Here storage areas are used to mark good solutions or to reinforce good routes, so that packets will be sent down the better routes available to them at a given time.

7.4.3   Logic-Based Reasoning

Logic can be used as a means to represent knowledge, and different types of logic programming can be used to learn from the past or to derive examples and knowledge from past data. A formal logic system defines a set of primitive symbols, axioms and rules allowing the formation of sentences by inference. An axiom is a proven sentence, that is to say one not obtained through inference. The system thus consists of any number of sentences built up through finite combinations of the primitive symbols—combinations that are formed from the axioms in accordance with the stated rules.[6] A number of formal logic systems with different levels of expressiveness, and with differing costs for their associated reasoning algorithms, have been devised.

---

[6]http://www.britannica.com/EBchecked/topic/213751/formal-system

In logic systems, knowledge and inference are separate, which allows inference to be domain independent. This is undoubtedly a major property. It means that once axioms and rules are properly defined, you just have to feed the systems with facts about the running systems and then actions to be undergone can be inferred. One issue is that even a 'simple' logic system, like propositional logic or first-order logic, can have complexities for some problems that demand important resources (propositional logic is decidable in polynomial time).

Logic systems can also represent facts, or fuzzy representations of facts, where the value of a statement is allocated a value between 0 and 1 or a probabilistic scale rather than simply being true or false.

There are in fact many formal logic approaches. Propositional logic is a simple declarative language allowing the definition of sentences from proposition symbols (facts) and operators. A sentence combines symbols (and other sentences recursively) with negation, conjunction, disjunction, equivalence and implication operators. Propositional logic has sufficient expressiveness to deal with partial information, using disjunction and negation. First-order logic is more expressive than propositional logic. It extends the syntax of propositional logic with universal and existential quantifiers in order to express sentences about some or all the objects of the world. The expressiveness of first-order logic has however a cost in term of inference complexity. In simple cases, problems expressed with first-order logic can be reduced to propositional logic problem when the domain of discourse is finite or can be discretised. More complex problems require complex algorithms to be used, which may not be compatible with the usual resources of an autonomic system.

Finally, let us mention constraint logic programming which can be applied to autonomic computing [19]. Constraint logic programming aims to satisfy constraints to prove the problem, that is, the solution lies in an answer that satisfies all the constraints. It is used for systems with many constraints such as timetabling and air traffic control-type problems.

Most of these techniques require a model of the world to be represented in the problem space. However this is extremely difficult to do and to do so accurately. Therefore some techniques that have been inspired by economics and probability theory have been devised that are applied when we have either incomplete or uncertain information. One such class of reasoning method that is popular with autonomic systems is that of Bayesian networks which have been used for inference, learning optimisation and decision-making. *Hidden Markov models* and *Kalman filters* are other examples of probabilistic approaches to perceive processes over time, ignoring useless data (noise) and aiding the prediction of events in the future.

Using logic to express models is always a challenge. It requires defining symbols representing the world (the managed artefacts and computing environment in our case), axioms and inference rules in order to capture some domain expertise. The transition from informal know-how knowledge and logic-based formalism is rarely straightforward. Also, inference algorithms can be extremely costly and largely exceed the available resources. Indeed many attempts to use formal systems in computer science fell short because of exceeding complexity of inference algorithms.

7.4.4 Classifiers and Statistical Learning Methods

Knowledge can be obtained through the grouping of data into classes or noticing groupings or patterns in data. Classification algorithms scrutinise examples or observations of phenomena, and by identifying patterns in this data, they derive sets of classes. At this point, the system has been 'trained' to classify the data so that when new data is given to the classification algorithms, they are in a good position and place that data in one of those classes and perhaps with a percentage representing the confidence in doing so. This placement of a piece of data in a class is the knowledge. For example, when an autonomic system has observed a high response time for a task and at the same time the CPU utilisation is quite low, then it can use this data to place the task's activity into a particular class—the class most likely being that the job is experiencing deadlock, for example. Essentially, this approach is making current decisions based on previous experience. Using our simple example, the system would have been trained with parameters that represented the characteristics about many previous tasks run on the computer. These would have been those that had a high response times and high CPU utilisation, low response times and low utilisation, high response times and low utilisation, etc. In turn, perhaps with the aid of the system administrator, the system would be told that the first set was typical of complex CPU bound jobs, the second set of high IO bound jobs and the final set would typify tasks in a deadlock situation. By classifying the data, one can feed a condition action (EA) rule which acts upon the detection of deadlock to bring the task back to its starting point releasing any resources it may have.

There are many examples of such approaches. *Neural networks* are used by many autonomic computing systems. Here the characteristics are modelled as neurons and links, or connections are made between these neurons to represent relationships. Classification occurs by varying parameters, weights on connections, etc. These values may change as the system 'learns'. Neural networks are used for time series prediction, fitness approximation, pattern and sequence recognition and anomaly detection in autonomic systems. Other approaches to classification are: *support vector machines* which have been used for reputation systems; *naive Bayes classifiers* which have been used to mine systems log files to derive knowledge for the autonomic manager; and *K-nearest neighbour algorithms* which have been used in decentralised pattern recognition for context awareness. Choosing the appropriate classifier for a given application is a tricky business.

7.5 Bayesian Networks Example

The purpose of this section is to provide an example using logic for knowledge representation and reasoning. We have chosen an example based on Bayesian techniques for they are very popular today to deal with uncertain environments. Bayesian networks are based on formal logic. In this section, we explain the basics of Bayesian networks by way of an example that can be applied to many systems that use utility as a means of decision-making in autonomic computing architectures. The example used is an amended version of the work on autonomic middleware from [20].

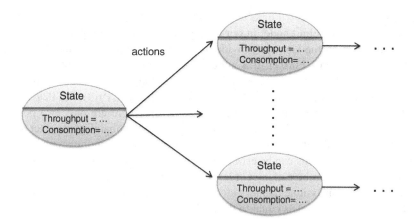

Fig. 7.11 Example of Bayesian network for autonomic service selection

In this example, we have an intelligent home that has a number of sensors that determine what the person in the home is doing. Each sensor is providing data regarding the person, such as the person's location or whether or not they are sitting or standing. This we call *context*, and each sensor is therefore a Context Provider (CP). Each sensor is also able to provide a quantitative value as to how well it can measure that context; this we call *probability of correctness* (*poc*).

To be able to derive the user's activity in this example, we need to combine data from different sources of the same type of context. That is, there may be more than one sensor (CP) that can provide us with the user's activity (e.g. pressure pad on the floor and/or a video camera in the room). Combining sensor data will increase the chances of correctly reporting the user's context. In our system, we wish the combination to deliver an output with a probability of correctness that takes into account the level of agreement between the different CPs given their individual advertised probability of correctness. From this, the autonomic manager can select the best combination of CPs to choose.

In this example, the goal is to take the context of all the Context Provider services for the context type 'activity' (in the sense of 'standing', 'sitting', etc.) and output a final context value that takes into account the value of all contest providers for this type and their probability of correctness each. This approach is applicable to any context with a finite set of discrete context values. The final output is based on probabilities; therefore, we use a probabilistic reasoning technique to solve this problem.

Bayesian networks are one approach to this problem and are frequently used in reasoning about autonomic management and decision-making. Further, efficient algorithms exist to perform inference and learning in Bayesian networks adding to its usefulness. Bayesian networks model sequences of variables and allow us to represent the relationship between the activity, the output of the CPs sensing the activity and the final output as a Bayesian network.

Figure 7.11 shows the Bayesian network of what we have just described. It is essentially a directed acyclic graph, where the nodes of the graph represent random variables, while the directed links represent the influential relationship that the parent node has on the child node. In our example, the activity being monitored has a direct influence on the Context Providers that are trying to determine the activity through their sensors. Further, the output of the CPs has a direct influence on the final output. To this end, we must define for each node its conditional probability given its parents. Thus, we define the probabilities $P(A)$, $P(CP1|A)$, $P(CP2|A)$... and $P(O|CP1, CP2,...)$. For simplicity, let us assume that there are only two possible values of activity: 'sitting' (si) and 'standing' (st). The probability of either sitting or standing is represented as the probability of an activity given the inputs from the sensors as $P(A)$, and this can be estimated by observing the frequency of the different final outputs (numbers of si or st *representing sitting or standing, respectively*).

Initially, we can assume that all outcomes are equiprobable; therefore, we set the probability of A given si as equal to the probability of A given st:

$$P(A = \text{si}) = P(A = \text{st}) = 0.5.$$

Let's also assume that we only have two Context Providers. The probability of the first Context Provider given the activity, $P(CP1|A)$ is the probability of correctness as advertised by CP1. If there is only one advertised probability of correctness, then we use that value for all possible context values (si and st in our example). However, we assume that in reality, different context values have a different probability of being correct, and therefore a single probability of correctness value is an approximation for the probability of correctness value of a specific context value. So, if on the other hand we have a specific probability of correctness value for each context value, then we can use these values for $P(CP1|A)$, that is, in our example:

$$P(CP1 = \text{si} \mid A = \text{si}) = poc(\text{si})$$
$$P(CP1 = \text{st} \mid A = \text{si}) = 1 - poc(\text{si})$$

and

$$P(CP1 = \text{st} \mid A = \text{st}) = poc(\text{st})$$
$$P(CP1 = \text{si} \mid A = \text{st}) = 1 - poc(\text{st})$$

Now, the same can be applied to $P(CPi|A)$ for any CP of this context type. Once we have chosen a definition for $P(O|CP1, CP2)$, this describes the strategy we use to combine the Context Providers to produce the final output, as we then select the output value with maximum probability $P(O|CP1, CP2)$. Finally, given $P(O|CP1, CP2)$, we can use the Bayesian network to find the most likely activity given the final output and its probability:

$$P(A = x \mid O = x) = \alpha P\left(A = x\right) \sum_{c_1, c_2 \in C} P(O = x \mid CP_1 = c_1, CP_2 = c_2)$$
$$P(CP_1 = c_1 \mid A = x)P(CP_2 = c_2 \mid a = x)$$

where C represents the set of all possible context values ($x \in C$) and α is a scaling factor that normalises the resulting probabilities $P(A|O)$ such that they sum up to 1. This result is obtained by applying the general form of Bayesian' rule with normalisation: $P(Y|X) = \alpha P(X|Y)P(Y)$.

Table 7.1 Conditional probability table, for example, with $|CP| = 4$ and $M = \{st, si, ld\}$

$A = st$	CP_1	CP_2	CP_3	CP_4
st	1	1	1	1
si	0	0	0	0
ld	0	0	0	0
$A = si$				
st	0	0	0	0
si	1	1	1	1
ld	0	0	0	0
$A = ld$				
st	0	0	0	0
si	0	0	0	0
ld	1	1	1	1

Table 7.2 Output for CP's CPT as in Table 7.1

CP_1	CP_2	CP_3	CP_4	O	$A = st$
st	st	st	St	**st**	1
st	st	st	St	si	0
st	st	st	St	ld	0
si	si	si	Si	st	0
si	si	si	Si	**si**	1
si	si	si	Si	ld	0
ld	ld	ld	Ld	st	0
ld	ld	ld	Ld	si	0
ld	ld	ld	Ld	**ld**	1

$P(A|O)$ can be used as a measure of the probability of correctness of the final output, and the definition of $P(O|CP1, CP2)$ determines how the final output depends on the output of the CPs.

Let's see how we can use this by constructing a conditional probability table for four Context Providers; see Table 7.1. Now we add the extra context of lying down (ld). The activities that the person in the intelligent home can perform (M) are standing (st), sitting (si) and lying down (ld). Then we can work through an example.

Table 7.1 shows the conditional probability table (CPT) for the CPs where we assume each CP always outputs the correct value (Sensors are notoriously unreliable, but for this first example, we assume they are new and with fresh batteries and therefore accurate). Table 7.2 then shows CPT for the output by applying the definition $P(O|CP1, CP2, CP3, CP4)$ (only combinations of CP that are at all possible are shown).

Now let's be more realistic. Table 7.3 shows the CPTs for the CPs. Now, each CP is 80 % accurate, that is, all CPs output the correct context with probability 0.8. Table 7.4 shows an extract of the resulting probabilities for the output. As you can see in the case where CPs output (st, st, st, st), if all CPs agree on the same context value, O's probability of correctness is very close to 1, far higher than the probability of correctness of each single Context Provider. This is the behaviour we want. After all, intuitively, it is far more likely that the output has a certain value if four Context Providers with high accuracy output this value (independently) than if we only have one CP that outputs this

Table 7.3 Conditional probability table, for example, with *poc* smaller than 1 and where all CPs agree on output

$A = \text{st}$	CP_1	CP_2	CP_3	CP_4
st	0.8	0.8	0.8	0.8
si	0.1	0.1	0.1	0.1
ld	0.1	0.1	0.1	0.1
$A = \text{si}$				
st	0.1	0.1	0.1	0.1
si	0.8	0.8	0.8	0.8
ld	0.1	0.1	0.1	0.1
$A = \text{ld}$				
st	0.1	0.1	0.1	0.1
si	0.1	0.1	0.1	0.1
ld	0.8	0.8	0.8	0.8

Table 7.4 Extract of final output given CP CPT in Table 7.3

CP_1	CP_2	CP_3	CP_4	O	$A = \text{st}$
st	st	st	st	**st**	**0.9995**
st	st	st	st	si	0.0002
st	st	st	st	ld	0.0002
si	st	st	st	st	**0.9827**
si	st	st	st	**si**	0.0154
si	st	st	st	ld	0.0019
...					
ld	si	st	st	**st**	**0.8**
ld	si	st	st	si	0.1
ld	si	st	st	ld	0.1
...					
ld	ld	st	st	st	**0.4961**
ld	ld	st	st	si	0.0078
ld	ld	st	st	**ld**	**0.4961**
...					
ld	ld	ld	ld	st	0.0002
ld	ld	ld	ld	si	0.0002
ld	ld	ld	ld	**ld**	**0.9995**

value. Note also that in the case where CPs have output (ld, ld, st, st), that is, half the CPs output context *c* and half context *a*, these two values are equally likely of being output, whereas si, while possible, is extremely unlikely. This is also the desired behaviour.

Consider now a more complicated example. Table 7.4 shows the CPTs for the CPs in this example.

Numbers in bold represent the probability of a CP's output given the real context, that is, the probability of the most likely value. Table 7.4 shows an extract of the output when we apply the definition $P(O|CP1, CP2)$.

Here, given the combination of output from CPs (st, si, ld, st), the most likely final output is $O = $st. This reflects the fact that, in Table 7.4, given an activity $A = $st, the most likely value of each CP is (st, si, ld, st) as emphasised by the probabilities in bold. This behaviour is also obtained in the cases (si, si, si, si) and (ld, si, ld ld) for the activities $A = $si and $A = $ld, respectively, as expected. Further, the probability of correctness of the final output is greater than the *poc* of any single Context Provider, so taking all four Context Providers into account does give us an advantage to using a single CP.

In summary, this example shows that through using a probabilistic reasoning approach, we are able to combine outputs from Context Providers with different values and probability of correctness and produce an output that has its own measure of uncertainty, which is determined by the uncertainty in the Context Providers. Further, taking multiple Context Providers into account produces better results than taking only a single CP.

7.6   Key Points

In this chapter, we have introduced the following important points:

- In order to exhibit self-administration properties, autonomic systems must rely on some form of knowledge about themselves, about the computing environment and about ways to solve problems.
- The general notion of knowledge is very complex. Its study gave birth to a philosophical domain of its own called epistemology. The classical definition of knowledge, adopted in this book, traces back to antiquity: knowledge is *true belief* that has been *justified*.
- We made a distinction between knowledge by acquaintance and knowledge by description. Knowledge by acquaintance is the result of a direct interaction with a person or with an object. Knowledge by description is a familiarity with someone or something that is acquired indirectly, by education, for instance. Knowledge can also be innate in the sense that someone possesses knowledge before acquiring it by acquaintance or by description.
- Self-management decisions have to often be made with incomplete knowledge. Managed artefacts are complex software constructions that cannot be completely known. They are apprehended through the *touchpoints* they offer, and only a limited amount of information can be collected. This is the same for the computing environment, which is often only partially known.
- Rule-based systems implement knowledge through simple event–condition–action rules and are capable of quick, simple reflex adaptations. Model-based systems maintain models of the managed artefacts and of the computing environment in order to produce more thoughtful actions. Goal-based systems introduce and use an explicit definition of goals in order to guide reasoning. Utility-based systems introduce utility functions in order to compare and rank states satisfying goals.
- Making models a key concern in autonomic computing is today a strong tendency. In particular, architectural models are built to drive many self-management

actions. These models reflect the system's structure and behaviour, its requirements and the system states required to match its goals.

- A great advantage of the architectural model-based approach to planning is that, under the assumption that the model correctly mirrors the managed system, the architectural model can be used to verify that system integrity is preserved when applying an adaptation.
- Models are built to support reasoning. There are a number of reasoning techniques well suited to autonomic systems. This includes programming languages, search-based reasoning and logic-based reasoning, which are discussed in this chapter.

References

1. Turing, A.: Computing machinery and intelligence. Mind **LIX**(36), 433–460 (1950)
2. Russel, S., Norvig, P.: Artificial Intelligence, a Modern Approach. Prentice Hall, Englewood Cliffs (2010)
3. Osogami, T., Harchol-Balter, M., Scheller-Wolf, A.: Analysis of cycle stealing with switching times and thresholds. Perform. Eval. **61**(4), 347–369 (2005)
4. Sharma, V., Thomas, A., Abdelzaher, T., Skadron, K., Lu, Z.: Power-aware qos management in web servers. In: RTSS'03: Proceedings of the 24th IEEE International Real-Time Systems Symposium, p. 63. IEEE Computer Society, Washington, DC (2003)
5. Dorigo, M., Blum, C.: Ant colony optimization theory: a survey. Theor. Comput. Sci. **344**(2–3), 243–278 (2005). doi:10.1016/j.tcs.2005.05.020. http://dx.doi.org/10.1016/j.tcs.2005.05.020
6. Chollet, S., Lalanda, P.: An extensible Abstract Service Orchestration Framework. In: Proceedings of the IEEE 7th International Conference on Web Services (ICWS 09), Los Angeles, CA, 6 July 2009
7. France, R., Rumpe, B.: Model-driven development of complex software: a research roadmap. In: FOSE'07: 2007 Future of Software Engineering, pp. 37–54. IEEE Computer Society, Washington, DC (2007)
8. OMG.: Unified Modeling Language (UML). http://www.omg.org/technology/documents/modeling_spec_catalog.htm#UML. Feb 2009
9. OMG.: Meta-Object Facility (MOFTM) specification, version 1.4. http://www.omg.org/cgi-bin/doc?formal/2002-04-03. Apr 2002
10. Herrmann, C., Holger Krahn, H., Rumpe, B., Schindler, M., Völkel, S.: An algebraic view on the semantics of model composition. In: Model Driven Architecture – Foundations and Applications. Lecture Notes in Computer Science, vol. 4530, pp. 99–113. Springer, Berlin/Heidelberg (2007)
11. Garlan, D., Schmerl, B., Chang, J.: Using gauges for architecture-based monitoring and adaptation. In: Working Conference on Complex and Dynamic Systems Architecture, Brisbane, Australia (2001)
12. Magee, J., Dulay, N., Eisenbach, S., Kramer, J. (eds.).: Specifying distributed software architectures. In: Proceedings of 5th European Software Engineering Conference (ESEC '95), Sitges. LNCS 989, pp. 137–153. Springer, Berlin/Heidelberg (1995)
13. Jackson, D.: Alloy: a lightweight object modelling notation. Softw.Eng. Methodol. **11**(2), 256–290 (2002)
14. Georgiadis, I., Magee, J., Kramer, J.: Self-organising software architectures for distributed systems. In: Proceedings of the First Workshop on Self-Healing Systems, Charleston, South Carolina, USA (2002)
15. Garlan, D., Schmerl, B.: Exploiting architectural design knowledge to support self- repairing systems. In: Proceedings of the 14th International Conference on Software Engineering and Knowledge Engineering, 15–19 July, Ischia Island, Italy (2002)

16. Garlan, D., Schmerl, B.: Model-based adaptation for self-healing systems. In: Proceedings of the First Workshop on Self-Healing Systems, Charleston, South Carolina, USA (2002)
17. Oreizy, P., Medvidovic, N., Taylor, R.N.: Architecture-based runtime software evolution. In: ICSE'98: Proceedings of the 20th International Conference on Software Engineering, pp. 177–186. IEEE Computer Society, Washington, DC (1998)
18. Dashofy, E.M., van der Hoek, A., Taylor, R.N.: Towards architecture-based self-healing systems. In: Proceedings of the First Workshop on Self-Healing Systems, Charleston, South Carolina, USA (2002)
19. Dearle, A., Kirby, G.N.C., McCarthy, A.J.: A framework for constraint-based development and autonomic management of distributed applications. In: Proceedings of International Conference on Autonomic Computing, 2004, pp. 300–301, 17–18 May 2004
20. McCann, J.A., Huebscher, M., Hoskins, A.: Context as autonomic intelligence in a ubiquitous computing environment. Int. J. Internet Protocol Technol. (IJIPT) special edition on Autonomic Computing 2(1), 30–39, Inderscience Publishers, Geneva, Switzerland

Evaluation Issues

8

Computer scientists, and the computing industries, rely on the ability to build systems and iteratively evaluate the design and implementational decisions that they have made during that process. As we have seen in previous chapters, an autonomic computing system can take many forms and as a consequence their evaluation, and moreover comparison, can be difficult. The very nature of some systems that emerge solutions adds further complexity to their evaluation. This chapter presents the challenges to evaluating an autonomic system, what to look out for and what others have attempted to do to aid this activity.

The chapter's aim is to enable the reader to be able to design tests and metrics that can be used to evaluate autonomic computing systems with a particular focus on the aspects that makes an autonomic system different from those without self-management features. As you will see, there is no single definitive metric that can be used in assessing the mechanisms of all autonomic computing systems.

P. Lalanda et al., *Autonomic Computing: Principles, Design and Implementation*,
Undergraduate Topics in Computer Science, DOI 10.1007/978-1-4471-5007-7_8,
© Springer-Verlag London 2013

8.1   Evaluating Autonomic Systems

We can assume that an autonomic system consists of a number of components that interact with each other and their environment. There may be a single autonomic manager that governs a large part of the system, or it may consist of a number of more localised managers that make decisions that emerge a global solution to maintain a goal (see Chap. 4). Either way, an autonomic manager must adapt to stimuli that originate from both within the system it governs and from outside that system (what we called its context in Chap. 2). Kaddoum et al. [1] describe these sources of stimuli as the dynamics that come from *exogenous* or *endogenous* changes. Endogenous changes are perturbations caused by entities within the system, whereas exogenous disturbances originate outside the system.

As discussed in previous chapters, autonomic features can be either designed as part of a new system build or retrofitted to a current or legacy computing system. The reasons for this addition are to ensure that the system meets certain goals, either more efficiently or more robustly or in a more cost-effective way. In designing an autonomic system, the aim is to have an operational system that essentially is able to reach a stable state, that is, to reach *homeostasis*. Homeostasis is an indicator of how well the ideal (or acceptable) state, as defined by the system goals, can be maintained given the exogenous or endogenous stimuli that act upon it. That is, it is a measure of how well the system can return to a stable state when disturbances, faults or perturbations have occurred.

It is already difficult to design a true evaluation for general computer systems, whether it is to understand the behaviour of a given system or to compare versions of the same system in terms of core functional capabilities. However, it is now necessary to also compare the autonomic components of the system. For example, there may have been a number of alternatives to the approach taken to build a given autonomic manager; differing intelligence algorithms will yield different results—some more accurate than others and some taking longer to compute. Therefore, an evaluation scheme would need to be designed to highlight both of these differences and not just the speed of the algorithm. That is, the metrics must be applicable and relevant—perhaps cost is no issue for some systems, for example, and so does not require reporting.

Further, other aspects of how a particular autonomic manager's logic fits with the system's overall architecture may need assessing or how this particular approach will scale, or is able to be reused by other system components, may also require evaluation.

This chapter will introduce the topic of evaluation from the viewpoint of the concepts of autonomic system appraisal rather than come up with definitive metrics. We assume that the reader has some basic idea of performance measurement in terms of standard measures of responsiveness and throughput of the functional aspects of the system. Nevertheless, Chap. 5 on monitoring introduces performance measurement metrics for general computing systems and is a useful refresher.

8.2   Evaluation Elements

8.2.1   Quality of Service

Service qualities may have been specified in a Service-Level Agreement. As introduced in Chap. 2.1.2, the goals of the system can be distilled from business process model and become manifest in a Service-Level Agreement (SLA). This is an agreement that exists between the software providers and clients, refined into Service-Level Objectives (SLO) that can be more easily monitored during runtime.

In terms of abstract ways to view the systems as a whole, quality of service (QoS) is possibly the highest level means to compare modern systems. It reflects the degree to which the system is reaching its primary goals. It is typically composed of a number of quantitative metrics, for example, percentage number of transactions that have a sub-second response time or decoding accuracy thresholds. More qualitatively, it can be a measure of user satisfaction that can then be distilled into user latency figures, numbers of users that continue using the system, etc.

QoS is a highly important metric in autonomic systems given they are typically designed to improve some aspect of a service. Most of the research in this field is looking at using autonomicity to improve performance (usually speed or efficiency). However, where systems wish to improve something less quantitative, for example, where a more personalised GUI is required for disabled people, or the requirements is to minimise the need for technical support staff, traditional metrics are found lacking. The notion of the degree to which an autonomic system is meeting its QoS parameters is therefore tightly coupled to the application area or service that is expected of the system. It can be measured as a single global goal metric (if the goal is as simple as that) or at the subservice or component level where each unit's ability to meet its local goals is measured. Most approaches to measure this for current autonomic systems have essentially taken the goals and refined them into more measurable, quantifiable, metrics.

The metrics that represent a service can involve systems efficiencies, response times, costs and usability. However, the ways autonomic systems are built bring other aspects of the system that can be measured that represent how well the autonomicity is measured. These metrics measure the system's ability to adapt to change, how well it maintains stability and how agile the system is to unexpected change. In the subsequent sections, we introduce these metrics.

8.2.2   Cost

Autonomicity costs, the degree of this cost and its measurement are not clear-cut. Currently, most performance studies of autonomic systems have measured the system's ability to reach its goal. However, more appropriately, the amount of communication, actions performed and cost of the actions required to reach that goal need to be noted.

For many commercial systems, the aim is to improve the cost of running an infrastructure, which primarily includes people costs in terms of system administrators and maintenance. This means that the reduction in cost for such systems cannot be measured immediately but over time and as the system becomes more and more self-managing. Therefore, measuring such costs, and in turn savings, is complex. However, using standard capacity planning techniques, there may be ways to estimate these savings to give a relative figure which can be used to compare approaches.

Cost comparison is further complicated by the fact that adding autonomicity means adding intelligence, monitors and adaptation mechanisms—and these cost in terms of not only processing time but also storage and memory (and all the maintenance costs typically associated with a computing system). For example, a Web server could have had autonomic features added to allow it to cope with fluctuating and sudden high demand (flash crowds) without lowering the user experience of the Web service. One would not only be interested in how well the system was able to cope with demand, but we would want a measure of the cost of adding these particular features (and a measure to allow us to compare approaches). It may be the case, as in [2], that the costs of adding both monitors to observe incoming Web traffic, and the mechanisms to analyse the resulting data and effect change, are outweighed by their benefits under *normal operation* only. As the so-called normal operation is the majority of time and is fairly predictable, it would appear that adding autonomicity is hardly worthwhile. However, perhaps there could be a case where loss of service under extreme conditions, for example, disaster recovery servers, would be so damaging that the cost was justifiable. So in some cases, the addition of autonomic features might even impact negatively on the system. However, under duress, the system would simply fail without the autonomic features, and it is there where the real benefit lies. Therefore, a measure of the added functionality that would otherwise not be achieved in a non-autonomic system would be useful. In the example above, the added functionality is obvious and is also the actual goal of the autonomic system. However, finding other added benefits might not be obvious and may be found in a serendipitous fashion, so it could be difficult to predict what to test for in advance in such cases.

The system's physical architecture also has an obvious impact on the cost of a self-managing system. For example, most solutions consist of a service that has autonomic features added as separate components that are interfaced to the managed element. For many of these, the analysis and planning is either hierarchical or even centralised; that is, the monitors or gauges are external to what they are measuring and the decision to adapt, and its supervision, is external to the managed element. Here the question is: is it fair to compare systems that use external computing hardware to run the autonomic services with those who run the autonomic services on the same system? With the former, costs could be in terms of the extra hardware and communications to that hardware. The saving is that the AI processing and autonomic data is residing on a separate system and therefore does not impede on the running system being managed. Extra processors dedicated to the autonomic services mean that they could be more intelligent, for example, checking the validity of a given reconfiguration in advance of that reconfiguration, or provide open intelligence where the autonomic decisions themselves are adaptive. So these benefits, and their future potential, versus their extra costs could be considered.

In more emergent, decentralised or agent-based autonomic systems, the intelligence can be tightly coupled with the functional logic of the main managed element and usually contained within the component or agent itself. Therefore, the self-management overhead is perhaps indistinguishable from the agent's core function, and therefore it is more difficult to separate out the costs of autonomicity—if that is sensible at all.

8.2.3 Adaptivity

To discuss this, we separate out the act of adaptation from the monitoring and intelligence that cause the system to adapt. Adaptivity can be something as simple as a parameter being changed, for example, changing the buffer size thresholds in self-configuration systems. Here the adaptation does not impact the system so much as for a component-based architectural reconfiguration. In the latter, a component may need to be hot-swapped where state is saved, the new component located and then bound into the system. Some systems are designed to continue execution while reconfiguring, while others cannot. Furthermore, the location of such components again impacts the performance of the adaptivity process. That is, a component object, which is currently local to the system versus a component (such as a printer driver), being retrieved over the Internet, will have significantly differing performance. Perhaps more future systems will have the equivalent of a prefetch of components that are likely to be of use and are preloaded to speed up the reconfiguration process. Intuitively standard metrics that measure responsiveness should be able highlight whether or not the time is being spent in adapting the system because the system becomes less responsive.

Adaptability can also be seen as a measure of how well the system can configure to cope with policy or goal changes after initial deployment. For example, over time, the goals of the business can change subtly, and this has a direct impact on the autonomic systems' requirements. This, therefore, has implications for the rules and policies that are derived from these changes. Not only does the autonomic system need to allow this change, those changes will have impact on the behaviour of the autonomic managers. How these managers will enable, and furthermore cope, with this is something that can be evaluated. What one should be interested in here is how those changes affect the systems' behaviour and whether this behaviour is what is both expected and welcome. This is a relatively straightforward process if the changes can be predicted in any way. However, there are many classes of system whereby their goal or usage may not be so predictable, and so testing the system for its ability to adapt in a meaningful way is non-trivial.

8.2.4 Time to Adapt and Reaction Time

Related to cost and sensitivity are the measurements concerned with the system reconfiguration and adaptation. The time to adapt is a measurement of the time a system takes to adapt to a change in the environment. That is, the time lag taken between the identification that a change is required until the change has been effected safely and the system moves to a *ready* state. Reaction time can be seen to partly envelop the adaptation time. This is the time between when an environmental element has changed and the system recognises that change, decides on what reconfiguration is necessary to react to the environmental change and getting the system ready to adapt. Further, the reaction time affects the sensitivity of the autonomic system to its environment (see next section).

8.2.5   Sensitivity

The aim of an autonomic system is to reach homeostasis, given disturbances, faults or perturbations. The degree to which the system is sensitive to its exogenous or endogenous stimuli is a measurement of how well the autonomic system *fits* with the environment it is currently sitting in. At one extreme, a highly tuned system will notice a subtle change as it happens and adapt (perhaps subtly) to improve itself based on that change.

Highly sensitive systems are also sensitive to system delays. For example, there may be a delay in the delivery of data from the monitors that indicate some part of the environment has changed. This could mean that a highly sensitive system would be currently adapting to system state data that is already out of date. Furthermore, the monitored data can represent a highly changing environment. Therefore, if a system is highly sensitive to its environment, it has the potential that it can cause the system to be constantly changing configuration, and the net result of this could be that the system is not getting on with the job at hand. We return to this in the stability discussion later.

To illustrate this, returning to our audio-server example (Chap. 4), there could be a number of parameters that affect the sensitivity of the system. For example, one could vary the disaster horizon which is a parameter that represents a threshold. The audio system used this as a means to calculate how soon it would fail based on how much audio data was currently in the player's buffer and how fast the data was coming in from the network. Fail in this case meant that the audio would go silent; the user lost sound. If it calculated that it was soon, corrective action would happen (it would ask that data is compressed more to speed up communication at the cost of sound quality). This adaptation costs in terms of performance also which needs to be taken into account. So if we have a less changeable network bandwidth, then that cost would be worth it. However, in more bursty networks, where the bandwidth is changing suddenly and many times, the system could cause an adaption that was not really required. Related to this, the audio system's bandwidth monitoring sample rates can also be varied. This indicates how much environmental data to monitor and store to predict changes in the bandwidth between the client and server. Lowering this value means that there is less monitoring data to be stored and processed, which in turn lowers the overheads of the autonomic system itself. However, lowering the amount of monitoring can also have the impact that it also lowers the sensitivity of the system and its ability to adapt to its environment.

Figure 8.1 shows the bandwidth observed by the autonomic audio player over time (blue line). We also plot two versions of the autonomic audio player. The first (red line) is the sensitive autonomic manager that takes many samples of the

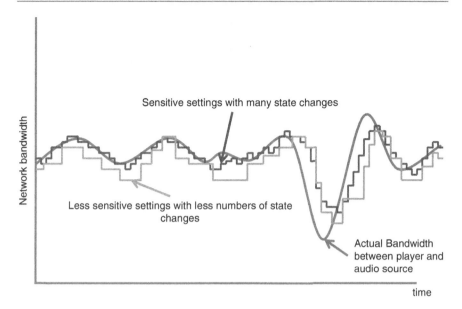

Fig. 8.1 Audio example showing how reducing samples and sensitivity equates to less state changes and highlighting that this equates to less bandwidth utilisation

environment (i.e. bandwidth measurements) and has low deviation thresholds such that the system tries to track the bandwidth and maximise the overall quality of sound delivered to the user over time. The green line represents a less sensitive version of the autonomic audio player. Here the sample frequencies are less and also the thresholds that indicate when to adapt are looser; therefore, the system configures less over time. The trade-off here is that sound quality is not optimal, but the cost of the autonomic system is actually significantly lower.

8.2.6   Stabilisation

Another metric related to sensitivity is stabilisation. That is the time taken for the system to learn its environment and stabilise its operation. This is particularly interesting for open adaptive systems that learn how to best reconfigure the system. For closed autonomic systems, the sensitivity would be a product of the static rule/constraint set and the stability of the underlying environment the system must adapt to. It is the time to reach homeostasis that is important here. To test this, one would ensure that the test environment contained parameters that cover edge conditions, values that are beyond the normal expected values of the system. From this, the tester can observe the behaviour of the system as it tries to adapt to best maintain goals under these extreme conditions. What the tester is wishing to observe is whether or not the system can get back to a steady state and how long this takes (see Fig. 8.2). As with every living organism, as the system ages, it may lose its ability to maintain homeostatic balance.

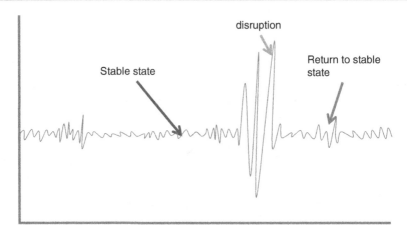

Fig. 8.2 Illustration of stability, disruptions and the return to stability. Compare this with control example in ctrl chapter

8.2.7   Failure Avoidance (Robustness) and Autonomy

Typically, many autonomic systems are designed to avoid failure at some level. Many are designed to cope with hardware failure such as a node in a cluster that is no longer responding. Some avoid such a failure by stopping and rebooting; others seek an alternative perhaps retrieving a missing component and installing it. Either way, the predictability of failure is an aspect that can require consideration when comparing autonomic systems. Some systems will be designed for their ability to cope with predicted failure but unable to handle failures that they are not programmed to identify or rectify. Systems that typically refine policies from goals are excellent at coping with predicable failure, as the methods to overcome this are programmed in the policies' associated actions. For example, a goal may be to ensure that transactions do not take over one second. Here the resulting policy could have the condition 'if node utilisation reaches $>= 70\%$' with the action being to 'bring up a new server node'. However, such mechanisms typically fail in unpredictable cases, and when they come across a situation (assuming they even recognise the situation at all), they can resort to some default action, such as informing the user. Other systems are designed to be able to cope with unpredictability. These tend to be systems that embed the autonomic features at the finer-grained lower levels and here typically the logic is highly distributed. Examples of such systems are those that perform routing functions in the Internet, for example. Here nodes in the system maintain routing tables to enable them to route around a node failure. Note that the notion of unpredictability is relative here; even the most autonomous system requires some programming of what to do when failure is detected.

Let us illustrate this by returning to our audio-server example. Recall that the purpose of this system was to adapt its audio encoding code depending on how it perceived the link between the audio server and the user at a moment in time. The overall goal is that there should never be a moment of audio silence during playback. To test how well this system is able to achieve this, we placed the system in a controlled environment. Here we would artificially mimic the communications link between the user and the server and vary the bandwidth available over the link. We would also change how quickly the bandwidth varied. This would test its ability to avoid periods of silence given differing environmental circumstances. The intuition is that the system would most probably be able to cope in situations where the bandwidth only varied slightly or in a predictable way. That is, the changes in bandwidth would fit obvious trends, and the variation in bandwidth would be minimal enough to allow the system to have time to identify the trend and quickly reconfigure to ensure perfect playback. One would expect that the system would adapt more gracefully compared with its operation in a more bursty network. We increased the parameters that reflected the environment to more stressful levels. In this case, the environment represented bandwidth fluctuation with extreme variation between high and low values. This experiment showed us that the system continued to operate correctly but was adapting up and down the codecs constantly, sometimes even missing an opportunity to adapt because it did not notice an instance of environmental change as it was still handling the previous adaptation [3]!

Therefore, one may wish to see how well the system is able to cope with less predictive situations. Tests would be designed with this in mind. One could choreograph a situation where nodes are switched off to mimic failure or a workload is ramped up to extreme heights and injected into the system. The use of randomness or distributions of values can be stretched to beyond expected limits to enable the tester to examine pathological cases. The measurement of the system's ability to cope could simply be in terms of how well certain quality of service metrics are met, which is obviously close to the application domain.

Related to this is the ability to compare how autonomous a system is. This would be a measure of not only how well the system can cope in less predictable situations but how much it relies on the outside world to do this. For example, the NASA pathfinder must cope with unpredicted problems and learn to overcome them without direct external help. Decreasing the degree of predictability in the environment and seeing how the system copes could measure this. Lower predictability could even mean it having to cope with things that it was not designed for. A degree of proactivity could also compare these features. The notion autonomy is also related to the conversation about how centralised and fully decentralised approaches to autonomic computing differ which we have later in this chapter.

8.2.8 Interfacing to the Outside World

Most autonomic systems that exist at the moment of writing are of a partially autonomic type, also described as the *basic, managed* and *predictive* levels in the Autonomic Maturity Model [4] (see Chap. 2.4.3). This means that some form of user interaction remains in the MAPE-K loop. Therefore, one needs to evaluate the systems' ability to communicate with external entities such as the technical support team, configuration managers, performance staff or even other extraneous pieces of management software (e.g. the operating system).

Autonomic systems also can have profound effects on how the user perceives the system. To illustrate this, we again return to our audio-player example. The goal of the system is to ensure that music is constantly delivered to the listener while maximising the music quality. To do this, the autonomic manager reacts to measures of network bandwidth by changing the encoding type (codec) of the music data to ensure this. If the bandwidth is bursty, the autonomic manager will swap from one encoder to another and then another and perhaps back again. This can form oscillations (see Chap. 3 on control), which means the system is state flapping back and forth between encoding components. The original goals to deliver music and to maximise the music quality still hold; the user will hear audio. However, to the human ear, this would sound dreadful, moving from high-fidelity sound to lower duller sound qualities and back again, like an old long wave radio. Therefore, a system that permits some damping of adaptation may be of more use. Nevertheless, a measurement of the user's perception is required beyond the more functional metrics representing the system's goal.

8.2.9 Centralisation Versus Decentralisation

Throughout this chapter, we have compared how different aspects of autonomous systems can be compared and have mentioned cases where the autonomicity is relatively centralised or more distributed. This section will focus on that divide more specifically as it is essentially a measure of the decision process within an autonomic system and an indication of which components are involved in that process. It also gives us an understanding of how local the decision-making process is or how a local decision affects external components that are also part of the same system. This is like measuring the butterfly effect discussed in complex systems. For example, in the situation where local decision-making relies on both data from other components and is required to communicate state to other components (e.g. a heartbeat), we wish to understand how much this communication can affect the other components. This can be in terms of performance, whereby the shared communication bandwidth is being saturated with housekeeping (control) messages, meaning the network is unable to get on with its core function which was to deliver application data (the *goodput*). It can also be in terms of behaviour where other nodes in the system are making decisions based on the outcome of a local node's behaviour and this permeates across the network; the impact ripples outwards, and this may not always be good.

In an emergent system, emphasis is focused on decentralisation, whereby the problem-solving power results not from the local actions but from the interactions of a group of autonomous entities instead. Here, the focus of autonomic behaviour is not local or node-based but lies in the *structures* representing an aspect of the system as a whole. This is sometimes described as the macroscopic properties of the system (rather than the microscopic local or node-based properties). Metrics would now be required to compare the system or the *structure's* ability to quickly and seamlessly adapt, for example, add or delete a new node to/from the system.

The common example regularly used to illustrate this is found in autonomic communications systems. A communications network is designed to route data packets from a source node to a sink node (e.g. similar to that found in Internet routing or sensing network routing). The elements of the network are nodes (which are computers and routers) and arcs (which represent the communications infrastructure, wired or wireless radio links). The network communications is multistaged whereby data hops over the arcs to the nodes. Each node has local knowledge regarding what it should do with that packet, but its logic is such that the structure (routing tree) emerges, to ensure reliable delivery of the data packet, and that the packet would be delivered over the shortest or quickest route to its destination. Here the system does not need to know about all the nodes in the network, just its neighbours. If it knows its best neighbour to send the packet too, then one can imagine that that packet will be sent over all the best links in the network to the sink. Therefore, optimising the delivery of that packet, that is, the route, emerges.

Evaluating such a system would involve its ability to cope with disturbances, malicious or not and temporary or permanent. In this example, there could be a node failure which means that the current fastest known route is no longer viable and the data is required to be rerouted around the dead node to ensure data delivery. Metrics to measure this would be throughput and latency based. Latency will highlight that the data had to be rerouted away from the shortest path and therefore the extra hops involved which will incur temporal costs. Likewise, if a new node is added to the system, this too will affect the *structure* in that many of the shortest routes may need recalculating; otherwise, the new node will be underutilised. The adaptation is to the structure of the system as a whole and not necessarily changing the behaviour of the local nodes themselves, though they need to have logic that knows to look for new nodes and route around nodes they no longer have contact with. For a fully distributed system, this would mean each node sending identification messages to each neighbour node to see who is there and then collectively build up routes. This is obviously an expensive activity increasing the numbers of control messages and limiting the ability to route the actual data. Therefore, when measuring such a distributed system, it is necessary to measure the ***goodput*** relative to the throughput as a result. This then highlights how much data is being sent over the network and how much is overheads.

8.2.10 Granularity/Flexibility

Similar to sensitivity, the granularity of autonomicity is an important issue when comparing autonomic systems. Fine-grained components with specific adaptation rules will be highly flexible and perhaps adapt to situations better; however, this may cause more overhead in terms of the global system. That is, if we assume that each finer-grained component requires environmental data and is providing some form of feedback on its performance, then potentially there is more monitoring data, or at least environmental information, flowing around the global system. Of course, this may not be the case in systems where the intelligence is more centralised or the monitored data is stored in a shared repository.

Granularity is important; take the example in [2]. Here the authors found that unbinding, loading and rebinding a component took a few seconds. These few seconds could be tolerable in a thick-grained component-based architecture where the overheads can be hidden in the system's overall operation and where change is not that regular. However, in finer-grained architectures, such as an operating system or ubiquitous computing where change is either more regular or the components smaller, the hot-swap time is potentially too much.

One question we may ask is: can systems that provide the same service be compared with each other if the granularity of autonomicity is different? Perhaps at a high level, yes. But let us unpick this a little further. If both approaches provide the same quality of service, the same ability to reduce costs, the same capacity to satisfy users, etc., is there a further cost? Of course, this further cost lies in the systems' ability to be maintained—an autonomic system and its autonomic features require maintenance too, just like traditional systems. If the granularity is fine grained, it usually means that there is tight coupling between the managed element and the management software. This adds extra burden in terms of debugging, updating and improving the overall system and therefore should be accounted for.

8.3   Some Evaluation Metrics for Emergent Systems

Emergent behaviours are those that arise from a number of (simple) processes cooperating to achieve a goal. Emergence has been proven in nature as an agile way to solve problems that involve many components as it has the ability and flexibility to adapt to situations that were unplanned. A natural example of emergent behaviour is found when birds flock; the flock is an entity that is used to transport numbers of birds for migration or to make the unit appear larger so that the individuals can be defended. Another advantage of emergence is that the rule base for the individuals is typically quite simple. It is for these reasons that the autonomic computing community has developed and adapted emergent algorithms to make the system more robust to failure, and change. One example of this is where gossip algorithms can be used to move heartbeats around the network of components. Here each node, component or entity in the network sends a message of its heartbeat to its neighbour and then that is passed on. When the network converges, it has a common understanding of the systems' heartbeat as a result. Emergent algorithms' behaviour also needs evaluating, and there are a number of metrics that can be used to do this; we list some below.

8.3.1   Price of Anarchy (PoA)

In many emergent systems, its components may collaborate by playing a game to solve a problem or evolve a solution. In such systems, the PoA is a measurement of the degree that the system degrades due to the selfish behaviour of one of the components. It is a gauge of how efficient these kinds of systems are at reaching a solution measuring the impact of 'selfishness' on the system as a whole. For example, consider the routing example given earlier. Here we wish to route data from one node to another. Our efficiency measure would be the average communications latency, the time for a message to reach its destination. Imagine we had two alternatives to determine the routes. The first approach would be the centralised one that takes the network's current details and uses algorithms that produce optimal routes for all nodes sending data to all other nodes in the system. Here the central authority will enforce every node along the computed optimal path to cooperatively forward the data packets. Alternatively, a decentralised version could exist (the more emergent version) whereby some nodes may not be willing to forward the data. This could be via gossip protocols as mentioned above. If we know or are able to reason about the performance of both approaches, the price of anarchy is then the ratio between the average communications latencies of each. Therefore, it is a measure of how well the system is able to evolve an optimal solution when some entities in the system show selfish/greedy behaviour or are not willing to participate.

8.3.2   Equilibrium

Equilibrium is a measurement of balance. It differs from stability in that we can have a system that is highly unstable but is currently in a state of equilibrium. For example, if we place a pin, sharp end down on a table, it is in a state of equilibrium (all the forces on the pin are balanced—the rightward forces are balanced by the leftward forces, the upward forces are balanced by the downward forces, etc.). However, the pin is unstable. Understanding this metric allows the tester to understand the degree to which the system under test has reached its objectives and how close to the optimum solution it has evolved.

One very popular example, named after John Forbes Nash who proposed it, is Nash equilibrium. The system is said to be in a Nash equilibrium when it has reached a state, again in a collaborative system, where each entity is assumed to know the equilibrium strategies of the other entities, and no entity can gain by changing only his own strategy unilaterally. This means that if a node or cell in a distributed autonomic system has decided on an autonomic management strategy to maximise its performance (say) and no other node can benefit by changing its own strategy (while the other nodes keep their strategies unchanged), then the current set of strategy choices (and the performance improvements that will result) constitute a Nash equilibrium. There are many variants of this metric and other equilibria, but these discussions are beyond the scope of this book.

8.4   Benchmarking

Finally, it may become necessary to bring these metrics together to form some sort of benchmark. There are two approaches this can take: either we can derive new autonomic systems benchmarks or we can augment current benchmarks to incorporate metrics that measure autonomic characteristics.

Benchmarking is the process whereby a system that is being tested is subjected to a synthetic (controllable) workload and its performance is measured given that workload. Therefore, the components of a benchmarking process are the system under test, the workload, the performance metrics, the component that measures the performance of the operational benchmark and the test results, as seen in Fig. 8.3. The design of the workload is central to benchmarking as it is this that 'tests' the system. It can represent what the system was designed to do, and thus, the results from the benchmarking process will show how well it is able to do that job. Here the workload will be designed to represent the typical use of the system. The workload can also test aspects such as how well the system can scale and work under stress. Here, the workload would be beyond the expected use of the system (as known at design time or under current usage), and the results will show where the system could potentially fail in the future.

An example of general benchmark is the Standard Performance Evaluation Corporation's (SPEC) benchmarking suites. SPEC is a not-for-profit organisation that produces standardised sets of performance benchmarks to evaluate computer systems. The results of running such benchmarks are sometimes referred to as

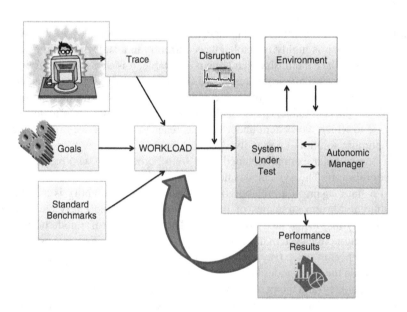

Fig. 8.3 The benchmarking cycle

SPECmarks. SPEC supplies a number of benchmarks that are a measure of the different aspects of computing from testing integer arithmetic in compilers (SPECint) to evaluating server energy efficiencies (SPECpower_ssj2008). Another popular example comes from the Transaction Processing Performance Council (TPC). These benchmarks evaluate the different flavours of database transaction processing applications. Interestingly, both SPEC and TPC were founded in 1988.

Benchmarking can be distinguished from the other evaluation techniques in this chapter, in that a form of technical agreement is made, perhaps between the industry and the user community, and this agreement represents mechanism to capture and report behaviours for *comparative purposes.*

Designing a benchmark for autonomic systems is not that straightforward. Given that the primary purpose of adopting the autonomic approach is to minimise the complexity in the development and moreover maintenance of complex systems, mere performance metrics driven by workloads are not enough. That is, other complexities exist that need testing.

One such example is 'configuration complexity' which is a measure of the level of complication involved with the configuration process of a system. Here, the configuration process could be the human configuration process, where the cost of the human whose job it is to support a system is given. Such a metric essentially measures how well the autonomic system can self-configure or better still how much we save by having the system self-configure over the human support. Therefore, the configuration process will typically involve computing, business and human systems' processes. However, the involvement, mapping and mimicking of these processes are inherently difficult to capture in a quantifiable way. Some approaches have combined automated methods (key traces and mouse movement tracking [5] of the humans involved); others use manual observation to produce the benchmark suite. Some benchmarks are also built by domain experts.

Benchmarks are supposed to be both reproducible and robust. That is, the benchmark should not be so open to interpretation or manipulation that would render systems incomparable. Worse, the benchmark should not make it easy for systems to be designed with the sole purpose of getting good benchmark scores. Though in reality, this is difficult to control and is an issue with benchmarking in general.

Runtime reconfiguration is carried out to maintain goals such as those pertaining to performance, security and failure avoidance. Benchmarks will then consist of datasets and associated background workloads that stress the system or inject disruption. It is important to note that that a workload for autonomic systems cannot be static. For example, instead of stating that the input load will be 100 connections/s, a benchmark for autonomic systems will have a ramped up load, such as 100–1,000 connections/s stepping up at 100 at a time, or a load that fits a distribution with a given mean, standard deviation, etc. The load is then run with the system under focus, and its ability to maintain its goal is monitored and evaluated accordingly.

8.5   The Autonomic Computing Benchmark: A Summary

There has been little progress in defining a definitive benchmark for autonomic systems, bar a small set of publications that very much come to the same inconclusive conclusions. In this section, we discuss the Autonomic Computing Benchmark as this is perhaps the most mature approach available at the time of writing.

To match the autonomic computing investment by IBM, a benchmark, aptly named the Autonomic Computing Benchmark, was released in 2008. This benchmark is described as using a 'fault injection methodology and five categories of faults or disturbances'. Though they describe the word 'fault' to imply an invalid operation and the word 'disturbance' as having the broader meaning covering invalid operations, intrusions, interruptions, events, etc., anything that alters system state, they use the words interchangeably. Two metrics are used to evaluate the system: the throughput index and the maturity index. The latter is a measure of autonomicity (as described in Chap. 2.4.3) indicating the degree of human intervention required in the task. Throughput measures the impact on quality of service expectations due to the injected disturbances.

As recommended in our early paper on autonomic system evaluation [6], the Autonomic Computing Benchmark essentially extends current representative benchmarking suites with mechanisms that pertain to autonomic features. To this end, the benchmark suite mimics a typical B2B (business-to-business application) and is designed essentially to wrap around current business application benchmarks such as the SPECjAppServer2004 Performance Benchmark, a popular J2EE performance benchmark from the SPEC organisation [7]. It covers a multicomponent application architecture and also takes *administrative* duties into account. The benchmark has three states: *baseline*, *test* and *check*. Essentially, the system must ramp up to a steady state to represent the *baseline* performance of that application under the given conditions. From this, disturbances are injected in a predefined sequence and the system is thus *test*ed. Finally, the *check* state double-checks that the changes the system made to maintain stability have had no other negative impacts on the system, such as transactions or updates lost and missing data. In between disturbance sequences, the system is allowed to 'recover' to a steady state to enable the user to trace the cause and effects of the disturbances more clearly.

Among the measurements that determine the notion of autonomic maturity is quantification of the quality of a self-healing action. Some self-healing actions can consist of mechanisms to avert the problem caused by a disturbance by routing around it or creating ways to bypass that process. After that, the system may instigate mechanisms to heal the problem, and the repaired system is reintegrated back into the system under test. Now given that self-healing systems have excised since before the term autonomic has been used and many systems have some sort of self-healing nature to them, one may not notice any change to the system because a component was able to continue operation with the fault injected into it. The example given is that of a RAID redundant disk array that is able to continue operation after a disk failure. That component is still operational, albeit in a reduced way that might cause problems in the future. This is what they mean by quality of repair. The system has not failed and is continuing to deliver data in, but it is not ideal or operating in an optimal way. To represent these phenomena, The Autonomic Benchmark judges that bypassing a problem does not constitute a full recovery and attributes a value to this and a score of any repair action taken. The intuition is that if no repair occurs (even if the system is running and stable), the resources available to the system are reduced. It allows those aiming to evaluate the system to get a better idea of the capability that the system has when facing any subsequent changes upon it. This metric was derived from The Autonomic Benchmark's authors, inspired by working with autonomic systems. It is a metric *they* found to be valuable and highlights both the complexity of deriving metrics for autonomic systems and that they can be metrics that are important to some users but not necessarily to all.

8.6   Key Points

- Autonomic computing is an engineering concept that has found its way in a myriad of computing fields. This chapter is a review of some typical examples of the sorts of aspects that would contribute to the evaluation of an autonomic computer system.
- We have illustrated the complexities in trying to measure the performance of such systems and compare them.
- We have presented the common components found in each of these types of system and from this derived a set of metrics and methods which we believe are a good starting point to compare autonomic computing systems.
- These we summarise as quality of service, cost, granularity/flexibility, failure avoidance (robustness), degree of autonomy, adaptivity, time to adapt and reaction time, sensitivity and stabilisation.
- We realise that some of these metrics are more general than others and some pertain to some autonomic systems and not to others.
- We also show that deriving new measurement systems or benchmarks from scratch is not necessarily the best way forward. Instead, due to the diverse application of autonomic systems, it may seem better to augment application-specific benchmarks to include metrics which evaluate the autonomic features of that system, for example, robustness, reaction speed and stability. Therefore, traditional benchmarks, such as the TPC benchmarks are now being used to measure autonomic DBMSs, but have been extended to test the specific autonomous nature of the system; for example the reaction times of the system are charted.
- It is interesting that to alleviate the maintenance and operation overheads of our modern increasingly complex computing systems, we require the addition of even more complexity. It is our argument that this complexity makes such systems much more difficult to evaluate than before, and therefore the need to derive correct robust repeatable methods and benchmarks is highly important and interesting.

References

1. Kaddoum, E., Gleizes, M.-P., Georgé, J.-P., Picard, G.: Characterizing and evaluating problem solving self-* systems. In: Proceedings of the 2009 Computation World: Future Computing, Service Computation, Cognitive, Adaptive, Content, Patterns, pp. 137–145. IEEE Computer Society, Washington, DC (2009)
2. McCann, J.A., Jawaheer, G.: Experiences in building the Patia autonomic webserver. In: 1st International Workshop "Autonomic Computing Systems", DEXA 2003, September 1–5, Prague, Czech Republic (2003)
3. McCann, J.A., Howlett, P., Crane, J.S.: Kendra: adaptive Internet system. J. Syst. Softw. **55**(1), 3–17 (2000). Elsevier Science
4. IBM Data Governance Council Maturity Model. http://www-935.ibm.com/services/uk/cio/pdf/leverage_wp_data_gov_council_maturity_model.pdf (2007)
5. 47RC23146 (W0403-071) March 10, 2004 Computer Science IBM Research Report. An approach to benchmarking configuration complexity Aaron B. Brown, Joseph L. Hellerstein
6. McCann J.A., Huebscher M.C.: Evaluation issues in autonomic computing. In: The International Workshop on Agents and Autonomic Computing and Grid Enabled Virtual Organizations (AAC-GEVO'04), 3rd International Conference on Grid and Cooperative Computing, Wuhan, China, 21–24 Oct 2004. Springer-Verlag, Heidelberg
7. http://www.spec.org/jAppServer2004/, url dated 26 Sept 2011

Autonomic Mediation in Cilia

9

Software integration is a well-known and very demanding activity. The purpose of this activity is to allow the interoperation of software applications that have been developed independently and often at different times. Such integrations are frequently required in software organisations in order to improve the existing computing infrastructures and provide new services.

Today, modular architectures are often used to design and implement integration solutions. Many are based on the notion of mediation, which focuses on the timely integration of disparate information sources and destinations. Most current solutions, however, are not autonomic. Updates are generally prepared offline by experienced developers and administrators and committed all at once in a static fashion. This requires some downtime and the availability of skilled administrators to deal with technical, low-level administration aspects.

Cilia is an autonomic mediation framework essentially developed by the Adele team[1] and currently used in collaborative initiatives like the Medical project.[2] This framework, designed with autonomicity in mind, allows the autonomic administration of mediation solutions. The purpose of this chapter is to show how the Cilia framework has been made autonomic, using many of the techniques presented in this book. This chapter also presents ongoing work offering further management capabilities, aiming to progress towards Cilia technology endowed with fully autonomic life-cycle management capabilities.

---

[1] Adele team, Grenoble University: http://www-adele.imag.fr

[2] The Medical project (http://medical.imag.fr) is funded by the OSEO and the *Conseil Général de l'Isère*. It is led by the Orange Labs.

P. Lalanda et al., *Autonomic Computing: Principles, Design and Implementation*,
Undergraduate Topics in Computer Science, DOI 10.1007/978-1-4471-5007-7_9,
© Springer-Verlag London 2013

9.1   Software Integration

Software integration has always been a recurring, expensive, time-consuming activity. Its purpose is to allow software applications developed independently, often at different times, and run on different computing infrastructures to interoperate. Integration is in escapable; the need arises as soon as an organisation looks for ways to extend or update its computing infrastructure. Existing applications, which cannot be redeveloped for obvious economic and operational reasons, have to be used by the new developments. These applications are usually called legacy applications. They can correspond to a program, a database, a device, etc.

Integration is a complex activity, but for a simple reason, the applications or devices to be integrated have not been designed and implemented for that purpose. As a result, data are represented in widely different ways, interfaces are mismatching, communication protocols are unlikely to be compatible, synchronisation mechanisms are absent, etc. In addition, software systems to be integrated have their own evolution pace, which reawakens integration problems very often.

Integration is a crucial issue in modern computing. Today's information systems are required to be very flexible in order to favour the rapid and frequent creation of new services. Integration is also key to pervasive applications. Such applications are run on distributed infrastructures, from small, communication-limited devices up to powerful servers connected via wide area networks. Building pervasive applications therefore requires integrating diverse devices embedded in concrete environments and also a number of services and resources made available via networks, like the Internet. This form of integration, which is prominent today, is made more complicated by the fact that the elements to be integrated are dynamic and heterogeneous.

As illustrated in Fig. 9.1, a commonly adopted solution is to encapsulate the integration code into software dedicated to this purpose. This centralised approach implements good software engineering practice. That is, technical code related to integration is kept separate from the applications that are required to be combined. The integration software provides a unique access point (often called an *endpoint* in the integration domain) for each application. Also, isolating the integration code can

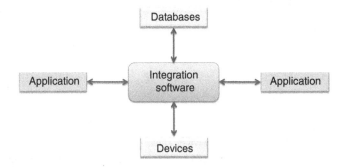

Fig. 9.1 Centralised integration architecture

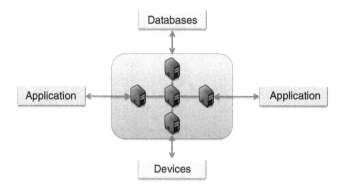

Fig. 9.2 Hub and spoke architecture (physical view)

facilitate change management. For instance, it is certainly easier to modify QoS properties (like security or persistency) of the integration since related code is kept in a single, well-identified place.

The integration issue has been around for decades. Through the years, various solutions have been proposed. The early ones, for example, those based on message-oriented middleware (MOM), were very technical and focused on data transport and communication. Enterprise application integration (EAI) systems are later, more general solutions that introduce the notion of adapted processes and business organisations. EAI can be seen as large integration frameworks based on the *hub and spoke* architectural pattern. This distribution architecture is illustrated in Fig. 9.2.

EAIs have been an undeniable market success, essentially in big companies. However, they have more recently faced criticism due to their operational cost and size. EAIs are often run by specialised, centralised departments, which can lead to heavy and slow business processes. Such departments are known to be overloaded with work and not able to swiftly meet project demands.

Researchers at Stanford University [1, 2] introduced a few years ago the notion of *mediation*. The mediation activity corresponds to the timely integration of disparate information sources. It has been used historically to integrate data stored in IT resources like databases, knowledge bases, file systems, digital libraries or electronic mail systems. Since then, the principles have been reused and applied to the integration of various software applications [3]. In the rest of this chapter, we will focus on this approach to design and implement integration solutions.

A mediation solution is generally implemented as a mediation chain. A mediation chain is decomposed into lightweight components called mediators that implement simple integration operations. Classically, mediators are used to implement operations like:

– *Communication alignment*. The purpose of this operation is to enable applications using different communication protocols to interoperate. It requires implementing protocol transformations such as those found in a *network bridge*.
– *Syntactic alignment*. The purpose of this operation is to homogenise data formats. It can rely on an intermediary format, often called a *pivot*.

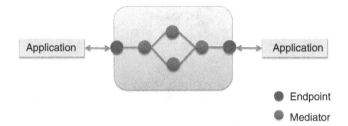

Fig. 9.3 Example of a mediation chain (logical view)

- *Semantic alignment.* The purpose of this function is to align data semantics. In the absence of recognised and used standards in a domain, applications develop different *ontologies* to represent (static and dynamic) knowledge.
- *Non-functional property alignment.* The purpose of this operation is to ensure certain quality properties for the integration, like security or availability.
- *Persistency.* The purpose here is to keep track of all exchanges between applications. The mediation layer can provide logging support for all requests, responses and data.
- *Monitoring.* The purpose of this function is to collect data for monitoring systems that verify that the expected quality of service is being achieved.

A mediation operation is usually performed by a single mediator. Many operations naturally lead to the chaining of a number of such mediators. Mediators can be executed on a single machine or distributed. In the latter case, communication middleware is needed to connect the mediators. Middleware can be based on RPC-like communication, on message-based interaction, etc. Figure 9.3 provides an illustration of a mediation chain with alternative paths.

Mediation solutions are required to be:

- *Efficient.* Time needed to perform integration operations should not impact the quality of the overall service provided by the integrated system.
- *Manageable.* The installation, configuration and management of mediation solutions have to be as simple as possible in order to reduce costs and risks.
- *Flexible.* Applications that have to interoperate change and their integration requirements evolve accordingly. Then, it should be easy to modify or add mediation operations in order to adapt at runtime the way applications are integrated.
- *Easy to use.* Programming and runtime models have to be simple. Once again, the point is to avoid complex solutions where integration code is hard to understand, fix and evolve.

In addition, today's solutions are often required to be deployable in various contexts, with disparate execution resources.

Many tools have been proposed in recent years. But, in most cases, mediation solutions are very technical and technology driven. Mediation chains still remain hard to build, deploy and maintain. They are difficult to change and reuse and this has an important business impact. This is because staff resources are required to ensure that changes are rolled out along the chain and the system might have to be taken offline thus lowering its availability.

Autonomic computing can obviously have a tremendously beneficial impact in this domain. The following sections introduce an approach to using an autonomic principles to system integration—the Cilia mediation framework.

9.2   Cilia

The Cilia framework[3] is an autonomic, open-source mediation framework [4, 5] developed by the Adele team. Its purpose is to simplify the work of integrators by offering a well-defined and limited set of abstractions to support design, composition, deployment and execution of a variety of mediation chains.

The Cilia framework takes the form of a domain-specific component model, including a specification language and a flexible execution environment. A Cilia component is called a mediator. Its purpose is to realise a single mediation operation like a data transformation, a security function and an aggregation. A Cilia component is characterised by a number of typed input and output ports. Input ports receive the data to be treated whereas the output ports forward the results of the mediation processing. Ports are the means to connect mediators and, thus, form mediation chains.

The content of the mediators is divided into three elements: a *scheduler*, a *processor* and a *dispatcher*. The purpose of the scheduler is to store the data received in the input ports and to apply a triggering condition. Simply put, the scheduler deals with all the synchronisation issues. When the condition held by the scheduler becomes true, all the data retained by the scheduler are sent to the processor. The processor applies the mediation operation to the transmitted data. The result of this operation is sent to the dispatcher, whose purpose is to place the results in the output ports. The dispatcher handles the routing aspect in the mediation chains (Fig. 9.4).

Schedulers, processors and dispatchers are Java classes that are developed independently. They are defined in a Java development environment and kept in a dedicated repository. In order to ease their development, abstract classes for schedulers, processors and dispatchers have been defined. Abstract classes define the methods to be implemented and, for some of them, templates to be used for the implementation. Cilia also supports the reuse of classes that have already been defined. This includes periodic schedulers, filtering processors, aggregation-oriented processors and content-based dispatchers.

Defining a mediator then comes down to assembling three Java classes (scheduler, processor, dispatcher) in a component envelope. This envelope is defined in terms of input and output ports and configuration parameters. A domain-specific language called DSCilia, based on XML, is provided for that purpose.

A composition of Cilia mediators is called a mediation chain. As previously said, the intent of a mediation chain is to perform all the mediation operations that are necessary to allow well-specified applications or resources to interoperate. A mediation chain is formed by a set of connected adapters and mediators. Adapters connect the resources to integrate to the mediators (see the 'endpoints' in Fig. 9.3). Their purpose

---

[3]The Cilia framework is available at https://github.com/AdeleResearchGroup/Cilia

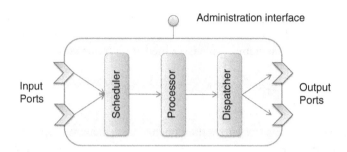

Fig. 9.4 Cilia mediator architecture

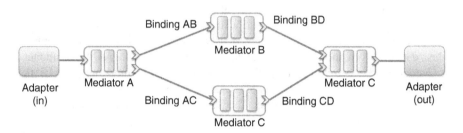

Fig. 9.5 Example of mediation chain

is to feed the mediators (and the destination resources) with data in the appropriate format and with the appropriate timing. Mediators constitute the heart of the chain since they implement the effective mediation operations. This is illustrated in Fig. 9.5.

Mediators (and adapters) are connected via *bindings*. A binding describes a connection between an output port and an input port. At execution time, a binding is realised by a communication protocol transferring data from a mediator (or adapter) to another mediator (or adapter). This protocol can be specified at deployment time but also at development time. Cilia supports local and distant communication protocols, including several message-oriented protocols.

A mediation chain is data-flow driven. Specifically, the computation model is the following. An adapter gets data from an application or a resource (using an appropriate protocol) and sends the collected data to one or several mediators. These mediators apply their operation to the received data as soon as the triggering conditions provided by their scheduler are met. Results are put in the output ports by the dispatcher and propagated to the next mediators. At the end, an adapter feeds an application or a resource (using an appropriate protocol) with the transformed data.

The DSCilia language permits straightforward definition of the mediation chains. Specifically, defining a mediation chain consists in specifying mediators and bindings between those mediators. This is done via domain-specific terms that are familiar to domain developers (integrators). Also, DSCilia permits the easy definition of the most commonly used enterprise integration patterns [6], which are part of the baseline knowledge for every integration engineer. Indeed, these patterns are often based on synchronisation and dispatching functions.

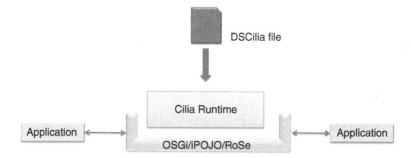

Fig. 9.6 Cilia overview

The Cilia execution framework is built on top of OSGi and iPOJO (see Chap. 6 about adaptation). It also includes RoSe, an open-source communication middleware that is able to dynamically import and export services.[4]

A mediation chain is created in the following manner (Fig. 9.6): a specification file, based on DSCilia, is transmitted to the Cilia runtime. These specifications are transformed into a number of iPOJO components definitions. At least five iPOJO components are created for each mediator: one component for the scheduler, one component for the processor, one component for the dispatcher and two components for the in and out communication ports (more components are created if different protocols are used by different ports). The defined iPOJO components are then instantiated and executed. From this point, the mediation chain is operational (and the desired integration is achieved).

Let us remind here that iPOJO relies on byte code manipulation to create extensible containers encapsulating the execution of Java classes. A container can host a number of handlers implementing non-functional aspects (handlers are triggered before or after a method call). As we will explain in detail, this feature is particularly convenient for implementing dynamic monitoring functions attached to a component.

To sum up, Cilia is a recent framework meeting the stringent requirements on software integration and well adapted to the implementation of commonly accepted integration patterns. The use of domain-specific concepts simplifies the creation and understanding of mediation chains. However, adapting Cilia chains to new runtime conditions still depends on skilled administrators and generally requires some downtime. In many domains, administrators are not available or service interruption is not an option. Autonomic approaches are therefore needed. This is why the Cilia framework has been partly redesigned with autonomicity in mind.

In the rest of this chapter, we concentrate on the autonomic features exhibited by Cilia, as needed in the context of this book. Above all, we focus on the way in which Cilia has been implemented in order to illustrate some of the techniques and

---

[4]The RoSe framework is available at https://github.com/AdeleResearchGroup/ROSE

approaches described in this book. For interested readers, extensive information about Cilia can be found on the Website (https://github.com/AdeleResearchGroup/Cilia).

9.3   Autonomic Cilia

9.3.1   Overview

Specifically, support for the following adaptations has been demanded during Cilia's requirement elicitation phase:
- A mediation chain can be dynamically added or removed.
- Configuration parameters of a mediation chain can be dynamically updated.
- A mediator can be dynamically removed from a running chain.
- A mediator can be dynamically added to a running chain.
- A mediator can be dynamically replaced within a running chain (hot-swapping).
- Configuration parameters of a mediator can be dynamically updated.
- Configuration parameters of the execution machine can be dynamically updated.
- An adapter can be dynamically replaced.
- Configuration parameters of an adapter can be dynamically changed.

These adaptations are required to address functional evolutions or to fix nonoptimal behaviours. Triggering an adaptation, however, requires a good knowledge of the running chains both in terms of specification and runtime behaviour. It also requires facilities to implement structural and behavioural modifications without data losses or broken control flows.

As illustrated in Fig. 9.7, the Cilia framework now provides a set of touchpoints to dynamically monitor and adapt the mediation chains under execution and some aspects of the supporting execution platform (essentially the service discovery functions). It also allows the construction of a configurable knowledge-base storing design and runtime information about the mediation chains and the platform under operation. This knowledge base provides a model of runtime phenomena, with trends and past data, and is intended for use by autonomic managers. This model is causal in the sense that modifications made on the model representation are reflected on the Cilia runtime and vice versa. Using this knowledge module is a very convenient way for domain engineers to create autonomic managers. Managers use high-level APIs provided by the knowledge module to get relevant information and trigger adaptations. Such approach does not demand to be familiar with the intricacies of Cilia; domain-specific mediation knowledge suffices to manage Cilia-based systems.

Many of the Cilia features are flexible and configurable. Monitoring, in particular, can be controlled in a dynamic way. This means that Cilia monitoring can be activated or deactivated globally. It also means that the elements to be monitored, and the way they are monitored, can be configured without interruption of service. Similarly, the knowledge base can be loaded or not, used or not, executed on a different machine (through REST interfaces) or not, etc. This allows developers and administrators to use Cilia features in accordance with their needs and objectives.

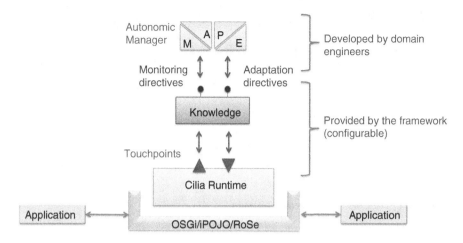

Fig. 9.7 Overview of autonomic Cilia

Expectations can obviously vary according to the runtime situation and to the problems that may arise, which is a typical property of administration systems.

It is important to remember that Cilia is a *framework*, which means that domain developers are in charge of the development of the mediation chains. To do so, they create mediators, bindings, chains, etc., in order to meet their requirements. But domain developers are also responsible for the development of the autonomic managers. In this context, the purpose of the framework is to provide facilities (touchpoints, design and runtime knowledge) to ease the work of the domain engineers.

As said earlier, the Cilia runtime, and the mediation chains, may be distributed across several machines. However, autonomic decisions are centralised in the sense that a unique autonomic manager is responsible for the management of the running mediation chains. We will see later in this chapter that more decentralised solutions involving multiple autonomic managers are also being investigated.

To implement the touchpoints and the knowledge base, the Cilia framework uses many of the techniques presented in this book (Chaps. 4, 5, 6, and 7). This is presented in the next sections.

9.3.2 Cilia Touchpoints

Now, let us see the interfaces that the Cilia framework provides to monitor the mediation chains and to adapt them dynamically. The Cilia framework offers a unique entry point called a *CiliaContext*. This interface is a façade, as defined in [7]. It provides general information about the Cilia framework and gives access to the *Builder* and *Application Runtime* objects.

For creation and modification purposes, the CiliaContext provides a *Builder* object. Builder is another well-known design pattern defined in [7] and often used in object-oriented frameworks for the creation of complex heterogeneous structures.

```
public interface CiliaContext {

        /* Version of the running Cilia */
        String getVersion();

        /* Start date */
        Date getStartUpDate();

        /* Object allowing the creation and update of mediation chains*/
        Builder getBuilder();

        /* Object allowing the dynamic monitoring of mediation chains */
        ApplicationRuntime getApplicationRuntime();

}
```

Listing 9.1 The CiliaContext interface (extract)

In our case, the Builder object allows the construction and update of the mediation chains and any of their constituents. Such creations and modifications can be made through a DSCilia file or directly in Java via what is usually called a Java DSL[5] (where domain-specific concepts are exposed through regular Java interfaces).

The *Application Runtime* object allows the management of the monitoring function for the mediation chains and any of their constituents. It provides methods to dynamically define the elements to be monitored, the information to be collected or received and the way to do so (monitoring policies).

An extract of the *CiliaContext* interface is provided hereafter in Listing 9.1.

Monitoring relies on the notion of state variables that are used to model the dynamics of the running chains. This approach draws its inspiration from control theory, as presented in Chap. 3. State variables are attached to global mediation chains but also to their constituents (mediators, adapters and bindings). Their values, called *measures*, are kept in circular lists in order to keep records of the past. The size of the lists is configurable and can be changed at runtime.

Measures can be kept in the knowledge base. Several policies are available to do so. For instance, values can be regularly sent to the knowledge module or simply provided on demand. Also, warnings and alarms can be defined on the state variables. When a measure exceeds a 'low' or 'high' threshold, a warning is emitted. When a measure exceeds a 'very low' or 'very high' threshold, an alarm is emitted by the Cilia runtime.

Specifically, the state variables attached to each mediator are the following:
– Scheduler start time
– Scheduler incoming data
– Processor start time
– Processor incoming data
– Processor outgoing data
– Processor end time

---

[5]Domain-specific language (DSL).

- Value of a processor field annotated by the developer
- Dispatcher start time
- Dispatcher incoming data
- Mediator execution time
- Number of messages sent out by a mediator

The monitoring and the modification functions require navigation facilities across the mediation chains. The Cilia framework provides such facilities to retrieve running chains and to browse them. LDAP filters can be used to search specific mediators (or adapters) in one or several chains. Once a mediator (or adapter) is selected, life-cycle management actions or monitoring directives can be applied.

To reiterate, touchpoints are of utmost importance. They have to provide ways to access the key elements of a running software system in order to observe it and to change it whenever needed. This challenge has been met in Cilia. Through the notion of state variable, it is possible to model the dynamics of mediation chains at a rather high level of abstraction, allowing problem solving to be conducted accordingly. Also, distinguishing adaptation and monitoring at the interface level, as well as at the code level, is important. It clearly separates concerns and leads to good decoupling, which is good for evolution.

9.3.3 Cilia Meta-level and Base Level

As previously indicated, Cilia is implemented based on iPOJO service-oriented components in its entirety. Domain-specific concepts specified with the DSCilia language (mediators, adapters, bindings, etc.) are transformed into a number of iPOJO components for execution. Model transformation, which is at the heart of many domain-specific approaches, often introduces an important semantic gap between what is specified and what is executed. In general, such approaches raise major administration challenges, especially when the links between specification and code-level artefacts are not preserved or are difficult to rebuild.

To cope with this issue, the Cilia framework internally maintains two levels (see Fig. 9.8): a *meta*-level and a *base* level [8] to follow the vocabulary introduced by the meta-object protocols (Chap. 6). Cilia's meta-level is made of interrelated Java objects representing the specified domain-specific concepts, such as chains, mediators, schedulers, processors and bindings. These objects can be seen as a direct transposition in Java of the domain concepts expressed in the DSCilia files. Cilia's base level contains the iPOJO components implementing and executing the mediation chains de facto.

The purpose of the meta-level is to represent abstract domain concepts and to link them to the code corresponding to their implementation. This level also provides a means to observe and manipulate the concepts and subsequently, their implementation. As illustrated by Fig. 9.8, the meta-level is a causal model: modifications to the meta-level are reflected in the base level and vice versa.

Of course, building and maintaining such an additional level of representation has a cost. On the other hand, it greatly enhances code monitoring and evolution

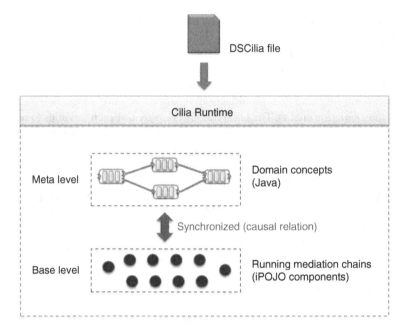

Fig. 9.8 Cilia meta- and base levels

support. The meta-level allows the dynamic definition of monitoring and adaptation strategies in domain-specific terms, which is essential when it comes to complex administration problem solving.

The base level thus contains the iPOJO components implementing the schedulers, the processors, the dispatchers, the bindings, etc. These low-level objects are never presented by Cilia through public interfaces. Yet these are the objects holding the runtime information that is needed to administrate the Cilia framework. They are also the objects to be manipulated when it comes to modifying a running chain.

The Cilia framework ensures synchronisation between the two levels. The base level follows what is specified in the meta-level, and the meta-level includes information coming from the objects at base level. The implementation relies on the *observer* pattern, as defined in [7], and on the notion of controller. As illustrated in Fig. 9.9, the specification of a mediator leads to the creation of three components:

– *SpecificationModelManager* stores the specification of a mediator at the meta-level.
– *MediatorManager*, at base level, creates and manages the iPOJO components implementing a mediator, that is, the scheduler (S in Fig. 9.9), the processor (P), the dispatcher (D) and the communication components (C).
– *MediatorControler* handles the causal relation between the model in the *SpecificationModelManager* and the implementation controlled by the *MediatorManager.*

MediatorControler is an *observer* of *SpecificationModelManager*. When registering as an observer, it provides *SpecificationModelManager* with a *callback* method that has to be called when the mediator specification is changed. *MediatorControler*

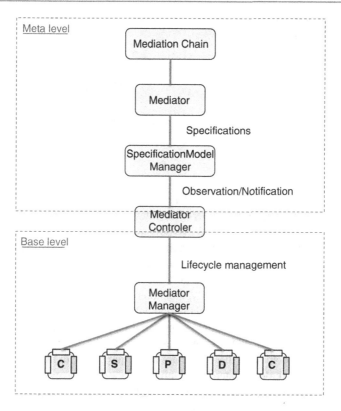

Fig. 9.9 Implementation of the synchronisation mechanisms

also transforms mediator specifications into management directives intended for the *MediatorManager*. The latter can be seen as a factory [7]. It creates all the necessary components and manages their life cycle.

9.3.4 Cilia Dynamic Monitoring

The monitoring functions are implemented at the base level and controlled by the meta-level. That is, the meta-level is in charge of activating/deactivating the monitoring activity, selecting the state variables that are needed, collecting the values of those state variables and deciding on the storage policy.

The base level implements the monitoring functions per se. It tracks and gets the relevant state variables and makes their values (measures) available to the meta-level. Implementation is based on the following principles (see Figs. 9.10 and 9.11):

– Each iPOJO component is augmented with a specific administration handler.
– Components of type *MediatorManager* have a monitoring API and must pass monitoring directives down to the iPOJO components they manage.

Fig. 9.10 Administration
handler in iPOJO components

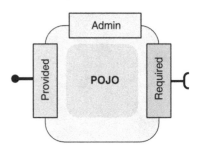

– Components of type *RuntimeModelManager* are linked to each *MediatorModel*.
  They contain the current measures of the relevant state variables of the monitored
  mediator.

Let us examine these three aspects in more detail. As previously explained, Cilia
concepts are transformed into iPOJO components for execution purposes. As any
iPOJO component, these components are executed in an extensible *container* where
handlers can be installed. Put simply, a handler is a piece of code that can be executed automatically before or after a method call.

A specific administration handler, containing monitoring capabilities, has been
added to every base-level iPOJO component. Thus, all the components representing
a scheduler, a processor or a dispatcher are now equipped with monitoring features
that can be activated, deactivated and configured. Concretely, every time a method
is called, the monitoring handler is awakened. Its purpose is to capture all sorts of
information about incoming and outgoing messages, like their size, their treatment
time and their required resources. Monitoring handlers are also able to track domain-
specific information. Such information is to be kept in a field of the POJO (like a
processor) and marked as monitored by the developers of the POJO. The notion of
administration handler is illustrated by Fig. 9.10.

The *MediatorManager* components, presented in the previous subsection, are
responsible for controlling in a homogeneous way the monitoring of *their*
attached components, which by definition pertain to the same mediator. The
purpose of *a MediatorManager* is then to transmit coherent monitoring directives to schedulers, processors and dispatchers and to appropriately combine
data collected from these objects.

Finally, a *RuntimeModelManager* component stores all the measures that are
emitted by the *MediatorManager*. Recall there are several strategies to send those
values: periodically, threshold-based, unconditionally, etc. *RuntimeModelManager*
components have a limited memory. They can store several measures for a given
state variable but not an extensive history.

The global monitoring architecture is illustrated by Fig. 9.11.

To sum up, monitoring is managed in a hierarchical way. The needs are expressed
at the meta-level, through APIs provided by the *SpecificationModelManager* component. Then, directives are observed by the *MediatorControler* and, finally, passed
on to the *MediatorManager* components. State variables values are collected by the

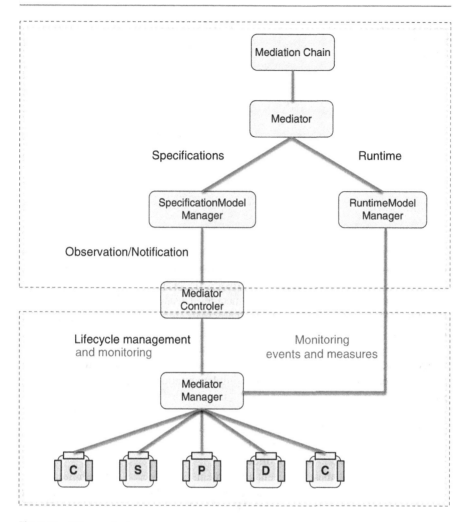

Fig. 9.11 Cilia monitoring

administrative handlers of the low-level components. Those values are consolidated by the *MediatorManager* component and sent up to the *RuntimeModelManager* component via the OSGi *EventAdmin* facility, a simple communication bus provided by OSGi.

9.3.5   Cilia Dynamic Adaptation

Regarding adaptations, the most ambitious goal of Cilia is to allow the dynamic modification of the chains topology. This requires preserving control flows and saving the data being processed, the messages in our case. Just like monitoring, adaptation

Fig. 9.12 Message
management in Cilia
schedulers

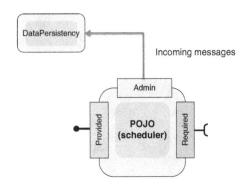

directives come from the meta-level. Concretely, the meta-level decides on the mediators to be modified, added, suppressed or swapped. Decisions are implemented by modifying specifications in the meta-level, using a domain-specific language (the DSCilia language or the Java DSL). Directives are transmitted down to the base level that has to realise modifications in the code.

The base level implements the adaptation functions per se. To do so, it implements a quiescence protocol, as discussed in Chap. 6, allowing the safe adaptations or replacements of mediators. Precisely, implementation is based on the following principles:

– All messages entering a mediator can be saved outside of the mediator.
– Components of type *MediatorManager* can be locked or unlocked.
– *SpecificationModelManager* provides a life-cycle management API, including start, stop, resume and remove directives.

Let us now detail these different implementation aspects. The administration handler of the iPOJO components that implement schedulers has been modified in order to store the data received by the schedulers outside of the components. Specifically, incoming messages (data) are first saved in a dedicated component called *DataPersistency* and then transmitted to the scheduler. This function is configurable: it can be activated or not. It is illustrated by Fig. 9.12.

In addition to that, a mediator can be locked. This operation is proposed at the *MediatorManager* level. When a mediator is locked, incoming messages are redirected to the *DataPersistency* component but are not transmitted to the scheduler POJO. This mechanism is used to put a mediator in a 'quiet' state, that is, a state where no computation is going on. When a mediator is quiet, that is, when it is locked and all the started computations are done, then it can be removed, and the stored messages can be sent to another mediator (a brand new one or an existing one). This prevents data losses during mediator hot-swapping or chain topology change operations.

Once again, implementing such a mechanism has a cost. Messages transmitted between mediators are intercepted, stored, managed, etc. However, this is the price to pay to be able to update a mediation chain without data losses or broken control flows. The mechanism can be controlled however. In particular, messages can be saved or not depending on the context, the importance of mediators, the past problems, the current issues, etc.

9.3.6   Knowledge Module

The purpose of the knowledge module in Cilia is to describe the running Cilia artefacts (chains, mediators, adapters, bindings, etc.) in terms of specification and runtime models. It can be seen as the 'K' in the MAPE-K approach presented in Chap. 4, architecture.

This 'K' is directly built by the Cilia framework and can be configurable (even disengaged if desired). It contains a selection of measures and events characterising a mediation solution over time that is corresponding to past and present runtime situations. For instance, it may record topological changes of the mediation chains, significant past values of specified state variables and current values of specified state variables. The definition of the information to be kept can be specified by auto-nomic managers through dedicated APIs. The autonomic managers can also directly use the touchpoints provided by the Cilia framework, but in this case, they have to build and maintain their own knowledge base.

Interactions between the knowledge base and the runtime are bidirectional. The knowledge base can explicitly fetch data through the monitoring touchpoints and subscribe to events originating in the Cilia runtime. Also, the knowledge can trigger adaptations on the runtime and get feedback.

As previously indicated, the model provided by the knowledge base—the 'K'—is causal. Modifications made on that model are automatically propagated down to the running chains and vice versa. For instance, suppressing a mediator in the model implies suppressing the corresponding implementation under execution in the Cilia runtime. Of course, a delay is necessary for an adaptation to be completed and for the results to be observable back in the K model. This has to be taken into account when measuring the effects of an adaptation, as explained in Chap. 8.

As illustrated by Fig. 9.13, the role of domain engineers is then to implement the mediation chains and the autonomic managers providing self-management features. If they decide to use the knowledge module for monitoring and adaptation purposes, they can concentrate on decision-making algorithms (see Chap. 7). Simply put, they 'just' have to dynamically configure the monitoring function, get runtime information and apply adaptations onto the knowledge module.

9.4   Towards Autonomic Life-Cycle Management of Cilia Chains

9.4.1   Challenges and Motivation

Life-cycle management comprises all operations necessary for getting an applica-tion from its specification stage to its execution stage. Often, life-cycle management must extend into the runtime for performing maintenance operations including

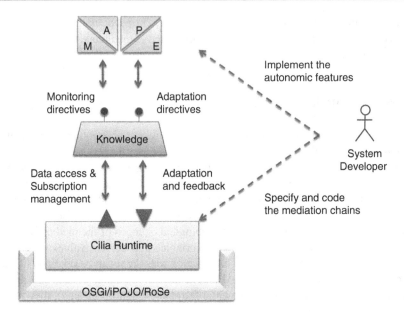

Fig. 9.13 Cilia knowledge base

updates, optimisations, repairs and extensions (see Chap. 1). In its current form, the Cilia framework supports the autonomic life-cycle management of mediation chains. It provides monitoring and adaptation touchpoints at two abstraction levels. First, mediation domain concepts such as chains, mediators and bindings can be manipulated through a configurable knowledge base. Second, the concepts from the underlying implementation technology (iPOJO) can be manipulated through the Cilia runtime. Autonomic managers can be built on top of these touchpoints.

However, in some situations, developing autonomic managers may require significant effort. Indeed, when mediation chains and their execution environment become complex, the corresponding life-cycle management logic is also complex, requiring expertise in both autonomic computing and mediation domains. Advanced solutions could facilitate the development and maintenance of autonomic management systems in the mediation domain. The main challenges to address for providing such solutions stem from key questions such as:

1. How to express the business-level objectives of autonomic life-cycle managers at a high level of abstraction? (See discussion on goals in Chap. 2.)
2. How to develop the system management logic that automatically attains the objectives?
3. How to develop the decision logic that uses monitoring information and enforces adaptation operations in order to attain the objectives in the presence of runtime change? (See Chap. 7.)

4. How to ensure that the decision logic can handle a large spectrum of changes?
5. How to render autonomic managers extensible in order to easily add new objectives and decision functions able to pursue them?
6. How to ensure the scalability of autonomic managers with the size, number and distribution of mediation chains and with the frequency of dynamic changes to adapt to?
7. How to ensure the life-cycle management of the autonomic managers so that they can follow the deployment of mediation chains and survive failures in the underlying platforms?

9.4.2 Model-Based Solutions

As introduced in Chap. 7, knowledge- and model-based approaches have been employed for facilitating various life-cycle management operations. Here we depict the applicability of some of these solutions to the life-cycle management of Cilia mediation chains. We show how increasingly evolved approaches can progressively address the aforementioned challenges.

Initially, model-based approaches were mainly devised for the deployment phase. Here, architectural models formally specify the application architecture, the available distributed platforms and the mapping of application components onto the platforms (e.g. [9]). An automatic deployment facility uses the model to deploy, instantiate and configure components onto the corresponding platforms. However, in these solutions, automatic deployment is executed off-line and subsequent model changes require full application redeployment. This type of solution can automate the deployment of Cilia mediation chains (challenges 1 and 2).

Having to deal with dynamic changes progressively pushed these initial solutions into the runtime and forced them to evolve in order to deal with a wider range of changes (challenges 3 and 4). This requires more sophisticated reasoning processes, which in turn requires more substantial knowledge of managed resources. Naturally, the use of architectural models was extended to enable the formal representation of system knowledge. Architectural reflexion was introduced to ensure that available knowledge constantly reflects the managed system state [10, 11].

Figure 9.14 depicts the general architecture of this solution type. It relies on two architectural models: a *reference architecture* formally specifies management objectives, and a *runtime architecture* maintains a causal relation with the managed system. In this context, the autonomic manager must ensure that the runtime architecture conforms to the reference architecture (goals). This approach has been defined as a stand-alone paradigm identified as models at runtime (known as M@R) [12, 13].

As the scale, desired adaptability and extensibility of the managed system increase, the aforementioned solutions must be further refined. Two important limitations must be addressed for this purpose. First, 'traditional' reference architectures may prove too restrictive. Indeed, defining concrete model elements, such as unique mediator component implementations, exact numbers of mediator instances, precise interconnections and strict platform mappings, severely limits possible system

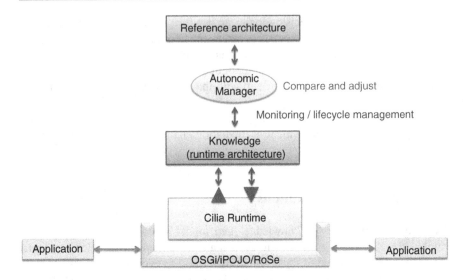

Fig. 9.14 Model-based autonomic life-cycle management

adaptations. Second, solutions that employ a centralised process for implementing life-cycle management eventually reach their scalability limits.

To address these limitations, an increasing number of research initiatives have started to explore the introduction of more abstract modelling for increased flexibility at runtime and decentralised control [14–17]. In some approaches, the centralised model interpreter is replaced by multiple independent processes, executing in parallel and interacting with each other so as to meet common goals. Coordination among decentralised processes relies either on a shared template, such as an abstract architectural model [14–16] or on a shared recipe, such as a set of rules [17].

9.4.3   The Cube Project

The Cube research project[6] aims to develop an autonomic life-cycle management solution that addresses the aforementioned challenges and that is applied to Cilia mediation systems. This subsection presents the main ideas behind the Cube initiative and indicates the subset of features that have been implemented in existing Cube prototypes.

Cube adopts an architectural model-based approach for managing software systems life cycle, as presented above, and introduces several extensions. Namely, Cube uses an *abstract architectural model*, called *archetype*, to define objectives formally, while leaving sufficient runtime flexibility to the life-cycle management

---

[6]Cube project is developed by the Adele team at University of Grenoble in collaboration with the S3 team at Telecom Paris Tech (Cube homepage: http://cube.imag.fr).

process (challenge 4). More specifically, administrators only specify general constraints that must hold in any runtime configuration of the managed system. This provides an increased adaptation leeway, as choices corresponding to archetype constraints can be postponed until runtime, when the actual system state and execution context can be known.

To ensure increased scalability, adaptability and robustness challenges (6 and 7), Cube's autonomic management process is *decentralised* and implemented as a set of self-organising agents; each agent manages a distinctive system part. The runtime model is accordingly split among the agents; each agent only maintains the model fragment reflecting its managed system part. The role of Cube's agents is to cooperatively create and continuously adapt an executing application whose overall runtime model conforms to the reference model (archetype).

Let's take a closer look at Cube's most significant characteristics. First, a Cube archetype is an *abstract* architectural model. This means that it includes several types of generic elements and alternative connectivity and deployment options. For example, mediator components are specified in terms of their abstract types rather than their concrete implementations. This means that the life-cycle manager (agents) can dynamically choose from a variety of alternative implementations when mapping a reference component type to an executing mediator instance. Suitable implementations can be discovered at runtime and introduced at any time during the managed system's life cycle. Similarly, abstract types can be used to define component interconnections and deployment platforms. For example, a deployment platform can be specified in terms of its minimum CPU performance and memory availability. At runtime, any available platform that features these properties can be used. If new platforms become available, Cube agents can discover and integrate them. In case of platform crashes or when energy consumption must be minimised, Cube agents can similarly migrate mediator instances to remaining devices. Cilia's support for safe mediator adaptations (without data losses) provides a valuable base that agents can rely on.

Consider now Cube's decentralised management process. Cube agents feature identical implementations and differentiate their behaviours at runtime depending on their role in the overall management process. Each agent receives an identical copy of the archetype and resolves an *archetype part* (or fraction) so as to create and maintain a corresponding *application part* (Fig. 9.15). At the same time, agents must coordinate their actions and self-organise in order to join their application parts into a coherent application.

Various agent design choices can be made notably with respect to the agent life cycles (challenge 7) and assignment of archetype parts. Regarding life cycle, agents can mutually create each other at runtime [18] or be created statically by an external process [19]. Regarding archetype partitioning, each agent may be assigned an archetype part that represents [18] (a) a component type, (b) a component instance [18], (c) a predefined part or (d) a dynamically determined part [19]. The current Cube prototype creates all agents via an external process; one agent is placed on each platform pertaining to the managed system (Fig. 9.15). Further details on the archetype specification, agent coordination and management process are available

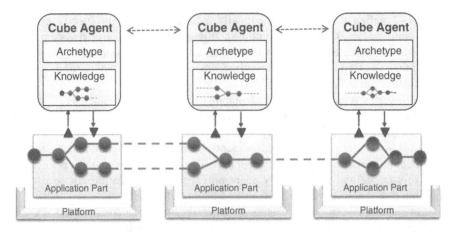

Fig. 9.15 Self-organising Cube agents controlled by a unique archetype

from [18–21]. Additional coordination solutions can be investigated based, for example, on gossip-based [22] or emergent coordination approaches [23].

9.4.3.1 Example

Let us consider an illustrative example of a Cube archetype and its life-cycle management process, in the context of a theoretical mediation application. Here, data collected from any *source*(Cilia Adapter in) must first be *aggregated* (via a Cilia mediator) and then transmitted to a *destination* (Cilia Adapter out). To improve performance, an aggregator may only accept data from a maximum of three sources. As sources join the system dynamically, the mediation chains must accordingly adjust their composition in order to integrate them. Figure 9.16 lists this example's archetype.

The archetype defines three types of mediator components (lines 6–8): S (source), A (aggregator) and D (destination). It also defines a number of constraints on these types. Namely, any data source must be connected to an aggregator (line 18), and any aggregator must be connected to a destination (line 19). When attempting to acquire an aggregator for a certain source, the agents in charge must first try to find an existing one (line 21) and then, if none is available, to create one (line 23). The same policy is specified for acquiring destination components. A final constraint limits to three the number of input connections that each aggregator may accept (line 26).

Figure 9.17 depicts the runtime model[7] of the mediation chains created by the agents after the dynamic insertion of eight data sources. The sources were added manually, triggering the agents to instantiate and interconnect of the necessary

---

[7]Cube's graphical interface shown here is based on the Prefuse visualisation toolkit—http://prefuse.org

Fig. 9.16 Cube archetype example

```
 1<cube xmlns:core="fr.liglab.adele.cube.core">
 2    <archetype id="cube.demo.ac-book" name="AC Book Demo"
 3        version="1.0">
 4
 5        <types>
 6            <core:component id="S" />
 7            <core:component id="A" />
 8            <core:component id="D" />
 9        </types>
10
11        <constraints>
12            <variables>
13                <var id="vs" type="S" />
14                <var id="va" type="A" />
15                <var id="vd" type="D" />
16            </variables>
17
18            <core:connect v1="vs" v2="va" />
19            <core:connect v1="va" v2="vd" />
20
21            <core:find-locally v="va" priority="1" />
22            <core:find-locally v="vd" priority="1" />
23            <core:create-locally v="va" priority="2" />
24            <core:create-locally v="vd" priority="2" />
25
26            <core:in-components v="va" max="3" />
27        </constraints>
28
29    </archetype>
30</cube>
```

Fig. 9.17 Example of Cube-based self-grown mediation chains

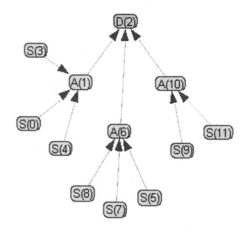

mediator components—aggregators and destination—in order to conform to the archetype. Mediators in the figure are labelled to indicate their types (S (source), A (aggregators) and D (destinations)) and their sequence number in the agent-based instantiation process (0 (first instantiated) to 11 (last instantiated)).

This example was kept simple for comprehensibility reasons. In a real scenario, the archetype would most likely be extended with additional component types—both mediators and platforms—and corresponding constraints (e.g. impose a single destination (D) instance for the entire application). Further examples and details on the archetype specification and agent-based management process can be obtained from the Cube project's Website—http://cube.imag.fr.

9.4.3.2 Discussion

By design, the Cube approach promises several advantages over related life-cycle management solutions. Conversely, the same design features that provide these advantages can also introduce certain drawbacks. In short, abstract reference models (archetypes) allow more runtime flexibility but provide less statically verifiable guarantees over the automatically determined solutions. The right level of abstraction must be found for each system in order to ensure the necessary balance between adaptability and control.

Similarly, decentralising the life-cycle management process and fragmenting the runtime model can provide clear scalability and robustness advantages. At the same time, decentralised control makes it difficult or sometimes impossible to obtain management solutions that are globally optimal. Furthermore, communication overheads required by agent coordination may impact global system performance; system development must consider additional challenges including convergence and stability. As before, the right compromise between complete, centralised control and long-term scalability and survivability must be determined depending on each managed system. Generally, Cube is mainly applicable to cases where the robustness of mediation chains in the long term is more important than instant system performance, even though a certain baseline performance level may be ensured. Conversely, the Cube approach should be avoided in cases where strong guarantees can be guaranteed via centralised control.

Concerning positioning with respect to related work, the Cube approach finds itself at the intersection of several research fields and subfields, of which we only mention a few at this point. For example, from a purely autonomic computing perspective, Cube can be seen as a solution for the autonomic life-cycle management for large-scale, distributed and highly dynamic mediation systems [18, 20]. With respect to the model-based software engineering field, Cube introduces a particular combination of design features, including model abstraction and control decentralisation, for providing increased runtime flexibility and scalability. Also, Cube is similar to the problem-centred approach presented, for example, in [24] or[25], where specifying a Cube archetype corresponds to posing a problem. From a bio-inspired system engineering perspective, Cube can be related to morphogenesis—the development process of biological organisms [21]. From this standpoint, Cube's archetype can be viewed as the equivalent of a biological genotype and the resulting application instances as the equivalent of biological phenotypes. From a self-organising and self-adaptive system perspective, Cube can be seen as a compromise between top-down and bottom-up approaches, where the archetype provides the means of controlling the global result of decentralised self-organising processes [19]. From a constraint programming perspective, Cube can be considered as a constraint-oriented solution, where the constraints are defined via the archetype and the constraint resolver is decentralised, allowing partial solutions to combine into globally conformant resolutions.

As a final note, it is important to note that most of the features presented for the Cube approach represent envisaged capabilities associated to the generic Cube proposal and have not yet been fully implemented or validated. Developments so far have focused on the initial instantiation of mediation applications from relatively simple archetypes. Two Cube prototypes have been developed for experimenting with possible design options within the general Cube approach. Both prototypes rely on iPOJO service-oriented component technology and target mediation systems as application domains. The latest prototype at this date, as presented in [19], is available from the project's Website. Future developments will become available at the same location.

9.5   Key Points

In this chapter, we have introduced the following important points:

- Cilia is an autonomic mediation framework that is made available for use and consultation at http://wikiadele.imag.fr/index.php/Cilia. The framework has been designed with autonomicity in mind. It is based on many of the techniques presented in this book.
- An autonomic system like Cilia is more complex than an equivalent system without autonomic features. As already said (Chap. 1 in particular), absorbing complexity cannot be achieved without any impact on the complexity of the software itself.
- Cilia mediation chains can be distributed across several machines, but the autonomic decisions are centralised since a unique autonomic manager deals with the management of all the running mediation chains.
- Cilia implementation is based on a meta-level and a base level. The meta-level contains Java objects representing domain-specific concepts like mediators, bindings and chains. The base level contains the iPOJO components implementing these concepts.
- Monitoring in Cilia is configurable and dynamic. Monitoring directives are expressed at the meta-level and are implemented at the base level. Monitoring is based on the notion of state variables (borrowed from control theory) that are used to model system dynamics. Adaptation in Cilia is also dynamic. This is made possible by the implementation of a quiescence protocol at the base mediator level.
- Cilia comes with a knowledge base that can be configured dynamically. The knowledge base contains information about the running chains and past events like topology evolutions. The knowledge base is a model providing a biased, partial view of the running artefacts.
- Cilia can be extended to support fully autonomic life-cycle management capabilities, facilitating the deployment, installation, instantiation, configuration, adaptation and repair of mediation chains. A related research project called Cube is being developed to provide such capabilities (http://cube.imag.fr). Cube relies on several important concepts, including model-based management, architectural reflexion and self-organising multi-agent systems.
- In Cube, management objectives are formally specified via an abstract architectural model, called archetype. Cube autonomic management aims to create and adapt application instances that conform to the archetype. This process is decentralised and implemented via multiple self-organising agents.

- Cube agents feature identical implementations and detain an identical copy of the archetype. They must collaborate in order to dynamically split the archetype among themselves. Each agent's archetype part defines its local objective; attaining this objective implies creating and adapting an application part that conforms to the archetype part. Agents must then self-organise so as to create matching application parts and combine them into coherent global applications.
- Cube's reliance on an abstract model (archetype) increases the runtime flexibility of applications that must conform to this model. Cube's decentralised management process (agents) increases the efficiency of local adaptations and repairs and reinforces overall system robustness and survivability.

References

1. Wiederhold, G.: Mediators in the architecture of future information systems. Computer **25**(3), 38–49 (1992)
2. Wiederhold, G., Genesereth, M.: The conceptual basis for mediation services. IEEE Expert **12**(5), 38–47 (1997)
3. Lalanda, P., Bellissard, L., Balter, R.: Asynchronous mediation for integrating business and operational processes. IEEE Internet Comput. **10**(1), 56–64 (2006)
4. Garcia, I., Pedraza, G., Debbabi, B., Lalanda, P., Hamon, C.: Towards a service mediation framework for dynamic applications. In: Proceedings of the IEEE 2010 Asia-Pacific Services Computing Conference, Hangzhou, China, 6 Dec 2010
5. Morand, D., Garcia, I., Lalanda, P.: Autonomic enterprise service bus. In: Proceedings of the Service Oriented Architectures in Converging Networked Environments (SOCNE), Toulouse, France, 5 Sept 2011
6. Hohpe, G., Woolf, B.: Enterprise Integration Patterns; Designing, Building, and Deploying Messaging Solutions. Addison-Wesley, Boston (2003)
7. Gamma, E., Helm, R., Johnson, R., Vlissides, J.: Design Patterns: Elements of Reusable Object-Oriented Software. Addison Wesley, Reading (1995)
8. Garcia, I., Morand, D., Debbabi, B., Lalanda, P., Bourret, P.: A reflective framework for mediation applications. In: Proceedings of the 10th International Middleware Workshop on Adaptive and Reflective Middleware, Lisbon, Portugal, 12 Dec 2011
9. OMG.: Deployment and configuration of component-based distributed applications specification. http://www.omg.org/spec/DEPL. Apr 2006
10. Cazzola, W., Savigni, A., Sosio, A., Tisato, F.: Architectural reflection: bridging the gap between a running system and its architectural specification. In: Proceedings of 6th IEEE Reengineering Forum (REF'98), pp. 12-1–12-6, Firenze, Italia, 8–11 Mar 1998
11. Cazzola, W., Savigni, A., Sosio, A., Tisato, F.: Architectural reflection: concepts, design, and evaluation. Technical Report RI-DSI 234–99, DSI, Università degli Studidi Milano, May 1999
12. IEEE Comput, Special issue on "Models @ Run.Time", **42**(10) (2009)
13. France, R., Rumpe, B.: Model-driven development of complex software: a research roadmap. In: Future of Software Engineering, pp. 259–268. IEEE Computer Society Washington, DC, USA (2007)
14. Georgiadis, I., Magee, J., Kramer, J.: Self-organising software architectures for distributed systems. In: Workshop on Self-Healing Systems, pp. 33–38, Charleston, SC, 2002
15. Sykes, D., Magee, J., Kramer, J.: FlashMob: distributed adaptive self-assembly. In: Proceedings of the 6th International Symposium on Software Engineering for Adaptive and Self-Managing Systems (SEAMS), pp. 100–109, Honolulu, 2011

16. Nafz, F., Seebach, H., Steghöfer, J.-P., Anders, G., Reif, W.: Constraining self-organisation through corridors of correct behaviour: the restore invariant approach. In: Organic Computing—A Paradigm Shift for Complex Systems. Autonomic Systems, vol. 1, Part 1, pp. 79–93. Springer, Basel (2011)
17. Ulieru, M., Doursat, R.: Emergent engineering: a radical paradigm shift. Int. J. Auton. Adapt. Commun. Syst. (IJAACS) **4**(1), 39–60 (2011)
18. Diaconescu, A., Lalanda, P.: Self-growing applications from abstract architectures an application to data-mediation systems. In: IEEE Symposium Series on Computational Intelligence (SSCI 2011) – IEEE Workshop on Organic Computing (OC 2011), Paris, France, 11–15 Apr 2011
19. Debbabi, B., Diaconescu, A., Lalanda, P.: Controlling self-organising software applications with archetypes. In: 6th IEEE International Conference on Self-Adaptive and Self-Organizing Systems (SASO 2012), Lyon, France, 10–14 Sept 2012
20. Diaconescu, A., Lalanda, P.: A decentralised, architecture-based framework for self-growing applications. In: Proceedings of the 6th ACM/IEEE International Conference on Autonomic Computing and Communications (ICAC 2009), Barcelona, Spain, 15–19 June 2009
21. Diaconescu, A., Debbabi, B., Lalanda, P.: Self-growing software from architectural blueprints. In: 3rd Morphogenetic Engineering Workshop (MEW 2011), satellite of the 20th European Conference on Artificial Life (ECAL 2011), Paris, France, 8–12 Aug 2011
22. Anthony, R.J.: Emergence: a paradigm for robust and scalable distributed applications. In: International Conference on Autonomic Computing ICAC, New York, 2004
23. Jelasity, M., Montresor, A., Babaoglu, O.: Gossip-based aggregation in large dynamic networks. ACM Trans. Comput. Syst. **23**(3), 219–252 (2005)
24. Landauer, C., Bellman, K.L.: Knowledge-based integration infrastructure for complex systems. Int. J. Intell. Control Syst. **1**(1), 133–153 (1996)
25. Landauer, C.: Problem posing as a software engineering paradigm. In: Proceedings of the 21st International Conference on Systems Engineering (ICSENG'11), 16–18 August, Las Vegas, USA, pp. 346–351 (2011). http://dx.doi.org/10.1109/ICSEng.2011.69

Future of Autonomic Computing and Conclusions

10

The purpose of this last chapter is twofold. First, it draws together the lessons we have learned about autonomic computing and the techniques that are used, at the time of writing, to design and implement self-managed software systems. Our purpose is clearly to help readers to understand, develop and maintain autonomic systems.

The second objective of this concluding chapter is to look ahead and foresee the future of autonomic computing, while also attempting to point out some of the most important challenges to address in order to attain the full autonomic computing vision. To achieve this risky exercise, we view the topic from the perspective of how autonomic systems will be engineered and how assurances regarding their behaviours can be made. We acknowledge that targeting system-level autonomy will presumably necessitate integrated solutions, incorporating multiple autonomic elements, each one dealing with different management concerns and operating at various granularity levels. In this context, we provide some examples of the more specialised fields of autonomic networking and autonomic machines. We also have a discussion about next-generation software engineering techniques, approaches and tools that would be required to meet future computing system requirements.

P. Lalanda et al., *Autonomic Computing: Principles, Design and Implementation*, Undergraduate Topics in Computer Science, DOI 10.1007/978-1-4471-5007-7_10, © Springer-Verlag London 2013

10.1   Autonomic Computing in This Book

We believe that autonomic computing is bound to change the way software systems are developed. This new field is addressing some of the issues resulting from the ever-increasing complexity of software administration and the growing difficulty encountered by software administrators in performing their job effectively. Undeniably, properly managing software systems is a considerable challenge for society and has to be handled urgently. The lack of appropriate responses to this issue could force us to reconsider our reliance on software to support our businesses and daily activities.

Autonomic computing can rely on advances in several scientific fields, sometimes very different from each other. In particular, autonomic computing is rooted in several (surprisingly) complementary fields, most notably including control theory and biology. To some extent, these two fields have paved the way to the *classical* autonomic architectures where a number of cooperating context-aware control loops can bring about a wide range of adaptations. Autonomic computing also relies heavily on software engineering best practices to dynamically structure, monitor and change software systems. In some way, software engineering provides the necessary techniques to implement the multiple control loop vision, and this can be said to be derived from biology in some instances. Further, autonomic computing is highly dependent on knowledge representation, reasoning techniques and learning as defined in various computer science fields like artificial intelligence or more distant domains like economics and psychology. From a certain perspective, these latter fields provide the means to reason about particular situations and make decisions regarding the possible courses of administrative actions to be undergone.

Yet, despite these influences, we believe that autonomic computing is a field in its own. Indeed, the runtime administration of software systems requires the definition of specific methods and techniques, still to be improved and explored. This is a formidable challenge, exacerbated by the complexity and variety of today's software systems and their execution environments, that will demand intensive research for the years to come.

In fact, because they seek to unburden system administrators and improve overall effectiveness, autonomic software systems are certainly more difficult to conceive and implement than systems without autonomic capabilities. Autonomic systems are expected to absorb the complexity of usually manual administrative tasks and provide intuitive, high-level interfaces for human administrators. Meeting this requirement leads to increased system complexity overall, albeit with the added advantage of minimising perceived system complexity for administrators and users.

This observation is certainly the main motivation of this book. Indeed, along with necessary explanations about the goals and origins of autonomic computing, we believe that it is of major importance to present, in a coherent way, the different techniques that are available today to design and implement autonomic software systems. Of course, given the large number of techniques that exist, as well as the high-quality projects in the autonomic computing area, we had to make tough choices regarding what we include and what we cannot possibly cover in one book. Decisions were guided by the rapid applicability of the techniques. In particular, we dedicated quite an important part of this book to review software engineering techniques and principles for architecting, monitoring, reasoning and adapting systems—for they are keys to software production in general. The rest of this chapter is concerned with longer term lines of work.

10.2 Alternative Autonomic Stories

In parallel to the general focus on autonomic computing, there have been a number of groups who have isolated a section of the general computing field and focused on self-management within those fields. Such work is more specific to the nature of the fields themselves but also overlaps somewhat with the general notion of autonomic computing that we present in this book. Two specific areas are autonomic communications and autonomic machines. The former is examining the subject from a more topological point of view, where the network is a graph that self-heals. The latter examines how one can imagine autonomicity right down to the very metal of the machine itself. To be autonomic, a large-scale distributed system will most likely have to integrate aspects of several fields, including autonomic communications, autonomic machines and autonomic software.

10.2.1 Autonomic Communications

The Internet is the interconnecting fabric that supports today's distributed computing resources. Interestingly, even before this current Internet was conceived, routing systems over the Internet's predecessor, Arpanet, had autonomic characteristics in terms of a form of feedback loop and implicitly monitored internal and external conditions. In 1969, Will Crowther, from BBN technologies, the company who won the initial Arpanet contract, used mathematical graph theory to design the Arpanet routing protocols. Using distance vectors, Crowther's protocol was both distributed and adaptive, designed to adapt to quickly changing network characteristics. External conditions were monitored in terms of delays, which were estimated by queue lengths at each link and a cost equated to those delays. Then routing decisions were made based on the end-to-end estimated costs of packet transfer; the theory being that traffic distribution should be balanced fairly on all outgoing links to a given destination as a result.

In 1983, Arpanet gave way to the Internet protocol suite we use today, TCP/IP. The flow and congestion control mechanisms used in this modern protocol work in a similar fashion to the Arpanet routing scheme (the reader is directed to the many sources of information on TCP/IP that describe in detail how this works). To this end, the protocols that compose the Internet can be described as self-organising, self-managing, self-optimising, etc., though they were designed long before the term autonomic computing was coined.

The autonomic capabilities of communication protocols such as TCP/IP manage to hide from programmers the complexity of the underlying network infrastructure. However, new-generation networks seem to raise additional challenges, as they develop in an increasingly hectic and decentralised manner, potentially integrating numerous protocols, technologies and administrative goals [1, 2]. In ubiquitous or pervasive systems, in addition to hardware and software heterogeneity, network dynamics increases dramatically as various communication-enabled equipments may frequently join, leave or move through the network. This significantly impacts the emerging network topology and usage patterns and can challenge traditional routing and discovery protocols. Finally, as network control becomes increasingly decentralised, traditional approaches to network configuration and security management become progressively inadequate.

While the potential benefits of new-generation networks are significant, addressing the ensuing challenges require redesigning many of the existing communication models and architectures, in order to render network services more flexible and dynamically adaptable, at the infrastructural, application and user levels. Meanwhile, global network dependability, trustworthiness and performance must be maintained. Therefore, autonomic communications research strives to endow next-generation networks with self-*capabilities that can handle significant heterogeneity, dynamism and decentralised control.

It is no surprise that a massively complex, planet-scale system like the Internet would be one of the first to truly embrace the principles of self-* as we know it today. Specifically, if one were to examine any text on autonomic networking, one would see that modern autonomic communications cover the areas that would generally map to those of self-knowledge, policy management, configuration management and network defence and security, and at this level, this approach resembles the approaches we present in this book. However, there is an obvious communications focus, which looks at the system in terms of its nodes and links (a graph view of the network topology), rather than components, services, software engineering, etc. Having said this, there is not a great deal of difference between the general and communications viewpoints—other than the devil being in the detail.

Obviously, core to the autonomic communications system is the knowledge that it obtains. As before, the internal and external environments are understood by sensing or probing; however, here it focuses on individual network elements, and therefore, self-knowledge can be obtained from switches and network interfaces. Configuration, both in terms of current and historic system state information, can also be derived from traffic flows or performance data. Self-knowledge then feeds the self-managing components, and the higher-level network goals then guide the runtime system in allowing it to control the network and to protect it from the many forms of attack.

The topological aspects of the communications system, such as the organisation and maintenance of the components of the computer network, can be managed in an autonomic way. This is typically driven through a database containing details, for example, network addresses, program versions and updates, and allows a form of automated configuration management. Currently, network administrators use tools or scripts to interface or maintain this resource. Historic data is also stored so that if a change leads to an undesirable state, the system should be able to rollback changes to the state the system was in prior to issuing the changes. Needless to say, configuration management interfaces with all of the other autonomic components in the communications subsystem.

The rules that govern the topological configuration management and how the self-knowledge is used are represented by the policy management subsystem. Policy management systems are used in general autonomic computing also. However, here it includes the specification, deployment, enforcement and reasoning about the policies that govern the activities that concern security, resource allocations and network configuration management. They are a means to define the relationships between network components, establish degrees of trust and define performance constraints, priorities, etc. They drive the mechanisms that respond to network attacks. Further, these defence components can also be dynamic and adaptive, proactively assessing the network infrastructure for risks and deriving defensive responses accordingly. Here, current network states must be dynamically understood and, where required, corrections to perceived risk taken, quickly! For example, this may mean that certain network packets may be dropped or ports temporarily closed on demand. Related to this are the components that define access to the different resources in the communications system. To ensure we trust the components wishing to have access to the network, authorization policies define what the component is allowed to do and how this will be implemented. Again this may be adaptive in that a component may be authorised to access something under some conditions, or contexts, but not others.

The ability for a network to scale is of paramount importance. This can be in terms of its ability to host many nodes and propagate data around a company or can even span a planetwide network, for example, the Internet. The intuition regarding how best to scale a network comes from ensuring that much of its operation is decentralised. Therefore, the main difference between autonomic computing in the general and autonomic communications approaches is that there tends to be a focus on more distributed and bottom-up methodologies.

Taking this a step further, currently there are many initiatives examining how bio-inspired paradigms might be applied to these aspects of the communications architecture. To enable this, the traditional tree-like hierarchical approaches to network architectures is giving way to a more compartmentalised approach whereby boundaries, based on technological and/or administrative aspects, are specified and the management function relates to the components and systems that reside within this boundary. Likewise, there is a move to make network functions behave like components that can be composed and recomposed in a flexible way. From this, control loops can be made to allow the system to become autonomic, flexible and adaptive.

Core to this ability is the opening of routers to become more flexibly controlled by software. This is known as software defined networking (SDN), and it seeks to make the network control plane remotely accessible and remotely modifiable via third-party software. Open protocols, such as OpenFlow, are an example of SDN. Previous networks viewed the network as a highly self-organising system that has been ideal in terms of allowing the Internet to both scale and be agile to environmental changes. However, this approach has a number of drawbacks in terms of being able to identify destinations by more semantic means (For example, I would rather send a file to my home computer wherever it is rather than having to know it is computer 176.27.230.111;

when the computer moves the address may change and I do not want to have to deal with that. Another example is that I would prefer to view the data in the network as having an entity, e.g. its a particular video stream rather than just a set of packets). Essentially, SDN decouples network control (routing and forwarding decisions) from the network topology (nodes and how they are linked). This means that these different aspects can be implemented using different distribution models whereby the control elements can become more sophisticated and can even be run on a different platform from the traditionally low-powered switch or router technologies of the past.

Finally, cloud computing, with its dynamics and complexity, brings increased network resource demands in terms of fast reconfigurations and flexible resource deployments brought about by the introduction of machine virtualization. Therefore, it is not surprising to see that the vast majority of research on autonomic computing remains with cloud and large data centre computing.

The topic of autonomic communications is very briefly introduced here; for fuller discussion of the topic, we direct the reader to comprehensive surveys of the subject [1, 3] or [2].

10.2.2 Autonomic Computing, Right Down to the Metal?

Described in the Autonomic Computing Blueprint [4], the Autonomic Computing Adoption Model outlined the architectural steps towards more highly autonomic capabilities of a system (Chap. 2). This spectrum ranged from the manual level, instrument and monitor level, analysis level, closed loop level for the IT environment and finally, the further closed loop level that includes the business processes. Crosscutting this is the scope which the autonomic functionalities cover. These range from the subcomponent level, instance level, multiple components of the same type and multiple components of different types, right up to the business level. Of course, they left open the definition of what a subcomponent would be, but it was assumed it would be a well-contained tractable software component with limited scope. However, there is evidence now that the notion of autonomic computing can be applied right down to the lowest edge of the software continuum where it meets the hardware.

One current example of this is the MIT-led Angstrom project.[1] To embrace challenges of extreme-scale computing, the Angstrom project's goal is to create the fundamental technologies necessary to overcome the primary challenges of energy efficiency, scalability, programmability and dependability. This project combines basic hardware and software research with chip and system fabrication research. It has two core foundations: a fully distributed factored architecture for both hardware and software and, more applicable to our discussion, a self-aware computational model called SEEC.[2] As such, it can be viewed as a system promoting autonomics down to the metal.

---

[1] Angstrom project (MIT)—Universal Technologies for Exascale Computing :http://projects.csail.mit.edu/angstrom
[2] SEEC: SElf-awarE Computational model.

Their assumption is that this system will run on energy-efficient multicore computers scalable to 1,000's of cores. Here they have taken a factored approach to both the hardware and low-level software and operating systems. For example, they use embedded memories consisting of low-voltage SRAMs capable of greater voltage and frequency scaling to significantly save energy. Dynamic cache-coherency schemes that can grow with the system have been developed and are again energy efficient, being able to adapt to system usage patterns. They describe this as a 4D approach to cache-coherency, which combines policy support and optimisations that depend on the operating context of the system at runtime. SEFOS[3] is the self-aware, operating system specially designed for such systems composed of 1,000 + cores. Given this assumption, they also provide support for 'helper threads', which assist the application's main threads of computation.

Using this factored hardware and systems software, the SEEC system relies on a goal-oriented computational model that abstracts traditional procedural programming into goals that are actuated in the self-aware, factored multicore system. SEEC explicitly incorporates energy and resiliency into the hardware, operating system, compiler and languages. In this way, the programmer defines goals such as 'correlate the weather and room temperature streams burning less than 10W', and the system should follow. Using methods based on machine learning and control theory, they are already able to show how their approach performs at orders of magnitude more energy-efficient and dependable architectures.

Key to this is the Angstrom support that exposes sensors and adaptations that traditionally would have been managed independently by hardware. This allows SEEC to control and coordinate hardware behaviours with actions specified by other parts of the system, allowing the SEEC runtime system to meet application goals while reducing costs (e.g. power consumption).

SEEC forms an observe–decide–act loop, much like the MAPE-K loop discussed in previous chapters. Here it continuously monitors its goals and resources using intelligence to map resources to meet goals given current system state. Every component of the Angstrom system, from applications to hardware, is designed to be autonomic in that all contribute to the specification of the observe–decide–act loop via an interface to specify goals and separate interfaces to specify actions (e.g. allocating processing cores or cache allocation).

To make this tractable, they simplify the systems monitoring function in terms of three application specified areas (goals): performance, accuracy and power. Performance is defined in terms of a target heart rate or latency between heartbeats. Accuracy is a measure of distortion from an application-defined nominal value over a given set of heartbeats. Then power and energy is specified as target average power for a given heart rate or between heartbeats. Actuation is then actions that happen in as low as the systems software and even hardware level as the associated interfaces of these are exposed. The most interesting part of this system is its decision-making capacity. It is required to make decisions about actions with which it has had no

---

[3] SEFOS: SElf-aware Factored OS.

prior experience and yet be able to react quickly, at runtime, to dynamic changes in application loads and resource fluctuation.

As stated in this book, we do not get autonomic computing for free; monitoring and decision-making are additional to the main computational load of the system and must either consume the same set of recourses or be off-loaded to additional computing resources. The Angstrom approach is to exploit the large number of processors in the system and combine this with its ability to control the power that those cores use. That is, to help reduce the costs of runtime decision-making, it pairs each main processor with a specialised, low-power core called the partner core. The partner core can inspect and manipulate state (e.g. performance counters) within the main core and has access to the event queues fed by event probes, and thus the autonomic decision-making is off-loaded.

In a similar fashion, the SpiNNaker project from Manchester University makes use of bio-inspired techniques, mainly from the human brain, to structure and organise billions of simple computing elements.[4] Their aim is to build a highly scalable parallel processing engine that is energy efficient. As multiprocessor and multicore systems have become the norm, we can imagine these approaches becoming mainstream in the future.

10.3   Autonomic Computing in the Near Future

'Prediction is very difficult, especially about the future'.[5] While this statement applies to any subject, it is especially true if that subject is fast moving like computing or if it has yet to be fully defined, as with autonomic computing. The danger with autonomic computing has always been that it might be seen as a fad and fade away to be remembered as something that got lots of funding around the turn of the millennium. The question that has to be asked is, has autonomic computing made an impact? Was the focus too broad (or too narrow)? Was the term overused or abused in some way?

ICT soothsayers describe a future where technology is highly pervasive. Sensors, actuators, RFID tags, etc., will be embedded in smart objects, people and their surrounding space. Networks will envelope these devices creating a decentralised cyber-physical world of systems of systems. All is dynamic, heterogeneous and complex yet tasked with one thing—to deliver reliable, efficient services. This world is much too complex for humans to manage. Automated system management is exactly what autonomic computing is about; therefore, it looks like there is a healthy outlook for this subject.

To examine what the future of autonomic computing will look like and what will impact the subject, we view the topic from the perspective of how such systems will be engineered and how assurances regarding their behaviours can be made. We also predict that the more specialist notions of autonomic communications and low-level systems, as discussed in the previous sections, will converge in a more tightly coupled way producing a much more complex yet agile sets of systems.

---

[4]http://rsif.royalsocietypublishing.org/content/4/13/193.full.pdf
[5]Niels Bohr, Danish physicist (1885–1962).

10.3.1 Engineering Autonomic Systems

Businesses no longer make proprietary software, yet businesses are supposed to manage, support and maintain software systems.

The effectiveness of autonomic computing is a product of new artefacts, such as languages, architectures, frameworks and standards, to support the development of autonomic systems. It requires new software engineering techniques to ensure that autonomic capabilities are easily and robustly integrated. This is because current software engineering techniques are designed and work well in the engineering of systems that exhibit a significant degree of predictability. Recall in Chap. 8, Evaluation, we mentioned the desirability to have an autonomic system that adapts or is at least able to cope with less predictable situations. Furthermore, autonomic systems and adaptive systems in general have the pertinacity to bring an element of change and uncertainty to the system, yet uncertainty is something we are still struggling with in the software engineering world.

Software requirements capture systems, such as KAOS [5],can aid the development of autonomic systems as they have been designed to extract system requirements from goals (see Chap. 4), but such systems have no explicit support for uncertainty. The challenge here is to be able to articulate what designers, or clients, would like the system to do but in a more 'fuzzy' way. That is, instead of saying 'the system must do...', analysts must be able to say 'the system could do this...'or alternatively 'try to achieve that...', 'as long as it maintains the following goals....', etc. Therefore, there is a need to be able to better specify requirements and be able to change these easily as the system develops and runs.

The ability to meet such fuzzy requirements implies on the one hand a clear separation between requirements specification and system implementation and, on the other hand, the ability of the system implementation to adapt to various changes in order to fulfil specified requirements. This further implies a need for formal requirement specifications (allowing autonomic managers to interpret them) and for self-describing implementation resources, such as software services or execution platforms (allowing autonomic managers to discover and integrate them).

Extensive system adaptation can be facilitated by the ability to seamlessly integrate parts that already exist into various system configurations. System integration has traditionally represented an important issue in software engineering. Static integration had to deal with difficult problems such as technological heterogeneity, distribution and syntactic and semantic interface mismatches between integrated elements. Dynamic integration must address additional issues, including resource discovery, dynamic binding and state management. Enabling autonomic managers to achieve extensive system adaptations by means of dynamic resource integration imposes consequent requirements on the design and implementation of system resources (e.g. support for open protocols, generic interfaces and self-description via public metadata).

Generally, having to deal with runtime changes, especially unpredictable changes, may mean that most software engineering activities, which were traditionally static, would have to progressively move into the runtime. Hence, requirement definitions may be provided, updated or extended at runtime. Autonomic managers must accordingly adapt the underlying system implementation so as to ensure the new requirements. Different system architectures and designs may be more suitable for meeting various requirements in diverse execution environments. Autonomic managers would have to identify and set in place the system architecture suitable in each context. Similarly, the system's component implementation, configuration and deployment would have to be reconsidered at runtime in response to changes in requirements, resource availability or user loads. Finally, and maybe most importantly, certain testing and validation activities may equally have to be carried out online in order to provide some indication of the system's current capacity to reach or approach given requirements. Indeed, addressing unpredictable changes would most likely imply dynamically implementing unpredictable solutions, which, by definition, could *not* be exhaustively tested and validated offline. Hence, runtime activities, such as testing, evaluation, reporting or rolling back to a previous stable state, may become increasingly essential in such dynamic settings.

The aforementioned considerations on dynamic change and adaptation concern both the managed resources and the autonomic managers administering them. Indeed, the autonomic management logic necessary for administering a certain set of resources, in a certain context, for reaching a certain goal, may also have to adapt to changes in those managed resources, their context or goals. Hence, the goals, implementation and deployment of autonomic managers may equally have to change during runtime. As before, dynamic integration of autonomic resources into complete autonomic managers could be applied here to increase management adaptability.

Interestingly, an autonomic manager that adapts a managed system may have to consequently change itself to manage the new system. For example, integrating a new component into the managed system may require adding new monitors and analysers to the autonomic manager. If the new component is placed on a remote platform, new autonomic decision logic may be necessary to find the best placement in the current environment. In such settings, the managed system and its autonomic management logic can mutually influence each other's adaptation and evolve incrementally towards a complete autonomic system solution. Layered architectures, similar to those proposed, for example, in [6, 7], seem suitable for supporting this sort of behaviour. Hence, additional layers of high-level autonomic managers can be introduced to control and adapt more basic managers, which interact directly with managed resources.

10.3.2 Managing Complexity

As autonomic systems grow, so does the complexity of the system. System complexity stems from the numbers of components to be managed and also from the potential heterogeneity and distribution of such components. Recall, adding autonomicity adds components and therefore complexity. One consequence of this is the sheer volume of data (e.g. metadata about the system's operation), which can also be highly heterogeneous and distributed. Data-mediation solutions can be adopted in such cases to implement monitoring and analysis functions based on hierarchical data processing and transport, such as discussed in Chap. 9, Autonomic Mediation in Cilia. The system's permutations of component interaction further complicate things, since components can no longer be managed in isolation without risking undesirable side effects; holistic management relying on integrate knowledge of the system's inner workings is required instead. Another difficult issue represents the growing numbers of constraints that represent the system's goals that have to be optimised. Goals may also be conflicting, requiring autonomic managers to define and optimise utility functions that account for such goals. Finally, the problem is exacerbated by dynamism, as managed systems are increasingly updated and extended at runtime. Autonomic managers must hence be able to administer systems as they dynamically change.

Overall, the ever larger scale, heterogeneity, distribution and dynamism of software systems render them increasingly complex. Managing complex software systems requires complex autonomic managers. There has been an increase in the body of research looking into this from a number of fields. New distributed optimisation techniques are coming forward, for example, control engineering, which is close to the heart of autonomic computing, which has been advancing. Here the problems of scale and complexity are being eased through the exploitation of hierarchical approaches to control. This way, the control loop interactions can be decoupled and their interactions, and subsequent interference, minimised. This limits the potential for damage from unexpected or unwelcome interactions that have not been accounted for. Control engineering has developed standard approaches to model and reason about feedback such as the Model Reference Adaptive Control (MRAC) [8] and the Model Identification Adaptive Control (MIAC) [9]. The decoupling hierarchical nature of a control system has many advantages, but there is a need to ensure well-defined links between the decoupled elements.

In addition to hierarchical solutions, approaches based on completely decentralised designs have been investigated for building complex autonomic managers. Research projects such as [10–12] aim to identify the key software engineering challenges involved in constructing complex autonomic managers and propose hierarchical or decentralised models, architectures and frameworks for alleviating these challenges. Notably such approaches can draw inspiration from fields such as multi-agent systems, proposing various techniques for agent collaboration or competition, and self-organising systems, studying the opportunistic self-assembly of systems from simpler elements. Finally, multi-criteria optimisation techniques can be adopted to manage multiple and possibly conflicting goals.

10.3.3 Who Guards the Guards? Trust and Assurances in Autonomic Computing

When computing moved towards systems that were well connected via networks (e.g. using the Internet), or open systems and services, there was a step change in the notion of understanding and trusting the system and ensuring it is secure and safe.

Autonomicity has the capacity to bring about a further step change. Here, concerning security, one can imagine a third party falsifying the parameters fed into the autonomic manager to make it adapt or change its operation in an inappropriate way. For example, if we had an autonomic audio player that operated like the one that we present in this book (see Chap. 4), there could be malicious third-party software sitting on the client machine, purposefully slowing down the packets being received in the audio client software, giving it the perception that the bandwidth was quite low. Then the system would adapt to this by lowering its compression codec. In turn, this lessens the quality of the audio playing but also frees up the bandwidth, which the malicious software could make use of.

This example shows that because the autonomic system is fed with environmental data and data from the managed resources, this open point is a place where vulnerabilities lie. Environmental complexity and system dynamism can render an autonomic system vulnerable even in the absence of explicit malicious behaviour. For example, even in a closed loop system, if the autonomic system cannot perceive the environment correctly, it will not behave well. So any self-managing system that is embedded in a dynamic environment has to deal with uncertainty. This is especially so if that environment is the physical world we live in. For example, this would especially apply to sensor networks embedded in a building or in a grape field or even just a system that has humans in the loop. Physical environments are by definition unpredictable; hence, at any point in time, there could be a mismatch between the models of the environment understood by the autonomic system and the actual environment. Furthermore, an autonomic system may have no control over other processes that influence its environment. Therefore, there is a movement to look at self-organising systems that exploit emergence to improve their ability to remain robust to dynamic operating conditions. Exploiting these principles is a promising direction to deal with uncertainty in decentralised autonomic systems.

This leads us to a conversation about what monitors the behaviour of the self-monitoring system? As we mentioned earlier, there is a movement, inspired by the emerging fields of distributed control theory that encourages the decoupling of the autonomic system into either hierarchies or collaborations of distributed systems. Yet, even in a distributive collaborative setting, sharing complete knowledge among decentralised adaptation managers constrains the scalability of the system. The alternative is to not share complete knowledge, but this means that each of the decoupled components only has partial knowledge of the system. That is, they are only interested in, and able to control, the bits they are responsible for. This limits the types of decision-making techniques that can be used to implement the knowledge component of the MAPE-K loop. For example, nonlinear programming and queuing network models rely on the availability of system-wide knowledge. With distribution, the lack of complete knowledge forces each self-adaptive unit to reach potentially suboptimal solutions when taken from the system-wide view. Nevertheless, we are beginning to see the development of algorithms that converge to optimal (or near optimal) solutions. However, in practice, engineering real-world solutions in this manner has shown to be extremely difficult, especially at scale. The extra complexity of such systems, coupled with decentralisation, dictating that no central authority exists, can make the behaviour of the system less predictable, and in turn, this may mean that the system is less trusted. In turn, as a potential advantage, inspiration from self-organising and emergent systems can be considered for enabling the construction of globally robust systems from a myriad of unreliable elements. Amorphous computing is one example initiative investigating this approach (Chap. 3). Yet, engineering such systems remains difficult and the current applicability of such approaches limited. Much more research is required in this area.

Another option is to introduce autonomic managers capable of administering other autonomic managers. This can be implemented as a higher layer of autonomic management that can monitor and adapt the basic layer of autonomic management. This new layer may also decide on the goals to be pursued and their priorities. The basic management layer represents a managed resource for the higher management layer. Overall, such autonomic system would be able to reflect upon its own autonomic behaviour and consequently adjust its decision logic. This enables the system to alleviate faulty conducts and adapt to external changes in order to best maintain itself within the viability limits defined by its goals. For example, supposing that an external environmental change renders the current management behaviour inefficient or dangerous, the higher management layer can detect the problem and adapt the basic layer so as to employ a different behaviour or strategy. This approach is compatible with Ross Ashby's ultra-stable system architecture (discussed in Chap. 3).

Gaining the trust of human users in what concerns autonomic systems is another important issue. Beyond psychological and sociological considerations, which are well beyond the scope of this discussion, autonomic systems could be endowed with several facilities that may help reassure their human clients. These mainly include a certain level of system transparency and the assurance that manual control can be efficiently re-established at any time. System transparency implies keeping human users informed of the system's state and success in reaching the goals via easy to understand domain-specific languages. Users should also be allowed to formulate customised inquiries on the system's historical information, including past faulty states, or the reasons for which a certain decision was taken. The ability to take manual control, and override various layers of autonomic management logic, may provide certain guarantees on the worst-case administration scenarios.

Finally, autonomic systems directly interacting with, or impacting on, human activity should have to be made more aware of human presence, core values and safety principles. Such capabilities will become essential for ensuring human safety even in the most unpredictable of situations. System self-awareness and human-awareness can help avoid catastrophic decisions being made by blindly following management strategies in reaction to a badly understood situation. As a complementary measure, Apoptotic Computing (Chap. 3) proposes a last resort for disabling autonomic systems that have gone out of control.

10.4   Conclusion

To return to our question, asking if autonomic computing was a fad of the new millennium. Given that data centres and systems that compose cloud computing infrastructures are already entirely instrumented and many of the management functions are now automated, we can say that there has certainly been an impact. At the software level, most component and service-oriented models, frameworks and technologies developed today provide inherent support for dynamic monitoring and adaptation, including hot-deployment, hot-swapping, dynamic bindings and configurations. These represent basic touchpoints which are essential for enabling the autonomic management of applications that rely on such platforms. Additionally, platforms provide an increasing variety of basic autonomic capabilities including automatic configuration, connectivity management, instance replication or downsizing. Indeed, as previously exemplified, several technologies had already started providing automatic management functions before the autonomic computing domain was explicitly defined. This only strengthens the position of autonomic computing, showing the progressive emergence of self-management issues in our ICT systems and the necessity to recognise and address them as first-order concerns in a dedicated domain. So, like most things that make sense, we can conclude that autonomic computing is subtly being added, as a natural solution, without celebration or pomp. It is here to stay and has a strong future [3].

How this future manifests is a product of the work that we present here in this book, combined with the growing body of work either described as self-managing, self-optimising, context-aware, self-adaptive or even simply autonomic. Further, as technologies and computer science as a whole grow, these new ideas can be influenced by and inspire the autonomic computing area. For example, we have seen in this book the degree of adaptability, agility and 'intelligence' an autonomic system has is closely tied to the improvements, heuristics and speed of computation of artificial intelligence systems. As machine leaning gets more sophisticated, faster to run, smart, etc., we will see more online adaptation, and this will also become more sophisticated. More system 'intelligence', combined with improved system awareness of administrative objectives and human values, will bring about more predictable and safe behaviours, which in turn will breed trust and reliability.

As another example, a complementary approach to traditional artificial intelligence is one that exploits self-organisation and emergent behaviour. A better understanding and capacity to govern this type of phenomena can equally provide a means of ensuring predictable results at the system level (even in the presence of unpredictability at the finer-grain levels). Hence, progress in these research areas can also benefit autonomic computing and enable the construction of dependable and trustworthy autonomic systems. After all, trust and reliability are core to the uptake of autonomic computing as we gradually take the human out of the loop.

Surely, as emphasised throughout this book, it is essential that humans can remain in control of their autonomic systems. System autonomy should allow them to do so, even if it is merely modifying high-level objectives or management policies, rather than repetitively intervening to fix low-level technical issues. Hence, there will also be a necessity to rethink human interactions with autonomic computing systems. Novel interfaces will have to be designed to reflect the autonomic system's capacity to follow higher management directives and to provide insights into its success status and reasoning process.

Significantly more research is needed to achieve the full vision of autonomic management in our increasingly complex computing systems [3]. Comprehensive solutions will require the integration of results from several research domains, investigating both natural and artificial systems. The necessity for cross-domain research provides a great opportunity for computer science advancements. Notably, it can help enrich software engineering with novel paradigms, algorithms and architectures inspired from other disciplines, which have already been confronted with the management of complexity and unpredictability (e.g. biology, ecosystems, economy, artificial intelligence or cybernetics). As indicated in the defining motivation of autonomic computing, the ability to introduce self-management capabilities in ICT systems is essential if we are to pursue the current trend of system development and computer embodiment within our society. Software engineering must evolve accordingly in order to provide the means to reason about, develop and maintain autonomic computing systems.

10.5   Key Points

This chapter discussed the following concluding points on autonomic computing:

- Autonomic computing will change the way software systems are developed. On the one hand, the change must be such so as to ensure that our increasing reliance on ever more complex computing systems remains safe and secure. On the other hand, the change must be such so as to preserve the current trend in the development of increasingly more complex computing systems providing ever better and more innovative services to our society.
- This book aimed to provide a coherent overview of software engineering principles and techniques that can be currently adopted for developing autonomic computing systems. Considering the overwhelming number and diversity of contributions to this domain, the presentation was necessarily partial. Included approaches were selected based on their maturity and rapid applicability.
- Many challenges remain before the full autonomic computing vision can be attained. More research is needed in autonomic computing and its related scientific domains.
- Software engineering must evolve in order to offer the necessary artefacts for facilitating the development of autonomic systems. The main challenges stem from the complexity of autonomic systems, exacerbated by the unpredictability of their execution environments. Most software engineering processes may have to be increasingly automated and/or pushed into the runtime.
- Self-management raises serious concerns with respect to the reliance and trustworthiness that can be placed on autonomic systems. Security and safety are here of utmost importance. In addition to necessary advancements in the autonomic processes themselves, acceptable solutions will most likely include additional safety-ensuring functions including a certain level of system transparency, support for external intervention and dynamic adaptation of its behaviour and possibly better 'awareness' of human objectives and values.

- Progress in autonomic computing seems tightly linked to advancements in its related domains, notably including artificial intelligence, self-organising and emergent systems. These can provide key contributions for ensuring the predictability, reliability and trustworthiness of autonomic behaviour.
- Existing management interfaces must evolve so as to enable the new types of human–machine interactions brought about by the autonomicity paradigm. Such aspects are tightly linked to progress in sociology, psychology and cognitive science.
- The important challenges raised by autonomic computing encourage interdisciplinary research opening valuable opportunities for computer science advancements. Inspiration from control theory and biology brought the feedback loop to the heart of the autonomic systems' architecture. Multi-agent systems promised inspiration for integrating multiple feedback loops into coherent systems. Further inspiration seems within reach from additional scientific domains, including economy, sociology or complex systems in general.
- Despite its notable inspiration from numerous existing domains, autonomic computing represents a well-defined research area with its specific challenges and dedicated solutions. Abundant research contributions and observable changes in system development practices clearly indicate the importance and perseverance of the autonomic computing domain.

References

1. Dobson, S., Denazis, S., Fernández, A., Gaïti, D., Gelenbe, E., Massacci, F., Nixon, P., Saffre, F., Schmidt, N., Zambonelli, F.: A survey of autonomic communications. ACM Trans. Auton. Adapt. Syst. (TAAS) **1**(2), 223–259 (2006)
2. Sestini, F.: Situated and autonomic communications: an EC FET European initiative. ACM Comput. Commun. Rev. **36**(2), 14–17 (2006)
3. Kephart, J.: Autonomic computing: the first decade. In: Keynote at the 8th International Conference on Autonomic Computing (ICAC), Germany, 2011
4. An architectural blueprint for autonomic computing. IBM Whitepaper, June 2005
5. Dardenne, A., van Lamsweerde, A., Fickas, S.: Goal-directed requirements acquisition. Sci. Comput. Program. **20**(1–2), 3–50 (1993)
6. Kramer, J., Magee, J.: Self-managed systems: an architectural challenge. In: Future of Software Engineering, pp. 259–268. IEEE Computer Society, Washington, DC, USA (2007)
7. Brooks, R.A.: A robust layered control system for a mobile robot. In: Cambrian Intelligence: The Early History of the New AI, pp. 3–26. MIT Press, Cambridge (1999). ISBN 10: 0262024683
8. Astrom, K., Wittenmark, B.: Adaptive Control, 2nd edn. Addison-Wesley, Reading (1995)
9. Soderstrom, T., Stoica, P.: System Identification. Prentice-Hall, Englewood Cliffs (1989)
10. Bourcier, J., Diaconescu, A., Lalanda, P., McCann, J.A.: AutoHome: an Autonomic Management Framework for Pervasive Home Applications. ACM Trans. Auton. Adapt. Syst. (TAAS) **6**(1), 8:1–8:10 (2011)
11. Maurel, Y., Lalanda, P., Diaconescu, A.: Towards a service-oriented component model for autonomic management. In: 8th IEEE International Conference on Services Computing (SCC 2011), Washington, DC, USA, 4–9 July 2011
12. Frey, S., Diaconescu, A., Demeure, I.: Architectural integration patterns for autonomic management systems. In: 9th IEEE International Conference and Workshops on the Engineering of Autonomic and Autonomous Systems (EASe 2012), Novi Sad, Serbia, 11–13 Apr 2012

Annex: Learning Environment

We have stated numerous times throughout this book that autonomic computing is a fast-growing and ever-changing field. Therefore, in true component-based software engineering fashion, we have abstracted out most of the dynamic components of the book that refer to the learning environment and exercises and placed these in an environment better suited to managing this dynamism—that is, they can be found on a Web page! We hope this Web environment will grow with the book, learning from the feedback that we receive from practitioners and students alike.

P. Lalanda et al., *Autonomic Computing: Principles, Design and Implementation*,
Undergraduate Topics in Computer Science, DOI 10.1007/978-1-4471-5007-7,
© Springer-Verlag London 2013

iCASA Autonomic Computing Learning Support Tool

We have designed a learning environment that allows students to develop, execute and test autonomic applications. This environment represents an autonomic pervasive computing application that simulates a *smart home*. A dedicated IDE (integrated development environment) has been designed around this, which allows the student to execute autonomic code in a runtime simulation that provides concrete, visual feedback of the behaviours that the student has programmed. We believe that the pervasive domain is very illustrative and easy to grasp for students in computer science. Also, it characterises requirements, such as device volatility, evolving QoS, mobility and environmental change that often motivate self-management.

Our challenge was to provide a learning environment that allows students to tackle the different challenges related to self-* applications that we discuss in this book. In doing so, we have defined a set of exercises illustrating the salient concepts that typify autonomic computing. These exercises are provided with explanations and complete corrected code. Interested students then can have the opportunity to develop a great number of applications beyond the exercises in a robust, dedicated environment designed to explore various aspects of autonomic applications.

Our learning environment is based on three elements:

- A dynamic execution infrastructure based on iPOJO (see Chap. 6)
- A simulation environment, called iCASA, simulating a *pervasive* house equipped with smart, volatile devices
- An integrated development environment based on Eclipse and facilitating the development of pervasive applications in iPOJO in the context of the simulated house.

In this learning environment, a student can develop autonomic applications in iPOJO in a well-defined domain (the pervasive house), download them to the execution infrastructure, start them and see the effects of their execution in the simulation environment. Evaluating the autonomic capabilities of an application is very straightforward since most actions, or absence of actions, appear in the simulation environment's graphical interface. For instance, a light is automatically switched on or off or nothing happens!

The learning environment is available on a Website associated with the book: self-star.net

It is packaged in such a way that it can be very easily installed on a students' workstation or laptop. However, these machines must be able to run (comfortably) Java and Eclipse.

In order to be reactive and to be able to provide regular updates, exercise sets are defined and corrected on the Website. Exercises descriptions and associate answers, including code, are then made available on the site only. Our purpose is to regularly update the site with new exercises and news versions of the learning environment (enhanced simulation capabilities, for instance).

The following sections briefly introduce the learning environment.

Execution Environment, iPOJO

The execution environment is based on OSGi/Felix and the iPOJO service-oriented component model. As explained in Chap. 6 (software adaptation), a major goal of iPOJO is to make the development of dynamic applications as simple as possible. To this end, the overall approach is to keep each of the code components as similar to a 'plain old Java object' (POJO) as possible. The code of a component (in Java) focuses on business logic, not on mechanisms for dynamism or other non-functional requirements so as to not confuse the student. We have chosen a Java platform due to the proliferation of Java courses in many undergraduate degrees.

iPOJO relies on the 'inversion of control' pattern[1] and provides an extensible component container that manages all issues regarding dynamism. In particular, it manages all the service-oriented interactions. Concretely, the container is responsible for publishing the services provided by a component and, conversely, for discovering, selecting and binding required services together at runtime.

Services used by a component can be selected anytime and changed in a context aware fashion. The binding policy is defined in abstract terms by the component developer (or the administrator) and implemented by the container. In that sense, a container implements an autonomic loop (it perceives the environment, decides on actions, executes actions) and can be seen as an autonomic element, as defined in Chap. 4 (autonomic architectures) (Fig. A.1).

Autonomic loops can thus be defined at the level of the component bindings. Programmers can explicitly define other control loops in an application. For instance, an autonomic manager can be simply defined as an iPOJO component able to monitor the other components and change them when needed. iPOJO provides the necessary programmatic APIs to dynamically load or unload new components, modify components features, etc. This means components playing the role of autonomic managers can adapt another component's life cycle.

The first exercises that we propose permit students to get familiarised with the iPOJO technology (additional material can be found on the iPOJO Apache Web

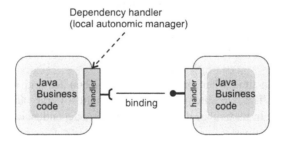

Fig. A.1 iPOJO dependency handler

[1] This is a software engineering practice where the component coupling, or object coupling in this case, occurs at runtime by the assembler object and not known at compile time.

page[2]). Then, subsequent exercises focus on the development of self-managed applications in iPOJO in the proposed pervasive environment.

iPOJO IDE

Learning OSGi/iPOJO technologies may take some time, even for good JAVA developers. Students need to get familiar with new concepts like components or services, but they also have to learn new development environments (including XML configuration files and annotations).

In order to allow students to more rapidly focus on autonomic concepts, we have developed an iPOJO IDE (integrated development environment) allowing the rapid and simplified development of iPOJO applications. This environment provides a set of facilities to assist the developer in the creation and deployment of iPOJO components. In particular, a number of classes and files are (partially) generated. Also, deployment can be fully automated. In that context, we had to make tough choices for the sake of simplicity. However, the IDE keeps all the iPOJO key concepts, and the projects managed by the environment are standard OSGi projects. Developers are free to access and edit them directly, making the tool an ideal transition tool to writing more complex OSGi applications.

The IDE is provided as an Eclipse plug-in. Eclipse is a very popular standard IDE for developing JAVA applications. Eclipse comes with many features supporting development through the use of plug-ins. For instance, it is possible to run applications on an embedded OSGi platform within Eclipse. In this way, it is natural and easy to use the Eclipse debugger.

The IDE assists developers in the different development phases:

– At design time for defining iPOJO components, their configurations and dependencies. Several wizards are provided to specify component types, provided and required services, service properties, configurations, etc. Also, the iPOJO configuration files are automatically generated.
– At implementation time for implementing components and the provided services. The IDE can generate template implementation classes to facilitate coding. Also, at any time, validity between component specification and their implementation can be verified. Finally, the IDE is able to reflect changes in the component specification onto the implementations without impacting the existing code.
– At compilation time when building the OSGi bundles and managing project dependencies. The IDE automatically manages most library and Eclipse project dependencies. In particular, it knows the iCASA dependencies and can import them automatically.
– At configuration time for configuring each component instances. The use of a wizard ensures that the configured properties have indeed been declared in the

---

[2]http://felix.apache.org/site/apache-felix-ipojo.html

component definition. This prevents a common problem when using OSGi where properties are identified by a single String that is disseminated across the code and configuration files—causing a lot of typos.
- At deployment time by making the deployment a one-click process. The user has the choice to deploy the application in an OSGi platform embedded within Eclipse or in a remote platform. If an application has already been deployed, the IDE does the necessary update. This makes application testing more straightforward.

iCASA, Smart Home Simulation Environment

The pervasive domain has been mentioned many times in this book—using it as a teaching support too in the real world would raise a number of practical challenges. First, sensors and devices are expensive, fragile and hard to install and maintain. Also, reproducing a scenario in a real-world environment is especially difficult as it depends on ground conditions and will take much of the student's time to configure. As this would not enable the student to learn about autonomic computing, this is not compatible with a classroom exercise.

For these reasons, we have provided a simulated environment enabling complete control of the environment and time. This is the very purpose of iCASA, a smart home simulator developed in the context of the Medical project ((http://medical.imag.fr). iCASA is based on OSGi and iPOJO and takes advantage of their versatility and dynamism. iCASA is provided as a set of modules and components (e.g. bundles and iPOJO components) that are deployed on a OSGi/iPOJO framework.

Using the iCASA, a smart home simulator, students have full control over:
- Time: it is possible to slow down, speed up or stop time during the simulation. It is therefore possible to simulate long-term actions such as energy consumption and skip to important actions.
- Environment: iCASA allows the definition of different 'zones' in a house. It also provides an administration interface to modify different physical properties such as temperature or luminosity of the different zones.
- Inhabitants: iCASA offers the possibility to insert or remove inhabitants from the environment. Inhabitants, who can be moved from zone to zone, may carry physical devices.
- Devices: they are accessible through standard service interfaces, and their configuration can be dynamically changed. They can be discovered and used dynamically by an application through the OSGi service registry. Devices can be simulated or real. At any time, the user can add or remove new simulated devices and modify their localisation in the rooms.

Specifically, iCASA provides:
- A graphical user interface: simulations are run on top of an OSGi platform and displayed in a Web browser. The interface displays a map of the house and the localisation of the different devices. It allows students to create and configure devices, create and move physical users and watch their actual configurations.

Synchronisation is automatically maintained between the GUI and the running platform ensuring that the interface is kept up to date.

– Scripting facilities: iCASA supports the scripts writing to control the environment. Scripts provide a convenient way to test the applications under reproducible conditions.
– Notification facilities: iCASA is event-based and is able to notify subscribers of any modifications in the environment.

Finally, iCASA is extensible: new types of devices (simulated or real) can be easily added. This enables teaching activities to be customised depending on the targeted domain. The current distribution is provided with a set of predefined simulated devices pertaining to the home-automation domains like light devices, presence sensors or sound devices. These devices are used in the exercises delivered with this book. This also means that the only limitation to the students' creativity is their imagination.

Full documentation about iCASA is provided on the Website.

Index

A

Active monitoring, 111, 112, 140
Adaptive maintenance, 9
Adaptive monitoring, 148–149
Administrator, 7–16, 20, 23–28, 31–33, 35, 36,
    40, 41, 52, 63, 83, 85, 89, 96, 97,
    99, 104, 112, 116, 169, 172, 173,
    191, 195, 208, 219, 235, 241, 242,
    255, 263, 264, 266, 280
Adoption model, 41, 42, 253, 268
Agents, 26, 57, 104, 196, 220,
    255, 273
Amorphous computing, 50, 51, 275
Analysis (in MAPE-K), 113–115
Angstrom project, 268
Apoptotic computing, 74, 275
Architecture, 2, 4, 14, 17–19, 44–46, 48,
    50, 53, 58, 61, 62, 71–73, 81,
    85–87, 91, 95–126, 130, 131,
    135, 136, 140–144, 147, 153,
    158, 165, 169–173, 188, 194,
    199, 202, 203, 208, 218, 220,
    227, 232, 235–237, 240, 249,
    251, 253, 264–268, 272, 273,
    275, 277, 278, 281
Architecture definition language, 202
Arpanet, 265
Artificial intelligence, 18, 19, 57, 58, 61, 62,
    82–89, 92, 105, 108, 117, 185, 190,
    264, 276, 277
Autonomic manager, 107
Autonomic communications, 39, 226,
    265–268, 270
Autonomic computing
    benchmark, 231–232
    influences, 58–62

B

Bayesian techniques, 208
Benchmarking, 229–232
Binary code, 154–159, 163, 164, 167, 169
Biology, 18, 25, 51, 57, 59, 61–74, 91, 264,
    277, 278

Autonomic element, 27–29, 33, 35, 40, 53, 85,
    95–108, 117, 120–126, 135, 153,
    181, 202, 263, 281
Autonomic manager, 77, 97–120, 122, 123,
    126, 130, 134, 136, 140, 142–144,
    146, 148, 149, 153–159, 162–164,
    166, 168, 171, 172, 185, 188–198,
    201–203, 208, 209, 217, 218, 221,
    222, 225, 242, 243, 251–253, 259,
    271–273, 275, 281

C

Central nervous system (CNS), 65, 66,
    71, 72
Cilia, 18, 19, 131, 147, 235–260, 272
Classifiers, 52, 208
CNS. *See* Central nervous system (CNS)
Code
    integration, 159
    upgrade, 168
Components off the shelf (COTS),
    12, 100, 111
Computing context, 28, 53, 96, 97, 104, 106,
    117, 129
Connectionist, 86, 87
Context, 3, 23, 59, 96, 129, 153, 189, 217,
    238, 263

P. Lalanda et al., *Autonomic Computing: Principles, Design and Implementation*,
Undergraduate Topics in Computer Science, DOI 10.1007/978-1-4471-5007-7,
© Springer-Verlag London 2013